Transformation Through Insight

Transformation Through Insight

Enneatypes in Life, Literature and Clinical Practice

Claudio Naranjo, M.D.

HOHM PRESS
PRESCOTT, AZ

Cover design: Kim Johansen
Layout: Bhadra Mitchell

Library of Congress Cataloging-In-Publication Data

Naranjo, Claudio.
   Transformation through insight : enneatypes in life, literature and clinicial
   practice /
Claudio Naranjo : Foreword by Will Schutz
        p.   cm.
   Includes bibliographical references.
   ISBN:0-934252-76-9
   1. Typology (Psychology) 2. Enneagram. 3. Psychotherapy.
I. Title
RC489.T95N37   1997
616.89—dc21   97-1010
                                                                          CIP

Hohm Press
PO Box 2501
Prescott, AZ 86302
1-800-381-2700
http://www.booknotes.com/hohm/

DEDICATION

To Oscar Ichazo

From whom I learned much more than protoanalysis
and from whom I received much more than learning.

ACKNOWLEDGEMENTS

I am specially grateful to Suzy, my wife, who in addition to contributing her story spent more time at the computer than I at my desk, kept reminding me of what needed to be completed and made of our life together a warm and happy nest for the book during its now ending egg-stage season.

I am also grateful to Dr. Peñarrubia for his autobiographic contribution, to Draco Maturana for his most appropriate cartoons, to my patients and students for the permission to publish the content of our gestalt sessions, to Victoria Sanjurjo for her gift of transcribing them, and to my editor Regina Sara Ryan.

CONTENTS

FOREWORD

Claudio Naranjo is singular. His worldly exploration of a variety of fields from a variety of countries has enriched our understanding of psychological events by helping to break us out of our provincialism. One of these contributions I had the opportunity to observe while we were both at the Esalen Institute in Big Sur, CA during the late 1960s and early 70s, when Claudio discovered a man named Oscar Ichazo in Arica, Chile, and persuaded a large and relatively distinguished group of people to follow him to Arica and experience Oscar for themselves. The influence of the Arica training was major in the human potential movement and Claudio deserves much credit for introducing it. His fertile brain and expertise in many fields has made Claudio a uniquely valuable contributor.

There is another valuable uniqueness about Claudio. He is one of the few people who have a simultaneous interest in both scientific and clinical approaches to human phenomena, and in the integration of the two. In this book he combines the theoretical model of the Enneagram with the wealth of his clinical experience with Gestalt therapy to enrich the theory. To insert a personal note, in my own work I have gone through an evolution in the use of categories for classifying people. On the one hand, they are valuable for pointing out syndromes of behaviors that occur together and often they suggest developmental reasons for this to occur. Readers usually can find themselves primarily in one of these categories and receive some personal insight from this. However, they often find that not all of the traits described in the "type" are familiar to them, and some traits from some types other than their own seem to fit themselves. Further, sometimes readers feel that if they are of one type they may have difficulty acquiring a characteristic of another type. These complexities have led me to advise people to use typologies as opportunities for personal awareness and to watch carefully their reactions to the description of their type and learn from those reactions more about how they feel about themselves. Further, if they want to acquire traits of a different type they have the ability to do that if they will focus themselves on figuring out how to do it. In other words, I suggest they use the typology as a way to strengthen their own self-knowledge and not see it as a terminal classification they are limited to. I also suggest to them that traits in their type that they cannot identify themselves with may (or may not) be those they are denying. I have not checked this use of the typology with Claudio, so it may well be he agrees with what I have found. If not, readers are left with the interesting problem of deciding for themselves how best to use this rich material.

I am sure the reader will find a rare feast in this book, another of Claudio's seminal contributions.

Will Schutz, Ph.D.
Author of *FIRO; Joy;*
Profound Simplicity and
The Human Element.

INTRODUCTION

In 1988, at the time of dictating *Character and Neurosis: An Integrative View* (Nevada City, CA: Gateways, 1990) I envisioned producing some kind of clinical book at a later date. Though I have already published one clinical book (under the title *Enneatypes in Psychotherapy* Prescott, AZ: Hohm Press, 1994, which title could be no less appropriate for the present volume), here is my first systematic, though incomplete, attempt.

From the domain of my own practice I have chosen to concentrate on one particular therapeutic form: that of Gestalt therapy. Each of the first eight chapters in this book contains a transcript taken from videos of my recent work with Protoanalytic Gestalt* and the last chapter includes a transcript from a workshop on dreams offered some fifteen years ago in Santiago de Chile.

As a complement to this microscopic account of the therapeutic process (provided by my experience as an enneatype-conscious Gestalt therapist), I also wanted to offer a macroscopic view through a series of more complete case reports. For this I have turned to a consideration of published accounts of psychotherapy.

Since a book on enneatypes in psychotherapy requires that the reader have a previous acquaintance with ego-types in light of the Enneagram, I have also included here (in the form of an opening section to each of its nine divisions) an account of the character styles themselves. Though I originally intended to do this through a reprint of a book based on fragments from my talks in Brazil workshops in the late eighties, and published by Dr. Alaor Passos, the abundance of books on the subject has prompted me instead to embellish that text through literary and biographic illustrations, some reference to social pathologies and a touch of humor, and then to excise a good part of the original material.

As it now stands, this book contains nine divisions, each with a similar threefold structure:

1. an introduction to one of the enneatypes,
2. a case report, with commentary, from the literature,
3. a session transcript illustrating enneatype-oriented Gestalt therapy.

This book has become more than I intended. Just as the descriptions of the enneatypes became more florid than I first envisioned, the entire volume exploded beyond its preconceived limits through the inclusion of some considerations on subtypes. Though I didn't intend to include this subject (except, to some extent, implicitly), I found it preferable to comment, as I proceeded, on subtype-related characteristics of the quoted biographic or therapeutic material. Yet, I have chosen to refrain from making the book still more complete by omitting more systematic coverage of the instinct-related variants of the enneatypes. The book has already become exceedingly thick, and I have from the very beginning of my writing planned to devote another book to this specific issue. Let me only mention here (for those who have not read *Character and Neurosis*) that Ichazo's protoanalysis* involves a three instinct theory, and that distinct varieties of every enneatype are distinguished according to the preponderance of the sexual, the relational or the self-preservation motive. More importantly, I have added to the original case reports from the classical literature (geared only to illustrate neurotic styles) a series of cases documenting successful psychotherapy; a psychotherapy that beyond symptomatic or adaptational cure has turned an individual to a truer life and a higher meaning. Thus, while originally I conceived a book on the human types, this current work became more and more a book on psychotherapy, and I am very pleased about it. The field of character-oriented therapy is growing, surely as a reflection of a living progress in the art, and I am satisfied to see my book as a contribution to this important development.

Just as twenty years ago it fell on me to be the vehicle for the transmission of some protoanalytic insight to a small group (from which the information seeped through into California, the Jesuit community and, increasingly, the world), lately I have been introducing protoanalysis to the psychotherapeutic community in the Latin world. This book seems a continuation of this work. It was originally conceived for publication in Spanish, though the development of events (and most particularly the interest of

Hohm Press) has caused it to appear first in English.

May this contribution to an ego-style conscious therapy be a ferment in the lives of those who work on themselves, and in the activity of those who help others in this turbulent world, so critically in need of transformed individuals.

Claudio Naranjo
Berkeley, CA

* Terms followed by an asterisk (*) are found in the Glossary.

1

ENNEATYPE 1

As far as I know, the first person to write schematic descriptions of character was Aristotle's successor Theophrastus, who also bequeathed us the first book describing character types. One type that he found interesting enough to record for posterity he called the "Oligarch."

Theophrastus defined "oligarchy" as a spirit of domination, aspiring to power and wealth. This apparently has nothing to do with anger — recognized by protoanalysis as the root motivation in enneatype 1. Yet, the anger of E1 is a passion masquerading as virtue; and, even the expression "angry virtue" — that I have used in reference to this perfectionistic and obsessive personality style[1] — would not be sufficient to describe E1, unless dominance (which in turn overflows into an interest in power and money) is taken into account as an anger derivative. Such is Theophrastus's emphasis in his all-too-patrician oligarch.

Theophrastus quotes his oligarch as declaring:

> We must meet and discuss these matters amongst ourselves, without the presence of the people. We must not accept insults and honors from the rabble. We must discuss these things amongst ourselves, and not depend on the opinions of the world.[2]

Here is an authoritarian and elitist character, whose thinking runs something like this: "We, the enlightened, must decide who is in possession of power, and not leave these decisions to vulgar people, who do not understand these matters." This is a position of virtue implying, "We are the good ones, we are the noble ones." It has a great deal to do with a feeling

1

of aristocratic nobility:

> The oligarch rarely goes out before noon, his tunic is carefully fitted, his nails are well-tended.

And, concerning appearance, the oligarch's concern is correctness — correctness with regard to forms. Lack of form is disgusting, much like sitting "...next to vulgar people, to plebeians."

Let us skip ahead some two thousand years and consider now a feminine character portrait, emphasizing a different yet overlapping set of traits. Along with the pilgrims in Chaucer's Canterbury Tales,

> There also was a Nun, a Prioress
> Her way of smiling very simple and coy.
> Her greatest oath was only "By St Loy!"
> And she was known as Madam Eglantyne.
> And well she sang a service, with a fine
> Intoning through her nose, as was most seemly,
> And she spoke daintily in French, extremely,
> After the school of Stratford-atte-Bowe;
> French in the Paris style she did not know.
> At meat her manners were well taught withal;
> No morsel from her lips did she let fall,
> Nor dipped her fingers in the sauce too deep;
> But she could carry a morsel up and keep
> The smallest drop from falling on her breast.
> For courtliness she had a special zest,
> And she would wipe her upper lip so clean
> That not a trace of grease was to be seen
> Upon the cup when she had drunk; to eat,
> She reached a hand sedately for the meat.
> She certainly was very entertaining,
> Pleasant and friendly in her ways, and straining

To counterfeit a courtly kind of grace,
A stately bearing fitting to her place,
And to seem dignified in all her dealings.[3]

Here the emphasis is on formality and refinement (already observed by Theophrastus), but interest in authority is only implicit in the statement that the nun is a prioress. Virtue is also implicit in her religious career, and we are made to feel that religiosity may be just an aspect of a more generalized striving for the best, ranging from table manners, through culture, to solicitousness and devotion. Just as in the case of the oligarch, but more subtly, we sense that excellence is contaminated by and serves a secret power-drive, and we feel that the ensign of "love conquers all" (in the Prioress's golden brooch) smacks of an ambiguity — with eros masquerading as pious charitas. While Theophrastus's portrait emphasizes an indirect expression of anger as power or leadership, in the case of the prioress it is the suppression of anger that is emphasized ("Her greatest oath was only 'by St Loy'"), and the defensive development of conscious benevolence and excessive correctness.

In still another attempt to portray the variety of human character, Samuel Butler, in the seventeenth century, presents the E1 in his portrait of a pedant "...who studies and uses words with the greatest possible respect, apparently for the sake of the words themselves, like an honest man who is not ruled by self-interest."[4] A concern for correctness in speech (good diction and the correct use of words) is typical of type1, and a veritable symptom. Such concern may be also taken as a symbol of something less specific, for what happens in speech also happens with behavior in other domains. A person who weighs each and every word is also a person who weighs each and every action — and thus behaves in an all-too-perfect way. Correctness itself becomes a virtue, whether in the person's words, or in her clothes or gestures. Yet, it is not just correctness of speech that is the target of Butler's caricature. His pedant is virtuously devoid of self-interest in his ("selfless") dedication to good diction and correct grammar.

What does anger have to do with pedantry? There is a superiority in the pedant (like in the oligarch), as well as the dynamics of seeking superiority to control; being entitled as "a person of merit." E1 people can make others feel uncomfortable with their mere presence. When people find themselves next to a pedant they often feel incorrect, as if they are lacking in something. Yet, it is not a matter of correctness only but just, moral virtue. It is benevolent anger, disguised with good intentions, which exhibits a *deliberate* (i.e. non-spontaneous) goodness — like that of school teachers (described by Dickens in his novels) whose severity claims to be justified by the pupil's own good.

Though E1 corresponds to the irascible or "wrathful" type, the name is not altogether adequate. To speak of an angry or resentful type fails to evoke the kind of person who is clean, honest, hard-working, respectful of social norms and compulsively responsible. Because of the inseparability of perfectionism from the mechanism of reaction formation, anger is the most effectively masked of passions; just as the power drive sometimes manifests as secret dominance, anger is masked by benevolence and commiseration. In the realm of current personality pathologies, here is (when the traits are extreme enough) the "obsessive personality disturbance," characterized by an excessive concern for order, cleanliness, moral issues and control. Since this designation is usually associated with the more pathological level of expression of the character style, "perfectionistic" or "perfectionism" seems the better description. Ironically, however, when years ago I used the expression "perfectionistic" (already proposed by Karen Horney) for an article submitted to the *American Journal of Psychoanalysis* (of which she was the founder), I was asked to change it; and I switched to "puritanical."[5]

A compulsive seriousness is typical of these people, who suffered great demands during their childhood development. Their parents may have pressured them for the sake of a brilliant academic performance — the achievement of good grades and exemplary behavior. Conforming to these demands, E1s have developed a kind of grim determination and responsibility. Because not everyone in the world functions so responsibly and with such respect for the rules, this type of person cannot help feeling that he or she is suffering from an injustice, carrying a greater load, or making a greater effort than the rest. Resentment is at the root of his tendency toward criticism, in general, as well as competitive superiority: however much he may criticize himself, he criticizes the rest of the world far more, and this leaves the individual on a relative platform of "exemplarity," with an aristocratic or "holier than thou" feeling. This superiority appears to be very natural in that it does not impress others as an arrogant superiority, but rather, as a sense of dignity or personal integrity.

"A person of character." The English invented this expression (which has become international), and which is particularly applied to this type. Here there is a clear effort to abide by socially-accepted norms and to develop self-control with regard to these norms. E1 is a social character, not anti-social. Although there is anger, it is placed at the service of that which is social, i.e., of how things *should* be done. The sense of duty is very strong.

In E6, in which cowardice or its denial is the issue, there is a subtype that is also characterized by doing his or her duty, but in a different way. E1 is more self-assertive; more self-confident, with little sense of guilt. E1s are not very tortured people. They rarely resort to psychotherapy; when they do, their aim is usually self-improvement, rather than the solution of existential problems.

But, let us return to anger — which Oscar Ichazo's protoanalysis posited as the emotional core of the personality pattern. Because anger is taboo for this character, they have great problems in expressing anger, however much resentment they may harbor, except when it may be justified as "righteous indignation." (In fact, the term "righteous indignation" was invented in the Anglo-Saxon world where this character is very frequent.)

Generally speaking, here is a person who enjoys fighting for good causes. It would be a mistake, however, to believe that the *cause* leads him to fight. In fact, quite the opposite: his aggressiveness *needs* a good cause in order to feel justified. The Crusader epitomizes this in his attitude of wanting to cut off the infidel's head in the name of civilizing the barbarian. Yet, in their intrusiveness or zeal for reform, E1s may not be aware of their aggression; they feel so idealistic, so moved by their devotion to the best. No perfection ever seems to be enough, and this self-demanding makes the person hard-working, reliable and willing to make great efforts for the progress of society.

There is also a high level of demand with regard to others. One of the unconscious dynamics of these people is the use of criticism as an indirect means of making demands. Where is the difference between criticism and demand? Demand is criticism oriented towards action, pointing out what is missing in order for the defect to be corrected. Often, it is not criticism for criticism's sake, but *requires* the person to act in a different manner. All this has to do with a demanding attitude, although the demand is often hidden behind moral principles, or general principles. Thus, for example, instead of saying, "I want," they tend to say "you must." They do not take responsibility for their own desires, nor are they so aware of them.

As mentioned already, the "perfectionist" has an ideal of himself or herself that is somewhat impersonal; she sees herself as altruistic, as not wanting things for herself, as generous and without self-interest. Consciously, this person appears to herself as lacking in self-interest, and she may also convince others, in spite of ordering them about and controlling situations. Of course, virtuous absence of self-interest becomes a passport to power — a strategy. Claiming to be clean to the point of near godliness, the E1 manipulates others through "morality" or, rather, moralism: "You *must be* ... "; "To the stake with you if you don't ..." The "clean" person's uncleanliness lies precisely in the manipulation that is involved in worshipping cleanliness. If you ask where the lack of virtue is to be found in this excessively virtuous person, you have to conclude that it lies precisely behind this excess of virtue: the use of virtue in order to stand out, to enjoy special privileges, to feel superior. Different from what it claims to be, the virtue of a Puritan is not loving goodness, but a means to buy love. It echoes the behavior of a child who, by behaving obviously well, is saying: "See how well I behave? Now give me what I deserve!"

In the *Enneagram of Society* I have illustrated the masquerading of unconscious selfishness into justice, and "I want" into "you must," with a description of a cartoon by Quino.[6] This cartoon depicts a demanding child wearing the wig of a judge, while a woman — whom we identify as a symbol of justice by the sword in her hand and the bandage over one of her eyes (yet, this justice figure conveys something of the pirate, since the bandage leaves her other eye uncovered)— uses the sword to cut, for the child, a slice from a big ham. In the cartoon alternative that follows, by Draco Maturana, the emphasis is on control through moral condemnation.

Type 1s are great arguers and defend themselves well. As children they played the role of good little children — i.e., "good little boy" or "good little girl." As adults, in their external appearance this same attitude prevails, but inside there is a great deal of rebellion and a great deal of competition.

Thus, there is a lack of harmony between conscious submission and unconscious rebellion, and this feeds anger and resentment further. E1 individuals are respectful people, good citizens; they honor institutions, obey the police, respect the traffic signs, do not shirk tax payment (or they do so less than others). Consciously, this is what they are like. Unconsciously they rebel, however, and then an inner conflict is generated, thus feeding resentment. Often, when joining an organization or an institution, these people start in a subordinate position. Gradually they rise until they reach positions of power as a result of their personal merits, and gain the acceptance of established power. But once they have reached a strong position, they feel that it is no longer necessary to be so accepting of power. Thus, they enter into the battle for power, become reformers and tend to "out-Herod Herod."

Another marked feature of E1 is the excessive control — rigidity and the inhibition of spontaneity. Of all the enneagram types, this is the most rigid. Just as they waste a lot of external energy on being hard-working and making great efforts, they also waste energy on keeping their "inner child" imprisoned. Their playful side — the part of the psyche that seeks pleasure — is underdeveloped. There is a contempt for pleasure because pleasure naturally conflicts with duty.

Aside from descriptive embodiments of the type in literature ranging from Chaucer's pilgrims to Aunt Betsy in Dickens's *David Copperfield*, a particularly insightful and dynamic view of the E1 character is found in Dostoyevsky's Katherina Ivanovna, in the *The Brothers Karamazov*. In chapter four, Dmitri (an E8), the eldest of the three brothers, tells the young Aliosha (an E9) of a time when he was lieutenant in a regiment. Dmitri was liked by many in spite of his outrageous behavior, yet he was disliked by the colonel. When he joined the battalion, all the town was talking of the return of the colonel's second daughter — "a great beauty who had just left a fashionable school in the capital." This was Katherina Ivanovna. She became "the belle of the balls and picnics," and once, when Dmitri approached her at an evening party, she scarcely looked at him, adopting a scornful expression. Dmitri told himself that he would have his revenge, particularly since, as he put it, "I felt that 'Katenka' was not an innocent boarding school miss, but a person of character, proud and really high-principled; above all she had education and intellect, and I had neither."[7]

Dmitri spent his time in drink and riot till the colonel put him under arrest for three days. (This was a time when Dmitri had received 6,000 roubles from his father.) Then, the colonel, accused of irregularities, was ordered to retire, and all his friends turned their backs on him. Dmitri found this the ideal occasion for revenge. He sent the disdainful beauty a secret message to the effect that, through the use of his money he was willing to rescue her father from disgrace if she would come to him in secret.

How can Katherina, the E1, be expected to behave in the face of this conflict between her aristocratic dignity and the opportunity to save her father from social disgrace and the prospect of serving as a common soldier in his old age?

Katherina decided to virtuously sacrifice her dignity, and though Dmitri was tempted to scorn her and take advantage of her distress, in the spur of the moment, he acted with nobility:

> I looked at her for three seconds, or five perhaps, with fearful hatred — that hate which is only a hair's-breadth from love, from the maddest love! I went to the window, put my forehead against the frozen pane, and I remember the ice burnt my forehead like fire. I did not keep her long, don't be afraid. I turned round, went up to the table, opened the drawer and took out a banknote for five thousand roubles (it was lying in a French dictionary). Then I showed it her in silence, folded it, handed it to her, opened the door into the passage, and, stepping back, made her a deep bow, a most respectful, a most impressive bow, believe me! She shuddered all over, gazed at me for a second, turned horribly pale — white as a sheet, in fact — and all at once, not impetuously but softly, gently, bowed down to my feet — not a boarding-school curtsey, but a Russian bow, with her forehead to the floor. She jumped up and ran away. (p. 135)

As a consequence of the event Katherina falls in love with Dmitri and offers to be his wife: "I love you madly," she says, "even if you don't love me, never mind, be my husband, don't be afraid, I won't hamper you in any way. I will be your shuttle. I will be the carpet under your feet. I want to love you forever. I want to save you from yourself." (p. 137)

In Dostoyevsky's analysis (voiced through Dmitri), however, she loves her own virtue, not the man. And through various hints, the author's text invites us to look upon her in the same light as the censor in Quino's cartoon who indulges in his erotic impulses under the disguise of a moral intent. At the end of the novel, when Dmitri is unjustly condemned to prison, Katherina's love of virtue takes the upper hand. She is not among those who believe in him; deceived by appearances, she takes the side of the accusers.

In the domain of biography, Confucius stands out as a teacher and preacher of filial piety, right intention and social virtues, and perhaps the most influential E1 in the Eastern world. In the West, Martin Luther is probably the most influential E1. Eric Erikson has said that Luther, by virtue of the anger inspired by his father, was able to defy the most powerful individual on earth — the Pope. Luther is of particular interest in that he became aware of the limitations of the perfectionistic attitude in his doctrine about the primacy of grace over good deeds in the process of salvation.

In *The Protestant Ethic and The Spirit of Capitalism*, Max Weber differentiates Western capitalism, especially that which developed in Anglo-Saxon countries (England and Germany), from the capitalism in the Latin countries of the south.[8] Anglo-Saxons are very industrious, ambitious and achieving. Not only do they exhibit a capacity for work, but also a reverence for work. Weber claims that the type of person who is efficient when it comes to accumulating riches and establishing his power in the world is one who has arisen in the context of the Puritanical culture that arose at the time of the Reformation. (Readers will surely be familiar with historical Puritanism and its intent to be "purer than the pure," or, as the Spanish saying goes, "to out-pope the Pope.") Puritanism is the movement that criticized traditional Christianity for being corrupt. Weber's claim is that this highly moralistic movement (in fact, the movement that permeated early American culture in New England) was also characterized by moral valuation of work. What Weber says of Puritanical culture is even truer of the puritanical psyche, however. The entire Western industrial development may be said to be highly related to a particular type of character — one who is not only puritanical; not only efforting to do things properly, attempting to be virtuous and inhibit his impulses (as the word *puritanism* implies); but a character driven by a "Faustian" spirit of conquest.

ANNA O.

As is widely known, the case of Anna O. (a patient whom Freud never met) was the turning point in Freud's career. When Dr. Josef Breuer was visiting this young patient, Freud was studying the nerve cells of the crayfish under a microscope. Yet, when the case of Anna O. was published (by Freud and Breuer in the *Studies on Hysteria*, ten years after the therapy took place), it became the stimulus for the formulation of many of the original ideas of psychoanalysis, including unconscious defenses, the sexual cause of neurosis, psychic trauma, conflict, conversion, transference and ambivalence. Besides, it was also Anna O. who originated the expression "the talking cure."

I imagine that it has been generally assumed, ever since, that Anna O.'s was a hysterical personality. I disagree: though her symptomatic neurosis is clearly the syndrome known as conversion hysteria, characterized by emotionally determined physical symptoms, I propose here that she embodies the obsessive rather than the hysterical personality style.

My argument is threefold. In the first place, it will be seen that her whole therapeutic process gravitates around the expression of anger, and the clinical account invites us to understand her symptoms as expressions of repressed rage. (Her paralysis, for instance, may be understood as an inhibition of the will to strike; her mutism, the blocking of the expression of an unacceptable rage.)

Secondly, Anna O. seems not to conform to Freud's generalization on the causes of hysteria. While he did not fail to observe the common occurrence of seduction and, generally speaking, sexual problems in his hysterical patients, Anna O. is a striking exception. She is an adolescent whose confessions contain no sexual experiences or thoughts. Breuer observed "...a complete lack of sexuality" in Anna O., and declared that she never spoke of love.

The case of Anna O. "proves that a fairly severe case of hysteria can develop, flourish, and be resolved without having a sexual basis," Breuer wrote in a letter to a psychiatrist, Auguste Forel, twelve years after *Studies on Hysteria* appeared.To this must be added, however, that although Anna O. never had a love affair, either before or after therapy, the forbiddenness of the erotic seems proportional to the bizarre fashion in which it found expression at the very end of her treatment, when her positive transference to her admirable and kind physician blossomed in the form of a false pregnancy (after a carriage-ride with him and his daughter in the park).

In terms of elucidating her character, more convincing than the material reported by Breuer and Freud is what we know today of Anna O.'s life. "Anna O." is, of course, not the real name of Breuer's client (as Freud revealed to his biographer and disciple Ernest Jones). Anna O. is Bertha Pappenheim, who became an extraordinary woman deserving a biography.[9] We happen to know more about her character through this biography than through Breuer and Freud, who gave us, as usual, a document not particularly revealing in terms of character.

The beginning of part II of Lucy Freeman's *Story of Anna O.* (which follows upon her clinical re-construction) could not have a more revealing title: "The Crusader." And, on the title page of this chapter, Lucy Freeman wants us to read a quotation from Bertha Pappenheim that shows a woman resentfully concerned with justice: "If there will be justice in the world to come, women will be lawgivers and men have to have babies."[10]

Bertha Pappenheim never again wanted to talk about her experience of therapy with Breuer. Perhaps she felt embarrassed by it; besides, the gains were doubtful. Breuer's repeated prescriptions of opium complicated her case with drug addiction after the therapy was completed, and though we don't know how she recovered, we do know through Freud's widow that Bertha went through dark times.

Bertha Pappenheim enters the realm of history as a person concerned with doing good. During the time of the pogroms in eastern Europe, she collaborated in the soup kitchen of a Jewish organization which provided shelter for orphans. Her biography portrays her as "irate at the injustice of persecution," and willing to take responsibility in helping those children who had lost their parents.

From ladling soup she went to reading to the children at the orphanage. Not only did she read, but she made up fairy tales to tell the children. These she collected under the pseudonym of Berthold in a volume called *The Rummage Store*. Then, on becoming aware that Catholic and Protestant women in Germany were more advanced than the Jews in the volunteer welfare activities, she decided that her work at the orphanage was more important than pleasure. Consequently, she took on administrative duties and, in time, became the director.

Enneatype III people are controlled and disciplined but pleasure-seeking and seductive, in contrast to E1 people who tend to be excessively austere and to undervalue the enjoyment of life. The latter is the picture we get from Bertha Pappenheim's life. At the point when she assumed directorship of the orphanage, we are told that "she walked each morning from the apartment where she lived with her mother, near the center of the city, to the Orphanage about thirty minutes away and put in a full day's work, sometimes staying until late in the evening."

What was her work like? We are told that "she expected the same discipline of the girls that she asked from herself, that she instituted strict washing, ironing, patching, and sewing routine, she would tolerate no tardiness at classes or meals. She insisted on impeccable table manners, allowed no disorder in the rooms. She kept meals simple, almost spartan, as though food were the first place to learn control."

It is no less consistent with the obsessive personality to be strikingly unaccepting of violence, and we know that Bertha Pappenheim placed a complete ban on corporal punishment. "Any employee discovered striking a girl was fired at once." Also coherent with the hypothesis of an obsessive rather than hysterical disposition is that, in spite of the responsibility that she took for the education of the girls under her charge, "she kept an emotional distance."

In Freeman's book the chapter that follows the one devoted to the orphanage is entitled "The Feminist." Here again we encounter a well-known E1 inclination. Just as the feminist movement today abounds in E4 women who are learning to turn their rage outwardly, early feminism and the suffragette movement was distinctly dominated by E1. Whereas today's women's movement has to do with the healing of excessive submissiveness, the earlier movement was characterized by the expression of the dominant, competitive and masculine tendencies in the perfectionist character.

"Her wish to be a man is evident in her writings," Lucy Freeman concludes (through studying Pappenheim's documents). Pappenheim also reflected, on the same basis, that "man was the enemy." She resented not having the education of a male child: "one of the smouldering resentments of her life was that she, along with all the young women of Vienna, had not been allowed to continue her education beyond high school." (p. 73) "She rebelled passionately against the age-old slavery, in which women had been held by the selfishness of men."   (p. 74) When she read Mary Wollstonecraft's *A Vindication of the Rights of Women,* published in England a century earlier, Bertha Pappenheim decided to devote her nights to the task of translating it.

The next chapter in her biography is entitled, "The Organizer," and it not only reflects the administrative abilities of E1 people, but Pappenheim's motivation to introduce improvements in what she saw. She understood "the need to modernize the welfare work carried on by wealthy volunteers." She felt critical at the efforts of her acquaintances to help in a disorganized, sporadic, unsystematic manner, and coined the phrase "careless charity" to describe this attitude. In time, she founded the Federation of Jewish Women and was elected president.

"The White Slave Rescuer," the title of Freeman's next chapter, is no less evocative of an E1 personality than the previous ones. Bertha Pappenheim became particularly concerned with young prostitutes, and it is easy to imagine that in this interest there converged pity and an intense preoccupation with those who were thrust on a path of degradation and immorality. "She wanted to protect Jewish girls from the traders who profited from the sale of their young bodies. She also wanted to help those who had become pregnant and would give birth to illegitimate children, but wished to live a moral life." (p. 91)

Though she felt disillusioned sometimes, Bertha Pappenheim refused to give in to her moods for long, and insisted that the women on her staff rise above their "moods" and physical ailments in the same way as she did. She often told her colleagues and friends a story that she emphatically approved; one in which we may see the reflection of her own forth-rightness. (Once more, this story is telling in connection with any doubts we might have concerning diagnosis of her personality.)

As the story goes, a bird is flying over a raging river during a severe storm, carrying his little birds one by one from their precarious nest to safety. As he flew with the first little bird, the parent-bird said, in mid-river, "You see how hard I struggle to carry you to safety. Will you do the same for me when I am old and weak?" The little bird replied, "Of course, dear Father," whereupon the parent-bird dropped his baby into the swirling torrents below, saying, "A liar shouldn't be saved." He did this to the second baby bird when it gave the same answer. But in reply to his parent's question, the third baby bird said, "Dear Father, I can't promise you that. But I promise to save my own little ones."

About this story Lucy Freeman remarks: "She [Bertha] enjoyed the honesty of the third little bird, an honesty that had saved his own life. In her own way, she too was living a promise to save her own little ones."

Toward the end of Pappenheim's life, after noticing that she was in pain, a board member asked her (during a meeting) whether her gall bladder had not been removed long ago. When she said this was not the case, the board member asked, "Aren't you going to have it out?" The reply was, "I have lived with it almost seventy-seven years, and I don't expect to have it out now." Lucy Freeman remarks: "that was all she would say, she never sought sympathy." (p. 163)

The "fighter" in Bertha Pappenheim became only more forceful as the years went by:

> She had not been afraid of the criminal middlemen nor of the merchants who trafficked in the bodies of young girls, and she was not afraid now of the thugs who had taken over Germany. She had to fight them too, for they were thieves and murderers. As she once wrote to Sophie, "Don't worry if not everyone understands what's right; do your duty and listen to your conscience." (p. 166)

Here are further relevant quotations on the issue:

> She had tried to fight the enemies in her life. It seemed her

entire existence had been a fight, perhaps that was what life was all about, a fight to help those with less strength. (p. 166)

Battle was her life element and the expression of her strength. She used a sharp rapier and did not spare the opponent, but she never misused the fight for small or personal reasons. Battle was as holy as was social work. (pp. 175-176)

Ottilie Schoenewald, the new president, wrote: "Bertha Pappenheim had the nature of a fighter in the highest sense of the word, a fighter for everything good and beautiful. Her aim was never 'Victory,' but progress, development towards something better, improvement of people and conditions." (p.177)

"I have often thought that if one has nothing to love, to hate something is a good substitute," Bertha Pappenheim wrote in a letter from Warsaw in 1912. (p.231)

Cora Berliner, in her memorial tribute, noted, "She enjoyed a fight. She provoked a fight ... She had an essential desire to fight." And: "A volcano lived in this woman, that erupted when somebody angered her." (p. 232)

I now reproduce the first pages of Breuer's momentous document, with which begins Freud's pioneering *Studies on Hysteria*. [11]

At the time of her falling ill (in 1880) Fraülein Anna O. was twenty-one years old. She may be regarded as having had a moderately severe neuropathic heredity, since some psychoses had occurred among her more distant relatives. Her parents were normal in this respect. She herself had hitherto been consistently healthy and had shown no signs of neurosis during her period of growth. She was markedly intelligent, with an astonishingly quick grasp of things and penetrating intuition. She possessed a powerful intellect which would have been capable of digesting solid mental pabulum and which stood in need of it — though without receiving it after she had left school. She had great poetic and imaginative gifts, which were under the control of a sharp and critical common sense. Owing to this latter quality she was *completely unsuggestable*; she was only influenced by arguments, never by mere assertions. Her will power was energetic, tenacious and persistent; sometimes it reached the pitch of an obstinacy which only gave way out of kindness and regard for other people.

One of her essential character traits was sympathetic kindness. Even during her illness she herself was greatly assisted by being able to look after a number of poor, sick people, for she was thus able to satisfy a powerful instinct. Her states of feeling always tended to a slight exaggeration, alike of cheerfulness and gloom; hence she was sometimes subject to moods. The element of sexuality was astonishingly undeveloped in her.[12] The patient, whose life became known to me to an extent to which one person's life is seldom known to another, had never been in love; and in all the enormous number of hallucinations which occurred during her illness that element of mental life never emerged.

This girl, who was bubbling over with intellectual vitality led an extremely monotonous existence in her puritanically minded family. She embellished her life in a manner which probably influenced her decisively in the direction of her illness by indulging in systematic day-dreaming, which she described as her 'private theatre'. While everyone thought she was attending, she was living through fairy tales in her imagination; but she was always on the spot when she was spoken to, so that no one was aware of it. She pursued this activity almost continually while she was engaged on her household duties, which she discharged unexceptionably. I shall presently have to describe the way in which this habitual day-dreaming while she was well passed over into illness without a break.

In July, 1880, the patient's father, of whom she was passionately fond, fell ill of a peripleuristic abscess which failed to clear up and to which he succumbed in April, 1881. During the first months of the illness Anna devoted her whole energy to nursing her father, and no one was much surprised when by degrees her own health greatly deteriorated. No one, perhaps not even the patient herself, knew what was happening to her; but eventually the state of weakness, anaemia and distaste for food became so bad that to her great sorrow she was no longer allowed to continue nursing the patient. The immediate cause of this was a very severe cough, on account of which I examined her for the first time. It was a typical *tussis nervosa*. She soon began to display a marked craving for rest during the afternoon, followed in the evening by a sleep-like state and afterwards a highly excited condition.

At the beginning of December a convergent squint appeared. An ophthalmic surgeon explained this (mistakenly) as being due to paresis of one abducens. On December 11 the patient took to her bed and remained there until April 1.

There developed in rapid succession a series of severe disturbances which were *apparently* quite new: left-sided occipital headache; convergent squint (diplopia), markedly increased by excitement; complaints that the walls of the room seemed to be falling over (affection of the obliquus); disturbances of vision which it was hard to analyze; paresis of the muscles of the front of the neck, so that finally the patient would only move her head by pressing it backwards between her raised shoulders and moving her whole back; contracture and anaesthesia of the right upper, and, after a time, of the right lower extremity. The latter was fully extended, abducted and rotated inwards. Later the same symptom appeared in the left lower extremity and finally in the left arm, of which, however the fingers to some extent retained the power of movement. So, too, there was no complete rigidity in the shoulder-joints. The contracture reached its maximum in the muscles of the upper arms. In the same way, the region of the elbows turned out to be the most affected by anaesthesia when, at a later stage it became possible to make a more careful test of this. At the beginning of the illness the anaesthesia could not be efficiently tested, owing to the patient's resistance arising from feeling of anxiety.

It was while the patient was in this condition that I undertook her treatment, and I at once recognized the seriousness of the psychical disturbance with which I had to deal. Two entirely distinct states of consciousness were present which alternated very frequently and without warning and which became more and more differentiated in the course of the illness. In one of these states she recognized her surroundings; she was melancholy and anxious, but relatively normal. In the other state she hallucinated and was 'naughty' — that is to say, she was abusive, used to throw the cushions at people, so far as the contractures at various times allowed, tore buttons off her bedclothes and linen with those of her fingers which she could move, and so on. At this stage of her illness if something had been moved in the room or someone had entered or left it (during her other state of consciousness) she would complain of having 'lost' some time and would remark upon the gap in her train of conscious thoughts. Since those about her tried to deny this and to soothe her when she complained that she was going mad, she would, after throwing the pillows about, accuse people of doing things to her and leaving her in a muddle, etc.

These *'absences'*[13] had already been observed before she took to her bed; she used then to stop in the middle of a sentence, repeat her last words and after a short pause go on talking. These interruptions gradually increased till they reached the dimensions that have just been described; and during the climax of the illness, when the contractures had extended to the left side of her body, it was only for a short time during the day that she was to any degree normal. But the disturbances invaded even her moments of relatively clear consciousness. There were extremely rapid changes of mood leading to excessive but quite temporary high spirits, and at other times severe anxiety, stubborn opposition to every therapeutic effort and frightening hallucinations of black snakes, which was how she saw her hair, ribbons and similar things. At the same time she kept on telling herself not to be so silly: what she was seeing was really only her hair, etc. At moments when her mind was quite clear she would complain of the profound darkness in her head, of not being able to think, of becoming blind and deaf, of having two selves, a real one and an evil one which forced her to behave badly, and so on.

In the afternoons she would fall into a somnolent state which lasted till about an hour after sunset. She would then wake up and complain that something was tormenting her — or rather, she would keep repeating in the impersonal form 'tormenting, tormenting'. For alongside of the development of the contractures there appeared a deep-going functional disorganization of her speech. It first became noticeable that she was at a loss to find words, and this difficulty gradually increased. Later she lost her command of grammar and syntax; she no longer conjugated verbs, and eventually she used only infinitives, for the most part incorrectly formed from weak past participles; and she omitted both the definite and indefinite article. In the process of time she became almost completely deprived of words. She put them together laboriously out of four or five languages and became almost unintelligible. When she tried to write (until her contractures entirely prevented her doing so) she employed the same jargon. For two weeks she became completely dumb and in spite of making great and continuous efforts to speak she was unable to say a syllable. And now for the first time the psychical mechanism of the disorder became clear. As I know, she had felt very much offended over something and had determined not to speak about it. When I guessed this and obliged her to talk about it, the inhibition, which had made any other kind of utterance impossible as well, disappeared.

This change coincided with a return of the power of movement of the extremities of the left side of her body, in March, 1881. Her paraphasia receded; but henceforward she spoke only in English — apparently, however, without knowing that she was doing so. She had disputes with her nurse who was, of course, unable to understand her. It was only some months later that I was able to convince her that she was talking English. Nevertheless, she herself could still understand the people about her who talked German. Only in moments of extreme anxiety did her power of speech desert her entirely, or else she would use a mixture of all sorts of languages. At times when she was at her very best the most free, she talked French and Italian. There was complete amnesia between these times and those at which she talked English. At this point, too, her squint began to diminish and made its appearance only at moments of great excitement. She was once again able to support her head. On the first of April she got up for the first time.

On the fifth of April her adored father died. During her illness she had seen him very rarely and for short periods. This was the most severe psychical trauma that she could possible have experienced. A violent outburst of excitement was succeeded by profound stupor which lasted about two days and from which she emerged in a greatly changed state. At first she was far quieter and her feelings of anxiety were much diminished. The contracture of her right arm and leg persisted as well as their anaesthesia, though this was not deep. There was a high degree of restriction of the field of vision: in a bunch of flowers which gave her much pleasure she could only see one flower at a time. She complained of not being able to recognize people. Normally, she said, she had been able to recognize faces without having to make any deliberate effort; now she was obliged to do laborious 'recognizing work'[14] and had to say to herself 'this person's nose is such-and-such, his hair is such-and-such, so he must be so-and-so'. All the people she saw seemed like wax figures without any connection with her. She found the presence of some of her close relatives very distressing and this negative attitude grew continually stronger. If someone whom she was ordinarily pleased to see came into the room, she would recognize him and would be aware of things for a short time, but would soon sink back into her own broodings and her visitor was blotted out. I was the only person whom she always recognized when I came in; so long as I was talking to her she was always in contact with things and lively, except for the sudden interruptions caused by one of her hallucinatory *'absences'*.

She now spoke only English and could not understand what was said to her in German. Those about her were obliged to talk to her in English; even the nurse learned to make herself to some extent understood in this way. She was, however, able to read French and Italian. If she had to read one of these aloud, what she produced, with extraordinary fluency, was an admirable extempore English translation.

She began writing again, but in a peculiar fashion. She wrote with her left hand, the less stiff one, and she used Roman printed letters, copying the alphabet from her edition of Shakespeare.

She had eaten extremely little previously, but now she refused nourishment altogether. However, she allowed me to feed her, so that she very soon began to take more food. But she never consented to eat bread. After her meal she invariably rinsed out her mouth and even did so if, for any reason, she had not eaten anything — which shows how absent-minded she was about such things.

Her somnolent states in the afternoon and her deep sleep after sunset persisted. If, after this, she had talked herself out (I shall have to explain what is meant by this later) she was clear in mind, calm and cheerful.

This comparatively tolerable state did not last long. Some ten days after her father's death a consultant was brought in, whom, like all strangers, she completely ignored while I demonstrated all her peculiarities to him. 'That's like an examination,'[15] she said, laughing, when I got her to read a French text aloud in English. The other physician intervened in the conversation and tried to attract her attention, but in vain. It was a genuine 'negative hallucination' of the kind which has since so often been produced experimentally. In the end he succeeded in breaking through it by blowing smoke in her face. She suddenly saw a stranger before her, rushed to the door to take away the key and fell unconscious to the ground. There followed a short fit of anger and then a severe attack of anxiety which I had great difficulty in calming down. Unluckily I had to leave Vienna that evening, and when I came back several days later I found the patient much worse. She had gone entirely without food the whole time, was full of anxiety and her hallucinatory *absences* were filled with terrifying figures, death's heads and skeletons. Since she acted these things through as though she was experiencing them and in part put them into words, the people around her became aware to a great extent of the content of these hallucinations.

The regular order of things was the somnolent state in the afternoon, followed after sunset by the deep hypnosis for which she invented the technical name of 'clouds'.[16] If during this she was able to narrate the hallucinations she had had in the course of the day, she would wake up clear in mind, calm and cheerful. She would sit down to work and write or draw far into the night quite rationally. At about four she would go to bed. Next day the whole series of events would be repeated. It was a truly remarkable contrast: in the day-time the irresponsible patient pursued by hallucinations, and at night the girl with her mind completely clear.

In spite of her euphoria at night, her psychical condition deteriorated steadily. Strong suicidal impulses appeared which made it seem inadvisable for her to continue living on the third floor. Against her will, therefore, she was transferred to a country house in the neighborhood of Vienna (on June 7, 1881). I had never threatened her with this removal from her home, which she regarded with horror, but she herself had, without saying so, expected and dreaded it. This event made it clear once more how much the affect of anxiety dominated her psychical disorder. Just as after her father's death a calmer condition had set in, so now, when what she feared had actually taken place, she once more became calmer. Nevertheless, the move was immediately followed by three days and nights completely without sleep or nourishment, by numerous attempts at suicide (though, so long as she was in a garden, these were not dangerous), by smashing windows and so on, and by hallucinations unaccompanied by *absences* — which she was able to distinguish easily from her other hallucinations. After this she grew quieter, let the nurse feed her and even took chloral at night.

Freud affirms that psychoanalysis originated in Breuer's treatment of Anna O.[17] It is remarkable, then, that such momentous exploration of an individual's mind appears, in retrospect, so blind to character. It is true that we are told that Anna O. is a persistent and obstinate young lady with energetic will power and a strong inclination to help the sick and the poor (enough to identify the preservation E1 style), but this understanding is very far from the psychodynamic awareness of modern psychoanalysis. Breuer's dismissal of his patient's insight into her own simulation suggests that he had fostered in her an understanding that transcended his own.

Some biographers, like Stephan Zweig, have the gift of being able to make historical characters speak according to their (the biographer's) insights into the character's personality style. Perhaps akin to the gift that Cuvier exhibited when he was able to reconstitute the shape of a prehistorical reptile from a few bones, such work is not fantasy, properly speaking, but an ability to move from inner dynamics to situational detail, such as is characteristic of writers who translate novels into movie scripts. Lucy Freeman is not only psychologically sophisticated, but has this gift, and I now quote some passages from her skillful reconstruction of the case.

On a hot evening in early July, he [Breuer] drove to the country home to find her mother very upset. "Now my daughter refuses to drink water," she said. "She is dying of thirst but she says she cannot touch a glass of water. She's living on fruit to quench her thirst."

He asked his patient, after hypnotizing her, "Are you thirsty?"

"Very thirsty," she said.

"Why can't you drink a glass of water?"

"I don't know." She shook her dark tresses.

"What prevents you from drinking?"

The nervous cough. Then, "I really don't know."

Perspiration ran down her cheeks, she seemed tortured by thirst. He handed her a glass of water. "Drink this," he said.

She promptly handed back the glass, her face distorted by disgust. "I can't."

The hot spell lasted six weeks and all that time she was

unable to drink, getting relief for her thirst by eating fruit. One evening she said to Breuer, "My brother thinks I'm crazy because I can't drink water."

Breuer occasionally caught a glimpse of a round-faced, red-haired young man with a rather morose expression, lurking in far corners of the house as though trying to elude him. He assumed this was her younger brother.

The day the heat broke, she greeted Breuer with a smile, saying, "My brother has gone back to Vienna. Now no one will make fun of me."

After he hypnotized her, Breuer asked, "Have you been able to drink water?

"No," she said. "And I've a tormenting thirst."

That word "tormenting" again. What tormented her so she could not drink a glass of water even though excruciatingly thirsty?

"What torments you?" he asked.

The words exploded from her parched lips: "That new governess! The one mother hired because she speaks English, so she can overhear what you and I say. I don't like her."

"She seems very pleasant," Breuer said.

"It's that horrid little dog of hers!" His patient's face held the same expression of disgust as when she had refused the glass of water.

"What's the matter with the little dog?" It looked like an innocuous white poodle who would not harm a crawling ant.

"He's a horror!"

"What did he do?" Breuer was puzzled by her intense reaction.

"The first day of the heat wave, the day the governess arrived, I went to her room to welcome her. And — "she paused, looked as though she had seen the most sordid sight possible, "there was this horrid little dog drinking water out of a glass she had placed on the floor!"

"What did you do?"

"I didn't do anything." Her eyes simmered with rage. "I wanted to tell her what I thought of the disgusting little creature.

But I held my tongue because I have been brought up to be polite to people, whatever their station in life. Though I felt like throwing something at her and her stupid dog!"

And, with these words, she seized an embroidered pillow with her left hand and hurled it venomously across the room as though it were a stick of dynamite she threw at an enemy.

Then, still in the hypnotic trance, she turned to Breuer, her fury and disgust replaced by a tranquil look.

"May I have a glass of water, please?" she asked. "I'm very thirsty."

Astounded, he stood up, walked into the kitchen, filled a glass with cold water, returned to her, handed her the glass. He expected her to push it away as she had done for the past six weeks as though she were suffering from hydrophobia.

Instead she said, "Thank you, Dr. Breuer," lifted the glass to her lips, daintily sipped the water.

He woke her from the trance, the glass at her lips. She set it casually on a table.

As he drove back to Vienna in the carriage, he thought in amazement of what had occurred. As the result of an accidental and spontaneous comment under hypnosis, a symptom that had persisted for a considerable time had cleared up. Or had it been "an accidental and spontaneous comment?" Was there a direct connection between her inability to drink water from a glass and the "horrid" little dog?

It had started when she saw the little dog drink from the governess' glass, a sight that disgusted and angered her. It was not until she was able, under hypnosis, to describe the scene, and speak of her anger and disgust, that she could once again drink from a glass.

She herself had given the clue when she spoke of something "tormenting" her. He persisted in asking what that torment was, and eventually she told him. Besides describing an experience, she spoke of feelings she had not expressed because she felt them impolite.

From then on, other symptoms that had returned upon her

father's death, vanished or improved. She suffered fewer hallucinations. The paralysis in her right leg disappeared and she could
walk without a limp. Breuer thought her mind much clearer, her
judgement improved.

But the talking cure was no quick, magical road to reality. At
times she would stop talking, obviously lost in fantasy. Once when
they sat in the garden talking, in the middle of a sentence she
stood up, ran to a tree, started to climb it. He followed and caught
hold of her, whereupon she resumed her interrupted sentence as
though nothing had happened. When he hypnotized her and
asked why she had run away, she said she had seen a large white
bird trapped at the top of the tree and had wanted to climb up and
rescue it.

She did rescue one animal. A relative had given her a large
Newfoundland dog to which she became very attached. One
evening as Breuer and she talked in the garden, the dog started to
growl, then dashed away from her side to attack a cat that was part
of the household feline menage.

She stood up, walked to the porch, seized what Breuer took
to be a whip and beat off the dog. Breuer could not help but
admire the way in which this frail girl, so beset by tormenting fantasies, quickly came to the rescue of the small victim. He then
noticed that what he had taken to be a whip was her riding crop.
Before her illness she had ridden horseback almost daily, an activity she very much enjoyed, she once told him.

August approached and this meant Breuer would take his
family on their summer vacation. He asked a physician who lived
near his young patient to substitute in his absence. On meeting
this physician, she seemed to like him, not ignoring him as she
had the earlier substitute.

On Breuer's return, he found she had permitted the physician to visit her though not to hypnotize her. But in spite of her
apparent acceptance of the substitute, she was again plunged in
deep depression. She would not talk to Breuer, even under hypnosis. He thought her excessive depression due to the lack of verbal release for her fantasies and feelings.

He told her mother, "I think you should arrange for your daughter to stay in Vienna for a week so I can see her every evening."

Her mother temporarily opened their new Viennese home. It was a different apartment from the one in which her husband had died and her daughter had fallen ill. She had not wanted to remain in the old one with its tragic memories.

Breuer was then able to visit his young patient every evening for a week, encouraging her to talk freely. The depression and rage that had accumulated during the weeks of his absence wore off and the former rapport was re-established.

The summer over, the household returned to Vienna. This meant Breuer would once again see his patient regularly. He hoped this would increase the effectiveness of the talking cure.[18]

Breuer was now confronted by several mysteries. Why could his young patient not live in the present? Why had a symptom — her inability to drink water — disappeared after her recollection, under hypnosis, of the scene of the little dog drinking from a glass?

Because of the way the symptom had vanished, Breuer wondered if each one of her physical symptoms might not be connected to an experience that had so disgusted or alarmed her that she had repressed both its memory and her feelings about it.

Perhaps, he thought, if he could persuade her to remember the specific experience each symptom brought to mind, all the symptoms — her cough, her poor vision, the paralysis of her right arm, her hallucination of snakes and death's heads — might vanish.

But this procedure would take up too much time in the evening sessions, time needed to help her overcome what he thought of as two sets of disturbances — her everyday irritations and her reminiscences of the year before. How could she possible cope with a third set of disturbances?

He was intrigued, however, by the possibility that each

symptom might be related to an experience that had produced an emotional reaction she could not express. It was a theory no one had ever proven, perhaps never even thought of. Breuer made a decision.

He would visit her twice a day — once in the morning and once in the evening, doubling the amount of time he was spending with her.

He explained what he wished to do. "I will visit you every morning and hypnotize you," he said. "After you have described whatever has been troubling you, or told a story from your private theater, or talked about your experiences on that day the year before, I will ask you to concentrate your thoughts on one symptom and try to remember the time, or times, this symptom appeared while you were nursing your father." He believed these five months constituted what he called the "incubation" of her illness.

"I will make notes on the morning visit," he continued. "Then, I will return in the evening at the regular hour and hypnotize you again. Referring to my notes of that morning, I will ask you to tell in detail all you remember about the time or times one symptom occurred."

She seemed delighted at his proposal. "I'll do my very best to try to remember," she said.

The next morning he followed the pattern he had outlined. He selected her poor vision, which at times amounted almost to total blindness, as symptom for the day.

"Can you remember the time, or times, while nursing your father, that your vision became blurred or you squinted?" he asked.

She thought for a moment, then said, "There was a night in November when I was reading and my eyes suddenly went so blurry I couldn't see the print. I had to put the book down."

She paused, added, "And a few weeks before that, one night I remember feeling so tired I could hardly see. But I managed to keep awake in case my father called for a drink of water or...." She stopped, blushed.

"Or what?" asked Breuer.

"In case I had to help him to the bathroom."

"Were there other times your eyes blurred?" he asked.

She thought again. She coughed. Then said, "Right after my father became sick, it was sometime in August while we were still living in the country, late at night he suddenly asked the time, and my eyes blurred."

That evening when Breuer returned to the apartment, he put her in a trance for the second time that day and asked, "What do you remember about the night your father wanted to know the time and your eyes blurred?" That experience lay deep in her memory. Though she had mentioned it last, it had been the first occurrence of her poor vision.

She spoke slowly, trying to remember. "I was sitting in the chair next to my father's bed and wondering if he were going to die from tuberculosis. I couldn't imagine living without my father. My eyes clouded with tears.

"I thought my father was asleep. Suddenly he asked, 'What time is it?' I tried to blink back the tears. I didn't want him to see them because he might guess how sick he was. I picked up his watch from the table by his bed. But I couldn't see the hands clearly. The tears blurred my eyes."

She coughed, went on. "I tried to see the time through the tears. I brought the watch close to my eyes. Its face seemed gigantic. I was conscious of squinting as I looked at it. It was quarter to twelve."

Tears came to her eyes, as though she were reliving the sad scene. With her left hand, now quite flexible, she took a lace handkerchief out of her pocket and daintily brushed away the tears. Breuer noticed her squint had again become very marked.

When he returned the next morning he found the apartment in an uproar. His young patient, who always lived in the previous year at night, had awakened screaming, arousing her mother, governess, and brother, insisting she had been taken from her old home to a strange place.

When he entered her room, Breuer noticed that her eyes

looked startlingly clear. The squint had completely disappeared.

"What happened last night?" She looked confused.

"I think perhaps that during my visit your recollections not only cleared up your vision but also your confusion about what year you are living in," he said. "When you woke in the middle of the night, sensing it was 1882 rather than 1881, the year in which you have been living at night, you found yourself in what you thought a strange room because you do not live in the same house as last winter."

"Please hypnotize me every evening as you leave," she begged, "and tell me I am not to open my eyes until morning. I don't want this to happen again. It's too frightening."

"If you wish," he said, and from then on he did so.

This worked well until one night when she woke crying as though her heart were breaking because she had found her beloved Newfoundland dog had died. But this time when she opened her eyes, even though the surroundings seemed strange, she did not become alarmed. When she told Breuer, he said, "That means you are now living more in the present than the past."

The second symptom whose psychic cause he tried to unravel was her nervous cough. After hypnotizing her in the morning, he suggested she recall the times she coughed at her father's bedside. In the evening, when she was in the trance, he asked, "What details do you remember about the first night you coughed at your father's side?"

She spoke as though in a dream. "I had just started to sit by his side at night and was not as yet used to the strange hours. Or to giving up a night's sleep, which meant I couldn't do anything during the day because I was too tired. It also meant I could never go out at night."

A pause. Then, "I suddenly heard the sound of music. An orchestra was playing next door. Our neighbors were giving a party to which I had been invited. I love to dance. I thought how much fun I was missing. Then I felt ashamed for being so selfish. I started to cough."

The following morning Breuer realized the persistent cough

that had plagued most of his visits had disappeared.

He then selected her deafness, what he described as her "passing habit of not hearing." He broke this down into seven categories, explaining, "Your inability to hear holds many variations."

In his first category, "not hearing when someone came in, while her thoughts were abstracted," she recalled a hundred and eight separate instances when this had occurred, remembering the persons involved, the circumstances, and often the exact date. The last experience she mentioned, the one furthest back in memory, was a time she did not hear her father return to his room after he had gone to the bathroom.

For Breuer's second category, "not understanding when several people were talking," she remembered twenty-seven instances. The earliest involved her father and an acquaintance.

To the third category, "not hearing when she was alone and directly addressed," she thought of fifty instances, the most remote having occurred when her father was forced to ask several times for some wine.

For Breuer's fourth category, "deafness brought on by being physically shaken," she remembered fifteen instances. The furthest back in memory was the night her brother shook her angrily when he caught her listening outside the door of her father's room.

For Breuer's fifth category, "deafness brought on by fright at a noise," she recalled thirty-seven instances. The memory she mentioned last was her terror when her father suffered a choking fit after swallowing some food the wrong way.

To Breuer's sixth category, "deafness during deep *absence*," she spoke of twelve instances. For the seventh category, "deafness brought on by listening hard for a long time, so that when she was spoken to she failed to hear," she remembered fifty-four instances.

Breuer noted that in each case the various experiences were so clearly differentiated in her memory that if she happened to make a mistake in their sequence she would correct herself and state them in the right order. If she did not do this, if he tried to hurry her onwards, she would stop talking.

Many of her experiences lacked interest or significance and were told in such detail that Breuer was certain she could not be inventing them. Some consisted of her reactions and sensations and could not be verified, but those that could he checked with her mother and found his young patient always accurate.

He noticed that when a symptom was being "talked away" it emerged for the moment with greater force. When she was trying to remember the times she could not hear, she became so deaf that for part of the visit he would have to communicate with her in writing.

The first time he had seen her she had been mute, and occasionally thereafter she would again fall mute for a day or so. Breuer now asked her to recall the times this had happened while she nursed her father.

"The first time I could not speak a word was when I had a fight with my mother," she said. "My mother accused me of leaving my father alone in his room for half an hour while I went downstairs to get something to eat in the kitchen. I knew I had been out of the room only ten minutes, and I was beside myself with fury but I didn't say anything."

She mentioned other moments when she held back anger at someone who accused her unfairly. Breuer concluded that she lost the power of speech whenever she felt angry after being unjustly blamed for something but was unable to speak up in her own behalf.

He found that the first cause of a symptom always seemed to be some sort of fright experienced while nursing her father. Often it was related to an oversight on her part, following which she became terrified at the thought her father might die.

Her cough, her disorders of vision, of hearing, of speech, were all "talked away" as she recalled the time the symptom first occurred and relived the feelings of that moment.

Breuer's wife was expecting a baby, their fifth child, and when he arrived half an hour late on the morning of March 11th, he apologized to his young patient.

"I'm sorry I was late," he said. "I was up most of the night.

My wife gave birth to a baby girl."

He could not quite fathom the look on his young patient's face, part consternation, part joy, part confusion. She said, "Congratulations, Dr. Breuer. You must be very happy."

"I am," he said. "Happy about the new baby. And happy you are feeling well once more."

He knew that remembering the experiences connected to a symptom was not always easy. There were times when she made a desperate effort, only to fail. No matter how hard he tried to help, she was the one who had to face the pain inherent in reviving buried memories.

But he sensed the greater pain would be in never recalling the memories. Then she would be crippled, perhaps forever, by the symptoms that served to suppress the memories and the feeling they evoked.

One memory refused to emerge. Breuer believed it lay at the root of her entire psychic illness — the hallucination of the snake and the death's head.

A hallucination might seem crazy to everyone else, he thought, but it was, to use her word, "tormenting" to the one who had to endure it. Breuer was determined to discover why the snake and the death's head terrorized his young patient.

One spring morning he hypnotized her and in accordance with their routine asked, "What were the times you saw a death's head?"

She thought a moment, then said, "One night when I was nursing my father, his face turned into a death's head."

Her father's face, then, stood for the death's head in her mind, as well it might, since he lay dying for months before her very eyes, and eventually his face, interred in a coffin, would be no more than a skull.

"Did this image ever occur to you before?" he asked.

She was again silent, as though searching deep into memory. Then she said, "I *do* remember another time!"

Her voice held the exultation that follows the sudden easing of pain, she had unlodged an experience embedded beyond supposed recall.

"When was that?" His voice as always was calm though he shared the exultation.

"Just after my father became ill. I was very tired because I never got enough sleep. I could hardly drag myself around days. But one afternoon I went to visit an aunt. I remember opening the door of a room in her house. Then falling to the floor in a dead faint."

"Why did you faint?"

"I don't know." She sounded puzzled. "I don't remember a thing."

"Perhaps this evening you will recall more."

That night, after he hypnotized her, he suggested, "Tell me about the visit to your aunt's home the day you opened a door, then fell unconscious to the floor."

"I don't remember anything more," she said, as she had said that morning.

Unlike other evenings, she seemed reluctant to explore the memory. But Breuer, sensing this to be the acid test of her treatment, of all the time he had given, of his belief he could ease her torment, persisted as forcefully as a compassionate physician could.

"Please try to remember," he urged. "This is very important."

"My mind is a blank. A white screen with nothing on it." She sighed.

"With all your strength, try to remember what you thought and felt as you entered that room," he insisted.

"I *can't* remember." It was a protest.

"Did you see something? Something so terrible it caused you to faint?"

She made the effort, a tortuous effort, because he asked, he pleaded, he insisted. Because she sensed it meant so much to him. And because she too was courageous.

The words came haltingly, as though spoken by a stranger, a stranger who possessed her, who fought against revealing what lay within.

"The...mirror," she said. "It ... was ... the ... mirror. It ... was ... in ... the ... mirror. It ..." She gasped, stopped.

"Go on." His words were whispered, he did not want to destroy the delicate thread that connected memory to memory.

A deep sigh flowed from her and now she spoke more naturally, as though telling a story. "When I reached my aunt's house, the maid asked me to wait in the parlor because my aunt was dressing. I opened the door to the parlor. The first thing I saw, facing me across the room, was the large oval mirror framed in gold.

"Gold ... like his hair, and your hair too, your hair has a golden tint. Not his hair as he was old and dying, then it was as white as the sheets on which he lay. But his hair when he was young, when he would play with me in the country garden and threw me up in the sky, and as I fell into his arms I would clutch at the golden hair for safety."

She stopped. He waited.

She repeated, "It was the mirror." Then was silent.

"What about the mirror?" he asked.

"When I flung open the door to the parlor, I expected to see the mirror and my face reflected in it. But instead I saw the face of my father. His hair was white, his face was twisted in pain, the way it looked so many nights while ... I ... watched ... over him." Her voice broke as though she could not go on.

Breuer's tone was firm, telling her she must. "Was that why you fainted?"

"No."

She retreated into silence. Again Breuer persisted. "What happened then?"

It was caught at last, the elusive, tenuous thread, as she said, "My father's face in the mirror turned into the face of death. A death's head. Leering at me. I screamed. Then I fell to the floor in a faint."

She was quiet, lost in fantasy. But she had remembered the first time she saw a death's head and if his theory was correct, she would no longer be haunted by this hallucination. She had relived the terror and fear of that moment and thus freed herself from its threat. She was feeling much better, all physical symptoms had vanished except for the paralysis in her right arm. This had decreased but still prevented full use of the arm.

He was hoping his visits might soon end. He sensed, especially since he had started the twice-a-day visits, that his wife resented the amount of time he spent away from his family. The summer before she had not complained of his long drives to the country. But during her pregnancy she had seemed irritable because he was not home in the evening. He did not wish to upset her even though he felt compelled to see his patient's treatment through to the end. He had been a pioneer in physiological research because of his persistence and now he sensed he might have made an important discovery about hysteria.

He thought his slim young patient very winning, with her expressive blue eyes, flawless white complexion and dark flowing hair. He admired her intelligence, wit, and charm, all of which seemed heightened as she shook off her symptoms. But he was devoted to his wife and five children, he would never dream of involvement with this young woman, about whom he occasionally spoke at home and about whom his daughter Bertha, who remembered the ride in the *Prater*, sometimes inquired.

He was therefore glad to hear his young patient say one morning in May, "June seventh is the anniversary of the day when I moved to the country last year, and by this June seventh, I am determined to be cured so you will not have to take that long trip."

"Fine." His voice held approval.

Since the June deadline was only a matter of weeks, they concentrated on trying to discover the experience that had caused the paralysis in her right arm.

"It first felt stiff one night at our country home as I was watching at my father's bedside. But I don't remember anything special about that night," she told Breuer.

No matter how often he urged her, under hypnosis, to recall more details, she could remember not one. Her mind seemed like cement hardened over the roots of recall.

It was June 6th, their next to last meeting, and still her mind refused to yield a memory. Breuer thought he might have to admit defeat on this one symptom.

Then he had an idea. "Let's rearrange the room to resemble your father's room in the country," he suggested. "Perhaps the similarity will help you remember what happened the night your arm first felt paralyzed."

"His bed was over there." She pointed to the center of a wall against which stood a small bookcase. Breuer took out the books, placed the bookcase to one side. Then he moved her light bed to the wall.

"His bureau was there." She pointed to the right of the bed, and Breuer, taking out the drawers, shifted her bureau to that spot.

"And I sat here." She indicated a space to the left of the bed. Breuer put a chair there to represent the one she had occupied in her father's room.

She sat in the chair beside the empty bed, he drew up another to sit beside her. Then he hypnotized her.

"Imagine your father lying on that bed," he said. "You are entrusted with his care. You have to make sure nothing happens to him, that he gets through the night without pain. To see he has enough water to drink, that he is kept warm, that he goes to the bathroom if he needs to.

"You sit there hour after hour, a dim light burning. No one else is awake — in the house, in the countryside. You are exhausted. You never get enough sleep. You want to close you eyes. But you are terrified that your father, a man you love deeply, may die if you fall asleep and fail to meet his slightest need."

At that moment Breuer wondered why she had been asked to take on such truly tormenting duties, why had her mother not hired the night nurse immediately and spared her daughter the horror of watching her father die under her very eyes? The family could well afford it, they were one of the wealthiest in Vienna.

His plan had worked, she was returning in memory at long last to that night. She was saying, her voice low, controlled, "I was exhausted. I was so tired I couldn't keep my eyes open even though my father had a high fever and needed to be watched carefully. It was a crisis in his illness. The local doctor had called in a surgeon from Vienna who was traveling there that night by train to operate on my father the next day. I had been left alone in the house, except for the maid. My mother had gone to Vienna for a few days. I don't remember why. I think some relative was sick. She was planning to return the next day in time for the operation."

Breuer decided the operation was probably the first time an incision was to be made in her father's back between ribs, to drain the fluid from the pleural abscess so he could breathe more easily.

"The maid had stayed with my father all day while I tried to sleep, though I couldn't. I was too worried. But that night, in spite of knowing how important it was that I stay awake because of his fever, I couldn't help myself. I fell asleep. I don't know how long I slept. But I woke with a start, feeling very guilty."

She stopped, as though it were all too much for her, both the original experience and the telling of it.

Breuer's gentle voice insisted: "What happened when you woke up? There you were, sitting in the chair by your father's bed. What did you see as you opened your eyes?"

She let out a sharp cry. "A snake! A big black snake! It was slithering across the wall. That wall!" pointing to the wall behind the bed. "It was going to attack my father. Bite him! Poison him! Kill him!" Her face contorted in terror.

"What did you do?" Breuer's voice was low.

"I wanted to drive it away, but when I tried to raise my right arm, which I had flung across the back of the chair as I slept, I found I couldn't move it. It was paralyzed!"

There was a soft moan, then, "I just couldn't ... move my right arm! I turned to look at it, to see what was wrong. Each finger was a little black snake. And each nail, a death's head."

She put her hand to her throat as though choking. "I was powerless to save my father. He would die and it would be all my fault. I tried to pray. But I couldn't remember a single prayer, all I could think of was the lines, from an old English nursery song — 'All the King's horses and all the King's men, Couldn't put Humpty Dumpty together again.' At that moment I heard the whistle of a train. There was only one train a night and I knew this one held the surgeon from Vienna who was coming to operate on my father.

"I forced myself to look at the wall behind my father's bed. The snake had vanished. My father was breathing naturally. He was all right. The snake hadn't attacked him. Then I looked at my right hand and saw fingers once more. And the nails were no longer death's heads."

She sighed in relief, appearing as exhausted as though she had once again spent the night by her father's bed.

Breuer, concealing his excitement at her revelations, asked quietly, "When was the next time you saw a snake?"

"The following afternoon when I played quoits on the lawn. Inside the house my father was being operated on by the surgeon, who had slept at the inn. He walked into my father's room early that morning, while I was still sitting there, and I was so upset from the night's experience that I didn't even hear him enter."

"My mother had come back from Vienna and ordered me to sleep for a while, then get some fresh air. So I went outside. I threw a quoit into the bushes by mistake. When I leaned over to pick it up, I thought I saw another snake. I screamed. And my right arm again felt paralyzed. Then I realized it wasn't a snake. It was only a bent branch."

"Were there snakes in the field behind your house?" Breuer asked.

"I saw a few when I was a little girl picking wildflowers for my mother. I would always run from them, afraid they would kill me."

"Do you remember other times during your father's illness when you saw a snake?"

"Occasionally I would see something that looked like a snake. A piece of rope on the floor. Or a long curly strand of black hair. And for a moment it would confuse me."

Breuer thought it probable that on the night she fell asleep by her father's bed, she had wanted to drive off the snakes with an

arm partially paralyzed by the sensation people call "pins and nee-
dles," caused by the unnatural position of her arm as she slept.
The paralysis of her right arm, spreading later to her left arm, then
both legs, became associated with the hallucination of the snake,
he believed, a hallucination that became more and more frequent
until finally both arms and legs were so afflicted she could not
move.

He woke her from the hypnotic trance. "How does your
right arm feel?"

She lifted it hight above her head.

"It's fine," she said. "There's nothing wrong with it at all."
(pp.31-53)

Anna O.'s protectiveness and high anxiety allow us to confirm her
personality diagnosis as that of the preservation subtype of E1, in which
excessive responsibility takes on the form of a passion for worrying and
fussing. From our knowledge of this character, we can imagine that her
intense "love" for her father entailed an intense and frustrated desire for his
tenderness and an intense motivation to deserve it, as well as an unconsciousness concerning what her need to try so hard was about.

Let us imagine, then, the situation of an over-responsible, father-
loving and frustrated Anna O., when put in the role of nursing her dying
father over months, from evening to daybreak. Obviously, the task is coherent with her dutifulness, yet intensely frustrating and anxiety-provoking in
its demand — particularly to a young girl inexperienced in nursing.

Only towards the end of his treatment (as Lucy Freeman tells us),
did Breuer wonder why such a wealthy family would put Anna in this position and not take a nurse. If the question did not arise in Anna O.'s mind,
this must have been due to her compulsive dutifulness. I am sure that it was
also an expression of the fact that Anna O.'s mother was also a spartan perfectionist. That Anna was angry about it is clear, and we may take her sickness to be a negative transformation of unconscious anger into psychopathology. Anna O. reported to Breuer that two personalities, or states
of mind, alternated in her: one civilized, the other naughty; and ill-temper
is no less significant a symptom than her pseudo-neurological disturbances.

A threatening skull is not an expression of a fear of her father's death, though its true significance may be screened by this more acceptable meaning: she is in dread of being attacked because she is full of unacknowledged rage. The hallucinations of skulls at the end of her fingers are revealing in this regard: deadliness is in herself. Yet, the reciprocal hostility between her father and herself would have been impossible to acknowledge in her puritanical milieu. Her muteness appears as something as bizarre as her hallucinations — a sickness unrelated to the reality of her situation.

Let me draw attention to the appropriateness of the alternative expression through which Anna O. refers to her "talking cure" — i.e., "chimney sweeping." This term involves a sense of something dirty in her, something that communication under trance cleanses. What is the nature of this cleaning? Let us take the example of her inability to drink water, that was cured when she connected it to the way her nurse's dog was drinking from a glass. Her disgust (supported by her character structure) was repressed, along with her anger at this dog and her nurse. When these feelings became acceptable, the symptom vanished. I think that her psychic "distress" consisted in anger, for the most part, like in this instance. Yet, "anger" itself was cleaned when expressed in the context of the warm intimacy of the therapeutic relationship.

Seemingly, the expression of anger itself was remedial (as when throwing a pillow cured her paralyzed arm); yet, this expression is itself the visible outcome of the less visible redemptive quality of acceptance by her internalized father.

Toward the end of her life, Bertha Pappenheim's acceptance of her own rage would make her able to stand up (successfully) to the Gestapo.

As she faced the uniformed storm troopers at Gestapo headquarters she stood erect as always, though she was in pain.

"One of the children you are responsible for has called Hitler a criminal." This was the accusation. It might mean death to them all, the children, the girls, the staff.

Her voice was matter-of-fact. "It is quite possible Maria said this. But you can't take her seriously. She's retarded. No one can be held responsible for what comes out of a defective mind."

She was so calm, she convinced the Gestapo. They let her go. (p. 166)

Of course, Anna's desire for her father's tenderness was transferred onto Breuer, her prestigious and attentive (probably E9) physician. She is twenty-one and he middle-aged and blond (as her father, as she remarks). Likely, Breuer felt more attracted to her than he reports, for we know that his wife was worried about his excessive attentions to Anna. After so many decades there is no way of telling what was the stimulus for Anna O.'s belief that she was going to have his baby, but I cannot doubt that she had established a strong, though not explicit, sexual transference by the time Breuer took her out for a carriage ride in Vienna's Prater, in the company of his own daughter. Every time Breuer needed to absent himself for some time, Anna's condition deteriorated in such a way that we sense that she was indirectly screaming for attention. (Though her whole illness bears the character of E1 shifted to E4[19] , it is in these moments that manipulation through suffering becomes most visible in the story).

This final manipulation through imaginary pregnancy precipitated the end of his visits. Freeman writes:

> He knew he must not see her again. He had to entrust her future care to others. He had gone as far as he dared. He could not jeopardize her, or himself, by trying to explore psychic realms no man had ever touched upon. He had been pioneer enough.

And then she ends her chapter with,

> Months later, the colleague told Breuer the young woman had become a morphine addict as the result of drugs he prescribed to calm her. A year later, Breuer heard she had been sent to a sanitarium.
>
> He wondered if it would not be better if she died and thus be spared further suffering.

Though the case of Anna O. can claim to be the most famous in the annals of therapy with an obsessive (though reputedly hysterical) personality, and does illustrate a near-psychotic expression of the displacement of the E1 to the E4 pattern, it is questionable to what extent it can claim to be a success.

Her therapy is not a case of character transformation; and we can hardly expect that more insight into her personality would have arisen from her relationship with a psychiatrist from the days before character had become a psychoanalytic interest. Besides, throughout the whole of Freud's work, his case reports are pale in terms of character description. He was, in this domain, less preceptive than Abraham, Adler, Reich or Horney.

Deciding to enlarge this present book through the addition of case reports illustrating less questionable therapeutic successes, I have selected two short accounts from Dr. Charles Berg (a British contemporary of Freud) who seems to have been specially competent with E1 individuals, for these are better represented than others in his work, *The Case Book of a Medical Psychologist*.[20]

TWO REPORTS FROM BERG

CASE: IX GOD VERSUS DEVIL

When I was about 19, the following thought came into my mind: I imagined God on His throne. I shook my fist at Him and said in imagination that I would prefer to go to the Devil.

Now, I certainly did not wish to go to the Devil, and why this thought should come bursting into my mind I do not know. I recalled it some weeks later and began to feel very guilty. In fact I thought I had committed an enormous crime against God, and I feared that I was damned. I could not get it out of my mind, and it has caused me agonies, day and night, ever since.

I might mention that, at that time (I was 19 years of age) I was very much in love with a girl. But, strangely enough, I was scared of her...too scared to give her any indication of my feelings.

Although I am now 36, I do not think I have made any progress since that time. I am still just as scared of women, and the feeling of guilt for the insult to God still keeps recurring in my mind.

When I received the above letter, it seemed to me impossible to help such a man by correspondence, and I therefore asked him to come and see me.

At the interview he said:

"My trouble has come to a head. I am again in love with a girl, and am too scared to give her any indication of it. I have a married friend about the same age as myself, and I have fallen in love with his daughter of 17.

"When they were on a holiday, I went all the way to Scotland, determined to declare my love. I spent a week with them, but found I could never bring myself to say a word. I got back, terribly disappointed with myself. I developed strange ideas that I was impotent. I have never had any experience, so I don't know if I am or not.

"What I have been brooding about is my inability to express what I felt so keenly. I am not particularly afraid of people in a group, or at parties, but I am scared stiff of a woman in any intimate relationship. Whenever I feel amorous towards a girl, I just seem to fall down, and can't do a thing.

"At 19, I was in love with a girl. That is when I got my obsession that has worried me ever since. The love petered out: the obsession has persisted. I had no interest in women for the next ten years or more, and then I fell in love with the present girl, when she was just a child of 14.

"Not only is there this fear of being in an intimate relationship with a woman, but I am also obsessed with the fear concerning that blasphemous thought. The reason for this seems to be that I had sold myself to the devil, merely by thinking this thought to myself. It is a fear of being possessed by the devil. I know it is rather absurd and based on the old theology. The devil seems to represent all that is evil or bad.

"The fear of selling myself to the devil takes my thoughts back to a dream I had at the age of 5 or 6 years. I was sleeping with my mother at the time. I woke up trembling very violently. I thought I saw a phantom fly across the room. It was like a flame, and yet it was like an imp grinning at me. It flew across the room and out of the window. I was scared to death."

Analyst: "What is the flame you would get if you were sleeping with your mother?"

Patient: "Love of my mother, I suppose."

Analyst:"What is the flame you would get if you were sleeping with a young lady?"

Patient: "Passion."

Analyst: "Would you?"

Patient: "No, I expect I should be scared to death, and trembling violently, like I was in the dream."

(*Silence*)

Analyst: "What are you thinking?"

Patient: "I was thinking to ask you what are the effects of masturbation. I started masturbating at the age of 10. At 15 or 16 I thought it was very wrong and sinful. Is this guilty fear of mine a matter of a bad conscience? I tell myself that the devil is merely a symbol, but there is a childish fear as though he were real, and a fear that I have committed myself to him. I often wonder why the thought ever occurred to me. Has it anything to do with the fact that I was at that time keen on this girl and too scared to do anything about it? I might have regarded the whole of sex as wrong. Perhaps I was saying this to God: 'If God forbids any expression of sex, I will have none of God, I will have the devil, that is Sex.'

"And then I got the reaction, and have since felt that any feelings of the kind had better be repressed.

"My parents were both rather tyrannical about the whole thing. Now my main concern is the idea or obsession that I am possessed by the devil."

Analyst: "Suppose you are?"

Patient: "That would mean that one would lose control of one's will."

Analyst: "What is natural?"

Patient: "Do you mean that what I am afraid of is my own

natural urge to live a normal natural life, and that that would include a natural expression towards a woman, and enjoyment of my work, and to have a number of friends around me?"

Analyst: "What for?"

Patient: "I naturally like people and company."

Analyst: "What for?"

Patient: "Well, I'd feel terribly nervous if I were left with one girl; I should not know what to say or do. I might feel the urge to tell her that I liked her, and on the other hand I'd be too scared to do anything about it."

Analyst: "Devils are not so scared."

Patient: "If it is the devil I am afraid of, would he lead to natural, normal love? If I were possessed of the devil I suppose I'd make love to her."

Analyst: "Is that what the devil would do?"

Patient: "I don't follow the trend of the argument."

Analyst: "Perhaps you did when you were 5 or 6, when you were sleeping with your mother, and saw the little devil fly across the room."

Here the session ended, but the patient was determined to come back the next day to continue it. He was given an afternoon appointment. But a few hours after he had left he telephoned, begging to come back that same evening. As I could not see him then he wished for an early appointment next morning. That, too, had to be refused. Finally, when he arrived at the appointed hour, he was still full of excitement and ideas.

He said: "I am better. I see it now. My fear of the devil that I have had since I was 19, or perhaps since I was 5, is nothing more or less than a fear of my sexual nature. The thoughts I have been having roused all sorts of specters in my mind."

Analyst: "For example?"

Patient: "I have been wondering if my fear is due to a fear that I might be cruel to the girl, or do her some physical injury...commit some crime.

"A few days ago I read of such a crime in the paper. A man

killed his wife. Such crimes, particularly sexual crimes, have always filled me with a sense of most utter repugnance and dread. Is that because there is something like that in me? Perhaps I am scared of a girl because I am terrified that my sexual feelings might run away with me, and I might not act rationally."

Analyst: "What might you do?"

Patient: "I might love her too much."

Analyst: "What would that lead to?"

Patient: "My desire would be to put my arms around her, and tell her I love her. But I was scared."

Analyst: "Does that seem so terrifying?"

Patient: "Well, I might lose control, and go too far."

Analyst: "How far might you go?"

Patient: "Well, I might have sexual intercourse with her: that would be going too far."

Analyst: "Would it?"

Patient: "Well, perhaps not as far as sexual intercourse. If that is the devil, perhaps he is quite a harmless devil. Perhaps the sooner I went to the devil the better."

Analyst: "If that is all there is to it, why is there all this scare?"

Patient: "Apparently all this time I have been afraid of being possessed by my own nature. The thing I want more than anything else is to lead a normal natural life. Since coming to you I have understood that this fear of being sold to the devil is nothing more or less than fear of my own nature on the one hand, and on the other hand a preference for it, which I have thought was preference for the devil."

"The whole amazing thing has become quite plain to me. It is amazing how the obsession left me last night after that talk with you.

"I had been fearing that having said to God that I would go to the devil, there was no turning back. Now I see that it was just two opposite parts of my own nature in conflict with each other. Part of my mind was synonymous with God, and I would allow no sexual expression at all. On the other hand, the devil was synonymous with sexual expression.

"At the time when I was in love with this girl at 19, I wanted sexual expression, and thus I turned to God and said, 'I will prefer the devil.' But immediately I thought that, I was frightened. I felt I was sold to the devil. I was so frightened that I have striven ever since to run away from the devil. And I am still afraid of girls.

"I have not yet told you that the real reason I came to you was a feeling I had last week — a feeling of fear that I might commit suicide. It is not that I have a desire to do so, but a fear that I might do it against my will."

Patient: "The only thing I can think of, except suicide in my present state of mind, is a fear that I might get hold of some girl and have sexual intercourse with her."

Analyst: "What happens then?"

Patient: "Sexual intercourse must terminate when ones desire is satisfied."

Analyst: "What happens when it is satisfied?"

Patient: "It is dead. It has led to its own suicide."

Analyst: "Is that anything to be afraid of?"

Patient: "No, I see it now.

"I tried to ignore all these things. At 19 I was so infatuated with the girl, yet so scared, that I could not approach her. The feeling was so strong that it seemed to bottle itself up. Thus it was all or nothing with me. So far it has been nothing. With the present girl, when I feel so strongly about her, I feel I must do something about it. I do nothing. I am afraid of that devil."

Analyst: "It does not look as though you have sold yourself to that devil after all."

Patient: "If it broke out, I would go wild."

Analyst: "And that is?"

Patient: "Possibly I might hurt the girl in some way. The thought occurs to me that in this frenzy I might kill the girl."

Analyst: "How would you kill her?"

Patient: "I might strangle her, with my hands round her neck."

Analyst: "What is it that you are strangling?"

Patient: "I am strangling my own feelings — my own feelings of a great desire for sexual intercourse with her."

Analyst: "So the girl stands for your desire which you are so afraid of, just as the devil stood for it. In this phantasy of strangling the girl you are dramatizing the struggle that is within your own mind. What might you do with the girl instead of strangling her?"

Patient: "Nothing — except sexual intercourse in the normal manner. But, surely, I would not have been so scared of that all my life. Can it be that I have been so scared because I am a sex maniac?"

Analyst: "Or an anti-sex maniac?"

Patient: "Last night ... you will appreciate that I was rather stirred up after my conversation with you ... I had an extraordinary attack of nasal catarrh."

Analyst: "What is nasal catarrh?"

Patient: "Congestion ... mental indigestion ... feelings which cannot obtain expression ..."

Analyst: "Expression of what?"

Patient: "Expression of nature...expression of my sexual nature. Nasal catarrh is also an emission of fluid. Is that a manifestation of congested sexual feelings?"

Analyst: "If so, they were rather at the wrong end, weren't they? Like the strangling."

Patient: "Are these the things the devil is doing to me? I have often had the crazy fear that one of these days I might come home and find him sitting in the chair waiting for me."

Analyst: "What does he look like?"

Patient: "Like the picture of Mephistopheles — a long, hooked nose, pointed chin, pointed ears, slit eyes, and a reddish face. In fact, the usual stage figure."

Analyst: "Thinking of that vision vaguely, what is the thought that comes into your mind?"

Patient: "I have got it! I told you, didn't I, that I used to masturbate from about 10 years of age to about 16? Then I stopped the habit with difficulty. It was after that, when I was in love with the girl that I said to God, 'I prefer the devil.' I suppose the same devil as I had given up. I had the idea that it had done me harm physically."

The letter which I wrote to this patient before I had ever seen him, in reply to his original letter, was as follows:

"The symptoms of which you complain such as 'Shaking your fist at God,' clearly reveal a conflict between two opposing sides of your personality. While you are trying to support the 'good' side, your 'lower nature' naturally feels unduly oppressed, and it is this which shakes its fist, as it were, at its oppressor, the other side of you.

"The measure of this oppression of one side of yourself may be revealed in your fear of the girl (i.e. the natural side of yourself—because this is what the girl stands for in your psychology).

"In other words, the measure of the repression of your nature can be gauged from the fact that you are 36, and still unmarried, and still with these conflicts about yourself."

The material which the patient provided in his three interviews only amplifies and confirms the conclusion cryptically put forward in my reply to his letter.

The case is chosen on account of the simple and clear conflict between the patient's sexual instincts on the one hand and his ego ideal on the other.

His life has evidently been an unusually successful attempt to mobilize his instinct energy on the side of his ego ideal, and against his sexual instincts. These latter he has identified with the concept of the devil.

It seems that only once did he willfully and consciously lean towards the latter, and the worry of this choice has obsessed him ever since. The reason why this obsession has persisted is because the energy of his sexual instincts has also persisted.

He succeeded in keeping sexual conduct at bay, by this persistent obsessional preoccupation of keeping the devil at bay. Thus, his obsessional activity had been a substitute for a normal sexual life.

The morbid factor in the situation had been the unusual degree of anxiety or scare of these instinct forces. This fear has transferred itself on to the natural object of this instinct (the girl), and thus he has always been scared of any intimate situation with a woman.

On account of the abnormally strong defenses against normal sexuality, the instinct "to do something to the woman" had been prevented from taking a normal conscious form, but has nevertheless been too strong to remain permanently repressed, and has therefore emerged, but in an altered or displaced fashion.

In fact, it is the familiar mechanism of displacement upwards which causes him in phantasy to do something with his hands, the upper part of him, to her neck, the upper part of her.

This abnormal travesty of the sexual act is then used as a rationalization for his fear of what his impulses will do to the woman, and, as it were, a justification for his continued repression of his instinct.

Helped by real insight into these mechanisms, a good deal of the morbid structure is already breaking down, even after a few interviews. With a further lessening of his anxiety it is a foregone conclusion that this patient will find a more healthy and happy method of releasing his natural energies than by maintaining his obsessional preoccupations. (pp.77-83)

CASE XIII: WHO AM I?

A young lady of 19 was brought to me on account of "strange feelings in her head."

She had been attending the mental out-patients' department of a hospital on and off for several years, but, nevertheless, during the last few months her condition had become considerably worse, and she was now unable to continue at her work (shorthand-typist), and moreover was unable to venture out of the house unaccompanied. Her parents rightly felt that they could not tolerate the thought of her being permanently invalidated at this youthful age, and that something more intensive than sporadic attendance at a mental out-patient department was necessary. Accordingly, it was arranged that she should attend for psychotherapeutic treatment three times weekly.

I saw a healthy-looking plump girl, very neatly dressed, almost circumspect in her appearance and deportment.

What struck me most at the first attendance was the very careful way in which she walked, as though she were picking her steps. It appeared subsequently that not only her movements, but also her every thought was carefully picked. There was a purpose behind this over-carefulness.

At this, and at all her subsequent sessions, she arranged herself precisely and complacently on the settee, and adopted a general demeanor of calm and contentment.

It was difficult to break through her calm, or to persuade her to abandon this over-carefulness, in action, speech or, it transpired, even in thought. When she can be persuaded to speak she says always the same thing.

"All that is in my mind is what I have already said to you before. There is nothing but the same feelings and the same thoughts."

Analyst: "Well, if you have nothing else to say, you must say that, even if you have said it before."

She says:

"The feeling is that I don't know who I am. My thoughts consist only of one thing all the time: a condition of puzzlement, as though I did not know who or what I am—as though I did not recognize myself, and cannot remember anything. My mind seems to consist of one thing only, and that is just a sort of feeling as though I am only just alive. That is all, and that I don't know anything else, except that I am just alive, and I am not always sure about that, but the feeling is with me all the time. It is as though it seems to put a sort of *stop* to all other thoughts and feelings. If I say a thing, or do a thing, I just can't imagine that I have done it. It does not seem to be me. There seems to be no connection between what I have done and me. It's as though I had no memory for anything that has happened, even if it is something I have done only a moment ago.

My mind seems to be occupied only with these strange feelings, and even these I seem to be holding carefully in check. But in spite of this they sometimes are inclined to reach a pitch, and then I feel at the moment that something terrible is going to happen. I feel that something is going to burst or explode in my head. I think that is the feeling I am trying to stop, and in consequence I have this feeling of something that stops me, that is always present in my head. If, in spite of this feeling to stop, I do get right up to this pitch, then it seems it cannot go any further, and I get awfully hot and confused. After that it goes back to the ordinary feelings again, the feelings of not knowing who I am, and of something stopping me. That is all."

These are the sort of statements that this patient makes over and over again, in part or in whole, after the first few minutes of silence, at the beginning of every one of her sessions. For some few weeks it seems that we shall never get any farther. The task of curing her, or even of making the slightest progress, seems hopeless. That stop, or full stop, in her mind appears to be stopping every therapeutic endeavor.

The question arises in the mind of the analyst, what is that stop stopping?

She herself has provided a partial clue when she says:

"I feel that something is going to burst or explode in my head."

That is, it would seem that she is stopping something from reaching a heightened intensity or climax.

In due course attempts are made to pass beyond a mere repetition of all these current mental experiences and feelings by pressing her with various questions. She is asked when she first experienced the condition which she complains of, and how it came about. She says:

"It suddenly came upon me, this feeling that I don't know who I am, at the age of 15, when I was looking at myself in the glass, and it has never left me since."

Analyst: "What had you been doing or feeling just prior to the event?"

"I can't remember. In fact, with these feelings in my head I have no memory at all for anything. Before that happened, I was perfectly well and happy. I wish I could get back to that state. I don't seem to be able to realize that I am the same person that I was before that happened. I was alive before that, and now I don't recognize myself."

Analyst: "Tell me about that liveliness. Did it feel nice to be alive?"

"I can't remember it; I can't remember what it felt like. There seems to be this stop in my mind which prevents me from knowing anything, from knowing what I was like, or what I felt, and even from recognizing who I am."

There can hardly be a more vivid account of the operation of repression within the mind than that which this patient is giving us. What is she repressing, and can we get her ever to give us an account of the conflict or fight with herself which led to such extreme measures as this, and to the persistent holding to these symptoms, rather than that she should revive the struggles and experiences which she has evidently been at such pains to forget? That these experiences against which she had struggled were very important to the feeling life of the psyche is beyond question from the fact that, with their successful repression, has gone a recognition of her own personality and the memory of everything that could be of importance to her feeling life. In place of it we have this new feeling life that is confined to the symptoms of which she complains.

One can only reply to her, as I did at one of her sessions:

"You do not recognize yourself, because it is not you. What has happened to the 'you' that lived before you were 15, when you were perfectly well and happy? Why can't you be the person you were then? The feelings that that person had, what was there about these feelings that you have been at such pains to forget, to put a full stop to—a stop which had ever since remained in your head? Evidently you prefer your present condition to the happy condition you had before you were 15, and against which you have fought so hard. At present you are clinging on to these symptoms lest you remember, and lest the mental experiences of that previous happy time come back to you and are remembered and re-experienced. What a fight you must have had against them!"

Nevertheless, the patient begins each session just as though it were again the first session. She enunciates the current feelings which comprise her illness, and claims that there is nothing else in her mind.

She continues:

"While I lie here and tell you about it the room seems to go round and round. It seems to make me giddy, as if there was something pressing on my brain the whole time. It seems to make me so dull."

Analyst: "Is it as though there is something you won't let your mind think about?"

(*Silence*)

Patient: "I can remember that when I was at school, and even up to quite recently, if ever anything was spoken about sex I used to get nervous. It used to make me terribly hot in my head, and my feet and legs would go cold. I wondered if others got the feeling. I thought it might injure my inside in some way. I used to worry about that. It seemed to push all the blood into my head, and then I could not think clear, and my mind would be dull."

Analyst: "That is the same as the feelings that you complain of now. And you say this was when you were in school. What age are you referring to?"

Patient: "I can't really remember. I think I used to imagine a lot of sexy things. I can't remember very well, but that seemed to be the beginning of it."

Analyst: "Tell me the sexy things you used to imagine?"

Patient: "Did I say 'sexy'? I don't know why I said 'sexy.' It was, I think, just when I felt nervous. I think it was just worry that something would do me some harm. Anyhow, my legs and feet would go cold and my head hot. I seemed all nervy at the time. And there would be this feeling of something hot rushing up to my head. I must have been only ten years of age when it started. There seems to be something that I used to like, but I can't remember what it was. All that I can remember is that it used to worry me. I had a queer feeling that some feeling I used to get would do me harm, would injure my inside. I knew that used to worry me a lot. Even then I felt somehow that it would affect me when I got married.

"I had some curious feeling that pushed the blood up into my head, and I know now that I felt that the blood that went to my head stayed there. I believe that it is from that that all these present feelings have developed. It does not seem clear up there at all. And now it has all died, and it is as though everything was stopped, except when things begin to reach that pitch, and then it stops them again. I have to stop things happening whether I want to or not. I don't really know what would happen to me if I were to relax. I feel that somehow I should completely lose my memory."

Analyst: "What is it that you are striving so hard not to remember? What have you tried to forget?"

Patient: "I don't know."

Analyst: "What would it be very unwelcome to remember?"

"Nothing...."

(*Silence*)

"Except...."

(*Silence*)

"The feelings I used to get at school. It used to worry me very much at the time. I believe it first happened when I was nervous or worried about something. I can't remember what used to happen to make me get these feelings, but I used to like it, and then I would worry in case it was injuring me. I used to think it was not right."

Analyst: "What are these feelings you refer to and never describe?"

"An irritation in my tummy that made the blood rush into my head and my feet go cold."

Analyst: "Where was the irritation?"

"In my tummy." But she puts her hand over her pubes to show the position.

57

Analyst: "What did you do about this irritation?"

"Nothing at all."

At the same time as she says this she unconsciously crosses her legs one over the other. This is the first movement of her legs which she has made during the sessions.

(*Silence*)

Analyst: "What made you cross your legs just now?"

"I don't know."

Analyst: "Put them back as they were, and keep still."

(*Silence*)

"I remember now. I used to make the feelings come. I always liked it, but I used to think it was wrong and that it might injure my inside. And it seems to me that while I was doing that that the blood rushed into my head and had stayed there ever since. I did it most if I was worried about anything, if I could not get my work done. My face used to get terribly hot.

"I'd cross my legs and work one on the other to work up the feeling. I used to think I worked it too far. I used to stop for a few minutes, and then do it again. It was like a magnet. It seemed to draw me to it. If there was any relief from it, it was not any good to me, because I used to think it was so wrong and unnatural, and yet, in spite of all that, I would do it again.

"In the end I would manage to stop it. Then my head would feel as if it were going to explode.

"I wish something would happen, but that is what I am afraid of, and that is what I am stopping. But I don't want to carry on like this, because now I am always at this final pitch.

"I suppose I did manage to stop it, for I have not done it for a year. But it is this past year that I have got this breakdown properly. It is true this past year I have been at this final pitch all the time, with this stopping all the time, and not being able to get on with my work or anything, feeling I have no memory, and unable to go out alone.

"It is only this last six months that it has been at its very worst, and I have had to give up my work and everything.

"I don't see how it can have anything to do with my boy

friend. I have known him for about eight months, and it got worse after we had become engaged—six months ago. But he left me three weeks ago to join the army, and the feelings have not gone."

Analyst: "Where are the feelings?"

"In my head."

Analyst: "And what use is the boy friend to those feelings?"

"Well, I do have other feelings when I am with him—sexual feelings. But I like being with him, and I can't say that I like these feelings in my head. The feelings in my head go on all the time since I stopped the leg-swinging."

Analyst: "In fact, it seems that the 'leg-swinging' is going on all the time inside your head, but with the worry predominant. You have just transferred it into your mind, but it goes back to its original position occasionally, while you are with your boy friend.

"Nevertheless, it gets no relief, and it returns to your mind with redoubled violence, when your boy is no longer with you. It seems that it is this extra stimulus during the past eight months which has made your condition more acute, so that you are incapacitated from work and ordinary mental activities.

"Your feelings are never fully relieved. They merely reach a high pitch of intensity, which you describe as blood rushing to your head. The point is that you hold it there unrelieved, and put all your remaining energy into the attempt to stop it from getting relieved. Thus you get the feeling of things having reached a pitch and also the feeling of stoppage.

"The attempt to stop the orgasm brings all hands to the pumps, and the effort is so successful that it stops everything else as well. This is the condition in which you have held yourself, and which you maintain all the time. It is the antithesis of the normal sexual cycle. In short, it is sexuality, constantly present, constantly being striven against, and displaced into your head to keep it more 'safely' from relief."

At a later session this patient behaved as follows:

She lay silent for several minutes, while her hand wandered unconsciously round the armholes of her sleeve, and then along her shoulders and neck. Finally, she said, "I have nothing to say to you to-day."

Analyst: "What is your hand saying to me?"

"Nothing."

She continued the movements.

Analyst: "Put your hands at your sides and keep them still, but put your feelings and thoughts into words for me."

"I don't know what to say, except the usual thing. I feel that I don't know myself."

(*Silence*)

Her hands again begin to wander, and her attention is drawn to it, and she is again asked to keep them still.

Presently, she says:

"Yesterday I had a great urge to do the leg-crossing, and this time I did it again, for the first time in twelve months. The old feelings came back, except that I didn't worry about it afterwards."

Analyst: "Tell me everything you thought and felt in the greatest detail."

"I have told you all I can remember."

(*Silence*)

"I did the same thing this morning, before coming here."

Analyst: "Why did you tell me only about yesterday? Why did you not mention to-day?"

"I thought telling you about yesterday would be sufficient. I can't remember anything about what I thought and felt yesterday. But I can remember about to-day's. To-day when the urge came I thought it might make my feeling in my head worse. Then I thought it could not be worse, and so I didn't worry so much about whether it happened. Still, I was going to get up and try and do something else instead, in order to stop it. But then I remembered that what I had been telling you suggests that I was stopping it that brought on this illness. And then I was really very pleased to think that I had an excuse to do it. Because I really wanted to do it very badly. So I worried no more about it, and I got a much better relief than ever before. Instead of making the feelings in my head worse, as I had expected, it made them better than they have been for a long time—at least for a little while afterwards. Although I cannot say it relieved them altogether."

Analyst: "It is easy to understand why you did the leg-swing-ings—but tell me why you stopped doing it?"

"I just thought I should not do it any more after a few min-utes."

Analyst: "Why did you stop it after a few minutes?"

"I wanted to post a letter, and I thought afterwards I would not catch the 1.30 collection. I wanted to get the letter off to my young man."

Analyst: "When did you write the letter?"

"Just before doing the leg-swinging."

She smiles:

"I keep thinking you are thinking that writing to him made me want to do it."

Analyst: "What do you think?"

"I think I liked it. At the time, even when I was doing it, I was thinking that probably it wasn't right to do it. I wish in a way that I did not have to do it."

Analyst: "You wished in a way that you had your boy friend making love to you instead. But, after all, in his absence this might be the best you could do. Thinking of him. Although it wasn't com-pletely satisfactory, because you were alone, you had the urge to get satisfaction at least on a physical plane. Did you get it?"

"Yes. I did to-day, though not yesterday; that is why I told you about yesterday and not to-day. Since then I have not thought about this illness so much, and I haven't had those feelings in my head nearly so much as usual."

PSYCHOPATHOLOGY

This is a case of Anxiety Neurosis, built upon a foundation of early sexual conflict.

The precipitating factor, which proved to be the last straw, was the additional sexual stimulation entailed in her courtship. This had the disadvantage of stirring up sexual tension without ever providing for its relief. In consequence, the opposition (the full stop within her mind which opposed the feelings reaching the pitch at which they would cause orgasm) was in turn reinforced from the super-ego as a whole, and was much intensified, absorbing any remaining available mental energy and resulting in exclusion from all ordinary forms of activity.

The fundamental cause of her condition, as distinguished from the precipitating and exacerbating factors of the last eight months, was the conflict which preoccupied her in her school days from the age of ten to fifteen.

The conflict began with the precocious development of the sexual urge, which she called "irritation in my tummy," and which she quite naturally relieved by the device of crossing and swinging her legs.

The fact that she adopted this rather indirect method of relief suggests that she was already inhibited from putting her hand to a prohibited region.

But the success of this method was only temporary, for the forces which prohibited the use of her hand soon became too active to permit even this mode of relief without making their voices heard. Thus, she suffered from feelings of guilt and its twin brother, morbid anxiety. In consequence, she conceived the idea that she was harming herself, and injuring her inside. It is interesting to note that, even at the immature age, she associated the idea of injury with the idea of marriage.

In due course the voices of opposition became stronger as the sexual urge itself became more insistent. By the time she reached the age of fifteen, the general opposition and worry associated with her mode of self-relief overbalanced at least the executive elements in the process of instinct relief. The leg-swinging was more often stopped than enjoyed. Nevertheless, the instinct itself was not thereby deprived of its dynamic energy. Already as a result of this opposition the conflict was being displaced from a sexual region to a disembodied or non-sexual locus. In other words, its head accompaniments were being felt as if no such thing as a sex-organ, or even the body, existed at all.

Thus she came to have sensations in her head, and so gradually became aware that they had nothing to do with the sex organs.

It was about this time that she looked in the glass and thought to herself: "Who am I?" She was already failing to recognize her sexual feelings, or in fact herself, as she had previously done. It is almost as though she were denying that she was the person who had felt sex feelings existed or ever had existed.

The advantage of this manoeuvre was that she could thereby free herself from the worry, guilt, anxiety and general distress of the conflict which was ever recurring in connection with her sexual instinct, and its demands for relief. One can gauge the suffering caused by the conflict from the fact that the head symptoms which displaced it were thereafter clung to with all the energy she could muster. In spite of their obvious disadvantages, they evidently had for her a great advantage in avoidance of distress over the previous condition from which she had fled, and to which she was reluctant to return.

It was only by the relief or partial relief of her guilt-feelings that she was prevailed upon at last to revive the old conflict, and perhaps to re-fight it this time with more tolerant appreciation of the needs of her nature, and less morbid stressing of the ideas of guilt, and the phantasies of punishment and injury.

Auto-erotic satisfaction had no real danger for her, for it could never be fully satisfactory, as it was not ego-syntonic. That is to say, it was at variance with her ego-instincts, and her social or heterosexual tendencies. She would always prefer normal love-making to such modes of relief, and when she became in a position to provide herself with these latter the habit, otherwise unavoidable save at the expense of her mental symptoms, would automatically give place to normal married life. (pp. 112-121)

Though Anna O's transformation through the experience of a deep crisis and Breuer's intervention may have been more profound than that of Berg's patients, the latter obviously contribute to an aspect of Freudian therapy that Breuer was uncomfortable about: the acknowledgment and relative liberation of sexual impulse. I now turn, according to the proposed structure of this book, to a single session of my own in which I carry out a more microscopic yet also broader assault on perfectionistic super-ego dominance.

THE HIDDEN TEETH OF CHAOS

Mrs. White had attended two enneatype psychology workshops with me before this session, and had recognized herself as a self-preservation E1. Significantly, she works as a director of air traffic. This was her first Gestalt session.

White: I feel anxious because I see myself with two parts. One cares about form, and that is the outer part: organized, rigid and controlled. And the other, that I've seen less and who I intuit is chaos, is a total chaos. It's so strong that I can't handle it and I faint.

Last night I dreamed about the chaos, the disorder, the dirtiness, shit — all of it. I saw a movie on TV, a passage in which a woman was fainting because she couldn't stand the death of her daughter. In the dream I'm totally regressed. I dream about my grandmother in a house that wasn't her house — in part it was; partly it wasn't. Dark, scary, a chaos; a total chaos of mess, of shit, of everything. And because I can't stand it, I faint. What follows is, who am I? Which one of them am I? What am I? What is there behind that?

Claudio: We already know that the perfectionist is the one that you're not.

W: But I can't stand the other one, she's worse.

C: The other one is the one you call the chaotic one, full of shit but ...

W: It's worse.

C: Isn't there a possibility that you are condemning her; that you are not doing her justice; that this could be an interference of your perfectionism?

W: But I feel and I am convinced that I cannot be in that chaos.

C: There's no doubt that at least it's going that way.

W: But I want to get to something else behind that.

C: It can be integrated, but we already know ...

W: They're incompatible.

C: But we already know that the path is one of integrating the shadow in the everyday person. So let's see how you can begin getting in touch. I think that the program would be to begin getting in touch with that. And, hopefully, to contact the experience deeply enough that you might possibly faint. But I think you won't faint anymore, for you will feel supported by us; maybe you won't get so scared in good company. The group is very strong.

W: Yes, but I hate it, I don't want a group; I'm completely isolated from everyone.

C: Groups have an effect much greater than what we imagine. I believe that groups help; they give an energy even though one feels isolated. Let's see ... with your memory. Get into memories of that experience, not for the sake of the experience itself, but for a moment in which you had that experience of chaos, dirtiness.

W: Maybe when I was a little girl, in my grandmother's house. It was a dark house, without order. My grandmother was very messy. I remember one time very clearly when I was a little girl, I was very young, in the girl's room ... Well, it seemed unbelievable to me that a person could sleep there. It was chaos.

C: The girl's room?

W: The maid's room.

C: Oh! the maid's.

W: One night they made me sleep there with her because a lot of people came, so we had to make room for someone and that was ... Sticking me in that place was like wanting to make contact with that same place. It's a little bit erased. It was like me putting myself in there, but not being there; not being in touch with anything; like being in the air.

C: Let's explore that environment. Imagine yourself as in a dream. You are that surrounding world of the maid's [room].

W: The maid was very good looking.

C: But her world, perhaps. What kinds of things would that maid do so that you can remember that?

W: I remember that she was a different kind of woman: she was blond with blue eyes, something that's not normally true of a maid, at least I didn't think it normal for a maid. And she apparently was clean.

C: She was apparently clean. How strange then that that place should produce such repulsion!

W: It was the room, not her.

C: The room.

W: It was the room and when I was there, that night, I didn't even realize that the maid was there with me.

C: That room expresses something for you. It's a chaos that you feel ...

W: It's that it was chaotic, a kind of half pantry with a bed ... something strange that I saw as very bizarre ... I never wanted to go in there.

C: What does it make you feel?

W: With a little window, a window that looked out over a patio; and it was a total mess. Well, I don't know if it was messy; it was disorder. For me it was disorder.

C: What would you call the emotion that that causes you?

W: Well, it's that I don't want to go in there. I don't want to.

C: Like revulsion? Like disgust?

W: Disgust. I can't make contact with that; I can't touch that or let that touch me. I can't make physical contact with that.

C: You can't make physical contact with that. [It's as if you are saying to yourself] "I don't want it to touch me, to get me dirty, to contaminate me." Keep developing that and see whether the memory becomes more distinct.

W: I remember seeing myself there as if I were ... I remember me in bed ... but I wasn't in the bed, I was like ... as if there were a space, a kind of chamber of air between me and the rest of the room because I couldn't be contaminated.

C: Probably it's lasted your whole life? Do you feel that there is a chamber of air between you and the group?

W: Yes.

C: Your world is a little like that; your world is like that room.

W: I have a kind of defensive layer of air that protects me from the rest.

C: So there had to have been something rather strong there, with that woman. Could it be something totally impersonal evoked by the way the sheets and everything were? Something like that?

W: I don't remember her. I remember that I had to sleep there with her, but I don't remember her. I remember myself with a bit of a ghostly image, like a kind of being and not being, because I didn't want to be; because if I was I had to become contaminated with all that.

C: Now imagine that you are that room, that contaminated environment. Personify it like an artist would, like a poet who give things a voice.

W: There's no space. Everything is full of things. It's very small. It's closed up. There isn't any air; it's dirty; it's dark, grey. There's no space, there's no space ... There are shelves with strange, weird things on them.

C: Imagine, give form to those things with your imagination: "There are shelves, there are things ..." What things?

W: Nothing had shape. Everything was vague.

C: "Everything is vague here, everything lacks shape here, in this darkness."

W: It doesn't have shapes.

C: And if it had shapes, it might look like what?

W: Shit.

C: "Everything evokes shit here. There is something in this atmosphere that evokes shit." C'mon, go on like that. Can you fish out some details? Is there a memory of shit, of a bed pan, of a smell?

W: It's as if everything is old.

C: Vulgar.

W: And the bed is so old and it's about to fall apart and I'm going to fall.

C: Any other association with the bed?

W: No, that I'm sleeping but without sleeping and then I've always had dreams in which I had dreams.

C: Let's see, imagine that the bed has been a witness to something filthy.

W: No.

C: No. Nothing filthy has ever happened in that bed ... ?

W: No.

C: How can you be so sure?

W: I am sure.

C: Well! There are truly clairvoyant people!

W: No, that I remember. Or I have total amnesia, but ...

C: No, I'm not saying that you were a witness; the bed could have been a witness to things when you weren't there in the room. It wasn't your room.

W: No.

C: It was a beautiful woman's bed. What do beautiful women do in bed?

W: I don't know.

C: Just as I already suspected.

W: The truth is that later this woman had to leave my grandmother's house because she became pregnant.

C: Oh, my friend! You weren't telling us the whole truth.

W: But I didn't know anything. I know that at some point she left and I intuited something.

C: You didn't notice anything because one shouldn't think about these things.

W: I sensed something.

C: Only in the shadows of your consciousness.

W: Then later she came back again. She had the child in her village and she returned to the house again, but then I was bigger.

C: And did you like the woman or not?

W: Vague memories, very vague.

C: No one can say that they're guilty for such vague memories. What I'm trying to say is that it seems to me that that vagueness is as if you didn't want ... as if you had put an isolating layer over the memories too. Let's see, another image. Another image from that experience. You knew that experience profoundly at some time. Evoke when was it ...? You don't have to know the name of the saint to tell the story, it's not so much the external [that matters]. Think of a scene where you were, maybe, even closer than ever to that emotion.

W: To what emotion?

C: Disgust, loathing, messiness ... so as to make you faint. When did you feel it so strongly so as to faint? Get into that experience and how it was at that moment. What was inside?

W: I'm going away from my feelings.

C: No, don't let it be with no emotion to ...

W: I don't remember scenes. Yesterday in the dream, I remember.

C: In your mind, how was it before you fainted? When you had that experience of fainting because you saw the filth.

W: In the dream?

C: Whenever it was, whenever you had that experience.

W: When I have had the experience of fainting it has been an unreal experience, with a very strange vision inside my head, as if my head was cut in a kind of zipper and would open, as if it were a zipper, and there was on the right side a very dark thing, something sort of very strange, I'd say, like a surrealist painting.

C: So the dark part was on the right side.

W: Yes, like a kind of triangular stain ... It had a peak here [*she points to the crown of her head*], and then it was bigger at the bottom, a little curved and black on the right side, and at that point I faint.

C: Could you evoke for a moment, just like that in silence, the blackness.

W: Yes, it's a curved triangle with a tip that's not pointed but rather curved; but that keeps getting bigger and along the bottom part there is like a saw.

C: Can you point to the bottom part for me.

W: The bottom part is here [*she points above the ear*] and it goes in like waves, like a mountain range ... and my head starts getting like a kind of ... this part here is wider. And it starts opening up into a mountain range ... But the jagged edge doesn't come from the top down, instead it comes from inside out.

C: Oh! The body itself is transformed into opposing saws.

W: Only in my head; everything is in my head.

C: But on both sides of the body?

W: No, they make superimposed, parallel saws, like three or four saws; and they come from inside out. They begin to get their points and then that black, dark part on the right is uncovered ... I feel very surprised, like it's very unexpected to see that, totally unexpected, and like I don't find any explanation, and then I faint.

C: But you already told us that that darkness isn't only chaos but something like shit, a dirty chaos.

W: Yes, but in this case it wasn't dirty.

C: It wasn't dirty, it was chaos ...

W: It was chaos itself, like the essence of chaos itself, but not shit; in that case it was the essence of chaos.

C: Okay, the essence of chaos. So, try to evoke ... that essence of chaos on your right side.

W: Well, it's like a dark stain.

C: Do you really feel that you have a stain inside of you?

W: Yes. I feel it.

C: Begin with that. "I have a stain inside of me ..." See what else you can say about that.

W: It's in my head, nothing else.

C: "A stain that is only my head."

W: Yes, only my head.

C: "My heart is clean."

W: Yes, it's only my head that has like a kind of ... I say tumor, but I don't know the word. It's chaos itself deep inside; it's there in my head. And it's as if my head were, I mean the shape, hydrocephalic. It gets bigger through here [*she points to her temples and up*] and it's chaos.

C: To me there is a great contrast between what one imagines of this chaos — the tremendousness of this chaos, this fearsome impurity — and the faint voice with which you speak. Do you know what I want to say? I feel that this side could use a little of that chaos.

W: Yes. But the contrast is because I can't bring that chaos out, the same as when I have aggression. I can't let it out and what I do is exactly that softness everywhere. Softness and amiability comes out my pores, when underneath I have murderous instincts, actual murderous instincts. I could kill someone.

C: It seems that you have to integrate this shadow into your everyday personality which is very dead. Do you have any idea how?

W: No, not yet. In these days I'm getting a little glimmer ... Or how to work on chaos and understand that I am also the chaos.

C: It seems to me that chaos and aggression shouldn't be too separate. Within chaos is destructiveness, that's why it's threatening. "Aggression," perhaps that might be a way to name it? Perhaps calling it "chaos" is like not knowing? As if in that darkness of the maid's room, where you couldn't see what was there, you didn't see the shapes, perhaps, that were there.

W: Exactly.

C: What do you think about a stain? Let's see, allow your fantasy to run it's course. What is there inside you that has to be kept at bay?

W: Well, I don't know.

C: Inside you there is a person who is ... What? How is that person?

W: Perverse.

C: Paint in [more details]. "Inside me there is a perverse woman ... "

W: Inside me there is a perverse woman with murderous instincts.

C: Now it's getting more interesting. Now the session is livening up.

W: But I can't express it; I can't ever express that.

C: Do you have an image of that perfect, I mean, perverse woman? Which one is the perverse one?

W: The perverse woman is the one who is very concentrated, measuring, controlling [herself] and waiting for the moment to kill. Of course, it's ter-rible! It's that everyone would reject me if I went through life like that!

C: [For the sake of] experiment let's take the position that you go through life like that. Affirm it.

W: Well, if I go through life like that, in the end they'll kill me.

C: No, don't say, "If I go through life like that ..."; instead try and see how it is to say: "In reality I go through life like that."

W: It's that I go through life like that.

C: Controlling and ...

W: And attacking.

C: And attacking.

W: But the aggression comes back toward me; I also feel it toward me. I feel it directly against someone in particular, but I also feel it against myself.

C: And why do you say "but"? "I feel aggression but..." Because that justifies you? Or because it makes you feel less murderous?

W: I feel aggression; but I can't express it because ... everyone would reject me.

C: If you're a goody-goody everyone would reject you?

W: If I attack, they reject me.

C: Poor thing! You can't go around attacking because you would be rejected ... [*He laughs.*]

W: The result is that I encounter rejection anyway because ...

C: Of course.

W: Because I go around with my perfectionism and a perverse look on my face. I go around trying to control everyone, especially at work, and of course, I encounter the consequent rejection because I go through life ...

C: So you wouldn't have so much to lose.

W: No. I know that the result is the same; I know it.

C: Sure. Better business to go around being the perverse one directly.

W: But I can't, I can't.

C: You lack practice.

W: It must be lack of practice.

C: Lack of psychotherapy.

W: Well, must be that.

C: Okay, let's do a little experimenting with perversion. How could you, in this moment, liberate a little ... give a little space to ... that held-back personality of yours?

W: At this moment I don't have a motive; on the contrary, I feel better now. I feel anxious, but better. Like it's not so perverse to be perverse.

C: It's not so perverse! It seems like a new idea is coming up for you.

W: Yes. Well, I'm not perverse, I feel perverse which is different. And sometimes I feel a terrible energy, a pull toward an impressive force; but other times I feel like the shittiest thing in the world, the most apathetic, lazy and idle person that exists in the world. Those two are always there.

C: I think that the apathetic one is the super-controlled one who no longer has energy to live.

W: No, that is true. And I think, "Why am I going to live? Big deal! The other one is too strong sometimes and she gets away from me."

C: She gets away from me too. How can we bring her into this room?

W: But she escapes because she's like pure aggression itself; it's aggression itself that escapes me. It's as if I were to become aggression and then it goes [away] ... it goes [away] ...

C: I suggest that you give that aggression an outlet in an attack on your everyday personality: the controlling and apathetic one.

W: She's a complete asshole.

C: Destroy her. Speak to your perfectionistic part with the knowledge of why, and with the emotion of the other one.

W: She's a complete asshole, because on top of [everything] she has the huge temptation of staying quietly at home, all safe, everything clean, everything orderly, but alone. It's a temptation that she can't resist.

C: You're still saying it in an obvious and very nice way. Now say it with an indecent voice. What would an indecent voice be like?

W: I can't.

C: Try to stop being the well mannered lady ... Speak from that emotion that wanted to make you faint.

W: It's that it's very strong.

C: Okay, use whatever you can.

W: It's just that I can't let out that voice, that energy, to tell her that she's a shit.

C: This emotion from this moment, you already have it, give voice to this emotion. It can also be from crying.

W: I think that she is completely timid. She always has that layer of ... as if she were wearing a layer of seriousness, as if she were defending an onerous land.

C: Speak to your perfectionistic side. You're the one who is suppressed; you are the chaotic one speaking to the super-orderly one.

W: Damn! I can't! It's that I feel like I'm a demon. I feel like I'm a demon, I feel like I'm a demon!

C: What does a demon feel?

W: The chaotic one is a demon.

C: And not the other one?

W: Not the other one; she's a shit.

C: The other one is a system of synchronized saws, from what I understood.

W: What did you say? Pardon me, I didn't hear.

C: The image that you gave us of the other one is one of successive saws. I think that the perfectionist is a demon made of saws; a cutting, organized person — *pam, pam, pam*— a machine that cuts. Tell the perfectionist that she's a machine that cuts flesh.

W: How am I going to tell her that? [She becomes overwhelmed.]

C: Try and see how it sounds to you if you say that to her.

W: But I have a horrible time getting it out.

C: Yes, you would do it very badly.

W: I feel like I'm making a scene on top of it.

C: It seems like you want it to look like you're making a scene.

W: And I'm doing it; of course, I don't give a shit. Well, ... You're a flesh cutting machine, asshole ... [*With a hurried voice and losing strength.*] It just can't be!

C: What can't be?

W: With that voice, it just can't be.

C: Well, things are learned little by little. Let's see, repeat with a little increase in volume.

W: You are a flesh cutting machine!

C: What did you feel while saying that?

W: A little better.

C: You could put more anger into it.

W: Yes, much more.

C: Let's see you put something into it that must not be very far away in you.

W: No. I'm disconnecting from it because I don't want to do it.

C: You don't want to do it.

W: So then I disconnect and if I disconnect I see myself here acting. Something I never do, so it's not a bad thing for me [to do], because I don't let myself do that either.

C: So, act as if you have a horrible self-image.

W: I have a horrible self-image, horrible! Because I see myself there in my neat house, very dignified, walking down the hall ... Terrible! On top of it my house is furnished like a typical 1. It's terrible!

C: And what do you feel, chaotic one, about that?

W: Well, I would throw it all to shit. I would love to break the plates, one after the other. The bad part is that they'd have to be picked up. I feel the need to break some plates that I don't like and because they are useful they have to be there. But then I don't feel like picking them up, because I'm lazy and I don't want to pick them up and it makes me crazy [to think] that one little piece of glass might stay stuck somewhere. I can't stand it!

C: Now I suppose that, as is common among humans, people provoke that anger in you more than anything else. People more than things.

W: Yes. Things also get me bent out of shape.

C: Principally, which things make you angry?

W: Well, sometimes I get angry about things! [*She laughs.*] No, people!

C: It's more people. Okay, could you identify one person, not by name, but by pseudonym?

W: By pseudonym ... Well, I'm not going to use a pseudonym. My dear mother drives me nuts — she's a 1 like me. I can't stand her.

C: Good, I would propose a therapeutic exercise: Send the cavalry after your mother right now.

W: I can't stand her and when I speak with her by phone, because she's some distance away, she makes me frenetic. I can't stand her because she even wants to control me over the *phone*. That's just *enough already*!

C: There is your mother and you are no longer going to put up with her. You speak to her.

W: I can't stand her.

C: Tell her that you can't stand her and elaborate that — develop it, really explain to her that you can't stand her; document it.

W: I can't stand you! Because all of your life you have been suffocating me and on top of it here's a typical phrase of yours: If I say I'm going to do such and such, I'm going to such a place, your automatic statement is, "What for?" My whole life you've been drowning me; I couldn't feel pleasure.

C: What would you call that attitude of hers?

W: Abortionist. You're abortionist!

C: "You are an abortionist."

W: You are an abortionist. You abort absolutely everything, all pleasure.

C: Repeat that accusation again, but this time with more force. And give her more details about how she is an abortionist.

W: You're an abortionist because you don't want to enjoy and because you don't want me to enjoy [anything]. You don't let me! You haven't wanted me to enjoy [anything]! And when I do I feel guilty, now less, fortunately. Because I have great desire and I feel passion and sexual desire intensely. Now I can evade her more. But when she is far away (this summer she has been outside Spain, she has been in Mexico for four months) I have felt fucking amazing. I don't want you to be here! The farther away the better! I don't want you to be here; I don't want you to be in Leon because from Leon you control me and from Mexico you control me less.

C: Do you feel she is controlling you right now?

W: Last night I spoke to her by phone and there is a subtlety ... It's the tone of her voice that controls me!

C: Okay, go back to that image.

W: And there is something curious. I'm on vacation during these days and I don't want to tell her because she thinks that a good daughter is obligated to go see her for part of her vacation. So I don't want to tell her so that she doesn't make me feel that obligation. And because I don't feel like going to Leon, well, I don't tell her.

C: That would be better than to be completely ...

W: It's that I feel like being astute, because until now I haven't been astute, I've been an idiot.

C: Good, it's better to be astute than nothing. Now take another step imaginatively, and speak to her from your reality. Imagine that your mother hears you and speak to her, not from the perfectionist, the good girl and all of the things she would like to hear, instead speak to her from the chaotic one.

W: Your daughter is practically a whore, and she has almost been one; and she hasn't been one because ...

C: "Because she has remembered something of you."

W: That's what is most ... I'm sure that that's the worst.

C: I would like you to repeat it, but now with more lusty details. Win your freedom right in front of her.

W: You think that I'm alone and I'm not alone. I have a lover! One I'm very satisfied with to boot!

C: That's it! Keep explaining your happiness to her and your pleasures.

W: I can be morbid. And I feel morbid and I love it.

C: Give her more explanations, about things that you wouldn't dare say to your mother in real life.

W: And I have taken drugs and I am very satisfied about it, and thanks to that I have experienced a ton of things; and I smoke marijuana when I feel like it, if I have it on hand, of course. Well, not when I feel like it.

C: I think that what you have told us is sufficient. Now imagine that she actually heard you. How would it be if your mother heard all that?

W: She faints!

C: Here is a case where we can appropriately speak of "finding the mother of the lamb."[21]

W: She doesn't faint. She dies!

C: Silently allow yourself to imagine the experience of your mother in the face of this monstrosity that her daughter has just told her; in the face of this combination of things. Maybe reliving it a little, you hear it little by little over again.

W: She would get pale, tense, rigid ...

C: Is she really hearing you? Your daughter has just told you ... What did she say? That she was practically a ...

W: That she was practically a whore.

C: That she is a whore, practically.

W: That she was, not now ... Now more, in essence more.

C: That now in essence you are more of a whore than ever. See how she receives that.

W: Because I need pleasure and because I like pleasure.

C: Try really, to get into her, imagine how it would be.

W: Well, it would be terrible for her because she totally negates pleasure. She does things because she has to do them but not for the pleasure. Then she gets some little bit of pleasure out of them, every now and then, because I can tell; but the minimum.

C: In other words, she feels, "I don't want to hear this. I don't want to hear this because one doesn't live like that."

W: No, she faces things, but she would get so pale and so rigid that she would die, really.

C: Now we'll imagine that she doesn't die yet. It would be convenient, but in the end.

W: I'd love it!

C: But we'll imagine that she heard you, she gets rigid and she speaks to you from that place.

W: And pale. Well, she would say to me, "That's not okay," like that.

C: "That's not okay." With what kind of a voice would she tell you that?

W: With the same that I say, "This is not okay." Calmly.

C: With a calm voice, softly. How does she feel? What does she feel? Does she feel anger, scorn or fear? Which? Or doesn't she feel anything, perhaps?

W: Maybe nothing, perhaps contained anger that she doesn't know she has, but, "That's not okay."

C: "That doesn't fit in my world." But your daughter's pleasure? Doesn't your daughter's pleasure matter to you at all?

W: My pleasure doesn't matter to her at all.

C: She's a bad mother.

W: Underneath I feel a little sorry for her.

C: She is a very hard person.

W: Her? Yes, very hard. And she is very demanding and tries to get me to do so many things. For example, two or three things in her life that she has tried to get me to do and I rebelled, of course, because she thought it was what was appropriate, what was perfect; and then I said No — well, I didn't say No, I moved away because I saw that if I stayed I would be under her yoke. But then there are contradictions.

C: Let's not get into that yet. She just said to you, "That's not done."

W: "That's not okay."

C: "That's not okay." Really experience that attitude and that emotion.

W: "That's not okay." It's as if she were sending me the message that I'm in mortal sin; that it's a sacrilege.

C: And she only tells you with unconscious anger?

W: Totally calm and totally controlled.

C: It's a saw that doesn't feel any more than a saw made of metal. She cuts your life; she ruins your life's pleasure for all your life, without saying anything. Does this inspire you a little to continue speaking to her from the space of the chaotic one?

W: It's that I pity my mother.

C: Poor little thing! She's a saw that doesn't know what she is doing!

W: She's made me in her image and in her likeness. She's poured herself out into me. She's controlled me, and she's suffocated me since always. Since she has no other way to fill her emptiness, she wants to fill it with her control over me.

C: You have to help her.

W: No. Not help her.

C: My proposition would be that although a part of you can understand her, we'll give that part some anesthesia so that we can concentrate on the other part.

W: The other one sees her as if she were a white snake. I've always hated snakes.

C: "You are a white snake."

W: Yes, she is a white snake, she is.

C: Speak to her.

W: Not me, her.

C: Yes, but tell her that she is a white snake.

W: You are a white snake.

C: Keep talking to her from your reaction.

W: You are white and cold. You've got the chill of death. You are dead. My hands are freezing. And her hands are freezing, and if she ever wants to take me by the arm and she touches my skin, she feels like a snakeskin to me. I've never touched a snake, but it terrifies me.

C: In other words, you have the urge to isolate yourself from her too. She too can contaminate you. Maybe she was the original contamination.

W: I suppose so ... it would make sense.

C: It's very probable that the first person in your life that made you feel, "Don't touch me," was a white snake like her. Tell her more, from that emotion, from whatever you feel; from not wanting to be touched.

W: She makes me cold; she gives me the feeling of death; she gives me the feeling of something under the earth. Like she's death. She's death itself.

C: What I feel could be useful to you ... .See what you think ... It seems to me that what's missing is something that will prompt you to react physically and intensely in a non-prescribed way to get you out of this lethal paralysis; and I would suggest that a few volunteers get on top of you, and you push your way through, not allowing them to pin you down. Take that as a symbol of winning your freedom, of not letting yourself ...

W: I don't feel strong enough; because when I feel that it might be possible, I cover up the emotion again.

C: Well, two things can happen. You can make it or you don't make it, but it will be a way of getting beyond your head.

W: [*Remains thoughtful, preoccupied.*]

C: What's going on?

W: I don't know, it's that it seems to me like ...

C: "A lady doesn't do that."

W: Okay!

C: How does this proposition sound to you — of being on the floor with people all over you?

W: Like if I do it I could feel it; I suppose that some day I'll be able to scream. I don't know. I want out! But it feels artificial to me.

C: Of course it is. It's an artificial situation but sometimes something real can happen.

W: I know that's true, but I judge it. It happens only when I'm motivated, prepared for it and etc., etc., ... Yes, I'm defending myself.

C: Well, for me it's okay.

W: Okay, I'll do it, okay?

C: Let's see, lie down over there and somebody big will pin her down so that it won't be easy for her to move. How many people? The strongest ones that are willing to hold down her hands, feet so that she can bring her strength out of nowhere.

[*White gets down on the floor. They hold her down and she begins to scream and cry.*]

W: What a bunch of beasts you are!

C: Let yourself go and let yourself do whatever comes.

W: [*She covers her face with her arm and she cries.*] Beasts! [*She keeps crying with a whine.*]

C: That sounded good to me, like you took a bit of freedom with that sob. [*Claudio gets down beside her.*] Develop that feeling like a relief. [*White calms down and gets up, she sighs.*] Tell us something about this feeling, about this moment.

W: I'm dizzy, I've never felt conscious dizziness.

C: You've taken a step forward: from completely unconscious fainting to the process ... How is it getting into it from that direction?

W: I felt that I was getting dizzy — dizzy from the oppression.

C: It seems to me that the dizziness is a not wanting to be conscious in the presence of your own temptation ...

W: Of getting out.

C: Of getting out, of fighting, of your own impulse to free yourself. You prefer not to see it. It is so repressed!

W: Yes, but I never felt dizzy from a conscious position, never. I've never gotten dizzy. Well only once but because I fell.

C: These are your *a posteriori* reflections, but what does it leave you with directly? What is your experience of this moment? While you breathe in a bit more freely ... a little teary, it seems ...?

W: I have felt the suffocation — the suffocation that I have felt so many times in more of a disguised way.

C: Now you have felt the suffocation more clearly.

W: Totally clear.

C: And a little relief.

W: And a little relief. The moment of screaming and of coming out reminded me of ... Also when I was a little girl I screamed and I had a lot of tantrums, that's how I got relief; but at some point they stopped and they didn't come back.

C: You became an adult.

W: Way too soon.

C: Good, we can leave it here. Like the first stroke of the drill.

White's symptom of fainting (much like the fainting of ladies of former times — when smelling "salts" were the fashion) is the external expression of her (and E1's) narrow-minded rejection of forbidden contents from consciousness. It is significant that in the course of the above-mentioned event, she knew for the first time what had happened during her earlier episode of unconsciousness.

The session above doesn't bring her to the point of liberating her angry impulses, but only to the urge for such a release; yet amounts to a relative liberation, particularly in the imagined dialogue with her mother and in her open-minded acceptance of her situation of physical struggle. I also think this session remarkable for how much insight she gains of the cruelty involved in her goody-goody perfectionistic self.

2

ENNEATYPE 2

Samuel Butler has given us a picture of a "Proud Man"— who "sets out his Feathers like an Owl, to swell and seem bigger than he is." He describes him as one who "has given himself Sympathetic Love-Powder, in consequence of which he has been transformed into his own Mistress." Also, as one who "commits Idolatry to himself, and worships his own Image." [1]

Yet pride is not always such a visible passion, and egocentricity may be successfully masked by generosity. In that case, the person's proud self-concept allows her to feel good or better, radiant, overflowing, full of herself — as if she had more than enough. This may also involve the conviction of having a great deal to give; that her mere company is a gift to other people.

In a woman (and this is an eminently feminine character, as well as one more common in women), the pseudo-abundance of E2 can be embodied in a maternal personality, and in the feeling that she, of course, has a great deal to give to babies; not only to her own children, but to children in general. Of course, she does not perceive that her generosity arises from her *need* to give and from how much she needs to be received. Characteristically, she *thrives on being needed*; for in this way she is confirmed as a person. Being needed implies that she is, more than merely okay, a great lover or a great parent or a great child — which implies not only beauty but love, a capacity for giving. It is not only a question of a seduction, for seduction is giving in order to receive later, or promising to give something in order to put somebody in debt; however seductive an E2, it is also true that the person receives (i.e., self-confirmation) *in the very act of giving*.

How generous behavior may uphold a proud image was keenly observed by Jane Austen, for she shows us such association between liberty and conceit in her picture of the ambitious Mr. Darcy in *Pride and Prejudice*.[2] I quote below a string of passages from the novel to convey an impressionistic picture of her character.

> Mr. Darcy soon drew the attention of the room by his fine, tall person, handsome features, noble mien; and the report was in general circulation within five minutes after his entrance, of his having ten thousand a year ... for he was discovered to be proud, to be above his company ... (p. 58)

> ... and coldly said: "She is tolerable; but not handsome enough to tempt me; and I am in no humour at present to give consequence to young ladies who are slighted by other men ..." (p. 59)

> ... where he could think with pleasure of his own importance, and, unshackled by business, occupy himself solely in being civil to all the world. For though, elated by his rank ... he was all attention to everybody. By nature inoffensive, friendly and obliging ... (p. 65)

> "... If he had been so very agreeable he would have talked to Mrs. Long. But I can guess how it was; every body says that he is ate up with pride, and I dare say that he had heard somehow that Mrs. Long does not keep a carriage and had come to the ball in a hack chaise." (p.66)

> His manners were pronounced to be very bad indeed, a mixture of pride and impertinence ... (p. 81)

> "...It seems to me to shew an abominable sort of conceited independence, a most country town indifference to decorum." (p.82)

"Can such abominable pride as his, have ever done him good?"

"Yes, it has often led him to be liberal and generous, — to give his money freely, to display hospitality, to assist his tenants, and relieve the poor. Family pride, and filial pride, for he is very proud of what his father was, have done this. Not to appear to disgrace his family, to degenerate from the popular qualities, or lose the influence of the Pemberly House, is a powerful motive. He has also brotherly pride, which with some brotherly affection, makes him a very kind and careful guardian of his sister; and you will hear him generally cried as the most attentive and best of brothers." (p. 125)

Since my statement in the early 70s that E2 people were "Jewish mothers," it has become widespread opinion that they are, most characteristically, "helpers." This is misleading, for the role of helper is even more characteristic of E9. In this highly emotional and romantic E2 character, "help" translates as "emotional support," and on the whole, the personality is better evoked through "lover" than "helper."

The role of seducer and the passion to attract may cause some to adopt an all-too-childish subordinate yet mischievous style, as is Nora in Ibsen's "Doll's House," who at the end of the play leaves behind her infantile and irresponsible role.[3] But most E2s are *both* tender and aggressive, and even adroit at making scenes. The "make love *and* war" motto is appropriate to their style — a hybrid of Venus and Mars. In some cases, aggression is compensated through extraordinariness and irresistibility; in others, like the familiar character of Scarlett O'Hara in *Gone with the Wind*, exploitiveness and selfishness are scarcely hidden under the mask of false love.

E2s pride is not usually the kind that derives its primary satisfaction from standing out among other people in a competitive manner. It is, rather, satisfied through love. It is in order to be loved that seductiveness has developed. I speak of seduction meaning not only eroticism, but, even more importantly, seeming to have more to offer than is the case. An important expression of it is that of promises that go beyond what will be delivered. "I will be by your side," or "I will love you, for the rest of my life," an E2 person will typically say; but these dramatic and usually moving vows are not necessarily kept.

Just as perfectionism is prominent in E1, false love is prominent in E2 — and this is true of narcissistic self-enjoyment as well as seductive benevolence towards others. One of its forms of expression may be flattery, and we recognize E2 in Butler's portrait of a flatterer, concerning whom he remarks that "he hangs bells in a Man's Ears, as a Car-man does by his Horse, while he lays a heavy Load upon his Back."

Some of the more problematic instances of E2 are diagnosed today as "hystrionic personality" — which is described as theatrical, impulsive, pushy, changeable, voluble, searching for novelty, inconsequent. There is something excessive about the expression of emotion of E2 people, be it tender or aggressive. Their enthusiasm too ecstatic, their fits of anger too manipulative. It is giving a false image for a purpose, emotion for an effect. Not surprisingly, the form of non-verbal deceit goes hand-in-hand with lying. In spite of a directness that may give an impression of uncommon truthfulness, these individuals are less norm-oriented than most, and lying may be a habit already in childhood.

I have met women about whom their mothers have said that when they were little, they were "not a liar, but highly imaginative." One of them, for example, as a little girl, would tell her little schoolfriends that she lived in a house where there was a swimming pool with a whale in it. All the children wanted to visit her in order to see this fabulous thing, yet she needed to keep them away. The recent movie "My Life," whose central character is proud, illustrates the same symptom; it shows how a boy convinces himself that there will be a circus performance in his backyard — only to be rebuked by his schoolmates when they are disappointed to see that it is not the case.

In the cartoon that follows, the humor lies in the sharp contrast between the commonsense judgment and the private judgment on a situation, based on a view of facts that has been altered through a substitution of feelings as if these were all that counted.

E2s are pleasure-oriented, cheerful, humorous, and perhaps a little wild. They do not accept restrictions easily and can be very invasive, not respecting limits either. They value freedom, and can easily confuse it with licentiousness. They rebel strongly against discipline, monotony and rigidity. Nothing clashes with E2 more than the severe and disciplined personality of E1. E2 rebels against correctness, against punctuality, order and what is predictable. E2 hates routine and ordinariness. Can you imagine a *femme fatale* standing in line? In a bank, for example, they will want to go straight to the manager. To be stuck with the fifth place in a queue is too much of an offense to their pride. They ought to enjoy the privilege of always being first and feel that they should never have to wait.

That desires are more important than principles can, of course, involve more or less anti-social behavior, as in the case of David Copperfield's admired schoolmate, Steerforth, who, like Dr. Faustus, allows himself to seduce and then abandon a girl at a time when this spells social ostracism and catastrophe. Or, in Scarlett O'Hara, whose never-too-scrupulous sense of honor allows her to read the letters that the man she is interested in writes to his wife, to whom she is the hidden rival.

A feature worth stressing, in view of how often it leads to interpersonal problems, is an excessive changeability in E2. Lack of consistency or coherence is not only the result of deceptive and seductive promising, and also more than the result of a distaste for monotony, routine and predictability; rather, it is a hunger for excitement — an excitement that feeds the self-concept. While we may say that we all have differentiated sub-personalities, with different and perhaps conflicting intentions, this is more true of E2. Also, in E2 there is very little communication between today's self and tomorrow's self. They tend to live in the present, yet this is not an instance of healthy present-centeredness. Most of us need to learn to live more in the present, and not so much in the past or in the future. Yet for E2, the present is a subterfuge. They live in the present because they don't want to think of the future consequences of their actions nor remember yesterday's commitment.

Recently I was reading a biography of Elizabeth Taylor. On the first page, the biographer shows through a string of quotations how all Taylor's five marriages were preceded by public declarations of eternal love, variations on: "This one is really the great love of my life."

I suppose that the most illustrious E2 individuals in history have been Alexander the Great, Julius Caesar and Napoleon; but in view of the association of the personality style with woman, I think it is most appropriate to concentrate here on one of the most striking women of all time: Cleopatra.

In his classic biography of Cleopatra, Emil Ludwig lets us know that already by the age of ten, Cleopatra learned from the failure of her submissive father that, "for a king, pride and haughtiness are above power itself," and that enslavement and submission are unworthy."[4]

When it was suggested to her by her advisors that she travel to Rome, like her father had done, to seek the restoration of her throne, she — "who knew how to choke her feelings when her interests were at stake, how to disregard her interests when it was a matter of 'self-esteem,' — ... immediately rejected the idea. It would be better to kill herself!" (p. 45)

Imperious Cleopatra let her court know that she would make her own decisions, and that her wishes were to be heeded.

"As bold as ingenious, audacious and cunning at the same time" she was cold in combat and assertive in the face of danger; but when it was night time she was completely transformed into a voluptuous and passionate lover — who was said to be a descendent of Venus.

There is a wisdom in the French expression *femme fatale* that fits the sexual subtype of E2 so well: though it has come to denote mostly irresistibility, it of course alludes to *dangerous* irresistibility.

Just as Zola's *Nana* stands out in literature as the *femme fatale para excellence*, so we may say that Cleopatra stands out among the women in history; and I see the situation most poignantly portrayed at that moment in her life when she claimed her bridal gift from Anthony after the latter had defeated Julius Caesar. She despised Anthony, and was set to use his weaknesses to dominate him. Writes Ludwig: "Before the map of the world, Cleopatra demanded her wedding gift: the ancient provinces that had belonged to the Pharaohs more than fifteen hundred years ago." (p.192) And he completes the reconstitution of the scene adding: "When she finished, he thought: what an expensive woman!" (p. 193)

A prominent feature of proud people is that of not acknowledging their needs — yet the same person who feels that asking for something would be "beneath her pride," can very well demand it or push for it. Once a spoilt child becomes an adult, he or she is always looking for privileges. They want to enjoy all kinds of care and for everyone to be at their beck and call. If they go to a restaurant, for example, they want the best table, and when they are offered a wine, they will accept it only after close scrutiny. They are demanding and capricious, sometimes with a capriciousness that is difficult to satisfy. I knew a six-year-old girl who was very spoilt, and I came to understand how this had resulted as a reaction to a temporary separation between her parents that made her feel neglected. From that moment on, her demanding and behaving in a trying way became an attempt to elicit proof that she was loved. It seemed that the more "difficult" she was, the greater was the proof of the love she sought to obtain, as if she thought to herself something like "they love me *despite* everything." The same dynamic explains the whimsical character of E2 no less than its willfulness. A proud person requires getting exactly what he or she wants, otherwise she will make a scene, cry, do anything in order to monopolize attention. (If, for instance, there was not enough butter on this child's piece of toast ... What an uproar!)

Though I have drawn on Scarlett O'Hara for literary illustration of E2, this account would not be complete without mention of the irresistibly attractive Carmen, who sings *"je brave tout, le feu, le fer et le ciel meme"* and *"mon coeur est libre come l'air."* ("I defy everything: fire, steel and even heaven," and "my heart as free as the air.")

Also, I want to include some selected paragraphs (from Dickens's *David Copperfield*) on "Little Dora," an embodiment of the explicitly egocentric infantile self-preservation subtype of E2:

"Will you call me a name I want you to call me?" inquired Dora, without moving.

"What is it?" I asked with a smile.

"It's a stupid name," she said, shaking her curls for a moment. "Child-wife."

I laughing asked my child-wife what her fancy was in desiring to be so called. She answered without moving, otherwise than as the arm I twined about her may have brought her blue eyes nearer to me:

"I don't mean, you silly fellow, that you should use the name instead of Dora. Only mean that you should think of me that way. When you are going to be angry with me, say to yourself, "it's only my child-wife!" When I am very disappointing, say, "I knew, a long time ago, that she would make but a child-wife!" When you miss what I should like to be, and I think I can never be, say, "still my foolish child-wife loves me!" For indeed I do.

Dora told me, shortly afterwards, that she was going to be a wonderful housekeeper. Accordingly, she polished the tablets, pointed the pencil, bought an immense account-book, carefully stitched up with a needle and thread all the leaves of the cookery book which Jip had torn, and made quite a desperate attempt "to be good," as she called it. But the figures had the old obstinate propensity — *they would not* add up. When she had entered two or three laborious items in the account-book, Jip would walk over the page, wagging his tail, and smear them all out. Her own little right-hand middle finger got steeped to the very bone in ink, and I think that was the only decided result obtained.

Then I would commence a practical demonstration, to which Dora would pay profound attention, perhaps for five minutes, when she would begin to be dreadfully tired, and would lighten the subject by curling my hair, or trying the effect of my face with my shirt-collar turned down. If I tacitly checked this playfulness, and persisted, she would look so scared and disconsolate, as she became more and more bewildered, that the remembrance of her natural gaiety when I first strayed into her path, and of her being my child-wife, would come reproachfully upon me, and I would lay the pencil down, and call for the guitar.[5]

In his dismissing of the social pathology of capitalistic society, Erich Fromm has spoken of a "principle of non-frustration."[6] He claims that the need for mass consumption that is part of our economic system "has been instrumental in creating a feature in the social character of modern man which constitutes one of the most striking contrasts to the social character of the nineteenth century." (p. 164) Fromm formulates this as a principle that every desire be satisfied immediately and no wish frustrated; and illustrates the expression of this in buying and the installment plan.

> In the nineteenth century you bought what you needed, when you had saved the money for it; today you buy what you need, or do not need, on credit, and the function of advertising is largely to coax you into buying and to whet your appetite for things, so that you can be coaxed. You live in a circle. You buy on the installment plan, and about the time you have finished paying, you sell and you buy again — the latest model. (p. 164)

Fromm goes on to discuss how the principle that desires be satisfied without delay has reflected sexual behavior, and gives credit to Aldous Huxley for giving it "its most poignant expression" in *Brave New World*, where one of the slogans used in the conditioning of adolescents is "don't leave for tomorrow the fun that you can have today."

Though E7 is almost as hedonistic as E2, I think E2 is more of a consumer, and the kind of person of whom it is most pertinent to say that (as Fromm proposes), loving fun consists mainly of "taking in"; "commodites, sights, food, drinks, cigarettes, people, lectures, books, movies — all are consumed, swallowed." (p. 166)

This impression of mine is congruent with the analysis of sociologist Colin Campbell, who replied (in 1987) to Max Weber's *The Protestant Ethic and The Spirit of Capitalism* with *The Romantic Ethic and The Spirit of Modern Consumerism.*[7]

SEEKING A GOOD THERAPY CASE REPORT

Just as I have illustrated the obsessive pattern with Anna O., a case history usually associated to hysteria, my first choice to illustrate psychotherapy of hystrionic personality was one in which the therapist, Dr. M. Scott Peck, emphasized an obsessive symptom, "a ritual." The case of Charlene, which consitutued the content of a chapter entitled, "Charlene: a teaching case" in Scott Peck's *People of the Lie*, is the most interesting I have found thus far in terms of displaying the E2 psyche with its typical aversion to rigidity, its manipulativeness and invasiveness.[8] Yet the clarity with which Dr. Peck perceives Charlene's psychopathoolgy is the result of a clash in personality styles and values rather than empathy, and I am inclined to think that the therapeutic failure reflected in this report can be explained on the basis of countertransference rather than on her therapist's view that his patient was not only emotionally disturbed but evil (and therefore needing exorcism rather than therapy).

Since Dr. M. Scott Peck refused permission to quote his material in the context of this book's theme, and also in view of my decision to seek instances of *successful* therapy rather than being content with the illustration of character in clinical practice, my search continued and I was surprised to discover how much more difficult it was to find a satisfying case report.

Writing about psychoanalytic treatment of the hysterical personality, Easser and Lesser have said that, "repeated inconsistency in the ability of the method to reverse the course of the hysterical symptoms has led to uncertainty, discouragement, disinterest, and in Freud's words, 'affords us a good reason for quitting such an unproductive field of inquiry without delay.'"[9]

I am not sure that it is appropriate to assume that Freud was prompted in this observation by the kind of personality that we today call "hystrionic," but Easser and Lesser certainly are addressing themselves to this neurotic style in their well-known paper. They write:

> On the one hand the hysteric theoretically is considered to have achieved the highest libidinal level for neurotic fixation, that is, phallic-oedipal, and on the other hand, the sufferers are regarded as frustrating, provocative, infantile, teasing, suggestible, irresponsible, non-intuitive, egocentric, non-productive citizens.

I began my search with Freud's cases, and found that only that of Dora could be considered a hystrionic personality. More than a document on therapeutic success, however, I regard it as an instance of how Freud's primary involvement in his theories limited his empathy.

I continued my search at the University of California library. Yet, after repeated visits to the catalogue and stacks, I was unable to locate a single detailed case report of successful therapy with an E2. Nor was I more successful after several inquiries with expert colleagues.

I could only find brief summaries in the journals, and mostly of brief therapies. John Andrews, for instance, illustrates a brief therapy focusing on a specific symptom: the character trait of being scattered — in turn, linked to the impressionistic cognitive style that distinguishes our E2 from E3.[10]

In the realm of books, what interested me most was a case of Dr. Peter Kramer's in his *Moments of Engagement*, which constitutes a rich and seemingly unintended testimonial to the Rogerian and, by extension, humanistic faith in therapy-through-relationship in which the basic ingredients are understanding the patient and unconditional positive regard.[11] Kramer begins his chapter telling us of his experience treating a man in his late thirties who had suffered terrible losses. Kramer had imagined that the patient needed to talk about his grief, but he would not express his feelings, and in response to the invitation to free-associate he only talked about business matters. After ascertaining that Kramer liked the patient, his supervisor urged him to "play along and trust his healing powers," and the man got well.

Rather than quote Kramer's therapeutic sessions with a school girl (in the description of whose problem and recent life events we intuit an E2), I'll just say that, not having time in his schedule for "another acting out borderline" he intended to see her only once. But she took an immediate liking to him, and he began listening to her story "not just for one session, but many."

> Wanting to become an object of neither rage nor dependent love, I made myself little known, except now and then to diffuse the transference. When on occasion things threatened to get out of hand, I quietly asked the patient whether she had not considered one or another practical course of action. She broke up with her [exploitative] boy-friend, put a new lock on her door, changed her phone number, and entered a course of study in which she moved rapidly to the top of the class. On graduation, she took an appropriate job and received promotion and raises.
>
> The therapist ventured no dynamic interpretations, nor followed

the traditional model of supportive therapy, yet profoundly affected a teenager with drug problems, whose father had introduced her as an incorrigible delinquent.

Kramer was at first not at ease with the idea that the best psychotherapy may sometimes be a matter of renting a friend, and at the time of writing was reconciled to it. Yet, it was a kind of whoring — but where else is such a friend to be found? It ended up by seeming fair to him, I would say, that therapists be not only friends but also professionals who charge a fee for their time and for the ability to understand, care and know how to respond skillfully to the patient's needs at the moment, for this takes long cultivation and ripening.

Thinking of the special case of E2 and its needs, particularly in view of the traditional medical-dominant patriarchal establishment and its obsessive vilification of the erotic type, I am attracted to the notion that a "rent-a-friend" approach might have a peculiar relevance or speciality. Since E2 thirsts for and offers pampering, might it not be that indulgence and sensitivity to a whimsical E2's wishes be no less effective than sustained severity?

AKERET'S TALE OF NAOMI

I had not quite given up on finding a substantial report on a case of successful E2 therapy, when at Berkeley's Cody's Bookstore I saw a new book. The title read, *Tales from a Travelling Couch*.[12]

Hours later, at home, I was happy to ascertain that its first chapter was not only a case of successful therapy (therapy that critically affected somebody's life, turning it from destructiveness toward the good, the true and the beautiful), but also a superb human and therapeutic record. I now proceed to quote, without further comments — though with some italicizing.

Midway through the Lincoln Tunnel I slipped *Sketches of Spain* into the tape deck and turned the volume way up. The castanets crackled around me like cicadas on a summer night, and then those mournful horns wailed in, pleading, soaring, filling the van. The piece has been one of my favorites since I first heard it in the early sixties — Miles Davis at his sinuous, soulful best. It is his and Gil Evans's riff on Joaquin Rodrigo's *Concierto de Aranjuez*, which was itself inspired by Spanish folk melodies. There are purists who put down *Sketches* as synthetic and false, a dilution of the authentic folk idiom. No me; for my money, Davis honed to the essence of that idiom and blew it true. But God knows I have never been accused of being a purist, not even thirty-five years ago, when I was just out of graduate school, freshly imbued with that most orthodox of doctrines, Freudian psychology.

An arch of brilliant sunlight appeared straight ahead of me, and I accelerated out of the tunnel, smiling as I circled up the ramp, Manhattan shimmering across the Hudson on my right. I was on my way to Miami, the home of Isabella Cortez, née Naomi Goldberg, one of my first patients at my first job, therapist with the counseling staff of the City College of New York.

I'd thought about Naomi hundreds of times over the past three and a half decades. She'd stuck in my mind like a first important teacher — or a first lover. From the start Naomi tested me, tested not merely my newly acquired psychological knowledge and technique but my flexibility of mind and independence of spirit — my mettle. Naomi was a test I was always afraid I'd failed.

She was the first destination on my itinerary.

The directions were simple: interconnecting parkways and turnpikes all the way down the Atlantic coast. I'd never even considered taking an airplane. Everything I needed was inside this van: tape deck, memo recorder, notebooks, a carton full of case records, my guitar. My traveling cocoon. I looked up at myself in the rearview mirror, saw a grinning bald head. My God, I hadn't taken a trip like this since I was a young man without wife or children — or grandchildren, for that matter. I felt giddy and more than a little apprehensive. I turned the Miles Davis tape up even louder. It was the last cut, a flamenco song called "Solea," Andalusian for "loneliness."

"Miss Goldberg is disruptive and provocative both in the

104

classroom and in student activities. Her behavior and dress are grossly inappropriate. Please see her immediately."

Naomi's referral had come to me in a manila envelope from Dean Yates of the college's Office of Student Life. Written in pen at the bottom of the page was a note from my boss, Dr. Briscoe, supervisor of student counseling:

> Robert,
> Take a full hour with this one. You may experience some difficulty.
> D.B.
> P.S. Miss G. has been told she's being seen for vocational coun-
> seling.

I'd like to report that I felt a flash of resentment at the deliberate deception of my prospective client that was admitted in that "P.S.," but that would not be accurate. My primary reaction was curiosity. The counseling service was so understaffed at the time that almost all sessions were limited to twenty-five minutes, even in some cases of students with chronic depression or excessive drinking problems. Why in the world did Miss Naomi Goldberg merit a full hour? Just how disruptive could she be?

There is something I must not forget: the year. It was 1957. Dwight D. Eisenhower was president. Gloria Steinem was in high school — a cheerleader, I believe. Most college girls wore circle pins on white blouses with Peter Pan collars; if they were particularly gifted students, they were encouraged to become teachers or social workers. *Nymphomaniac* was the technical term for women who were as avid about sex as men. I was thirty; I had just begun to lose my hair.

I tried to locate a free private office or unoccupied classroom for my first appointed hour with Miss Goldberg, but none was available, so I had to settle for my personal quarters, a thin-walled six-by-six cubicle in the midst of a maze of identical cubicles occupied by mathematics professors. Through these walls I would often hear sudden and enthusiastic rapid-fire bursts about X's and Y's, polygons and googoleplexes. It was as though a devotee of Kafka had been commissioned to design a space for the most intimate human exchanges.

At precisely 10:00 A.M. the buzzer in my cubicle sounded. Before I could rise, Naomi Goldberg walked through the door.

To say that she was an attractive young woman would not begin to capture the effect that Naomi created as she swung into my tiny office. She was stunning, a voluptuous, long-legged beauty with raven hair and fiery dark eyes that locked on mine immediately. She was wearing neither a circle pin nor a Peter Pan blouse, but rather a crimson wool sweater over a skintight body-length black leotard. She raised her shoulders in a gesture somewhere between a shimmy and a shrug and smiled.

"Mmm, it's warm in here, Doctor," she said in a throaty voice. "Mind if I slip this off?"

Without waiting for a reply, she crossed her arms in front of her, grasped the lip of her sweater, and slowly pulled it up, undulating first her hips and then her torso as she wriggled free of the garment. Clearly she was not wearing a bra under her leotard. With a flourish she dropped the sweater onto the floor. Her eyes had never left mine. She shook her long hair behind her and smiled again, triumphantly. Defiantly.

Yes, "disruptive in the classroom" seemed within the realm of possibility.

And yet, although dazzled by Naomi's entrance, I did not feel in the least aroused by her. To be sure, I was well prepared: I had been repeatedly warned by my mentors about seductive patients; I had been trained not to give away any sexual feelings I felt for them. But the truth was I hadn't experienced any sexual feelings that I needed to conceal from Naomi.

Were my instincts that professional already? Or was it something else? Sexual behavior without any genuine sexual intent or feeling often does not elicit a response. *The body knows the difference*. Mine did. What I had just witnessed was only a performance, albeit a bravura performance. I wondered what real feelings lurked behind it.

Naomi had seated herself in the metal office chair directly

across from mine. Our knees were almost touching. Her posture remained provocative, her facial expression insolent. I leaned slightly forward and, as matter-of-factly as I could manage, said, "So, how are you feeling, Naomi — happy?"

Instantly her face went blank, then terrified. It was as if I had asked her the most devastating question in the world.

"God, no!" Naomi blurted, and she immediately began to cry. She bawled long and loudly, tears flooding down her cheeks, and I suddenly remembered my mathematics colleagues behind the thin walls on every side of us.

Go ahead and listen, damn you! I thought defiantly. That sound you hear is truer than any of your calculations!

It was the sound of utter despair.

This time I did have to subdue a powerful natural desire: to embrace this devastated young woman — to let her cry against my shoulder. But of course, I followed the dicta of my training and simply nodded sympathetically, occasionally supplying her with a fresh tissue. When Naomi's torrent of tears finally subsided, I asked her what it was that made her so unhappy, and a second torrent erupted, this one of venom.

"I hate my life!" Naomi began shrilly. "I hate this goddamned school and everybody in it. Goody-goodies and policemen, all trying to control me! I detest my mother and my father and the whole goddamned neighborhood I live in ...."

She went on for several minutes, the litany of malice expanding to include virtually everything and everybody that touched her life, and although her own name was missing from the list, it was abundantly evident that above all, Naomi Goldberg hated herself.

Close to the end of the hour Naomi suddenly went quiet and, for the first time, lowered her eyes from mine.

I waited several moments, then asked softly, "What is it, Naomi?"

Although I was a freshman in this business, I knew that sudden withdrawal near the end of a session sometimes signals the coming of a powerful revelation — a bombshell just before escape.

Naomi raised her eyes but remained silent. I offered her the thinnest possible smile of encouragement. I knew that a gesture too large could be read as a demand, an invasion, and she would clam up completely. Again I waited.

"I was born into the wrong family," Naomi said finally in a low voice.

I nodded, trying not to let my disappointment show. The "wrong family" line sounded fairly banal to me, more like a variation on the then-popular complaint "I'm having an identity crisis!" than a bombshell revelation.

"I'm serious." Naomi went on more loudly, her eyes hardening. "Somebody has made an incredible mistake."

"Exactly what kind of mistake?" I asked benignly.

"Jesus, aren't you listening to me?" Naomi barked. "I said I was born into the wrong family!"

"You mean, you think you were adopted?" I ventured.

"God, no! *It goes back much further than that!*" Naomi said, obviously annoyed by the banality of my response. "It's a much bigger mistake than that!"

I was completely perplexed: "further back than that"? Whatever could she mean? And was now the right moment to press the question further?

The buzzer sounded, signaling the arrival of my next patient. I was reprieved.

Naomi stood, picked her sweater off the floor, and slung it over her shoulder, then opened my cubicle door and sashayed out. In the doorway of the cubicle next to mine, my woolly-haired mathematician neighbor gazed at her slinking by in her leotard, his jaw sagging. At that instant Naomi stopped, pivoted at the waist, and smiled seductively at me.

"Same time next week?" she intoned, her dark eyes flashing.

I nodded.

Looking utterly scandalized, the mathematician hurriedly closed his door.

There is magic in the first encounter with a patient; you get a slice of everything to come. In just fifty minutes I had witnessed both Naomi's flamboyant femme fatale persona and the pathologically low self-esteem that lurked just beneath it, both her shamelessness and her shame, and even, in her "incredible mistake" remark, a hint of her overwhelming desire somehow to escape from herself. It seemed a reasonable guess that Naomi had constructed her brazen exterior as a protective response to traumatic rejection as a child.

The next time Naomi came to see me, she made another dramatic entrance — a double twirl through the door before alighting gracefully on the metal seat across from me. She was again wearing a black leotard and tights, this time overlaid with a man's white shirt open to the waist, where it was tied bolero-style. There was no "striptease" this time — a good thing, too: I didn't have unlimited confidence in the discrimination of my body's responses.

She was eager to get right down to business, to tell all. All it took was this and the following two sessions for me to put together a fairly detailed picture of how Naomi Goldberg had developed into such a painfully unhappy young woman.

Naomi had indeed been mercilessly rejected by her mother, a seamstress named Miriam. Everything about Miriam's one and only child displeased and disappointed her, starting with Naomi's sex (Miriam had "prayed" for a son, but God had "punished her" with a daughter) and her physical appearance (Miriam could never forgive Naomi for being so "swarthy." If she had to have a girl, couldn't she at least be "blond and blue-eyed"? This latter was just one example of the mother's wholesale rejection of her own — and hence her daughter's — heritage. Both Miriam and her husband were first-generation immigrant Ashkenazi Jews with characteristically dark hair and dark eyes. How in the world could Miriam even imagine having a blond, blue-eyed child?

A possible answer to that question — albeit totally false and irrational — came in the cruel refrain Naomi had frequently heard her mother spouting to the neighbors ever since she was a toddler: "She's no child of mine, that one; we found her on the doorstep!"

Above all, Miriam condemned Naomi's behavior; she was appalled by the fact that Naomi could never act like "a proper young lady." Naomi was constantly being chastised for being too jumpy, too fidgety. She could never just walk but had to skip and dance; she could never talk softly and demurely as a young girl should but had to screech and babble and sing and swoon. Again, their ethnic heritage was an issue here.

"[Mother] always complains that I talk like an immigrant," Naomi told me. "That I use my hands too much and talk too loud-ly. Like a Jew, she says. I talk too much like a Jew."

By the time she was ten, Naomi was an inveterate tomboy. She wore pants — extremely rare for girls in those years — and often hid her hair under a cap. She played stickball, rode a bicycle, sneaked into movies, and got into street fights with boys her age in their lower-class neighborhood. Her mother was outraged.

"That's when she started telling me I was crazy," Naomi told me. "All the time — 'You're crazy! You belong in a nuthouse!'"

Of all the verbal abuse her mother hurled at her, this stung Naomi the most.

Throughout her childhood Naomi found solace in books and in the occasional Sunday company of her father. She read pre-cociously and voraciously. *The Arabian Nights* was a special favorite. She also recalled another book that she read over and over at the age of ten: it was the true account of a Belgian Jewish girl who spent the war posing as a Catholic in a convent school.

Naomi's father, Carl, a waiter in a delicatessen, was a weak man totally intimidated by his wife. On Sundays, his one day off, he would often take Naomi away from the house, fishing and hiking. On a few of these occasions Naomi was mistaken for a boy by other fishermen; her father got a big kick out of this bit of mistaken iden-tity and gave Naomi a boy's name, "Tony," to keep the ruse up when this happened. Naomi recalled these Sunday excursions with bittersweetness, for her father abruptly withdrew from her when at the age of twelve she began to develop sexually. He acted as though she'd suddenly become repulsive. The Sundays of solace came to an end.

Now, when Naomi would dance about the apartment with her young breasts bouncing under her sweater, her mother had a new epithet for her: "Whore!" At the time Naomi literally did not know what the word meant, but defiantly — and quite deliberately, she recalled — Naomi went straight from being a tomboy to a bombshell, dressing as provocatively as possible. Men began to stare at her, to whistle and make suggestive remarks.

"I loved it from the start," she told me. "Loved the commotion I made. Loved the power it gave me."

She also admitted to loving the way other women reacted to her. Naomi reserved a special contempt for these women.

"All those good girls in their tight brassieres looking at me from the corners of their eyes as if I'm scum — they have no idea how *numb* they are inside! How *dead*!"

But at home her father, too, had taken to calling Naomi a whore, and it hurt so much that she frequently cried herself to sleep. Sometimes the torment was so intense that she felt as if she were "cracking up inside." Soon the manner in which all men responded to her sexiness could prompt bouts of self-disgust. Still, she'd be damned if she'd give in to anyone — least of all to her mother — and behave like a "little lady."

"I'd rather die!" she declared to me.

Naomi's first sexual relationship was with a married man when she was fifteen. Since then she'd had several affairs, all of which she claimed to have enjoyed — up to a point.

"They were short and passionate, the way affairs are supposed to be," she told me. "Of course, they all ended the same way — when the guy would try to put me on a leash. First men want you because you're sexy. Then after they've got you, they want you to act like a prim little pussycat. They get jealous and mean. Or worse, they get jealous and pathetic."

Unsolicited, Naomi reported to me that she reached climax easily in intercourse, usually several times.

In these succeeding few sessions Naomi had not again alluded to the notion of being "born into the wrong family," though I found myself thinking about that line from time to time. I decided that she'd revealed more by it than I'd originally given her credit for, that it was an expression of all the rejection she'd endured growing up, a deeply felt metaphor that helped her make sense of her emotional abuse and abandonment. I imagined that it was a conscious and perfectly harmless "safety valve" fantasy that allowed her occasionally to escape the pain of that rejection: "I am not really an ugly and awful daughter, I'm just in the wrong family" — like the ugly duckling in Hans Christian Andersen's story that turns out to be "a very fine swan indeed." I did not attach any more importance to it than that.

At the beginning of our fifth session Naomi strode unceremoniously to her chair, sat down, looked earnestly into my eyes, and said, "I have something important to tell you, Akeret: I am not who you think I am."

I raised my eyebrows inquiringly.

"I'm Isabella Cortez de Seville," Naomi said. "Actually, the Contessa Cortez."

I searched her eyes for a wink or a twinkle, any clue that she was playing with me again. Nothing.

"At least that is who I was in the eighteenth century," Naomi want on. "You know, before the mistake."

I could guess, of course, what "mistake" she was referring to: being born the child of Carl and Miriam Goldberg in The Bronx.

I smiled benignly, but my pulse accelerated.

"The moment this woman — this clairvoyant I met in Greenwich Village — told me who I really was, I knew it was true. The whole thing just fit. Of course, I am an aristocrat — or at least I was an aristocrat until I was kidnapped."

I clung to my smile as Naomi went on to explain that as a beautiful young contessa she had been carried away by Gypsies. Fascinating, I thought — an escape fantasy within an escape fantasy. Perhaps that was the result of a hidden fear that the first fantasy would not hold, that it needed a safety fantasy to fall back on when reality threatened to puncture it. In any event I was fairly sure this was a sign that Naomi felt her fantasies were vulnerable. As if reading my mind, she shot me a hard, critical look.

"That's who I really am, Akeret! This —" She gestured at herself with both her hands. "This really is an awful mistake, and I've got to do something about it before it's too late. I have to get back to the real me."

There was not a doubt in my mind that at some conscious level Naomi believed everything she had told me. I still hadn't uttered a word.

"You think I've got a mental problem, don't you?" Naomi suddenly blurted, her eyes wide. "You think I'm screwy, don't you?"

I swallowed hard. There are standard professional options for handling this question. I could remain silent. I could bounce the question back to her: "What do you think, Naomi? What makes you wonder if you have a mental problem?" Or, "What exactly do you mean by 'screwy'?" I could ask her how the question made her feel or if the question elicited any specific memories (of course, it did). In short, I could legitimately respond in any number of ways except by answering the question directly.

"Tell me, Akeret? I need to know," Naomi said beseechingly.

"Of course, you're not screwy," I replied with an easy smile. "Lots of people believe in reincarnation."

With that, Naomi let loose a marvelous, musical laugh, and tears of relief appeared in her eyes. I was absolutely sure I had given her the only response I could have and still retained a trusting, therapeutic relationship with her; any other response would have cast me in the same role as her mother, whose ultimate control over Naomi was to threaten her sense of sanity.

But suddenly I was overtaken by panic. My God, what had I done — traded in a rare opportunity to help my patient test her sense of reality for the short-term satisfaction of her trust and gratitude? Wasn't I, in effect, encouraging a possibly dangerous fantasy rather than helping Naomi examine it for what it was?

"Of course, who you were in an earlier life is quite a different story from who you are now," I said evenly.

"*Who I am now?*" Naomi snorted, her face gone hard and sullen again. "You mean this cesspool? This life of endless shit?"

Before I could pursue the thought any further, another tirade of pain and bitterness came gushing forth, and I decided it was best to leave the challenge alone for the time being. Anyhow, I reminded myself, believing in reincarnation doesn't necessarily make one any more deluded than, say, believing in an afterlife. And more to the point, the very fact that Naomi was continuing to rant about the pain of her Bronx childhood proved how very real that part of her life was to her.

It was during this same session that Naomi recalled how, when she was just a toddler, her mother would often flounce around the apartment bare to the waist, proudly wagging her large breasts back and forth. Miriam would do this only when her husband was out and she and Naomi were alone. One day years later, after Naomi had begun to develop sexually, she deliberately imitated her mother, dancing around the apartment with her young breasts exposed.

"[Mother] slapped me hard across the face — four or five times," Naomi told me. "And with every slap she said it again: 'Whore!' 'Whore!' 'Whore!' 'Whore!' "

This child had been punished for being a girl instead of a boy, then for being a boyish girl, and finally for being a sexy young woman. There was no way for her to win. And on top of all these confusing and abusive messages, Naomi had clearly been "commissioned" to act out her mother's secret sexual desires, which obviously included exhibitionism. I remember thinking what a wonder it was that for all of these burdens and in spite of all her difficulties in relationships, Naomi seemed basically secure in her sexual identity and in her sexuality.

Toward the end of the hour Naomi gave me a sidelong glance, then started to giggle.

"Hey, I thought you were supposed to be giving me vocational guidance in here," she said.

"What did you have in mind?"

"Well, in case you're interested, I just started taking dance lessons."

"Sounds like fun," I said. "Ballet?"

"Flamenco," Naomi replied. She suddenly stood, raised both her hands above her head in a graceful arc, snapped her fingers, threw back her head, and laughed. Then she strode out of my cubicle.

Above all, I knew I had to help Naomi rebuild her ravaged ego. I figured if we could rescue her self-esteem, she would no longer feel the need to escape into fantasies of contessas and Gypsies. I would not have to risk alienating Naomi by trying to disabuse her of any fantasy identity because that identity would simply fade away on its own once she felt better about being herself. Certainly she might continue to hate her family and regret her personal circumstances, but she would not need to see them as some kind of cosmic mistake that required a magical solution.

So over the next three months I encouraged Naomi to keep focusing on all the abuse and rejection she had endured as a child and continued to endure at home as a young woman. She was furious and rightly so, and she knew I put no limits on her expression of this fury. She could scream, she could cry, she could talk filth — and I would still be there. I was the parent who would *never* reject her no matter how hard she tried to shock me.

Whenever I could, I would point out how Miriam's rejection of Naomi had translated into Naomi's own low opinion of herself and ultimately into her self-hatred. I carefully led Naomi back to rediscover her feelings as a small child hearing her mother berate her dark hair and complexion. Naomi reexperienced the way she would automatically incorporate Miriam's contempt for her appearance into her own perception of herself; it literally transmogrified the image she saw in her mirror.

Gradually I began to weave in evidence that Miriam herself was riddled with self-hate, that, for example, Miriam's contempt for her daughter's appearance was the result of her warped perceptions of *herself*. We began to see that Miriam's self-hate was in turn born of her own rejection as a child, that Miriam rejected in Naomi what she had learned to hate about herself.

"It's an ugly legacy she's passed on to you," I told Naomi one day. "Shame begets shame. It's like a bad seed that gets passed from one generation to another."

"How in the name of God do you break the chain?" Naomi

asked.

"We're doing it right now," I replied.

In fact, Naomi *was* changing. By her own account, she was beginning to feel happier more of the time; she'd finally made some friends in school, people she felt she could talk to; she was having fewer crying jags, fewer bouts of depression and self-loathing. And although the battles at home continued to blaze daily, Naomi said they did not make her "go crazy" as often as they once had. She recounted how she had recently come home from a date at three in the morning to be met at the door by her father, who'd spit in her face, once again calling her a whore.

"I started to cry, like always," Naomi told me. "And I started to scream at him, but suddenly it was like I was watching the whole scene from the ceiling and there was this broken man spitting and sputtering because he was so terribly unhappy and lonely. It was sad, very sad, but it didn't hurt me anymore because it had nothing to do with me."

Naomi was also forging ahead in school. She had advanced to the highest level in Spanish language, and this in turn had qualified her for a graduate course in Spanish literature and culture. She was now taking dance three afternoons a week, waitressing evenings in a Village coffee shop to cover the cost of her lessons. Now, more often than not, she wore a skirt and sweater over her leotard. She didn't mention contessas or Gypsies again the entire spring. (pp. 19-33)

Since it would be too much for Akeret's publisher and for mine that I transpose his whole chapter into my book, I will summarize the rest.

Naomi decided to go to Mexico for the summer, but her mother refused to give her permission, and the resulting quarrel ended in Naomi leaving home for good. Naturally, this was the end of her therapy and Akeret only saw her briefly some months later when he received the short visit of Isabella Cortez. Naomi had so completely metamorphosed that Akeret appropriately thought to himself: "If one's performance is one's entire waking life, at what point does that willful suspension of disbelief [appropriate for good performance] become delusion?" (p. 41)

Naomi then gave her former therapist an impressive performance of flamenco, and he reflected: "As I watched Naomi dance, there was no doubt in my mind that she was endowed with more radiance, more power, more life energy as a young Spanish dancer than she has ever possessed as the desperately unhappy daughter of Miriam and Karl Goldberg from the Bronx." (p. 44)

Some thirty years later, Akeret visited Naomi in New Orleans as part of the follow-up project of which his book is the report. The pink sign at her address read "The Pampered Poodle." Unconscious of being watched, she "looked bright, expectant, full of life. And in that she seemed totally peaceful and unfraid, sitting there in her poodle parlor, she looked remarkably innocent to me." (p. 46)

I skip to the beginning of her tale of her life since therapy.

"I danced with the Ballet Nacional for twelve years. It was incredible, Robi, the highest of highs. I danced, and they loved me. My picture was in the papers all the time. People in the street, they'd call out, 'Isabella! Isabella!' Being a star flamenco dancer is like being a movie star over here. I had princes chasing after me, princes and playboys. We toured everywhere: South Africa, Australia, Hawaii, all over the Continent. I loved every minute of it. After two years I was one of the premier women dancers in the company. After six I was married to the ballet orchestra's lead guitarist, Antonio."

I leaned back, smiling, as Isabella went on, regaling me with stories of her fabulous career. From time to time she would jump up, rush to another room, and return with a program or a poster or a scrapbook of newspaper clippings. Last she brought out a photo album.

"Here I am at our mansion in Seville. Sixteen rooms. Beautiful gardens, eh?" She pointed at a photograph of herself sitting on a wrought-iron chair in front of a blaze of bougainvillaea. "You would have loved that house, Robi. It was once a contessa's, can you believe that?"

I grinned in amazement — the "Contessa Isabella Cortez" at

her mansion in Seville. Isabella turned the page to a photograph of the mansion's terrace. A sharp-featured man with a shock of black hair sat holding a guitar, an older woman standing behind him with one hand on his shoulder. The woman held her handsome head high, as if she were royalty. She looked remarkably like Isabella.

"Who is she?" I asked.

Isabella hesitated, her face flushing.

"It's Mother," she said finally. "She came visiting once."

I nodded.

"She read about me in the papers and sent a telegram saying how proud she was and all is forgiven, that sort of thing. In a way it was my dream come true. She said she wanted to visit, and I couldn't resist. I just had to show her my house, my husband, this whole wonderful life I had."

"And your father?"

"He was dead. He'd died a few years after I left, although I didn't hear about it until much later," she said.

"How long did your mother stay?"

Isabella shrugged. "A few weeks, I guess."

She immediately turned the page. On this one was an enlarged photograph of a group of beautiful barefoot women dancing in a village street.

"Here I am in Andalusia, dancing the real flamenco with the other Gypsies," she said cheerfully. "They couldn't believe I was actually American."

I felt a chill cross my shoulders. I looked straight into Isabella's eyes but didn't say a word.

"I never felt completely at home there, Robi." She went on rapidly, her voice lower. "The Spanish are so rigid, especially the men. They call it macho. I call it uptight. My heart bled for all the Spanish little girls, the daughters of my friends. They lock them up like silverware. No one ever takes them fishing. These poor niñas have two choices: to grow up to be a lady or a whore. There's nothing in between. Over there they all act so cultured, but it's just an act. They never want to know what you are really like — what's deep in your soul."

I literally held my breath. I had a hundred questions I wanted to ask Isabella at that moment, but I remained silent.

"Did you ever hear the expression 'Beware of what you desire, for you will surely get it'?" she asked.

"Yes."

"Well, that's exactly what happened to me. Everybody loved me over there. They completely accepted me as Spanish. And I was — I was Spanish for the first few years. Spanish through and through. I mean, how else could I have danced like that? I never had to work at it. It just all came naturally to me, like déjà vu. But after a while my American side rebelled. It wanted to come out again."

Isabella shrugged and smiled at me, her dark eyes gleaming.

"Your American side?" I repeated, my pulse racing.

"Yes, you know — my wild side. That part of me that won't stay still, that won't be put in a box. That's my American side. It just wouldn't be stifled, know what I mean?"

"So — so you returned to being your old self," I said, desperately trying to sound as casual as she did. "Back to your American self, Naomi Goldberg."

I watched her face intently as I said that name. She didn't bat an eyelash.

"Oh, no, it wasn't as easy as that," she replied animatedly. "It was a real struggle. A battle royal, actually. I mean, I don't know about anybody else, Robi, but I've got lots of selves inside me, all fighting to be the star. And I've always got to referee between them, pick the parts that feel right at the time. My Spanish side and my American side still get into skirmishes now and then."

Isabella cocked her head to one side.

"But isn't it wonderful, Robi? I mean, the way you can be so many people in one lifetime?"

She delivered this line with the smiling nonchalance of Shirley MacLaine on a late-night talk show.

A wild laugh burst out of me; I couldn't have held it in if I'd wanted to. So this was it, the denouement, the answer to the question that had been haunting me for all these years — all these decades: At fifty-three years old, Isabella Cortez, born Naomi Greenberg, in radiant good health and in possession of her own business, a fine house, and a full range of emotions, thinks it's just grand that you can pack a whole bunch of lives into one. That, in the end, was apparently the sum total of her "delusion."

My God, whatever had I been worrying about?

"What's so funny, Robi?" Isabella asked.

"Me," I replied. "Sometimes I think I make life far too complicated. I guess it comes with my line of work." (pp. 48-51)

TIME TO GROW UP AND BE SERIOUS

In my search for a therapeutic session to illustrate E2 in the protoanalytic Gestalt situation, I first selected one after which the patient felt elated about insights that had arisen from my confrontation of her manipulativeness. In the end, however, I opted for trusting my intuitive sense that this was mostly false or fabricated insight prompted by an ambitious pursuit of recognition, though this might be difficult to demonstrate through the written transcript alone.

I turn, instead, to the transcript of two seemingly less dramatic but perhaps no less significant mini-sessions that took place in the course of a single group meeting. The subject — the grandson of a very illustrious man — has grown up under the protection of his aristocratic and wealthy family. Now, in his twenties, he needs to begin to earn his own living and senses that he cannot any longer bask in borrowed glory. The main feature of our first "round" is the acknowledgment of the "spoiled child" issue, and a measure of disidentification from it. The second revolves around the split between the seductive surface personality and a covert competitive antagonism. Short as the therapeutic experience was, it involved a practical demonstration that through a freer expression of his childish mischievousness he can also distance himself from compulsive disdain and achieve a better contact — with himself and others.

Sonny: I would like to work. I feel very stubborn. When I go out and meet someone I get very stubborn. When I am alone and dreaming everything goes very well, and when I have something to do, I don't get to do it. But now I finally have to do; I have to manage to get things done. I cannot continue living out of my family things and in the family fairy tale. I need to be able to get my own things done.

C: To do something with your life.

S: Yes. I mean, to do things well; but when it comes to really doing them, it is too difficult.

C: Do I hear that you carry a strong spoiled child in you?

S: Yes, very strong, almost perfect [*laughing*].

C: I think that to work on this issue you could begin by dramatizing this spoiled child a bit.

S: [*laughs, nodding in agreement, then continues to smile without speaking*]

C: He seems to be a very happy child, very charming.

S: Yes. I can present it in very charming ways. I become proud of him.

C: What are the characteristics of this charming child in you? I have the impression that he is quite marvelous.

S: Yes [*smiling brightly*].

C: It seems that he feels very important.

S: Yes, yes, important.

C: [*continuing to read his gestural language*] He seems to be saying: "You can help me, it will give me pleasure if you help me."

S: Yes, it is a very demanding child.

C: And what is the problem?

S: Problem?

C: It seems that having a spoiled child in you involves a problem.

S: Yes, it is a problem because ...

C: Now that you are a grown up it becomes a problem.

S: Yes, now that I am 21 ...

C: Yes, some people get stuck ...

S: I am afraid. Always in the beginning, when I begin something, it is okay, but then, going on, I just can't ...

C: I have the impression that if you talk to this spoiled child now ...

S: Talk to him? To the spoiled child? [*hesitantly*].

C: You are bound together, you can't separate, but you have many things to say to him, I suppose.

S: "Spoiled child, you think you can fool everyone, huh? But you will not succeed, you will get the bill of what you are doing, and a very heavy one!"

C: That sounded like a divine pronouncement, yet very charmingly said.

S: [*laughs, and after a pause, more seriously*] "You are faking, and they believe you; you are charming but in fact you are not working ... "

C: Do you have some advice for him?

S: Yes. "Work more, be more professional, more serious, more responsible."

C: Yes, some people have a "topdog"*[see Glossary] that they have to become free from, but here I get the feeling that there is the little boy who has the advantage. You are being ruled by your underdog who is used to running your life, and you are beginning to realize that, however pleasurable, that is not good any longer.

S: Yes, Yes ... [*gestures to convey that he is satisfied with the transaction and returns to his seat*]

By the end of the group meeting, when I say that there is still time for a short session, he says:

S: I don't feel comfortable. It is not terrible. I feel in my body that I am not feeling well, I am restrained, closed down.

C: Yes. Well, you got something by going into the sense of being a spoiled child. We did a bit of work with your spoiled child, moved on a bit ...

S: Beginning to answer to him and to get rid of him was very rich, but does not feel sufficient. It is sticky [*bending his body*].

C: Is it sticky?

S: Yes, something needs to move.

C: What is the feeling? Do you need more freedom?

S: I want to tell more. Because I look very happy, very friendly, but I don't feel very friendly. There is also some aggression.

C: One has to be very sharp to pick up that aggression, because you come

123

on so smilingly and charming.

S: Yes, that is the situation. I am always very charming and nice ...

C: And you even feel that it is too hostile to say: "I feel stuck, I haven't come to complete satisfaction."

S: I feel more comfortable saying that I am not completely satisfied, and also that I feel some aggression — not against you. I feel more comfortable to tell the truth.

C: Yes, yes. But would you like to go a little further?

S.:Yes [*moves the chair to place it in front of Claudio, smiling*].

C: What do you feel now?

S: I feel my body, it is sticky. I want to let this energy loose. I would like to feel more permeable, more light, more smooth. But I also feel that nothing is going to happen.

C: Let's see what is your fantasy.

S: The fantasy at first is not to make this smiling face, and to seem that everything is okay. I want not to say that everything is wonderful; it is problematic and I am somehow aggressive and not content with the situation.

C: So, here and now, you are not satisfied.

S: Yes, I am not satisfied, and even if you don't like it, I am not satisfied.

C: And are you satisfied now, telling me this?

S: No, I am not satisfied, and I don't want to smile and make a joke of it. I feel some aggressiveness in my body, and I don't know against whom or what [*smiling*].

124

[*Pause*]

C: Could it be me?

S: [*bursts into laughter, then becomes silent*]

C: You seem to be censoring now. What is going on?

S: It is stupid, but the first thing that comes is that it is you, but then — you are the therapist.

C: It is okay. So continue in the same attitude, and whatever presents itself, whatever you see yourself doing, report it and express dissatisfaction about it.

S: I think it is stupid. You are a nice man, but behind comes this little boy who is trying to make a joke.

C: So show us this mischievous little boy that wants to make some joke. Maybe I can survive it.

S: He is saying: "He is not so clever. I can go around him; find the point where he is not so good." I know this very much from him [the little boy]. He looks for some points in others like "he doesn't look so good," et cetera. And I don't want to be like this; to go always against authority, and wanting to be the authority. Stubborn. Like I always feel I am a good artist, better than other famous artists, and so forth. It doesn't work well. I want·to feel more in contact with what I am and not with these labels I put; these values I make up for me.

C: Is this attitude something you could experiment with while you are here?

S: Yes, yes. [*Pause*] As I sit with you I can accept ... I feel more contact.

C: It seems you have to allow yourself to criticize before saying "yes."

S: Also, when I say it, I go back. [*Pause*] I feel better now, more contact. It is very difficult being in contact with respect.

C: You are too proud to allow yourself to express enthusiasm towards others.

S: Yes!

C: Your child is used to being at the center. [*Pause*] You seem to have accomplished something.

S: Okay, very good, thank you.

The transcript above illustrates well some of the traits of a preservation E2 — i.e., the "infantile" variety of self-importance in which dependency, irresponsibility and charm are in the foreground.

Brief and simple as the sessions were, they may be expected to be effective for the confirmation that they involved, for the subject, that he needs to develop responsibility and that he can trust the impulse to a more genuine expression of his feelings.

3

ENNEATYPE 3

Ichazo called the character on point 3 of the enneagram an "ego-go" in reference to its achievement drive and active disposition. It was well caricatured by Feiffer in a cartoon that shows a big man in a series of activities throughout the day. The caption over each image is a repeated word that suggests drivenness. First, "swim, swim, swim"; then, "tan, tan, tan"; later, "play, play, play"; next, "eat, eat, eat;" then, with a glass in his hand and an elegant jacket, "party, party, party"; while driving his car home, "home, home, home;" and in the end "rest, rest, rest" — conveying, of course, that for this character, even relaxation is experienced as a means to an end and becomes a task.

Not always is E3 primarily an achiever. At least sometimes the success is not pursued through performance but through sexual attractiveness. The victory that the sexual subtype is interested in is one of sex-appeal and beauty rather than of money or prestige. Which is not to say that it is less competitive in its pursuit than a business executive is in work matters. Here are a couple of E3 pictures of this sort taken from La Bruyere, master in character description, who lived in a courtly atmosphere of ostentation and glory at Versailles:[1]

"Menippe" is a bird decked with different feathers which are not his. He does not speak, he does not feel; he repeats sentiments and speeches, even makes use of other peoples' wit so naturally that he is the first to be deceived by it, and often thinks he is expressing his taste or explaining his thought, when he is only the echo of someone he has just left.

"Narcisse" is appropriately the name La Bruyere gives another of his characters:

> ... he has his hours of toilette like a woman; everyday he goes regularly to mass at the Feuillants or the Minimes; he is a man of honest conversation ... He carefully reads the *Gazette de Hollande* and the *Mercure Galant* ... He walks with women in the Plaine or at the Cours, and he makes visits with a religious punctuality. To-morrow he will do what he does today and what he did yesterday; and thus he dies after he has lived.

Though the most elaborate portrayals of vain character in fiction are Thackeray's clever and manipulative Becky Sharp in *Vanity Fair* and Flaubert's *Madame Bovary*, it is not on these texts I will be drawing for literary illustration, but on a masterful miniature: a somewhat condensed version of Katherine Mansfield's story "A Cup of Tea".[2] It shows a woman for whom being found the prettiest is no less a ruling passion than for Snow White's mother. This is how it begins:

> Rosemary Fell was not exactly beautiful. No, you couldn't have called her beautiful. Pretty? Well, if you took her to pieces. ... But why be so cruel as to take anyone to pieces? She was young, brilliant, extremely modern, exquisitely well dressed, amazingly well read in the newest of the new books, and her parties were the most delicious mixture of the really important people and ... artists — quaint creatures, discoveries of hers, some of them terrifying for words, but others quite presentable and amusing.
>
> Rosemary had been married two years. She had a duck of a boy. No, not Peter — Michael. And her husband absolutely adored her. They were rich, really rich, not just comfortably well off, which is odious and stuffy and sounds like one's grand-parents. But if Rosemary wanted to shop she would go to Paris as you and I would go to Bond Street ... Today it was a little box. He had been keeping it for her. He had shown it to nobody as yet. An exquisite

little enamel box with a glaze so fine it looked as though it had been baked in cream. On the lid a minute creature stood under a flowery tree, and a more minute creature still had her arms round his neck. ...

She always took off her gloves to examine such things. Yes, she liked it very much. She loved it; it was a great duck. She must have it. And, turning the creamy box, opening and shutting it, she couldn't help noticing how charming her hands were against the blue velvet ...

But the shopman had already bowed as though keeping it for her was all any human being could ask. He would be willing, of course, to keep it for her for ever ...

The discreet door shut with a click. She was outside on the street gazing at the winter afternoon. Rain was falling, and with the rain it seemed the dark came too, spinning down like ashes ...

One ought to go home and have an extra-special tea. But at the very instant of thinking that, a young girl, thin, dark, shadowy — where had she come from? — was standing at Rosemary's elbow and a voice like a sigh, almost like a sob, breathed: "Madam, may I speak to you a moment?" "Speak to me?" Rosemary turned. She saw a little battered creature with enormous eyes, someone quite young, no older than herself, who clutched at her coat-collar with reddened hands, and shivered as though she had just come out of the water.

"M-madam," stammered the voice. "Would you let me have the price of a cup of tea?"

"A cup of tea?" There was something simple, sincere in that voice; it wasn't in the least the voice of a beggar. "Then have you no money at all?" asked Rosemary.

"None, madam," came the answer.

"How extraordinary!" Rosemary peered through the dusk, and the girl gazed back at her. How more than extraordinary! And suddenly it seemed to Rosemary such an adventure. It was like something out of a novel by Dostoyevsky, this meeting in the dusk. Supposing she took the girl home? Supposing she did do one of those things she was always reading about or seeing on the stage, what would happen? It would be thrilling. And she heard herself saying afterwards to the amazement of her friends: "I simply took her home with me," as she stepped forward and said to that dim person beside her: "Come home to tea with me."

The girl drew back startled. She even stopped shivering for a moment. Rosemary put out a hand and touched her arm. "I mean it," she said, smiling. And she felt how simple and kind her smile was. "Why won't you? Do. Come home with me now in my car and have tea."

"You — you don't mean it, madam," said the girl, and there was pain in her voice.

"But I do," cried Rosemary. "I want you to. To please me. Come along."

The girl put her fingers to her lips and her eyes devoured Rosemary. "You're — you're not taking me to the police station?" she stammered.

"The police station!" Rosemary laughed out. "Why should I be so cruel? No, I only want to make you warm and to hear — anything you care to tell me."

Hungry people are easily led. The footman held the door of the car open, and a moment later they were skimming through the dusk.

"There!" said Rosemary. She had a feeling of triumph as she slipped her hand through the velvet strap. She could have said, "Now I've got you," as she gazed at the little captive she had netted. But of course she meant it kindly. She was going to prove to this girl that — wonderful things did happen in life, that — fairy godmothers were real, that — rich people had hearts, and that women *were* sisters. She turned impulsively, saying, 'Don't be frightened. After all, why shouldn't you come back with me? We're both women. If I'm the more fortunate, you ought to expect ..."

"Let me help you off with your coat, too," said Rosemary. The girl stood up. But she held on to the chair with one hand and let Rosemary pull. It was quite an effort. The other scarcely helped her at all. She seemed to stagger like a child, and the thought came and went through Rosemary's mind, that if people wanted helping they must respond a little, just a little, otherwise it became very difficult indeed. And what was she to do with the coat now? She left it on the floor, and the hat too. She was just going to take a cigarette off the mantelpiece when the girl said quickly, but so lightly and strangely: "I'm very sorry, madam, but I'm going to faint. I shall go off, madam, if I don't have something."

"Good heavens, how thoughtless I am!" Rosemary rushed to the bell.

"Tea! Tea at once! And some brandy immediately!"

The maid was gone again, but the girl almost cried out: "No, I don't want no brandy. I never drink brandy. It's a cup of tea I want, madam." And she burst into tears.

It was a terrible and fascinating moment. Rosemary knelt beside her chair.

"Don't cry, poor little thing,' she said. "Don't cry." And she gave the other her lace handkerchief. She really was touched beyond words. She put her arm round those thin, bird-like shoulders.

"Now at last the other forgot to be shy, forgot everything except that they were both women, and grasped out: "I can't go on no longer like this. I can't bear it. I can't bear it. I shall do away with myself. I can't bear no more."

"You shan't have to. I'll look after you. Don't cry any more. Don't you see what a good thing it was that you met me? We'll have tea and you'll tell me everything. And I shall arrange something. I promise. Do stop crying. It's so exhausting. Please!" ...

Rosemary lit a fresh cigarette; it was time to begin.

"And when did you have your last meal?" she asked softly.

But at that moment the door-handle turned.

"Rosemary, may I come in?" It was Philip.

"Of course."

He came in. "Oh, I'm sorry," he said, and stopped and stared.

"It's quite all right," said Rosemary, smiling. "This is my friend, Miss ...?"

"Smith, madam," said the languid figure, who was strangely

still and unafraid.

"Smith," said Rosemary. "We are going to have a little talk."

"Oh yes," said Philip. "Quite," and his eyes caught sight of the coat and hat on the floor. He came over to the fire and turned his back to it. "It's a beastly afternoon," he said curiously, still looking at that listless figure, looking at its hands and boots, and then at Rosemary again.

"Yes, isn't it?" said Rosemary enthusiastically. "Vile."

Philip smiled his charming smile. "As a matter of fact," said he, "I wanted you to come into the library for a moment. Would you? Will Miss Smith excuse us?"

The big eyes were raised to him, but Rosemary answered for her: "Of course she will." And they went out of the room together.

"I say," said Philip, when they were alone. "Explain. Who is she? What does it all mean?"

Rosemary, laughing, leaned against the door and said: "I picked her up in Curzon Street. Really. She's a real pick-up. She asked me for the price of a cup of tea, and I brought her home with me."

"But what on earth are you going to do with her?" cried Philip.

"Be nice to her," said Rosemary quickly. "Be frightfully nice to her. Look after her. I don't know how. We haven't talked yet. But show her — treat her — make her feel —"

"My darling girl," said Philip, "you're quite mad, you know. It simply can't be done."

"I knew you'd say that," retorted Rosemary. "Why not? I want to. Isn't that a reason? And besides, one's always reading about these things. I decided —"

"But," said Philip slowly, and he cut the end of a cigar, "she's so astonishingly pretty."

"Pretty?" Rosemary was so surprised that she blushed. "Do you think so? I — I hadn't thought about it."

"Good Lord!" Philip struck a match. "She's absolutely lovely. Look again, my child. I was bowled over when I came into your room just now. However ... I think you're making a ghastly mistake. Sorry, darling, if I'm crude and all that. But let me know if Miss Smith is going to dine with us in time for me to look up 'The Milliner's Gazette.'"

"You absurd creature!" said Rosemary, and she went out of the library, but not back to her room. She went to her writing-room and sat down at her desk. Pretty! Absolutely lovely! Bowled over! Her heart beat like a heavy bell. Pretty! Lovely! She drew her check-book towards her. But no, checks would be no use, of course. She opened a drawer and took out five pound notes, looked at them, put two back, and holding the three squeezed in her hand, she went back to her bedroom.

Half an hour later Philip was still in the library, when Rosemary came in.

"I only wanted to tell you," she said, and she leaned against the door again and looked at him with her dazzled exotic gaze, "Miss Smith won't dine with us tonight."

Philip put down the paper. "Oh, what's happened? Previous engagement?"

Rosemary came over and sat down on his knee. "She insisted on going," said she, "so I gave the poor little thing a present of money. I couldn't keep her against her will, could I?" she added softly.

Rosemary had just done her hair, darkened her eyes a little, and put on her pearls. She put up her hands and touched Philip's cheeks.

"Do you like me?" said she, and her tone, sweet, husky, troubled him.

"I like you awfully," he said, and he held her tighter. "Kiss me."

There was a pause.

Then Rosemary said dreamily: "I saw a fascinating little box today. It costs twenty eight guineas. May I have it?"

Philip jumped her on his knee. "You may, little wasteful one," said he.

But that was not really what Rosemary wanted to say.

"Philip," she whispered, and she pressed his head against

her bosom, "am I *pretty?*" (pp. 584-591)

I think that the most original statements concerning our E3 have been those of Erich Fromm who coined the concept of the "marketing" orientation of personality. By this he meant not just a personality involving a gift for selling, but that of those who, along with their services or merchandise, also sell their personality in the personality market. A doctor, for instance, has far greater chances of being successful if he has the kind of personality that people can place their trust in. His success may be increased if his *presentation* of himself is that of a correct, efficient person whom people feel they can rely upon.

In American character there is much of this. Just as the market of goods is supported by advertising, personal success is enhanced by the subtle or not so subtle self-advertising of cultivated appearance and a programmed pleasant attitude. This involves a character orientation in which the experience of oneself is that of being merchandise. The person's values are too much those of the market. Intrinsic values are eclipsed by borrowed values: what is fashionable, what everyone approves of, or what sells.

The passion for the cultivation of a good image is frequently called "narcissism," but more commonly and colloquially, vanity. It involves the drive to shine, attract attention, either through the development of sex-appeal or through achievement or success. When the latter is the case, it is typical of E3 to focus on success in relation to established, universally accepted criteria. While E2s do not need to convince the world of their worth, since they have such a good opinion of themselves, E3s make efforts. They are active, alert, striving people, to the point of stress disorders and high blood pressure. This can take place in sports, social life or in any other field. In school, they get the best grades. They are efficient people. They do things well. Just as they attracted their parents' attention during their childhood, they later strive to stand out before the world. The practical efficiency of E3 is an alternative to the good behavior of E1. While type 1's "good behavior" is oriented towards the moral ideal, in the case of E3, it is useful behavior and skillful performance. People striving for such excellence in achievement invest a great deal of energy in coming and

134

going, and in doing so many things; though they find it difficult to be with themselves. They have very little capacity for inwardness and for inner silence. They have to be doing something in order to fill time, and they do not leave themselves time for being with themselves.

Another aspect of E3 is social brilliance which is instrumental in their climbing up the social ladder — as is so well analyzed by Thackeray in his "novel without a hero" about Becky Sharp and her status seeking.[3] In this social variant of the enneatype, the trait of knowing how to approach people is particularly developed, and the very name "Becky Sharp" evokes her personality style: cold and calculating, precise and direct when speaking, with a quick, agile and organized mind.

Executives and business people often seem to need to be like that. They are diligent people, observant of detail, attentive, smiling, reliable, efficient; and also, they have a precise sense of timing.

Types 2, 3 and 4 are the most emotional characters in the enneagram, generally speaking; but just as E2's false feelings are positive and E4's negative, those of E3 are neutral. Thus, the more pathological E3 is the least emotional of the three, for rational and practical considerations override their emotional life. Only when they are more developed, healthier, do they allow their emotional side to appear, for they no longer need to be permanently in control, and come to transcend the emotional lie involved in their implicit claim to be their smiling, self-assured *persona*.

In a general fashion, we might say that E3 experiences a polarity of self-confidence/insecurity. They are people who cannot be characterized as insecure. (Insecurity is far more typical of E5 and a sub-type of E6.) E3 individuals recognize insecurity, but they also know how to disguise it and produce an impression of self-confidence. They know how to carry on. They have learned early in life to look after themselves, and have developed autonomy. They know how to look after their own interests. Implicit in this is that they do not trust in things working out of their own accord, or developing naturally.

While they are optimistic, the optimism is in regard to their own capacity for carrying things out; not the type of optimism that abandons itself to luck, or to the care of others.

Not only are E3 people active and good at getting things done, they are also good organizers. This is the personality of many executives, mostly in the business world, but also in government. Former president Reagan's life — of salesman become actor, and then governor and president — illustrates the typical skills of E3 and the importance of keeping appearances in politics.

Another domain in which E3s excel, aside from business and government, is that of entertainment and show business, since they have a talent for acting and a liking for display and applause. The case of Marilyn Monroe is of special interest, not only as representative of a whole class of E3 Hollywood "sex goddesses," and a case of exceptionally successful exploitation of a sexual E3's passion to attract the opposite sex, but because of the wealth of information — in some forty biographies and intelligent commentary — that she aroused in view of her excellence and fame.

Norman Mailer speaks of her as "the angel of sex," for, he observes, she "suggested sex might be difficult and dangerous with others, but ice-cream with her."[4] And Diana Trilling wrote, "she suggested such a purity of sexual delight. The boldness with which she could parade herself and yet never be gross, her sexual flamboyance and bravado which yet breathed an air of mystery and even reticence, her voice which carried such ripe overtone of erotic excitement and yet was the voice of a shy child — these complications were integral to her gift. And they described a young woman trapped in some never-never land of unawareness." (quoted in Mailer, p. 17)

As for Marilyn herself, she claimed:

> ...the truth is that I never deceived anyone. I have sometimes allowed men to deceive themselves. At times they didn't care to find out who and what I was. Instead, they invented a character. I didn't bother to argue with them. It was obvious that they were after somebody who was not me, and when they realized this they blamed me for disappointing them and deceiving them.[5]

Perhaps some deception is involved in this disclaiming deception to such an extent, yet it is clear that Marilyn Monroe suffered from the constraints that her Hollywood-given image imposed on her and on her life beyond the movies. She was fully conscious that in Hollywood a woman's virtue was of lesser consequence than her hairdo, and we may take it as part of her sanity that she was bitter about being judged for appearance rather than being. No matter how much being a good actress reinforced her self-esteem, there came a time when she could say that, "the important thing is what you feel about yourself as you live what comes up day after day." (p. 19)

But her life, as Graham MacCann puts it, "had become a complicated tangle of public and private appearances, an exploitation of personality that demanded her impersonation of the 'Marilyn' image that her audience demanded at the moment." And this to such an extent that Lawrence Olivier remarked that, "she was exploited beyond what anybody could have endured." (p. 20) She became the best-selling star in the world — but she also rebelled in the face of an excessive manipulation, and on one occasion sought to demolish her public image.

During the thirties and fifties, the distance between the stars and the public diminished as the fiction of "ordinary" characters was created, and characters of the past were coupled with the basic values. Male stars, thus, were photographed during their times of leisure in the countryside, and women stars were presented as if they had enough time to be devoted mothers. The management of success, inseparable from profit, then involved the Hollywood stars in the straightjacket of a fictitious life, with little place for spontaneity. Given this context, the extent of Marilyn Monroe's suffering may be taken as a sign of her healthy yearning for authenticity.

It is not surprising that type 3s should be good salesmen and advertisers. Not only do they know how to manipulate their own image, they also know how to affect the image of others — not only to elevate but also to denigrate; they have a great skill in hurting or defaming without seeming to intend it. (As in "poisonous compliments." This is the typical high society aggression, such as when, for instance, one lady says to another: "You look lovely, dear, what a marvelous figure! Who would guess how many years have gone by!") They know how to offend deeply; how to hit the bull's-eye, without losing elegance of form.

Seen from outside, the superficiality of type 3 is easily perceived. There is simulation, and seems to be a kind of "plastic quality," a facade without depth. Appearance engages the person's surface, and being so concerned with formal perfection and what others approve or disapprove, they lose touch with their own depth.

Though the character seems to have been prominent in the days of La Bruyere and in the environment at Versailles, it is no less prominent today in the United States, where a shift in the modal personality seems to have occurred in the "Roaring Twenties" from the earlier traditional and puritanical (E1) to the highly achieving, fast moving "outer directed" E3. "Outer directed" (an expression introduced by Harvard sociologist David Riesman) is, of course, an apt description of this kind of person, who is inclined to follow public opinion and adapt in his or her taste to what is fashionable. E3 is an extroverted kind of person, who does not consult ideals or tradition so much as the prospect of approval; one not so interested in self-fulfillment, or even in fulfilling his own taste, because it is more important to be approved of, or admired; a person who wears his religion, his opinions, "on his sleeve," so to speak, to clothe himself in them, and for whom appearance eclipses being. The doll stereotype, be it Barbarella or Barbie, is an echo of E3.

The E3 character of the United States is nowadays visible in a wide array of manifestations ranging from fast food restaurants and supermarkets through the Hollywood advertising industry to technocracy (i.e., the rule of technological values to the detriment of human and ecological considerations). Most serious among the social consequences of the "marketing orientation" of personality may be, however, a world surrendered to market values and money considerations.

TWO CASES FROM LOWEN

Though Alexander Lowen's book *Narcissism* constituted a response to a generalized interest prevalent since the eighties, the picture he presents of narcissistic personality through his cases is quite different from what is labeled as such by Kohut, Kernberg or the DSM-IV.[6] Without engaging in a discussion on the various meanings of narcissism in the literature, let me state that Lowen's narcissist is most often our E3 — the vain, appearance-minded character (whom I have found usually diagnosed as "rigids" by practitioners of bioenergetics). Lowen's own feeling-full and expressive personality seems to have contributed to making him a good

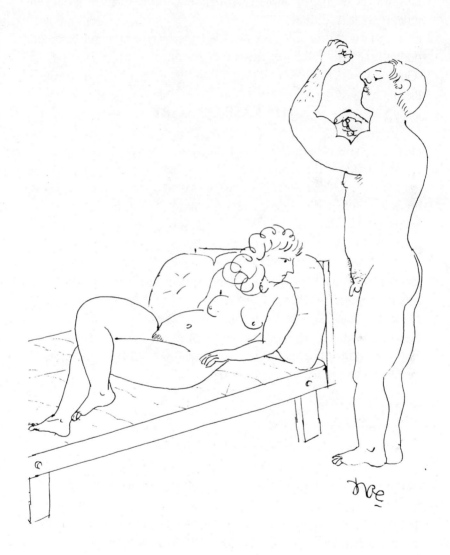

therapist in the case of the "cold and calculating" rigid and perfectionistic E3; particularly since he seems to understand image issues, as "heart-centered" people typically do.

I extract from his book two cases to which he brings his good eye both for the body and the expression of emotion.

THE CASE OF MARY

I was consulted by a woman, Mary, who had had a breakdown after a threatened breakup with her lover. She was very attractive looking — her face was well formed, with a strong jaw, a full mouth, and widely spaced eyes; her body was rather petite, very trim, with shapely legs. Her smile was warm and inviting. At least this was my impression when she directed her attention to me. When she looked away and was quiet, however, a pathetic look crept onto her face. The same pathetic quality was apparent in her body. Her chest seemed narrow and tight, her waist so constricted that it almost divided her in half. Somehow, she had no belly and her pelvis was surprisingly small, given that she had had two children (in an earlier marriage). Her body looked so tiny and undercharged that I thought, "No body. She is a nobody."

The idea that Mary could be considered a nobody was contradicted by her seeming command of her movements, her ideas, and her words. Her will was strong, and she knew how to use herself. From the age of five, she had trained to be a ballet dancer, and although she had never danced professionally, she considered herself a dancer. Knowing this, I realized that when she turned on her charm as she looked at me, it was a performance. She became a vivacious, dancing doll; indeed, her body and her face had a doll-like quality. This was the image with which she was identified and which she tried to project. When she dropped her act and looked away, she became a pathetic, lost creature, a nobody. The role of the image was to compensate for a diminished sense of self, but its effect was the reverse. By directing all her energies to maintain an image, Mary impoverished and diminished her real self.

Even though Mary recognized the weakness in her sense of self (she got depressed easily, she was overwhelmed by any strong feeling), she was not prepared to give up her image. She sensed the power in it — a power over men. Though she was past thirty-five, Mary portrayed herself as more a girl than a woman. What men were attracted to, and even fell deeply in love with, was a cute, dancing doll-girl who was openly seductive. After a relationship developed, Mary became completely dependent on the man. She oscillated between the pathetic little girl, who needed to be cared for and protected, and the seductive, dancing doll, whom men wanted to possess.

If we ask what is the reality of Mary's personality, we must answer that the image of the dancing doll is as real as the image of the pathetic little girl. In effect, Mary has a double personality in the sense that she presents two different faces to the world. One face is a mask like a doll's face that is devoid of feeling. The other face expresses her true feelings and is therefore a true representation of the self. The doll's face reflects an ego image and the pathetic little girl's face reflects the self-image. One face is put on by an effort of the will, while the other is a spontaneous manifestation of the inner being. This splitting of Mary's personality would justify the diagnosis of borderline condition.

Although diagnostically Mary would be seen as a borderline personality, in my opinion, the diagnosis is less important than understanding Mary — who she is, who she pretends to be, and why she developed a split in her personality. The image is really a part of the self. It is the part of the self that faces the world, and it takes its shape through the surface aspects of the body (posture, movement, facial expression, etc.). Because this part of the body is subject to conscious control by the will or ego, it can be modified to conform to a particular image. We can speak of a false self set up against the true self, but I prefer to describe the split in terms of an image that contradicts the self, and to see the basic disturbance as a conflict between the image and the bodily self.

Why did Mary give up her bodily self in favor of an image? Although the sacrifice was not conscious, she had decided her

141

feeling self was not acceptable. I found that she couldn't cry and couldn't scream. She had no voice to express feelings. Her speaking voice sounded flat, unemotional, and mechanical. It was clear why Mary became a dancer. Unable to use her voice to express herself, she turned to movement. But that avenue, too, was circumscribed. She began to study ballet at five years of age with the support and encouragement of her mother, who wanted Mary to be outstanding and bring some credit to her. Mary was completely dominated by her mother and terrified of her. Yet she insisted to me that she had no angry feelings toward her mother, who had done so much for her. The degree of denial in this statement is typical of narcissists. Having accepted and identified with the image of the dancing doll which she saw as being special and superior, she couldn't admit to "bad" or angry feelings which would contradict this image.

Her father adored his little dancing doll, but his adoration was coupled with a sexual interest in her. At an early age, Mary was aware of her ability to excite her father, but any sexual feeling on her part had to be denied to avoid her mother's jealousy and her father's negative reaction (from guilt). She mentioned that when she was a teenager, her father would become very upset if he saw her kissing a boy. Without any support from her father for her feelings, Mary surrendered herself to her mother and identified with her in contempt for her weak father. Having made the surrender, she could compensate for the loss by creating an image that gave her sexual power over men without the vulnerability engendered by sexual feelings. Images can only be deflated, not hurt.

In a borderline personality, such as Mary, the discrepancy between the image and the bodily or feeling self is wide enough to pose a danger of emotional breakdown. Mary had been hospitalized before consulting me. Fortunately, I was able to help Mary get in touch with and release some of her sadness by crying. This enabled her to break through the denial, see the reality of her being, and make a connection to her bodily self which gave her a strength she had not previously possessed.

In my therapeutic approach called bioenergetic analysis, the

142

individual's connection to his or her bodily self is achieved through direct work with the body. Special exercises are used to help a person feel those areas of the body in which chronic muscular tensions block the awareness and expression of feeling. Thus, in Mary's case, one of the exercises used was to have her lie on a bed and kick with her legs while loudly yelling "no." She had never been able to protest the surrender of her bodily self, and she could not reclaim that self until she had voiced that protest. Despite the fact that she was a dancer, her kicking movements were uncoordinated and without force while her voice was small and weak. She felt the constriction in her throat which prevented her from making a loud, full sound. It also restricted her breathing, which decreased her metabolism and lowered her energy. I could palpate the constriction as a spasticity of the scalene muscles on the sides of her neck. The technique I use to reduce this spasticity is to apply a light pressure with the tips of my fingers to these muscles while the person is making as high-pitched a sound as possible. When I did this with Mary, she broke into a loud scream which continued for some time. After several screams, she broke into a deep sobbing as the tension in the muscles of her neck relaxed and the feeling of sadness broke through. Following this release, her protests by kicking and yelling were stronger and more forceful.

People in trouble need to cry. While it was relatively easy to get Mary to cry because her body was not heavily armored, one faces considerable difficulty with narcissistic men who pride themselves on being able to take it without breaking down. The muscular overdevelopment results in a tight, hard body which effectively inhibits the awareness and expression of soft or tender feelings. In such cases, it often takes considerable work with breathing to soften the body to the point where crying can occur. Once the person lets himself cry, it is not too difficult to evoke the anger which has been suppressed. Sometimes, releasing the anger by having a person hit the bed with a tennis racket or the fists may open the sadness and produce the crying. I have described some of the exercises and body techniques in my previous books. I must emphasize that these exercises are not mechanical. They are effective in changing personality only when they are coupled with a thorough analysis, including the interpretation of dreams, and when they follow from an understanding of the personality as it is expressed by the body.

In other patients, such as narcissistic characters, the ego is able to maintain control and avoid a breakdown because it is less completely split off from the self. Yet props, like alcohol, may be used to maintain a certain denial of reality, as can be seen in Arthur's case. (pp. 39-43)

THE CASE OF LINDA

Linda, a woman close to forty, consulted me because she had been severely depressed some years ago and was afraid this was going to happen again. When she entered my office, I was impressed by her appearance. She was an attractive woman, strikingly but tastefully dressed, with a shapely figure. She smiled easily and seemed free in her manner. Granted, her voice was slightly husky, without much range of tone. Still, it was hard to believe, at first glance, that Linda had any serious problems.

Her major complaint was that she didn't seem to be getting anywhere in life. She had held the same job for a number of years. Although it was a creative position and paid her well, she felt unfulfilled. She thought she should move on, get a job with more responsibility and more money. But she didn't know what else she wanted to do. She was also dissatisfied with her personal life. She had never married and felt desperate about the prospect of never having a family. Yet she wasn't sure if that was her most important goal. She was confused about her direction in life, caught between her desire for a career and her wish for a home. Some women, she commented, achieve both, but she hadn't attained either. On the surface, Linda seemed to have the potential for both — brains and beauty. What was wrong?

Linda's present depressive reaction had begun just after the breakup of a relationship with a man. She hadn't been in love with him; she herself had terminated the relationship because it wasn't going anywhere. Nevertheless, she experienced the breakup as a failure and became depressed.

The first cue I had to Linda's problem was her voice. I had noticed its lack of resonance. I could not sense any excitement in her voice; it sounded unalive. When I remarked on this to Linda in our first session, she replied, "I've always been ashamed of my voice. It doesn't sound right." The voice, as I have indicated, is one of the main channels of self-expression. The lack of resonance in her voice suggested a lack of feeling in her body.

Since Linda had said that she was unhappy and frustrated about her life situation, I suggested that she try to express some feeling about this. Could she voice some protest about her fate? I asked her to lie on the bed[7] and kick her legs against it as a form of protest. To kick about something means to protest. This is one of the regular exercises in bioenergetic therapy. All patients have something to kick about. Neurotic individuals suppress their feelings, and kicking is one way to help them express these feelings. The voice is also engaged in this exercise. With the kicking, the person is told to say "No" or "Why?" Both words imply a protest. I specifically directed Linda to raise her voice as loud as possible, letting it come out as a yell or scream.

Linda tried the exercise, but her kicking was mechanical and her voice sounded weak. It lacked any note of conviction. She complained that she had no feeling of protest in her, so she couldn't do the exercise properly. Did she have any feeling of sadness which she could express by crying? She didn't feel sad and she couldn't cry. Nor could she feel any anger. In fact, she didn't feel any emotion strongly enough to be able to express it. That was her problem.

I realized that Linda's appearance was a facade. She projected the image of a successful woman of the world, but the image did not correspond to her inner being. I could guess that in her inner being she felt herself to be a failure. The fear of failure had led to her first depressive reaction. For some reason, the image was so important to her that it absorbed most of her energy, leaving her without the strength to express herself with feeling as a real person in the world.

To help Linda, I had to understand both the exact meaning of the image and its relation to her sense of self. What was the image of success so effectively concealing? Why and how did it assume such an overriding importance in Linda's life? What did failure signify? It is insufficient to answer these questions in general terms. The narcissistic image develops in part as a compensation for an unacceptable self-image and in part as a defense against intolerable feelings. These two functions of the image are fused, for the unacceptable self-image is associated with the intolerable feelings. It was only as Linda's therapy progressed that we came to understand the exact meaning and role of her success image.

Therapy is a process of getting in touch with the self. Traditionally, the approach to the self has been through analysis. Every therapy must include a thorough analysis of the patient's history to discover the experiences that have shaped the patient's personality and determined his or her behavior. Unfortunately, that history is not readily available. The suppression and denial of feeling result in a repression of significant memories. The facades we erect hide our true selves from us as well as from the world. But analysis has other material to work with, in addition to remembered history.

The analysis of dreams is one way to acquire additional data. Then there is the analysis of present-day behavior, especially as it is evidenced in the therapeutic relationship. This relationship is often a highly emotional one because feelings toward important figures from the past, like the parents, are transferred to the analyst. Through analysis patients come to see the connections between their adult attitudes and actions and their childhood experiences. This traditional approach, however, is limited because it is too dependent on words, which are themselves only symbols or images.

Getting in touch with the self involves more than analysis. The self is not a mental construct but a bodily phenomenon. To be in touch with oneself means to sense and be in touch with one's feelings. To know one's feelings, one has to experience them in their full intensity and that can only be done by expressing them. If the expression of a feeling is blocked or inhibited, the feeling is either suppressed or diminished. It is one thing to talk about fear, another to feel the fright and scream. Saying "I am angry" is not the same thing as feeling the emotion surge through one's body. To truly feel one's sadness, one has to cry. This is what Linda was unable to do. She had choked off her sobs and her screams. She had swallowed her tears. The chronic tension in her throat affected her speaking voice, making it sound unalive.

In addition to verbal analysis, then, Linda's therapy involved working with her body physically to reduce its rigidity, to deepen her breathing, and to open her throat.

I have mentioned earlier in this chapter some of the exercises I use — kicking the bed while saying "no" as an expression of protest and hitting the bed to express anger. These are expressive exercises. They would also include reaching out with one's hands to touch, to call for mother or to ask for help, and reaching out with the lips to kiss or suck. Most people have a lot of trouble reaching out; they are inhibited by a fear of rejection which is structured in tensions around the shoulders and the mouth. I also use a number of positions to help a person feel his body from head to toe. The simplest of these is a standing position with the feet parallel and about six inches apart, the knees slightly bent, the weight of the body on the balls of the feet, the belly out and the pelvis slightly back. If the person will breathe easily and deeply with the shoulders relaxed, he will feel himself down to his feet. It is the position to which one lets oneself down from the rigid holding of oneself up. Many people doing this exercise feel some anxiety about letting go or letting down. One can then sense how tightly one holds to maintain control. Another position, called grounding, enables a person to feel his contact with the floor or earth. The person bends forward and touches the floor with the points of the fingers. The feet are parallel and about twelve inches apart, the knees slightly bent. Again, breathing deeply and freely is important. If one feels one's legs in an alive way in this exercise, they will vibrate as the current of excitation flows through them. The vibration reduces the tension in the legs and gives the person a sense of aliveness in the lower part of the body. All exercises must be attuned to the needs of the person as they are manifested in the expression of the body. Such work with the body aims at and facilitates the release of feeling. And this release often brings to consciousness a significant memory from the past. The release of feeling removes the block in the function of perception.

After a number of sessions and considerable work, Linda broke through her throat block. As she noted, "I was able to cry with deep sobbing, and I experienced a lot of sadness. I recalled that as a child I was so frightened because Mom and Dad argued so much. I was terrified that either he would hurt her or she him. I always tensed up in bed when they were arguing, petrified or terrified that one of them would get hurt, possibly killed. But I couldn't express my feelings, my fear, or my pain. Did I subconsciously want Daddy to kill Mother so I could have him all to myself?"

In the following session we looked at this problem more closely. Linda commented on the two areas where she felt stuck — her love life and her career. At the time she was living with a man who was still attached to his ex-wife, who drank and didn't have a place of his own — not even a mailing address. She remarked, "I feel stifled that he is still with me all the time. I think I love him, or at least I need him." With respect to her work, she said, "I'm having a problem with my career — I need a change. I don't want to be doing the same thing next year or five years from now, and that frightens me. I am really desperate. I'm not feeling suicidal, but I have bouts of despondency." When I asked her if she felt like a failure, she replied, "Of course I do." I then asked if she was able to cry about it, and she began to sob softly. She said it made her sad to realize she had shut off her feelings.

As we turned to the relationship with her father, the question of sex came up. Linda recalled, "When I was a child, I felt that masturbation was evil. I felt sneaky sitting on someone's knee — possibly an uncle's — and feeling good. But I have no memory of

148

my father's physical affection — he never held me.

"My parents would accuse each other of being wrong," she continued, "and I as a child had to listen to each side separately. They would complain about the other to me, a little ten-year-old child, and tell me how they felt. Naturally I suppressed ever expressing how I felt. I never had the courage to tell them to shut up when they were arguing. It was an intolerable situation. I feel he was the instigator since it was his gambling that brought on the arguments — and at the same time, I could not tolerate her when she argued. I used to go to bed at night with a pillow over my head to shut off their screaming. I even remember that when I was about six or eight, I wanted to commit suicide because I couldn't stand the arguing. I was afraid he would hit her. But they never really hit each other."

Linda's story, however, did not seem complete. She reacted to the conflict between her parents as if it had a nightmarish quality. She described it as "intolerable," saying she was petrified and had wished to "die." Yet parental arguing is too commonplace in and of itself to be a horror story. Why, then, do many patients report their experience of parental fighting as a horror? The child fears that such arguing will result in one of the parents being killed. Linda indicated this fear, which I then related to the Oedipal situation. She had suspected the connection. In the Oedipal period, at three to six years of age, children have death wishes against the parent of the same sex. At the same time, the child feels terribly guilty about these feelings and tries to reject them. I thus assumed that Linda had been afraid her father would kill her mother because on some level she wished he would so that she could have him all to herself. On a conscious level, however, Linda turned against her father and wished he would die. She even said that she still wished this, for it would make her mother's life much easier. But in turning against her father, Linda also turned against herself, against her love for him and against her sexuality, which was an expression of that love. At least, this was my hypothesis. To test it, I checked her feelings toward me, for as her therapist, I was a father surrogate.

As Linda lay on the bed, I leaned over her, with my face about twelve inches from hers. As our eyes made contact, I could sense that she looked at me with a positive regard. I asked her if she would like to kiss me. (I don't kiss my patients, but I do permit them to express their feelings verbally.) Linda said she was afraid to kiss me, that it was improper and "dirty." But as she said this, she began to cry and sob. She was in a conflict about her feelings. If she could not accept them, she could at least protest. So I suggested that she kick the bed and scream "Why?" After this exercise, which she did with some feeling, Linda felt some release.

In the next session, I asked Linda to reach up and touch my face. Here are her words about the experience as she recorded it in her notes after the session: "Big breakthrough came when I had to hold his face and tell him I like him. I couldn't do it. The words were choked in my throat — they wouldn't come up — and when I finally got them out, I cried. I really cried hard before I was able to say anything. I could not say 'I love you.' I could not bring the words up past my throat. But as I sobbed, I said, 'What am I afraid of? Why can't I say I love you?' I can really feel my sadness."

I told Linda that I sensed she didn't feel she had a right to burden anyone with her sadness. Her attitude in the face of sorrow was to put on a "happy face," to keep smiling. She then remarked, "My parents told me all their problems and how upset they were. I naturally felt I shouldn't share any of my upsets with them. Consequently, I pushed all my sad feelings down. Why couldn't I tell my parents I was unhappy and sad that they argued all the time and felt miserable? I can see now why I have such a neurosis about my voice and throat — including a great fear that I could develop throat cancer. I never felt like an articulate person."

After this session, in her notes Linda wrote, "I was finally able to break down. It was sad and painful, but I felt uplifted and wonderful when I left — and remained so the rest of the day."

We can see now that Linda's image and her inner reality were opposites. The image presented to the world was one of a worthy, competent, and successful person. She was a "somebody." Unfortunately, Linda didn't feel worthwhile; she didn't feel she had the right to express herself as a person, to have a voice in her own affairs. Had she felt this, there would not have been a problem. But at the beginning of her therapy, I couldn't tell what she felt. She had suppressed all feeling. Only after the experiences I have described was she able to open up and reveal her inner self.

The true sense of self is determined by the feelings of the body. And it is reflected in the body's expression. I mentioned that Linda was an attractive woman. In one respect, however, her body was misshapen. Her pelvis and buttocks were too heavy and too large. There was a passive quality about this area, and in fact, it was difficult for her to move her pelvis easily and freely. Linda was aware of this difficulty, having experienced the passivity of the lower part of her body during sexual encounters. (She had never reached a climax with a man during sexual intercourse.) The passivity related to a feeling that sexually she was "there" for the man but not for herself. When we discussed the significance of her pelvic immobility, Linda remarked that her mother had the same problem. Was she, then, identified with her mother? "I suppose we're alike in some way," Linda replied, "but I've always tried to be different from her." The difference was expressed in the role that Linda adopted, in the image she projected. The similarities, however, came out on the bodily level and in patterns of behavior that were unconsciously determined. Both women were sexually passive, suggesting deep feelings of sexual guilt, which foster feelings of inferiority and inadequacy. Belonging to the modern generation, Linda rebelled against her "fate," in contrast to her mother, who accepted hers, married, and raised a family. But Linda had to pay a price for her rebellion — namely, no marriage and no children.

I posed a question earlier about Linda's image: What was its exact meaning? To be a successful woman meant to be different from her mother. Failure meant that she was no better than her mother. But how does the idea of competition between mother and daughter (or father and son) arise? I do not believe that it is natural.[8] In the natural order, children tend to emulate their parents, not compare themselves with them. Competing with or comparing oneself with a parent implies an equality of level. Children can only feel equal to their parents if they are treated as equals by one or both parents. Both parents did this to Linda, sharing their problems and anxieties with her. The parent who looks for under-standing and sympathy from a child treats the child as an equal, placing the child in an adult position. A similar situation occurs when a parent shows that he or she is sexually excited by a child. In both cases, the child is seduced and used. The effect, however, is to make the child feel special. That is what happened with Linda.

Linda's therapy continued to progress in a satisfactory man-ner. She was able to sense and express more feeling. She cried more easily and more deeply about her past and present life. Through the body work with her pelvis, she developed more sex-ual feeling. Then, she met a successful man, unlike her previous lovers, who was interested in marrying her. Her marriage necessi-tated a move to another city, and her therapy with me ended.

Linda' case illustrates a number of points about narcissism. The grandiose self-image that characterizes the narcissist compen-sates for an inadequate and ineffective sense of self. It represents a conscious effort to be different (better), but it fails to change the basic personality or the self. The self is a function of the body's aliveness; it is not subject to conscious control. All one can do con-sciously is to alter one's appearance — in effect, change one's image — and this has only a superficial effect on the personality, just as changing one's clothes does not change one's body under-neath. More profound change requires the expression of the sup-pressed and denied feelings. To do this, one must release the chronic muscular tensions that block feeling and raise the repressed memories to consciousness. (pp. 64-73)

FROM WANTING-TO-SHINE
TO FEMININITY

In producing the first draft of this book I had disregarded Lowen's cases as too brief as illustrations for E3, in a series that began with Anna O.

and continued with Scott Peck's Charlene. Not finding something both elaborate and rich in characterological detail in the professional literature that I surveyed (beginning in Freud's *Studies in Hysteria* and ending in a computer search of successful therapy cases in hysterical personality), I decided to select an account written by a patient rather than her therapist — more precisely, an annotated extract of Cherry Boone's book *Starving for Attention*.[9] It seemed fitting that E3 be illustrated by a media personality and fitting, too, that the sub-title of this document on the achieving personality style already told the reader about the author's triumph over disease. As for the title itself, it felicitously condenses a double meaning. "Starving for attention" suggests being attention starved (and thus animated by a passion to be seen), yet more specifically announces a case history in anorexia nervosa — a disease that involves a willingness to starve for the sake of an attention-getting body-image.

Since, I am sorry to say, my publisher's request to quote extensively from Cherry Boone's material as an illustration of E3 was declined, I have had to fill the gap with an unpublished report: a therapeutic and spiritual autobiography written some years ago by my wife Suzy in view of a somewhat different book that I then had in mind.

I will let the document speak for itself, limiting my commentary to the remark that here is a story of transformation in which the decisive influence was the exposure to my work (at a time preceding our coming together); and the decisive factor was the sincere acknowledgement of her destructiveness, self-deceit and mistakes.

Let's give her a name, a name that will please her, give her value, and be remembered forever; a name to be known all over the world and even beyond ... That's what she is — a star from beyond.

Star-from-Beyond created herself, impelled by need — her need to shine in order to survive. However, the reason for her brilliance was absolutely secret. Nothing and nobody could ever be let into the secret that her brilliance was achieved with great effort, cunning and perseverance. This brilliance had to appear to be authentic, unique, unequaled.

The world she lived in did not deserve her trust, but had to lie at her feet. To achieve this, any means were allowed. There were no rules ... no morals to stop her from reaching her aims.

Her arduous apprenticeship included many lessons, and was systematic and self-taught. She had to learn on her own, for to show that she needed to learn with or from somebody else would have been to reveal her mystery, her aura of perfection; it would force her to admit that there was somebody who could teach her something. This was quite out of the question. When she didn't know something, she would observe patiently with a knowing look, and after having absorbed sufficient information, she would then deliver subtle lectures full of apparent wisdom.

The world was her school — constant observation of all and everyone, especially of people's shortcomings, each person's "Achilles heel." Everybody had one, and would reveal it (it was simply a matter of time); and then she would use it to her convenience to place herself in an outstanding position.

The primary lessons she learned early: how to be useful, interesting and altogether irreplaceable. She had the necessary tools for this: beauty, quick reasoning and an acute and precise perception of what went on around her. The rest developed gradually.

The question behind her apprenticeship was always the same: What does the other person like, need or want? She would discover this quickly; an equation easy to solve. (Nothing was impossible for Star-From-Beyond.) She knew that once the hook was cast, the fish would surely swallow the bait. Her aim was always firm, precise; her timing always accurate.

Star-From-Beyond was born pure and innocent, like any baby, but did not remain an innocent child for very long. Soon she was forced to face an urgent need: to hide and swallow her terrible fear of the falling bombs that destroyed her world and distanced her mother from her. Alone and helpless, unable to imagine the possibility of feeling welcome, sheltered and protected, she lived in terror.

She was born in the middle of a war (1944) ruled by darkness, and her mother was unable to provide even the slightest stability. Thus, her first feelings were that this world was cold and cruel. She had to defend herself as well as she could.

Everything in her environment should have led Star-From-Beyond to believe that she was destined to be a loser. One terrible event followed another, making it inevitable for her to undergo situations of extreme suffering and loneliness. Her father was unable to be near her in the first months of her life, as he was hindered by the critical situation of persecution and violence.[10] She could hardly remember the one occasion in which she embraced this father she had so longed for — the single time, when he looked at her with sad, tired, resigned eyes, and spoke affectionate words that became engraved on her memory as a balm of love. Before she was six months old, a new bombing put an end to the chance to have a father. He died, and she was forced to live with a "never more" that marked her existence, turning what could have been love into disbelief and contempt for feelings. This loss, experienced as such premature abandonment, led her to look for a substitute, in one form or another.

Her mother had difficulties in supporting herself, suffered continuously, and constantly proved her incapacity and unavailability as a parent. So, Star-From-Beyond turned to another possible source of help — her older brother. He frustrated her attempts to approach him, however, too taken up with his own difficulties and anguish.

Not yet two years old, a new misfortune befell that innocent little body. She was the victim of poliomyelitis, and as a consequence was left with a shrunken leg. More deaths, a decimated family, concentration camps, Communist domination, flight from her country, leaving behind possessions, memories. Her mother took her to a faraway place where she could not understand the language. Finally, at the age of five, she found herself in a strange house, where she was left in the care of cold hands. She cried desperately, calling to her mother, without any reply, without anyone to comfort her. That was when she stopped crying and decided: "I WILL NEVER CRY AGAIN! NOBODY WILL COME AND HELP ME! I CAN'T TRUST ANYBODY!"

This decision marked her path from then on. She decided she would not be a loser, but would triumph despite everything. She would show the world she could win, that only the weak fall; the strong overcome misfortune and carry on.

With a strength drawn from her deep suffering and pain, a Star was born — a Star that would have to shine without anyone's help. This was possible only at the cost of burying her pain, her needs, her fear, her deep sadness and loneliness. Quickly she substituted her perceptions of what pleased others for all that was genuine about herself. Her smile and her friendliness were constantly praised; her availability and her capacity for work were extolled; her intelligence and constant optimism were always well received. The world belonged to the strong, to those who never had problems, and she would be the best, the most talented, the most beloved; whatever the cost.

But then, a new person entered her life — a person who allowed Star-From-Beyond to maintain a small degree of trust in love, and in her fellow man. She found a new father in her mother's second husband. What a lovely man! He was her guardian angel, who welcomed and cherished her. She loved him from the first moment. He gave her her first toy.[11]Her first poem (written at the age of nine) was dedicated to him, with the title "My Father." She saw tears in his eyes as he read it. From this moment on he became the father she had so longed for.

Star-From-Beyond experienced many difficulties during her adolescence — she realized that physical beauty also meant having nice legs, and she didn't have them. There was no way to solve this problem, unless ...

She could get all the men she wanted by so bewitching them that they would forget that one of her legs did not belong to the perfect whole she presented. She learned to use complex tricks to reach her aims, and that "the ends justify the means." Seduction became her most frequently employed and least visible weapon. Her sex life began very early, and she gave men everything they wanted, and more than they could have imagined. Nevertheless, the game was always implicit, wordless, cautious and patient. Since she could not fight out in the open, nor compete as an equal, her strategy was camouflaged with attributes that had nothing to do with sexuality. She kept her strategy so hidden that she herself was convinced that sexuality was less important, and thus convinced others more easily. This was the only way to escape from direct confrontation, where she would most certainly lose, for deep inside herself she was afraid that someday someone would tell her she was no good as a woman because she had a crippled leg. She showed off her skills and played intensely with them all, but kept her most important motivation (and weapon) under lock and key (to the extent that she herself did not consciously admit to it).

Meanwhile, the force moving her as a young girl, and over the following years of her life, was, without a shadow of doubt, the search for love from a man, i.e., the confirmation that she was desired, loved, and the main focus in the life of the man she chose as a partner. Each one of her qualities (and they were many) served an ultimate motivation: recognition from a man. Her social and professional brilliance was an achievement placed on a silver platter at the service of seduction.

Professional success, the fact that she was independent, self-confident, capable and active was constantly accompanied by the implicit question: When will the day come when you will prove to me that I am the queen of your heart?

There were men in her life who succumbed to her seduction, who loved her passionately. Nevertheless, she was not satisfied, she wanted more and more, or she wanted something different from what was within her reach. In fact, she wanted the impossible. Somehow, the vicious circle was already at work, for in her innermost self she could not believe in the love she received, since the object of that love was but an artificial image. Her real self remained hidden, lost on the way. And the search continued — untiring, arduous and compulsive, through the windings of a labyrinth that still remained to be recognized as such. And so, thirty-three years of life passed. Star-From-Beyond felt perfect. Everything she did fit in with her plans of success and full public recognition. She was a perfect housewife, a perfect mother, a perfect wife, a perfect friend, a perfect professional, a perfect lover. Perfection meant the total capacity for being what the other person wanted, dreamed, imagined. And that was life. Everything was under her control. An admirable and admired woman.

However, an unexpected interference arose. Her husband began to free himself from her subtle and firm rule, and set out on a new, unknown path.

She had lived in holy ignorance. What a shock!

She tried, then, with all her means, using all the mechanisms within her knowledge, to keep up her *status quo*. But, it didn't work. Soon, she found herself drawn into a new world. Her daily routine, her values ... all were shaken. And Star-From-Beyond did not know how to stay on her feet. Most of all, she did not know how to maintain her brilliance in the middle of all this confusion.

Quickly, however, she reintegrated into these new values, to which her husband resonated. Since she was a creature of her own making, she had the enviable capacity to adapt to new circumstances, and to place herself at the head of them. Her thought was, "Ah! So that's it ... Very well. Let's go, I can do it. Nothing is impossible for me."

She never asked herself what *she* wanted. She overrode her own feelings, burying them deeper and deeper — knowing that to have feelings or desires was very dangerous. To have feelings would make her vulnerable, leaving her at the mercy of someone else's rule; basically, she could get hurt. So she kept her feelings only to herself, where nobody, absolutely nobody, could get in.

This zeal for hiding, concealing and substituting what the world wanted for what she really wanted became a trap of which she was unaware. She was so busy being the best, the most adaptable and the most desirable, that she forgot herself.

She had buried her own feelings, her own values, her real self someplace, and had neglected to mark the way. She was no longer able to return to them herself. What is more, she did not even recall having hidden these parts of herself. She was so busy promoting herself, being somebody so special, and keeping the world at her feet.

This work was so great that it took up her whole being. She crystallized into this role and became the slave of the power of admiration she exercised over others.

And then, everything changed — she began to go to therapy. She went through a crazy period in which her marriage was open (her body and her bed no longer had a master), still trying to keep up with her husband's new interests, as well as in the hope of trying to make up for the imminent failure of her marriage. Finally, she separated from her husband. She remarried, moved to another city, changed jobs.[12]Star-From-Beyond became involved in a new career, becoming a therapist. More importantly, she became a seeker. There was something more to search for, though she did not know exactly what.

Yes, everything changed, but mainly on the outside, thanks to her capacity for adapting to and overcoming events. Her slogan remained the same: to make her presence known, to be loved, desired and basically necessary.

Despite her involvement in something new, with far wider dimensions than before, and although she was living in an environment in which the name of the game was evolution, change, transformation, spirituality ... Star-From-Beyond did not allow herself to be touched. Her armor remained practically intact. A couple of scratches here and there, but nothing to really tear her down from her throne.

In one area she allowed herself a little relaxation, and tenderness — with her children. She had four children from her first marriage and two more adopted from her second husband. These children were her stronghold of love. They didn't pose a threat to her. They were innocent beings, like she herself had been once. It was possible to feel them in her arms, to show them love and affection as a human being who could open her heart. Her heart beat along with these little hearts that were a part of herself. That, somehow, kept her in touch with something human, in the middle of that invented war of lights and fireworks that she believed to be life.

Many, many frustrations in the impossible love with a man!

She could not understand how a man who had the honor of being by her side did not become the man of her dreams — the most perfect of men, the one who would finally rescue her and take her back to her most secret hiding place. She could not understand how he too let himself be deluded by her brilliance, her perfectly devised luminosity, which gave her nourishment and nourished her relationships. She waited and waited, she schemed and schemed so that he would finally tear off her mask, despite herself.

She fell deeply in love with the man who would be her second husband, to the extent of dropping everything and following him to a strange city, leaving behind her home, her family, her work, her friends, her material possessions. She also left without any guarantee, for he did not love her; he barely enjoyed her company, but felt safe thanks to her abilities. Nevertheless, the challenge was stimulating, and having to prove that she could conquer him was exciting. She would never give up. Now, more than ever, her greatest motivation (even though it was not obvious) was to finally manage to be loved.

Star-From-Beyond looked for love although she did not admit that she needed it greatly. Moreover, her games were so compulsive, she was so tangled up in them that she always ended up finding herself a prisoner. Her suffering, her frustrations and continuous dissatisfactions were a total incoherence, an enormous paradox in the face of her image of constant well-being. When she finally obtained her partner's love she destroyed the relationship. She blamed him for arriving too late and accused him of everything that had attracted her most about him. She killed his self-esteem and with great superiority handed him over to another woman, once again distorting failure and turning it into an apparent victory.

Little by little a new, practically-unknown, being began to emerge; one who had been asleep for almost an entire lifetime. This "somebody" began to pull at her sleeve, to face up to her, to create conflict and doubt. Star-From-Beyond realized that she was not alone; actually, she was barely in command of this body, of this life.

Light-of-the-Horizon began to rise.

Star-From-Beyond was used to competing, to manipulating, to using any strategy, but this other being did not resemble anything she knew. And that was how the war between the two began; a ferocious war, in which Star-From-Beyond would use any weapon to maintain her rule over her territory.

Little by little, however, Star-From-Beyond was revealed by Light-of-the-Horizon ... her games, her tricks, her way of life, until then unquestionable.

Star-From-Beyond suffered one shock after another, was tripped up over and over again. Seeing that many people in the world behaved like she did ... that she was not unique ... that all her pretended luminosity, sagacity, singularity, were commonplace, just part of some silly little pattern, mediocre and perfectly detectable; this left her dumbfounded, perplexed, paralyzed.

Nevertheless, she did not give in easily, but renewed her strength and went to battle. It was not like her to give up, even less to surrender. Failure was not a part of her curriculum.

Light-of-the-Horizon proved to be made of quite different material. Her existence was not comparable ... could not be defined within a known environment. She did not fight with the same weapons as Star-From-Beyond. In fact, she did not use weapons, she used her presence; and Star-From-Beyond did not trust her. The only thing Star-From-Beyond knew was that she had to survive on her own. She could not count on anybody. She did not know what surrender meant.

Once again, in a rapid, astute and efficient manner, Star-From-Beyond overrode the situation, using her own unmasking to suit her own purposes. The more she showed what she knew about herself, the more "they" would leave her alone and at the head of things, thus she avoided confrontations, humiliations and, at the same time, could once again be THE BEST, the top student. She knew how to camouflage herself. Now the reputation built up over a lifetime was at stake. She would never surrender everything she had won. It was worth anything. She would risk everything, as long as she remained the only valid Star in this sky. And thus she remained on the throne for over a year.

Light-of-the-Horizon observed patiently and made note of the extraordinary deeds of Star-From-Beyond. What an effort! What energy Star wasted in distorting, denying, turning truths into lies, turning the obvious into arguments calculatingly designed to silence any voice that dared confront her!

Star-From-Beyond was no longer so self-confident, so in command of herself, but she would not admit this under any circumstance. Her fatigue and doubts were perfectly justifiable; she always found reasons, or others to blame, thus staying on her pedestal.

Gradually, Light-of-the-Horizon removed the veils, one by one. As each one was slowly lifted, a new battle took place. Suffering, conflict, pain — Star-From-Beyond was not prepared to lose her brilliance, and tried with all her might to keep those veils covering up a much greater light; a light that she glimpsed, and which would certainly obscure her forever.

She spent more than a year fighting this battle, and darkness prevailed. No light, outside or inside. Light-of-the-Horizon's light could not yet be seen, and Star-From-Beyond's light had proven false, senseless and basically embarrassing; too explicit and empty to allow her any credit.

It was a year of going downwards. The tables were turned and nothing was left standing. It was not possible to continue on such false, such deceitful, such degrading premises.

Then, Light-of-the-Horizon's dignity broke through like a flying arrow that pierces all obstacles and calmly reaches its target. It was necessary and urgent to begin anew. Yet, she did not know from where to begin, nor how. The only certain thing was WHAT WASN'T. However, even now there was another, more unknown aspect of Star-From-Beyond that had not really been identified; it made its appearance, emerging from the ruins of her defeat. Star-From-Beyond seized the merits that had resulted from Light-of-the-Horizon's courage in putting an end to all the roles that had been played, and approved these merits, turning herself into an unconditional ally and showing off her glory in her insistent vanity; she was the only one great and victorious enough to carry off such a feat.

And, to get Light-of-the-Horizon out of the scene, she tried to deal her a death blow, pretending to be a fearless and unequaled seeker in an absolute, unmovable surrender — completely absurd, stupid and suicidal — into the hands of a pseudo-master ruled by such a clever and seductive ego that he made her feel astonished, perplexed, and at the same time glorified, swollen with pride. This man placed Star-From-Beyond back on the brilliant throne that had almost slipped out of her control. He promised her the moon and the stars, used a powerful and hypnotic energy, and took advantage of all her characteristics, in the name of what promised to be the "definite encounter" — the end to all her seeking and anguish. He maneuvered to have her at his service during a time of madness — egos set loose, out of control. The horse led the carriage aimlessly and the coachman had no chance of imposing his will.

This was a period of euphoria, "great discoveries," contagion from a blinding energy that made any interference by Light-of-the-Horizon impossible. There was no room for discernment nor common sense. It was an avalanche coming closer and closer. Then, a deep silence and an enormous emptiness — in the darkness of not knowing, with the uselessness of self, with a disinterest in life, with despair and loneliness. It was chaos, disillusionment, exhaustion. Nothing was worthwhile. And, as a final resort, a deep hatred for all humanity and mainly for God, who had led her into this sea of slime in which she felt trapped, defenseless and impotent. Certainly, this was a hatred that had always been buried, under lock and key, never allowed; incompatible with her intention of triumphing in life by making herself adored, loved, desired and admired.

Light-of-the-Horizon, who reeled and tried to stay on her feet, without perishing in this terrible hurricane, saw Star-From-Beyond as an invincible monster — a monster who had the capacity to deceive everything and everyone; who used any means in order to attain her end; who did not measure the consequences.

A monster who must be vanquished, defeated, dominated and domesticated.

Light-of-the-Horizon knew clearly that this was a war of life or death, and that *her* life was at stake, not Star-From-Beyond's. She knew she could not kill Star-From-Beyond, or she too would die. Light-of-the-Horizon had to survive, win and rule over the battlefield, bringing Star-From-Beyond over to *her* world, giving her the only nourishment she needed, and had never had, the food she had searched for untiringly, that would satisfy and calm her, bringing peace and harmony. Yes, it was LOVE.

Light-of-the-Horizon carried love with her. She was made of love. Her constitution was love. It was necessary to win by means of love.

Quite suddenly, God appeared, by means of Light-of-the-Horizon, illuminating the darkness! Star-From-Beyond finally surrendered to the obvious. With deep humility she asked God for forgiveness for all her errors, for all her arrogance, for so much destruction. She abdicated. She tore down the enchanted castle. The artificially created star disappeared from the illusory sky.

Ah, the unequaled brilliance of an eternal LIGHT that does not need any effort to be! This light does not need feeding nor recharging. It is, and gives its brilliance, its energy, because that is its nature and function.

Well ... This is me and this is my life. Love conquers any barrier — sooner or later. Love removes any mountain — whatever the obstacle, however arduous the task.

My ego is a part of me that had been trained with a suicidal goal. However, once it has been dominated, once I have gotten to know it and it has calmed down, it has become an element that can be lived with, intrinsically, as well as an essential ally on my journey through life. All the characteristics that previously were at the service of a vicious circle, in search of an absurd and impossible objective, today fit in and cooperate with the divine plan. Now my ego harmoniously lends its service in consonance with the love emanating from the light arising from the union of all beings — a light that is the presence of the Creator in the heart of every living being.

Star-From-Beyond and Light-of-the-Horizon have one single name: Suzy.   (Mojacar, 22/09/90).

❦

A little over four years later I am completing this report with the purpose of updating it. When I wrote my story I was emerging from a ten-day solitary spiritual retreat, which for me was an experience of the highest importance. It was like a parenthesis, a division of the waters, undergone after two years of having been immersed in hells and purgatories, and genuinely having devoted myself to admitting the acts of destruction I had brought about in my life and in those relationships most important to me. I had set myself the task of taking a one-year full retreat from all the activities I had been involved in (professional, conjugal, social, Sufi group, etc.). And, in this decision, I included abstinence from any kind of sexual relationship, because I did not want to lose my way in casual relationships as a means of escape from tensions. The loneliness was very difficult, the inactivity depressed me increasingly; nevertheless, the greatest surprise was discovering how much I needed sex, for only now could I realize this, since I had never (from the age of sixteen on) lived without. It was a difficult time, but I held out firmly; at the end, it turned out to be valuable. The retreat was like a culmination after the darkness; the grace of finally glimpsing a faint light at the end of the tunnel. I remember identifying with the story of Gilgamesh, when he walked "miles and miles on end, and there was only darkness before and behind him."

Several therapeutical contexts determined my course. The first one was my experience with the Fischer-Hoffman process (in 1977) that connected me for the first time with the importance of my parents' influence on my life. Second was the discovery of the existence of an essence inside me — a spiritual part, that I had been completely unaware of, due to my tendency to be absolutely practical and concrete, and to focus only on what happened outside, without any interest, or any time, for anything abstract or untouchable, or for anything that could not provide me with immediate benefits. Until then I had considered this type of thing a "waste of time."

I consider that the ten years I spent as a disciple of Omar Ali Shah, within Sufism, allowed me to work hard, using my capacity for discipline in order to turn towards a spiritual practice. I learned to cultivate patience and to accept that changes would not take place when I wanted them to. I learned to meditate daily and to carry out the exercises suggested, thus preparing myself for what would come later. However, my ego swelled up extremely during this period and any conquest or advance was credited to egoic characteristics such as, "I am the best, I am the most advanced member of the group, I am one of the top *murshids**; I have been given responsibilities and authority over others; I have direct communication with the master, etc." This contributed considerably to the crystallization of the Star I had been cultivating.

With the appearance of the Enneagram in my life (in 1987) and the influence of the work carried out with Claudio Naranjo, little by little I dismantled my castle, until I arrived at what I have described above: a fall into absolute darkness and the feeling of not having any way out.

In September 1989 I had my first experience of true contact with love, with divine energy that entered my heart by means of love, after a petition of profound forgiveness to God for all the madness and aberrations undergone until then. It was a moment of great humility and of ridding myself of any kind of defensive mask. I felt my heart — that until then had been locked up in a shiny glass box (transparent, pretty, luminous, but uncommunicable) — freeing itself of this prison that made up the basis of my ego, and returning to its human condition. It was the moment in which the calculating machine dressed up in the guise of Star-From-Beyond was beaten by Light-of-the-Horizon, and my essence was finally able to appear — calm, peaceful and, above all, loving.

It was a time in my life in which I had given up on any kind of romantic relationship with a man. I was separated from my second husband and I felt that I had to remain on my own. Just then the love that I felt pouring out of me met the eyes of a man — a man whom until then I had considered a master, whom I respected and admired, but whom I had never seen in any other manner. And to put the finishing touch to the repetitions in my story, I was falling deeply in love with somebody who did not love me. I resolved to be faithful to my feelings, and above all, I decided to learn from everything I had experienced previously, and not to make the same mistakes over again, even though I had to go through such familiar phases once more, constantly tempting me with the same vicious "solutions." I followed a similar course to the previous ones. I used the capacities within my reach; I made use of my courage, my self-confidence and the belief that I would be able to conquer a place next to this man who had turned up for me without my looking for him. However, I was not going to allow myself to get entangled in the harmful, destructive passion. The vanity of collecting conquests and recognition had to be totally dominated. I established as my top priority giving this man my love, making him happy, but above all, staying clean inside, never again using illegitimate games, being absolutely transparent with regard to my feelings, whatever they might be.

Now, every time he looks at me, smiles and confirms that he is happy, my heart is filled with joy, and gratitude illuminates me, giving me the assurance to carry on. I have been living almost exclusively for him and I feel privileged in being able to be useful to him, and in having the chance to accompany him in his daily life.

I feel that God has granted me a fresh opportunity, and over these last few years, since I wrote the first part of this story, I gradually held my ego in, working constantly in order not to allow my life to be ruled anew by falseness, by lies, by self-deceit. There were many times when I could easily have fallen. I underwent various tests, but I feel I came out victorious. And today, I can say that I am a winner. Not the winner I had always set myself out to be, but a winner in love — a silent, unnoticed, humble winner, without a scepter or a crown; a winner who is profoundly grateful for the opportunity granted.

My ego is there, I live with it daily. It tries to trip me up whenever there is an opportunity, but love has been stronger, and this has given me an emotional stability and the capacity to live quietly, using the characteristics that are inherent to me in the right situations, without any other end or excuse. The nourishment that has kept me going has been in merely being a woman — feminine, capable of following her man, of being receptive, honest and loving.

I had a reunion with my mother in the last period of her life; it was like a blessing from heaven. My mother and I met again exactly where we had left off. We completed the cycle of life. We recognized each other; we converted our mutual and deep love, without veils or illusions ... with reality, with clarity, with understanding, with gratitude, and above all, with love and respect. Forgiveness was no longer necessary, for it had been granted a long time ago. It was a moment of reunion on a level where everything is absolutely right. And we said goodbye, knowing that she would always be my mother, and I her daughter. Ever since her death I have felt her more present than ever, and on discovering myself as a daughter I discovered what being a mother involves in another dimension.

My relationship with my children changed drastically. Between us a kind of complicity arose, an exchange of experiences, a mutual learning, accompanied by loving. I feel that I respect their decisions, their right to create their own lives. I do not allow myself the compulsions of "teaching, educating, correcting, directing." We have experienced moments of great joy, depth and love. Life has taken me far away from them physically; nevertheless, I feel that my being, my daily life, includes them so strongly that often the separation hurts. I am trying to live with the pain and to create conditions for communication and exchange to make up for the lack of more everyday contact.

I have followed the same direction in my relationships with those nearest to me, who are few — my brother, my sisters-in-law and my brother-in-law, my nephews and nieces, my ex-husbands, my ex-mothers-in-law and a few friends who were able to realize that I was not merely a superficial and empty shell. Today these relationships are a treasure in my life and I keep them as precious jewels that I was lucky enough to receive in this life.

My relationships with people have become highly selective — I prefer to be with whom I feel it is possible to have communication and growth, rather than to be the popular and superficial figure in all environments. I almost completely gave up my career, where I had achieved a notable position. I acquired experience that I now make use of in opportunities that appear in a natural manner, without any wish for projection in the professional world. I am at peace with the people I feel I have hurt most; I have experienced that it is possible to rescue what was most beautiful and loving. I feel that I am a happy person — in my simplicity and anonymity.

There is no longer a search for the miraculous. The miracle, for me, lies in every day that I wake up — I open my eyes and realize that God lives in my heart. I go through my day, carrying out my tasks, and I close my eyes when the day is done with the same realization, and with this prayer on my lips: "Thank you, God, for all I have received, for the chance to live in peace and give the best that is in me."

(Madrid, 5/11/94)

BREAKING ONE'S BEAUTIFUL IMAGE

Linda: I can begin by telling you about a dream that I wanted to tell you last week, and then we could see what happens.

Claudio: Tell me the dream.

L: The dream is that I was going out one night and I returned home very late, around 3 or 4. Everything was very dark; there were no lights in the neighborhood and so I was very scared because I had the presentiment of someone's presence. I was in my car and I got out and saw two individuals — Rambo types, very strong — who were coming after me. So I started to run for the doorway, I quickly opened the door, I slammed it shut. In an instant they were already at the door pushing it, and so, very terrified I went up to my flat. I went up in the elevator and they went running up on foot. I was thinking all the time that they were going to get me. Then I went in my home. Just as I had done in the doorway, I slammed the door in their faces. At home, only my mother and eldest son were there. I knew that these individuals were going to begin beating down the door and that they weren't coming to rob me, but that they were coming to kill me. They wanted to kill me.

They began pounding on the door and I felt the need to protect myself with my mother, but I knew that she could not protect me, that she wasn't of any use to me. My mother was saying things to me and I was saying, "But what are you saying, Mom?" I wasn't paying her much attention. I was thinking how to hide my son so that nothing would happen to him, but I knew that they weren't going to do anything to my son or to my mother, that they were coming for me.

So when they had finally managed to break down the door, I woke up and I woke up with the feeling of fear; my body trembling and my legs trembling and it shocked me a lot because I have had those kinds of nightmares — very strange, worse — which have frightened me a lot, but I had not felt that bodily sensation in a long time. [It really surprised me.]

C: Obviously, you woke up as an escape, as a way of avoiding the end of the dream.

L: Yes, once I had a dream...

C: Let's stay with this. I want to ask you to imagine that you don't wake up; imagine that you continue sleeping and dreaming, and see what happens ... if there is no censorship, if there is no escape from the dream and all of its catastrophe. Live through it. Visualize it.

L: Well, I would have picked up a weapon to defend myself.

C: Describe it as you speak, as if it were happening to you right now. "I look for a weapon to defend myself with ..." And describe where you are, everything you see.

L: I feel that they break down the door and so I quickly go into the kitchen and pick up the knife for cutting ham, the one that cuts best. And I grab it, but I run out; I am going to hide in any case because I think that they are stronger than me and the knife isn't going to be of any use. Well, it'll help me to feel a little more secure, or more insecure, I'm not sure.

I hide behind the door and when they go into the bedroom ... But of course one goes into the bedroom. Because they are jointly looking for me and because they are very smart, one goes to look in one bedroom and the other goes to look in another. One comes into the bedroom and I am behind the door and at that moment I come out running, from behind the door, but I encounter the other one in the hallway. And so I threaten him with a knife, but he goes like that at me with his muscles [*gesture of shrugging off*] and punches the wall, and in that moment I am left without strength ... But I don't want them to catch me!

C: Are you standing?

L: Yes, I am standing and also the other one is coming up behind me and I can no longer fight.

C: Go on ...

L: I try to throw the one that is coming in front but he is very heavy for me. Well, okay, I kick him in the balls. I go out over the top of him and I leave on the run ... My son and my mother are in the living room and the three of us run out of the house. But there wasn't anybody on the street!

C: Let's see, go on. You are in the street. What happens?

L: It could go on for a long time.

C: A little more.

L: We go on running and they're coming behind us, but they can really run and my mother gets tired. I become very nervous because I know that my mother has nothing to do with this, that it is me they are after. I would have to leave my mother behind.

C: I don't think she would be in much danger if it's you they are after.

L: Well, I leave her behind. I keep running ... [*long pause*] ... It's just that it makes me really scared because they are going to catch up to me!

C: Dare yourself to live through it, with all the fear it causes ... A conscious nightmare instead of an avoided nightmare.

L: But it's just that I don't want to let myself be killed.

C: You could fight ...

L: I know that I don't have a chance with them.

C: They probably will kill you. What I am asking you to do is to consciously live through the death fantasy.

L: But I don't want to die. I'm not going to be able to.

C: You are already pulling yourself out of it just like you pulled your persecutors out of your dream, putting it off for the future.

L: Once I also had a dream. Again I was with my mother going along on a highway on the coast; it was a beautiful day. We were going in a bus and the bus was falling into the sea and I knew we were in the sea and that we were going to drown; but then within the dream I said: "No. This can't be, we have to get out of here." Then, all of a sudden, a ramp appeared under the sea and the bus got out and we continued on our way. And here I get that sensation...

C: That you won't be able to; there won't be any *deus ex machina* or magical means that can appear. Dreams are dreams, not too logical and if you are the dreamer ...

L: If I want it to come out well, I'll kill them and that's it. But it's just that I can't kill them because they are very strong!

C: Then we will try to understand what is happening. Why a part of you has turned against you so fatally. Get inside the persecutors and see what's behind that. What are they looking for, what do they want? Why are they after you?

L: I don't know.

C: Describe yourself as if you were one of the persecutors. What kind of person are you as a persecutor? Beginning with the most concrete aspect of the dream.

L: As if I were the persecutors?

C: Both or one of them.

L: I am very bad, I am terrible, I am very violent and I want to knock off Linda just because, just for the pleasure of knocking her off, of killing her. I want to kill her and that's it; because I think it's better that I kill her; it's better that she be dead.

C: You know a lot about the gestalt perspective, that these assassins in dreams are the assassin part of our own selves, so the work that lies ahead is to see how much you can make that conscious; put yourself inside that part and make it more conscious. I would propose something to you; that you play a little irrationally, "I feel like killing Linda" and repeating that phrase and see what comes out if you go into that emotion. Continue imagining that you are the persecutor and seeing what content arises. Whatever other things occur to you, alternate with the phrase, "I want to kill her"; and the more you let yourself be surprised and you don't censor yourself, the better.

L: It seems to me that you have become my persecutor now. I don't know if it's going to come out.

C: If it comes out it will amount to an exorcism of the persecutor; it will leave you.

L: I want to kill Linda because she doesn't deserve to live.

C: Continue repeating that and exaggerate it.

L: I want to kill Linda because she's stupid, she's an idiot; a vain, proud, vile person.

C: Connect it up with things out of Linda's life, document it.

L: I want to kill Linda because she doesn't do anything, she does a lot of things but she doesn't *do* anything; she's an idiot and she's wasting her time.

C: How are you going to kill her? With a bullet? Or are you going to wring her neck? What do you anticipate doing when you catch her?

L: Well, I'm going to smash her face, that face that she looks at in the mirror so much, so that she won't look anymore. I'm going to begin with the face.

C: Keep going into your hate toward Linda and the things it inspires you to do.

L: I'm going to stab her in the heart so that she understands. She is going to feel everything. She'll find out!

C: Ah! You want to kill that Linda who doesn't understand; she who does not feel.

L: I'm going to give her a kick in the cunt so that she realizes. I'm going to annihilate her! I'm going to smash her to bits and see if she finally gets it together and does something! Since she doesn't do anything. Well, I'm going to kill her! I'm going to fuck her good!

C: Go on ... even if you repeat things you have already said, now raise the intensity. Put more into your voice, into your gestures, give your hate more of a catharsis. Break her face ... "I kill you because ... I'm killing you because ..."

L: It's just that I'm embarrassed.

C: When one leaves behind embarrassment such good things happen that afterwards one doesn't regret it ... And remember that you need to lose control.

L: It's very hard to lose it.

C: Let that completely irrational little girl out, blindly.

L: It's that fucking little girl that I want to kill.

C: Let her be the assassin now [*referring to the irrational one*]. She's going to kill the one that doesn't want to lose control.

L: Who, the little girl?

C: Yes. That little girl is a potential assassin. She doesn't like the vain one; she doesn't love the one that doesn't "get it," [*that doesn't understand*].

L: [*raising the tone of her voice*] I'm going to kill you asshole, I'm going to smash you to bits, I'm going to smash your breasts, your face, your body, everything, so that nothing is left for you to show off, asshole! Who do you think you are? Idiot! What kind of an act are you performing in your life? Stupid little girl! I'm going to tear you apart, I'm going to leave with nothing. See if you finally see something more than looking at yourself in the mirror and putting creams on your face! Stupid little girl! Idiot! You're going to get it! Do something at once with your life, asshole, you are asleep! What good is that to you? What good are all those things to you? Are they worth anything? Are you proud of yourself? No, right? Well, I'm going to kill you for that, because you are not worth anything, not one cent. You're not worth one cent you filthy asshole!

C: Do whatever you consider necessary to kill her imaginatively. I don't know whether by blows or … So that you will feel, "I've killed her."

L: I don't know if I will be able to kill myself.

C: I think that one, potentially, is free to — at least in stages, like layers of the onion — free to take steps …

L: It's that that is very difficult for me. I am and I feel very much in a trance, but there is something that is not working.

C: Imagine that you have killed her, or perhaps imagine that you shoot her. Can you do that?

L: Yes, but don't I have to see it in a scene?

C: Like Rambo, like one of those persecutors, machine gun her and feel that it's you that kills that internal character.

L: I imagine it to be me.

C: Yes. Play all you want with the images so that you feel it.

L: It's that she doesn't die.

[*Linda sits with her eyes closed imagining. Long pause.*]

C: What has happened?

L: There was a moment when she had died but I couldn't stand it.

C: Ah! Tell me about that. How is that?

L: It's that I couldn't stand killing her.

C: Killing her or living without her?

L: Living without her.

C: Keep talking about her. Tell her that you want to kill her, but that you cannot live without her. Explain to her this situation in which you find your-self.

L: I want to kill you, but I only want to kill you partly.

C: Explain more to her.

L: There is one part of you which I like a lot, but there is another part of you that I don't like at all: the part which is still like a dependent little girl, the part that doesn't choose.

C: That is the part you don't like, but that is the part that you are when you don't kill her; it's your dependent little girl. You cannot live without her because you could end up alone. It's the one that survives in the end.

L: She always survives.

C: Well now. Imagine that ten years have already gone by, and there you are, hating your vanity to death; not being able to live without it. What do you feel? Or twenty years more, perhaps.

L: Oh no! [*desperately*]. No, no! I just can't imagine even ten or twenty more years because I feel there is a part of her that dominates me, but there is another part, also very important, that wants to get out of that place.

C: And there are good intentions.

L: They continue to struggle, but they have good intentions!

C: Good intentions. A struggle that is worthless.

L: And you think that the other can win, that the vain part can win?

C: What do you think?

L: Yes.

C: I believe yes.

L: Yes, yes she can, she has rather more power than the other one.

C: Imagine yourself at seventy.

L: I can't imagine myself so old.

C: And you haven't done anything in all your life, so I don't know how you would feel.

L: Well, very bad.

C: You have lived for the image of the moment, before the eyes that pass by, the eyes that come and go.

L: Yes, but what do I do? How do I get out of that place?

C: What could it be? When I suggested, for example, to live through the catastrophic scene which you avoided in your dream and you didn't do it, so as not to lose your composure.

L: No, I didn't feel that it was that.

C: What did you feel?

L: No. There was a moment when I did feel it, but then finally, when you told me that I should shoot her, I felt that I couldn't.

C: That was a different moment; then you were no longer able.

L: I wasn't thinking. It was real that I couldn't, I was blocked.

C: Blocked when the moment comes to let out your aggression toward yourself. I think that is part of the vanity system that lives on this so pleasant island of emotional neutrality, relatively happy, pleasant or pseudo-pleasant at the cost of amputating part of life.

L: I don't know, sometimes it's like that, but sometimes not.

C: No.

L: At other times it is pleasant because it is simply pleasant and I feel that it is so.

C: So we will continue. Is there hope? Is there not hope?

L: I do want there to be hope.

C: And what do we do now? From where could we make progress with this dream? Okay, you already lived through the scene as the aggressors ... First you had them in that hall in front of you, impotent ... that led to your declaration of hatred ... I suggest that you now be the one who has lived through all this persecution and is panting and scared, and who has received the machine-gun fire of all this hatred.

L: That I should put myself in the role ...

C: You, the persecuted one, confront this person that hates you to death and who hates all those things that have been mentioned ...

L: Well, I don't understand why she can hate me like that, if all of what I do is only to please others, so that others will like me; and I want to make them happy and I want to be happy too. I don't understand those assassins that are coming to get me.

C: Tell them that you don't understand them; that it seems completely irrational to you.

L: I don't understand why you're after me; why you want to kill me. I haven't done you any harm.

C: Now be the assassin again trying to make her understand. Now you, assassin, make the good girl understand, the one that thinks she is so good ... Give her your perspective. You who hate her to death, make her understand your murderous hatred.

L: Look, I'm fed up with good little girls. I eat good little girls feet first; and you are not a good little girl. You act like the good one, which is different; but you're not. I'm going to kill you for that, because you're not a good girl, you act like the good girl!

C: Take off her mask. Bring her out of her deception.

L: Pleasing everyone, being very pleasant, never ever letting anyone down, always keeping your composure ... but what of it? What do you really feel? Do you really feel that? You're a phoney! You're filthy! No, right? Well, I'm going to make you swallow all of that stuff, you're going to swallow all of it! You get it?

C: You who want to kill her, don't just tell her that she is not such a good little girl. She is a bad little girl! It's not only that she has false love. Speak to her about something that's worth killing her for; something that makes you feel that she is not a good person. Unmasking her, I think, would be that; not just telling her that she's not so good, but that she is bad.

L: You are not so good, Linda, you are not so good, because you don't love your mother; you don't love her, Linda, so you are not so good. You don't love your mother and you can't stand her; you hate her, you haven't forgiven her, even after doing the Fischer-Hoffman Process you haven't forgiven your mother; and that's not something one can live with. You can't go through life like that.

C: If you hate your mother, you hate all other beings? If you don't forgive your mother, you don't forgive anyone? Is that what you are saying?

L: No, I can forgive others.

C: Go on ... You are being very understanding now when you say, "Look, you are not so good because you don't love your mother." I would incite you to go beyond the literal meaning of such words and to take an extreme position. "Linda, you hate everyone, you don't have the capacity to love; you are cold ... " Use it like a suction pump, and see what comes out ... Use that form, even though it may not be true. See what things it may bring up, what content emerges, what accusations ...

L: I want it to come out of me, and it's not because [I'm afraid] of losing my form, it's that I want to really feel it.

C: Get inside that character that emerged from your dream, and feel what he feels. Why does he want to eat you feet first? What kind of good little girl is this who makes him so furious?

L: What kind of good little girl is Linda? That she can't forgive her mother, that she hates everyone. What kind of good little girl is Linda?

C: Come on, get closer to the point.

L: What kind of good little girl is Linda? What a good little one she is, always the good little girl, the well-behaved little girl. And in reality what? You're a filthy, pleasing phoney! You don't love anybody! You only love yourself, you're only out for yourself, for your bullshit. You are an idiot, a conceited person, you think you are better than everyone else. You are incapable of enjoying the moment; you're always acting, asshole! Quit the act already, asshole! [*She kicks the chair.*] Quit the act, idiot! Always posing! [*She begins making sexy poses.*]

C: Keep going like that, answer her ...

L: [*She continues making sexy poses.*] Let's see what it's like ... smiling ... [*She gets angry.*] Asshole! The pose has to be natural, it has to be something that comes from here [*she points at her heart*], from the guts, from the cunt, from the tits, from everywhere. Asshole! Idiot!
 I am going to flatten your face, asshole, you've got me fed up already, Idiot! [*She stands up and stomps the floor without letting go of the chair.*] I don't want to see your face anymore, not in the mirror, not anywhere! Idiot! Fucking conceited bitch! Son of a bitch! You think you're better than everyone. Why? Because you put your eye makeup on well? Idiot! [*She gets up, stomps the floor and spits.*] I'll spit on you, then you'll die. Under the dirt the worms are going to eat you and no one is going to see any image. What image is going to be seen under the dirt! With the little worms all through you, you are going to be adorable. You'll see when the worms eat you up! You'll see how attractive you will be!

C: It looks like the other one is winning.

[*Linda laughs, she leans on her knees and she covers her face.*]

C: Put yourself in the role of the underdog and tell the other one how you feel in these moments ... You are the vain part. The vain part that has been stepped on; that internal aspect of Linda. What are you feeling toward your assassin?

L: [*covering her face and crying*] I do that so that they will love me. I do all that so that they will love me, so that they won't leave me; so that people will notice me; so that I won't go unnoticed and so that they won't forget me.

C: Would you get good results from marketing that option? Would it be efficient for them to love you that way? Would it be the best life?

L: What?

C: The vain little girl of course wants to make people love her, and she doesn't have bad intentions. But, I ask you, with the perspective you now have of your life, does it work for you? Is it an option?

L: No, because I no longer believe it.

C: No, of course. So then you must make that little girl understand, she who is almost as primitive as that instinctive assassin; you would have to make that good little girl understand another perspective; you need to get through to her. Can you perhaps communicate with her telepathically? Transmit to her your understanding, and see if there is another way she can be?

L: Well, yes. She should do something real because she feels it or because she wants to do it, not because she is looking for other peoples' love.

C: Give her good advice.

L: That she look for her own self, that she love herself. That she shouldn't

182

value herself for the image for which others love her; that others love her as she is; if not, then she doesn't deserve their love.

C: Do you love her? The one who is talking at this moment?

L: Yes.

C: Perhaps you can transmit that to her so that she can learn to love herself.

L: I think that you have to love yourself, in the first place.

C: "I will try to make my affection help you to love yourself."

L: I will try to help you with my love so that you can love yourself a little more.

C: Make a declaration of friendship and collaboration, that you will teach her to grow and to transform her behavior.

L: I am going to show you how to grow, Linda; I am going to help you, I promise.

C: What are you going to help her with? If you take away her vanity, what are you going to give her?

L: Well, I'm going to give her love.

C: The capacity to love herself. Speak to her further in a tone of advice and alliance.

L: The only thing that matters is love and love is not obtained like that, Linda; love is gotten by being authentic, being yourself, loving yourself, really loving what you are doing in each moment, really being present in each moment, not by projecting an image or a pose. Love yourself!

C: Continue with the moment, continue with this, with how you are feeling now and loving yourself in the moment. Giving your friendship to Linda, who is sitting here, in this moment. Go on with what you feel, with what you do, with what happens inside of you.

L: Well now, I don't know, I'm experiencing a tranquil moment.

C: You are saying it as if it were an inadequate response. "I don't know, I'm experiencing a tranquil moment." As if you should be doing something. Should you be agitated?

L: No.

C: Can you love yourself in this peaceful moment?

L: I think so.

C: Do you understand what I am asking you? That you stay in touch with the moment, that you put into words whatever happens here and now — what is your body doing, what is your mind doing; and giving yourself love in this moment, giving your self appreciation moment after moment.

L: Well, I'm going to love you, Linda, because if I don't love you, who is going to love you? I have to love you myself and help you.

C: What are you doing in this moment, besides talking to your internal Linda?

L: Caressing her, feeling her. [*She caresses her thighs and knees.*]

C: Keep saying what you feel and do.

L: I am going to help you get over your anxiety and blocks.

C: And what are you doing in this moment?

L: Letting myself be.

C: No. You are talking to your neurotic aspect, you are talking to your personified childhood neurosis. I told you to describe what you feel and what you do; one of the things that you are doing is speaking to her.

L: But how do you mean neurotic aspect?

C: I don't know. You were talking to the immature Linda, let's say. Is that what you are doing?

L: Yes.

C: Now I tell you: Don't tell yourself to do one thing or another, instead describe what you do and see what you want to do, that can be an option. What happens if you ...?

L: Well Linda, the Linda ... It's just that I don't know which Linda! The Linda that wants to grow, that wants to be grown up and doesn't want to depend, not to have this dependence on others; she wants to be herself, she does not want to depend on her husband or on her mother, nor on anyone. She wants to be herself. She wants to be herself and to be able to share with others, but first be herself.

C: I feel that there was a clear step in this session, from one state into another; to a state in which your face became radiant (like Tamia's face did in the last session), you got some meat on your bones, you became filled up with life. After getting that far, what I notice most is that when I tell you: "Go on with what you feel and what you do," in no moment you let yourself do nothing; it's as if you are giving yourself a therapeutic task, you are going on with that internal dialogue. As if you were doing something, even more focused *on doing* than on the awareness of *what* you are doing. That would be something further to work on, but in another session. I think we have come to a good fruit. You could continue this. Write this pact out.

L: I will try. Thank you Claudio.

185

❦

The first stage in the transcription above was Linda's description of a dream; the second part, an attempt to daydream a continuation to this dream — which enabled her to realize her avoidance of being a witness to the killing of herself, in the dream.

In the session it seems as if nothing is happening for a long time: she is running away just as she did in her dreaming. Once she identifies with her persecutor, she goes deeper into the experience of the dream, and then it is not just a pure savageness that she finds: she can contact, through the mirror of the dream, her self-hate; particularly the hatefulness that she directs against her vain self, that is obviously that of a sexual E3 — too concerned with her appearance and not finding meaning in life beyond wanting to be liked by other people.

The first element of therapy that takes place here is bringing her rejection of her neurosis more to the foreground. What in the dream had seemed so monstrous then turns out to be a transformation of something healthy in the first place: wanting the death of her ego, and not of her real self.

At last she does, in some way, enact the killing of her ego, and mobilizes a more vehement aggression toward her vain personality. But, then, it seems as if even her awareness of self-hatred is split off from her vain sub-self, and the next part of the work is an internal communication: the attempt to integrate the aggressor and the victim.

Linda moves forward to the extent in which she gets it. We might say that she intellectually knows all this (all that she is putting into the mouth of the aggressor), but still there is a split-off part of her psyche that gets to know it a little better toward the end. Also, towards the end, she comes to confess something more substantial: it is not only that she does not love her mother (which is an important confession, because of the importance it has for her) but that, more generally, she is feelingless and cold. That kindles a desire to really develop love for herself and for others. Even if this ability has not matured at this point, she is left with an orientation toward the growth of love and an alliance with herself in that regard. That alliance, that dramatized friendship toward herself is, of course, a beginning of self-love.

Finally, in the last part of the session, I propose that she stay in the present. Though there is a bit of talking to herself, it is essentially a time of dwelling in a tranquil and warm state — which is the proof that something has shifted in her awareness. Not only did she break her "nice girl" image during the session, but because she is left in a harmonious state, we feel that she has got somewhere.

4

ENNEATYPE 4

In Farid Ud-Din Attar's *The Conference of the Birds* (which was an inspiration to Chaucer's *Parliament of Birds*), different character styles are represented allegorically.[1] The author (a great Sufi who had a deep influence on Rumi) shows how each character interferes with the quest that constitutes the ultimate goal of his own life. When, at the beginning of the book, after the hoopoe explains to the other assembled birds the need to set out on a long journey to find their king (invoking Mohammed's dictum, "Seek knowledge, even in China"), it is the nightingale who first objects:

> The amorous Nightingale first came forward almost beside himself with passion. He poured emotion into each of the thousand notes of his song; and in each was to be found a world of secrets. When he sang of these mysteries the birds became silent. "The secrets of love are known to me," he said. "All night I repeat my songs of love. Is there no unhappy David to whom I can sing the yearning psalms of love? The flute's sweet wailing is because of me, and the lamenting of the lute. I create a tumult among the roses as well as in the hearts of lovers. Always I teach new mysteries, at each instant I repeat new songs of sadness. When love overpowers my soul my singing is as the sighing sea. Who hears me forsakes his reason, though he be among wise. If I am parted from my dear Rose I am desolate, I cease my singing and tell my secrets to none. My secrets are not known to everyone; only to the Rose are they known with certainty. So deep in love am I with the Rose that I do not even think of my own existence; but only of the Rose and the coral of her petals. The journey to the Simurgh is beyond my strength; the love of the Rose is enough for the Nightingale. It is

for me that she flowers with her hundred petals; what more then can I wish! The Rose which blooms today is full of longing, and for me smiles joyously. When she shows her face under the veil I know that it is for me. How can the Nightingale remain a single night deprived of the love of this enchantress?" (pp. 14-15)

In E4, envy is the most characteristic element at the motivational level. Envy involves a painful comparison between self and others that may be felt as worthlessness, competitive rage or an excessive striving for merit. Envy can be focused on specific people — as, for example, a brother or a sister; or generally, as with envy of the opposite sex, or envy of the privileged or wealthy.

But, most characteristic of type 4 is an exaggerated suffering. While E2 — the hystrionic personality — is dramatic, E4's drama inclines to the tragic side. Fritz Perls would speak of some envious women as "tragedy queens," wanting to point out how they use suffering to enhance their own importance, and attract attention through their frustrated needs.

In the first years of our lives we were all familiar with weeping for attention. Just as all babies cry to attract mother's care, E4 is a personality in which this feature is exaggerated in a manipulative fashion. Suffering is exaggerated in order to attract an attention which is otherwise not forthcoming. We may speak of a "seduction through suffering" (just as effective as a seduction through pleasing) as is clearly illustrated by Flaubert's description of Rodolphe's conquest of Mme. Bovary:

And they talked about the mediocrity of provincial life, so suffocating, so fatal to all noble dreams.

"So," said Rodolphe, "I just get more and more engulfed in gloom as time goes on ..."

"You do!" she cried, in surprise. "I thought of you as being very jolly."

"Of course — that's the impression I give: I've learned to wear a mask of mockery when I'm with other people. But many's the time I've passed a cemetery in the moonlight and asked myself if I wouldn't be better off lying there with the rest ..."

"Oh! And what about your friends?" she asked. "Have you no

thought for them?"

"My friends? What friends? Have I any? Who cares anything about me?"

And he accompanied those last words with a kind of desperate whistle.

Then once again Madame Bovary took Rodolphe's arm, and he went on as though talking to himself:

"Yes, so many things have passed me by! I've always been so alone! Ah! If I'd had a purpose in life, if I'd met anyone with true affection, if I'd found somebody who ... Oh! Then I wouldn't have spared any effort; I'd have surmounted every obstacle, let nothing stand in my way ...!"

"It seems to me, though," said Emma, "that you're scarcely to be pitied."

"Oh? You think that?" said Rodolphe.

"Yes," she answered, "because after all you're free" — she hesitated — "rich ..."

"Don't make fun of me," he begged.

"Do you really not know," he said, "that there exist souls that are ceaselessly in torment? That are driven now to dreams, now to action, driven from the purest passions to the most orgiastic pleasures? No wonder we fling ourselves into all kinds of fantasies and follies!"

She stared at him as if he were a traveler from mythical lands. "We poor women," she said, "don't have even that escape."

"A poor escape," he said, "since it doesn't bring happiness."

"But do we ever find happiness?" she asked.

"Yes, it comes along one day," he answered.

"Yes, it comes along one day," Rodolphe repeated. "All of a sudden, just when we've given up. Then new horizons open before us: it's like a voice crying, "Look! It's here!" We feel the need to pour out our hearts to a given person, to surrender, to sacrifice everything. In such a meeting no words are necessary: each senses the other's thoughts. Each is the answer to the other's dreams." He kept staring at her. "There it is, the treasure so long sought for — there before us: it gleams, it sparkles. But still we doubt; we daren't believe; we stand dazzled, as though we'd come from darkness into light."

As he ended, Rodolphe enhanced his words with pantomime. He passed his hand over his face, like someone dazed; then he left it fall on Emma's hand. She withdrew hers.[2]

The E4 is a characterological disposition in which the person frequently finds himself or herself in genuinely painful situations. Somehow, a negative anticipation ends up creating an external reality that confirms that expectation; so to speak of "imaginary suffering" would not be to the point. Indeed, there are people whose subjective tendency has led them to be operated on five ... six, ... or seven times, and obviously, surgery is never a pleasant thing. There are people who give the impression of attracting bad luck, and they really do suffer genuine accidents, real tragedies. "Self-defeating" is an appropriate concept, even though the operation of self-defeat may be unconscious or seemingly mysterious.

It would be an incomplete statement to say that the unconscious dynamic in E4's suffering is only seductive. Suffering and the expression of frustration may be a substitute for demanding, it may be geared to the induction of guilt, or it may be punitive, i.e., "See how I am suffering because of you!" It is a stratagem for creating guilt. Think of the mother who says to her son: "When I die you will understand me," or, "Your insensibility is going to kill me," or, "One of these days I am going to have a heart attack because of you," etc. Also, suffering may be "masochistic" — in the sense that the person is willing to take on excessive pain or frustration out of a need to be loved or to be deserving of love.

In general, the story of this character begins with painful circumstances during childhood. This is true for all of us, for it can be said that all our problems date back to childhood; yet in E4 there is more dwelling on the past, more nostalgia and a keen sense of the value of what was missed — often (and most characteristically) real losses have acquainted the person with mourning early in life. Unlike other people who forget and resign themselves, E4 individuals harbor a keen sense of "lost paradise."

There are people who, in the face of a painful situation, reduce their needs. Others develop an austere strength. Others withdraw from the world. Yet, in E4 a strong desire remains, a desire for love that turns into an excessive dependency, a sort of "love-addiction." Love becomes something too necessary, without which life is a tragedy. The reason lies not only in past frustration, but in an ongoing psycho-dynamics: love is sought as a compensation for a lack of self-love, a condition of intense, chronic self-rejection and frustration. Because of this, too, these people find it hard to endure affective solitude. For them, loneliness entails the pain of confirming their poor self-image. Orientals (mainly in the Japanese culture) hold that, in the West, we attach too much value to romantic love. It has been said that we allow romantic love an excessively monolithic place in our lives, out of proportion to its real value. Whatever may be the importance of romantic love in our culture, it is true for type 4 that there is an excessive reliance on love as a solution to everything.

Envy goes hand-in-hand with feelings of inferiority, guilt and shame. E4 people tend to see themselves as stupid, clumsy, ugly, and sometimes even repulsive — physically or morally. They go through life with a sense of being a sort of fairy-tale monster. And, since chronic frustration involves conscious or unconscious anger, the E4 person has reason to feel venomous, wicked, witch-like, etc. Yet, all these monster personifications of the shadow self also reflect an intense self-denigration. Just as E2 people elevate their self-image, E4 bring themselves down.

The subtypes of E4 are as differentiated as the varieties of E6, and there is a sharp contrast between the angry (sexual) and the sad (social); while the first is complaining and explicitly demanding, the latter is too shy to express his or her desires, except through an intensification of suffering — as if to convey, "See how much I need help?"

The angry (sexual) type was caricatured by Dickens through Mrs. Grumble, in *David Copperfield*. Freud, in his psychoanalytic work, observed the pattern in his description of "those who feel exceptional" — by which he meant those who feel that life is in debt to them and that this gives them the right to advantages. He gives Shakespeare's Richard III as an example. The shy and melodramatic personality pattern may be illustrated by Proust — both in his biography and in his nearly autobiographical Marcel, the narrator of *The Remembrance of Things Past*.

While in Proust's work the interest goes far beyond the merely characterological, it is a very rich document in E4 psychology; the prevailing emotion is nostalgia. Proust begins his covertly autobiographical novel by describing how he craved his mother's kiss every night in order to be able to go to sleep. When his mother would not come to give him his good-night kiss, he would raise an uproar. He would cry and cry, and sometimes his father had to intervene. Despite being a kind, forbearing man, his father considered this behavior intolerable; the little boy's demand for maternal care was too extreme. He believed the child was too spoilt, too effeminate, too attached to his mother; and Proust remained like this throughout his entire life. His mother's death, when he was already an adult, was a devastating tragedy for him, for he had lived clinging to her his whole life, and she had looked after him until her death. He even developed a psychosomatic ailment, asthma, which increased his need for care. Due to this condition he could not be alone. Neither could he go out into the world; for the world was for him full of threats, an inhospitable place, too unlike a mother's bosom. Thus Proust, for the rest of his life, lived behind closed doors, spending most of the time locked up in his room.

I quote from Miller's psychoanalytic study of Marcel Proust:

> His friends, impressed by his intellect, were bothered by his exaggerated need for affection, his readiness to take offense, his undue humilty combined with a suppressed tendency toward biting sarcasm, his archaic qualities, affectation, and yearning for acceptance in aristocratic society. Later, a phrase, "to Proustify," was used by his friends, connoting overobservance of social amenities.[3]

Whether shy or forward, shameful or hateful, E4 is a hyper-sensitive personality, seeking protection and over-protection, and suffering disproportionately from lack of consideration or recognition. As in the case of E2, E4 is an emotional type, and one aesthetically inclined. In both E2 and E4, romantic, sentimental, emotionally intense and violent expressions of emotion are characteristic; not only in regard to suffering, but also in the case of joy. Sexual E4 persons are usually arrogant, despite the fact that they have a generalized sense of inferiority and are prone to guilt. Take, for example, the vision of Oedipus in Pasolini's film. His way of standing in the road along which his father's carriage approaches might be through the attitude of an E8 person, but E4's arrogance (as well as protest and invasiveness) is more visibly an over-compensation. There is a conscious pain of feeling misunderstood, and an arrogant attitude is adopted in order to be recognized. Among talented people there is often an attitude of "misunderstood genius." Even a budding genius can feel this way, arrogantly demanding a worship reception even before revealing his work — as was the case of Rimbaud.

Throughout his entire life Rimbaud seemed to think everything was allowed to him. Much of the time he felt abandoned and misunderstood, and his tendency to believe that those who accepted him *to a point* needed to accept him *fully*, greatly complicated his social life in his hometown and eventually brought about rejection from practically everybody. Of his enigmatic decision to quit poetry at an early age, one of his biographer's writes:

> Rimbaud was thoroughly modern: he wanted success, fame money, the *direct* admiration of his readers. Before the impossibility to reach such objective in a middle-range future, he decides that the best revenge will be in wealth.[4]

Not only is an artistic tendency common in E4, but also a less specific interest in culture and an aspiration to social refinement, to the point of affectation or snobbishness. These tendencies are not only an expression of envy (in the sense of a desire to incorporate something good) but of a wish to suppress or cover-up a shameful sense of violence (perceived as gross or ugly). E4 individuals may be full of obsessions and full of rules about how things should be. And, of course, they are easily subject to frustration or disappointment, for they are so needy — regardless of whether such neediness is expressed imperiously (as in Proust's Baron de Charlus) or deviously, as in Marcel's "playing sick."

Their need for being treated in a very special manner, and the normal friction produced by the differences between people, causes E4 to be very easily hurt; and this is complicated by their many implicit notions about what coexistence should be like.

Just as there is a sharp contrast between the assertive and the shy forms of E4 (bad vs. sad), these two forms of excessive attachment differ from a third personality style — the self-preservation subtype — that is neither melodramatic nor overtly competitive. I have characterized it as "counter-dependent" — in analogy to the counter-phobic variety of E6 (in which fear is scarcely conscious). Envy is less apparent in such cases, and just as the aggressive form of E4 in its arrogance resembles E2, this counter-dependent form resembles E1 in its greater autonomy. Here oral demands are retroflected on the self, and the person is more masochistic than melodramatic: she can take on much pain without wincing, and can suffer a great deal in order to *deserve* love.

Just as Proust illustrates the hypersensitive and sickly social subtype of E4, and the sexual is illustrated by the arrogant Rimbaud, we find the counter-dependent pattern (of the preservation subtype) in Tolstoy. He alternated between sensuousness and stoicism, tortured himself physically as a teenager and morally as an old man, analyzed himself mercilessly in view of perfecting himself, and, after the death of his brother, renounced art as deception. We may say that Tolstoy's humanitarism — which was to become Gandhi's foremost inspiration and the prelude to Marxism in Russia — echoes an empathetic and nurturant disposition typical of the long-suffering, counter-dependent E4; being one who protests for the sake of others, E4 is typically sensitive to the needy, the dispossessed and the victims of injustice.

Such was the personality of the great Van Gogh — who began his work-life as a missionary, then sacrificed himself to poverty for his vocation and individual expression, cut off one of his ears after a fight with Gauguin, and in the end took his own life. It was also that of the heroic Lawrence of Arabia. Just as Van Gogh once held his hand in the fire to prove something, young Lawrence used to put out matches between his fingertips as practice of stoic imperturbability.

Horney's expression "the solution of modesty" could well apply to Lawrence (T.E. Shaw) who, after being disappointed that the British were not truly interested in the Arab cause, sought to become an anonymous soldier, and changed his name. As for his masochistic austerity, "He tested himself to the limits, making himself independent of regular food and sleep, swimming on frozen Winter nights, and bicycling non-stop until he collapsed with exhaustion." During this time his aversion to everything physical became intense, and in one of his letters he wrote, "that the world would be a better place without human beings: we are all guilty alike, you know ... isn't it true that the fault of birth rests somewhat on the child?"; that the only rational conclusion to human argument was pessimism; that he would not even engage in sports as they were a physical activity; that his mind galloped down twenty divergent roads at once; that his only relief was to go for a ride on his Brough motor-bike, and hurl it at top speeds along the road for hour after hour.[5] In this condition of extreme mental distress, it is probable that T.E. invented the myth of an uncle who made terrible demands upon him, and enlisted the help of another Tank Corps recruit, John Bruce, in making sure that the demands — which included tests of physical endurance, and even birching — were carried out; the medieval saints, whose lives T.E had read, had flogged their bodies to keep them in subjection. We have to thank the tenacity characteristic of the self-preservation E4 that, after losing the manuscript of his monumental *The Seven Pillars of Wisdom* in a taxi cab, Lawrence wrote the book again. Speeding on his motorcycle was like an addiction, and he died trying to avoid hitting a child on a bicycle in front of him, while a truck was coming in the opposite direction. He fell and fatally injured his brain.

Today, psychotherapists usually diagnose E4 as "masochistic-depressive" personality, self-defeating personality or borderline personality, and this type looms large among those who seek professional help for psychological symptoms or life problems.

That the personality pattern is popularly recognized is clear from the jokes and cartoons that it has inspired. Thus, William Steig's "... lovers" is mostly a series of variations on the over-dependent, over-grieving and forlorn E4, and Feiffer has offered many vignettes of the character through his ballerina. From Feiffer I borrow a cartoon (see next page) — in a perhaps not too successful, self-critical and slightly desperate attempt to bring this section to a happy end.

SOLITAIRE

The case history below is exceptional, as it is written by a psychoanalyst with a gift for writing — Robert Lindner, widely known as the author

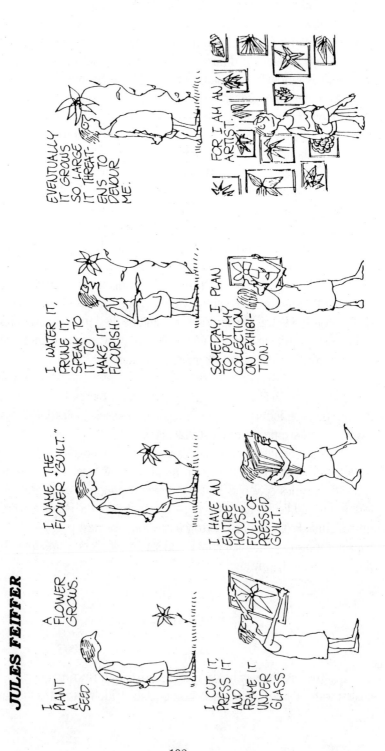

of *Rebel Without a Cause*. I quote from his book *The Fifty Minute Hour* where it is introduced (most appropriately, for an E4 woman) by the title "Solitaire." Just as a case of anorexia was mentioned in connection to the E3 chapter, here is a case of bulimia. The chapter opens with the description of Laura after one of her eating binges.

> "Look at me, you son-of-a-bitch!" she cried. "Look at me and vomit! Yes — it's me — Laura. Don't you recognize me? Now you see, don't you? Now you see what I've been talking about all these weeks — while you've been sitting back there doing nothing. Not even listening when I've begged and begged you for help. Look at me!"[6]

For diagnostic purposes, the vignette above would be enough to acquaint one with the psychology of the enneatype. Though in contemporary clinical practice, she would probably be diagnosed as "borderline," here is our sexual and hateful, demanding variety of E4. As will be seen in the passages that follow, she (at the same time) insults the therapist for his failure, pleads for his attention through critical need, vindictively condemns him and, by becoming a monster, rebels, frustrating his wish for therapeutic success. Hers is a kamikaze maneuver of nearly destroying herself in order to destroy another.

Bulimia was the condition that brought Laura to seek help, and may be understood as the physical acting out of that painful sense of lack that many envy-centered persons describe as located at the pit of the stomach. Bulimia may also be viewed as inwardly turned oral-aggression — as it is not only the acting out of an incorporative impulse, but an act of self-aggression. The combination of self-loathing and frustrated demanding in an intensely tranferential situation complete the picture.

Here are some excerpts on how Laura describes her symptom:

> Suddenly, it hits me ... It seems I can be doing anything at the time — painting, working at the Gallery, cleaning the apartment, reading, or talking to someone. (p. 81)

> I think it begins with a feeling of emptiness inside.

Something, I don't know what to call it, starts to ache; something right in the center of me feels as if it's opening up, spreading apart maybe. It's like a hole in my vitals appears. Then the emptiness starts to throb — at first softly like a fluttering pulse. (pp. 81,82)

I become idiot with terror, I feel as if I'm going to become nothing, become the emptiness — get swallowed up by it. So, I've got to eat. (p. 82)

Most of the time I eat myself into unconsciousness. I think I reach a state of drunkness, or something very like it. Anyhow, I pass out. This is what usually happens. Once or twice I've been stopped by exhaustion. I couldn't open my mouth any more, couldn't lift my arms. And there've been times, too, when my body just revolted, refused to take in any more food. (p. 83)

Lindner opens his account of Laura's psychotherapy telling us of:

... stormy months for both of us, each analytic hour tearful and dramatic as Laura recited the story of her life. In the recount- ing she could find no relief, as many other patients do, since it was a tale of almost endless sorrow in which one dismal incident was piled up on another.(p. 83)

He goes on to report that, although he is used to hearing the awful stories of abuse, neglect and unhappiness that people usually bring to an analyst, he was "moved by Laura's narrative and could hardly help express- ing his sympathy." Not that he verbalized the feelings she aroused in him,

...for the discipline of these long years of practice and the experience gained through the many errors I have made safeguard against such a gross tactical blunder; but in small ways of which I was largely aware I communicated my compassion to her. With Laura it turned out to be a serious mistake. Typically misreading my attitude for one of pity, hardly had the analysis begun than she set out to exploit this quality and to demand more and more of it. (p. 83)

As is typical with E4 (and "borderline") love relationships, so too in the transferential situation Lindner's patient upbraided him constantly for his "coldness," "stonelike impassivity" and his "heartless indifference" to her sufferings. She would,

> ... begin with one of her moving chronicles, to the telling of which she brought a remarkable histrionic talent; then she would wait for some response from me: when this was not forthcoming in the manner she desired, she would attack me viciously. (p. 84)

I don't doubt that Lindner's observations are correct in regard to Laura's manipulation for attention, for I know the pattern he describes as universal to its type; yet, however much his description may evoke the image of a clean surgeon who keeps asepsis with great impeccability and however much he invokes the doctrine of neutrality and for the sake of the expected psychoanalytic results, I suspect that a conflict of characters is subtly at play. Due to Lindner's success as a prison psychiatrist, from his documented daring, contactfulness, social involvement and success with "toughies," I suspect him to have been an E8; if so, it has not only been the analytic rule that explains his upbraiding himself for an excessive compassionateness. For the arrogant-vindictive (to use Horney's term) not only suppress their own dependency, but also look down on the dependent traits and behaviors of everybody else.

Whatever the personality support for Lindner's therapeutic behavior, I form the impression that his frustration of Laura's transference expectations was both an agent of the therapy and the trigger to her crisis; and therapeutic in the end.

Of course, frustration would not be therapeutic if the stimulus were not properly used by an insightful therapist in the service of insight. Lindner's report in this case, however, is essentially an account of a process of insight growth.

A substantial aspect of Laura's therapeutic process consisted in the reminiscence and insight into painful memories. Central among these memories was that of the day when, after being insulted by her mother, her father left her childhood home, never to return. Clearly, from the description of the scene, her mother's personality, like her own, was also one dominated by hateful envy and its passion for violent protest. I quote:

"I'm thinking," she began, "about the night my father left. Have I ever told you about it?"

... It was raining outside. The supper dishes had just been cleared away; Laura and her brother were sitting at the dining-room table doing their homework. In the kitchen Freda, the oldest child, was washing up. Their mother had moved her wheelchair into the front bedroom, where she was listening to the radio. The apartment, a railroad flat on the edge of the factory street, was cold and damp. A chill wind from the river penetrated the windows, whistling through newspapers that had been stuffed into cracks around the frames. Laura's hands were stiff with cold. From time to time she would put her pencil down and blow on her fingers or cross her arms, inserting her hands beneath the two sweaters she wore and pressing them into her armpits. Sometimes, just for fun and out of boredom with her sixth-grade geography lesson, she would expel her breath toward the lamp in the middle of the table, pretending the cloud it made was smoke from an invisible cigarette. Across from her Little Mike, intent on forming fat letters according to the copybook models before him, seemed unaware of the cold as he labored. Laura could tell which letter of the alphabet he was practicing from watching his mouth as lips and tongue traced familiar patterns.

When the door opened, Little Mike glanced up at her. Their eyes met in a secret communication of recognition and fear as heavy footsteps came down the hall. Bending again to their lessons, they now only pretended to work. In the kitchen Freda closed the tap so that she, too, could listen.

In a moment, they heard their father's grunting hello and a mumbled reply in kind from their mother. Then there was a creak of the springs as he sat heavily on the bed, followed by the sharp noise of his big shoes falling to the floor when he kicked them off. The bedsprings groaned again as he stood up.

"Peasant," they heard their mother say over the music from the radio, "if you're not going to bed, wear your shoes. It's cold in here."

"Let me alone," he replied. "I'm not cold."

"I'm not cold," their mother mimicked. "Of course you're not cold. Why should you be? If I had a bellyful of whisky I wouldn't be cold either."

"Don't start again, Anna," he said. "I'm tired. "

"Tired," she mocked. "And from what are you tired? — Not from working, that's for sure."

"Oh, shut up, Anna," he said wearily over his shoulder as he walked through the doorway."

When her father turned to one of Laura's sisters to get some supper, her mother interfered: "Wait! Don't listen to him!"

She glared balefully at her husband, her thin face twisted with hate. When she spoke, the veins in her long neck stood out and her whole shrunken body trembled.

"Bum! You come home to eat when you've spent all the money on those tramps. You think I don't know. Where've you been since yesterday? Don't you know you've got a family?" (pp. 85-87)

When, after some more of the same, Laura's crippled mother realized that she had gone too far, she desperately tried to dissuade him, but it was too late: he made true his threat of leaving for good if he were not allowed to get some food from the kitchen, and the children never saw him again.

Lindner's account of the transaction following these shared reminiscences illustrates the typical vicious circle between demandingness and frustration:

"Well?" she said.

"Well, what?" I asked.

"Why don't you say something?"

"What should I say?"

"You might at least express some sympathy."

"For whom?"

"For me, of course!"

"Why only you?" I asked. "What about Freda, or Little Mike, or your mother? Or even your father?"

"But I'm the one who's been hurt most by it," she said petulantly. "You know that. You should feel sorry for me."

"Is that why you told me this story ... so that I'd feel sorry for you?"

She turned on the couch and looked at me, her face drawn in a grimace of absolute malice.

"You don't give an inch, do you?" she said.

"You don't want an inch, Laura," I responded quietly. "You want it all ... from me, from everybody." (pp. 88-89)

This exchange with Lindner, in turn, exacerbated Laura's complaint:

"You give nothing. You just sit there like a goddam block of wood while I tear my guts out!" Her voice, loaded with odium, rose to a trembling scream. "Look at you!" she cried. "I wish you could see yourself like I see you. You and your lousy objectivity!" (pp. 88-89)

And further along:

"You see?" she shouted. "You say nothing. Must I die to get a word out of you? What d'you want from me?" (p. 89)

That Lindner was both well-trained and exceptionally gifted, the next segment of his case report shows. Laura came back. Here is Lindner's summary of the first year or so of psychoanalysis:

During the first year she made only few — and those very minor — advances so far as her symptoms were concerned, particularly the symptoms of depression and sporadic overeating. These persisted: indeed, for several months following the "honeymoon" period of psychoanalysis — when, as usual, there was a total remission of all symptoms and Laura, like so many patients during this pleasant time, believed herself "cured" — her distress increased. The seizures of abnormal appetite became more frequent, and the acute depressions not only occurred closer to each other in time but were of greater intensity. So, on the surface, it seemed that treatment was not helping my patient very much, even that it might be making her worse. But I knew — and so did Laura — that subtle processes had been initiated by her therapy, and that these were slowly, but secretly, advancing against her neurosis. This is a commonplace of treatment, known only to those who have undergone the experience of psychoanalysis and those who practice the art. Externally, all appears to be the same as it was before therapy, often rather worse; but in the mental underground, unseen by any observer and inaccessible to the most probing investigation, the substructure of the personality is being affected. Insensibly but deliberately the foundations of neurosis are being weakened while, at the same time, there are being erected new and more durable supports on which, eventually, the altered personality can rest." (pp. 89-90)

Even though for the first year the therapeutic process was a trying one, Laura had already found a promising relationship with an eligible young man by the time she reported the following dream:

"Well," she said, "this is what I dreamed ... I was in what appeared to be a ballroom or a dance hall, but I knew it was really a hospital. A man came up to me and told me to undress, take all my clothes off. He was going to give me a gynecological examination. I did as I was told but I was very frightened. While I was undressing, I noticed that he was doing something to a woman at the other end of the room. She was sitting or lying in a funny kind of contraption with all kinds of levers and gears and pulleys attached to it. I knew that I was supposed to be next, that I would have to sit in that thing while he examined me. Suddenly he called my name and I found myself running to him. The chair or table — whatever it was — was now empty, and he told me to get on it. I refused and began to cry. It started to rain — great big drops of rain. He pushed me to the floor and spread my legs for the examination. I turned over on my stomach and began to scream. I woke myself up screaming."

Following the recital Laura lay quietly on the couch, her eyes closed, her arms crossed over her bosom.

"Well," she said after a brief, expectant silence, "what does it mean?"

"Laura," I admonished, "you know better than that. Associate, and we'll find out."

"The first thing I think of is Ben," she began. "He's an interne at University, you know. I guess that's the doctor in the dream — or maybe it was you. Anyhow, whoever it was, I wouldn't let him examine me."

"Why not?"

"I've always been afraid of doctors ... afraid they might hurt me."

"How will they hurt you?"

"I don't know. By jabbing me with a needle, I guess. That's funny. I never thought of it before. When I go to the dentist I don't mind getting a needle; but with a doctor it's different ..." Here I noticed how the fingers of both hands clutched her arms at the elbows while her thumbs nervously smoothed the inner surfaces of the joints. "I shudder when I think of having my veins punctured. I'm always afraid that's what a doctor will do to me."

"Has it ever been done?"

She nodded. "Once, in college, for a blood test. I passed out cold."

"What about gynecological examinations?"

"I've never had one. I can't even bear to think of someone poking around inside me." Again silence; then, "Oh," she said, "I see it now. It's sex I'm afraid of. The doctor in the dream *is* Ben. He wants me to have intercourse, but it scares me and I turn away from him. That's true ... The other night after the concert he came to my apartment. I made coffee for us and we sat there talking. It was wonderful — so peaceful, just the two of us. Then he started to make love to me. I loved it — until it came to having intercourse. I stopped him there; I had to, I became terrified. He probably thinks I'm a virgin — or that I don't care for him enough. But it isn't that. I do — and want him to love me. Oh, Dr. Lindner, that's why I need your help so much now ..."

"But other men have made love to you," I reminded her.

"Yes," she said, sobbing now, "but I only let them as a last resort, as a way of holding on to them a little longer. And if you'll remember, I've only had the real thing a few times. Mostly I've made love to the man — satisfied him somehow. I'd do anything to keep them from getting inside me — poking into me ... like the needle, I guess."

"But why, Laura?"

"I don't know," she cried, "I don't know. Tell me."

"I think the dream tells you," I said.

"The dream I just told you?"

"Yes ... There's a part of it you haven't considered. What comes to your mind when you think of the other woman in the dream, the woman the doctor was examining before you?"

"The contraption she was sitting in," Laura exclaimed. "It was like a — like a wheel chair — my mother's wheel chair! Is that right?"

"Very likely," I said.

"But why would he be examining her? What would that mean?"

"Well, think of what that kind of examination signifies for you."

"Sex," she said. "Intercourse — that's what it means. So that's what it is — that's what it means! Intercourse put my mother in the wheel chair. It paralyzed her. And I'm afraid that's what it will do to me. So I avoid it — because I'm scared it will do the same thing to me ... Where did I ever get such a crazy idea?" (pp. 93-95)

In the next paragraphs Lindner endeavors to show us what insight he and Laura formed, concerning the origin of this crazy idea at the pre-verbal level of her own development.

It arose out of sensations of terror when she would awaken herself during the night, shocked from sleep by the mysterious noises her parents made in their passion, and incapable yet of assembling these sounds into a design purporting the tender uses of love. The heavy climate of hate, the living antagonism between her parents, made this impossible; so the sounds in the night — the "Mike, you're hurting me," the moans and cries, the protestations, even the laughter — impressed upon her the darker side of their sex, the brutish animality of it and the pain. And when the disease struck her mother a natural bridge of associations was formed between the secret drama that played itself out while Laura slept — or sometimes awakened her to fright — and the final horror of the body imprisoned on the chair.

I explained this to Laura, documenting my explanation with material the analysis had already brought out. For her, the interpretation worked a wonder of insight. Obvious as it may seem to us, to Laura, from whom it had been withheld by many resistances and defenses, it came as a complete surprise. Almost immediately, even before she quit the couch at the end of that hour, she felt a vast relief from the pressure of many feelings that had tormented her until that very day. The idea that sexual love was impossible for her, the idea that she was so constructed physically that the joys of love would forever be denied her, feelings of self-dissatisfaction, and numerous other thoughts and emotions collected around the central theme of sex — these vanished as if suddenly atomized.

"I feel free," Laura said as she rose from the couch when time was called. "I think this has been the most important hour of my analysis." At the door she paused and turned to me with moist, shining eyes. "I knew I could count on you," she said. "And I'm very grateful — believe me." (pp. 95-96)

It is this that becomes the focus of the next pages in the report.

"Laura," I said, "you seem very anxious to get me to reject you today. Why?"

"I told you — because I hate you."

"I understand that. But why are you trying to make me reject you?"

"Do we have to go through that again?" she asked. "Because that's my pattern — according to you. I try to push people to the point where they reject me, then I feel worthless and sorry for myself, and find a good excuse to punish myself. Isn't that it?"

"Approximately. But why are you doing it here today?"

"You must be a glutton for punishment, too," she said. "How many times must I say it? — I hate you, I loathe you, I despise you. Isn't that sufficient?"

"But why?"

"Because of what you made me do over the week end."

"With Ben?"

"Ben!" she said contemptuously. "Of course not. What has that got to do with it? All that happened was that I went to bed with him. We slept together. It was good ... wonderful. For the first time in my life I felt like a woman."

"Then what ...?" I started to say.

"— Keep quiet!" she interrupted. "You wanted to know why I hate you and I'm telling you. It's got nothing to do with Ben or what happened Saturday night. It's about my mother. What we talked about last time ... That's why I hate you so. She's haunted me all weekend. Since Saturday I can't get her out of my mind. I keep thinking about her — the awful life she had. And the way I treated her. Because you forced me to, I remembered things, terrible things I did to her ... That's why I hate you — for making me remember." She turned on her side and looked at me over her shoulder. "And you," she continued, "you bastard ... you did it purposely. You fixed it so I'd remember how rotten I was to her. I've spent half my life trying to forget her and that goddam wheelchair. But no; you won't let me. You brought her back from the grave to haunt me. That's why I hate you so!"

This outburst exhausted Laura. Averting her head once more, she lay quietly for some minutes. Then she reached an arm behind her.

"Give me the Kleenex," she commanded.

I gave her the box of tissues from the table by my chair. Removing one, she dabbed at her eyes.

"Let me have a cigarette," she said, reaching behind her again.

I put my cigarettes and a box of matches in her hand. She lit up and smoked.

"It's funny," she said. "Funny how I've clung to everything I could find to keep on hating her. You see, I always blamed her for what happened. I always thought it was her fault my father left us. I made it out that she drove him away with her nagging and complaining. I've tried to hide from myself the fact that he was just no good — a lazy, chicken-chasing, selfish son-of-a-bitch. I excused him for his drinking and his neglect of us all those years. I thought, 'Why not? Why shouldn't he run around, stay out all night, have other women? After all, what good was she to him with those useless legs and dried-up body?' I pushed out of my head the way he was before ... before she got sick. The truth is he was never any different, always a bum. Even when I was small he was no good, no good to her and no good to us. But I loved him — God! how I loved that man. I could hardly wait for him to come home. Drunk, sober — it didn't matter to me. He made a fuss over me and that's why I loved him. She said I was his favorite: I guess I was. At least he made over me more than the others.

"When I'd hear them fighting, I always blamed her. 'What's she picking on him for?' I'd think. 'Why doesn't she let him alone?' And when he went away, I thought it was her fault. Ever since then, until Saturday, I thought it was her fault. And I made her suffer for it. I did mean things to her, things I never told you about, things I tried to forget — did forget — until this weekend. I did them to punish her for kicking him out, for depriving me of his love. His love!

"Would you like to hear one of the things I did? I've thought this one over for two days .... Maybe if I tell you I can get rid of it."

... Everyday on the way home from school she played the same game with herself. That was the reason she preferred to walk home alone. Because what if it happened when the other kids were around? How would she explain it to them? As far as they were concerned she didn't have a father. Even on the high-school admission blank, where it said: "Father — living or dead — check one," she had marked a big X over "dead." So what would she say if, suddenly, he stepped out of a doorway, or came around a corner, or ran over from across the street — and grabbed her and kissed her like he used to? Could she say, "Girls, this is my father?" Of course not! It was better to walk home alone, like this, pretending he was in that alley near the bottom of the hill, or standing behind the coal truck, or hiding behind the newsstand by the subway entrance ... or that those footsteps behind her — the ones she kept hearing but there was no one there when she turned around — were his footsteps.

The game was over. It ended in the hallway of the tenement house, the same house they had lived in all of her life. If he wasn't here, in the smelly vestibule, on the sagging stairs, or standing expectantly on the first-floor landing in front of their door, the game had to end. And he wasn't: he never was....

She heard the radio as she climbed the stairs, and her insides contracted in a spasm of disgust. "The same thing," she thought, "the same damned thing. Why can't it be different for once, just for once?" With her shoulder she pushed open the door. It closed behind her with a bang; but Anna, sleeping in her chair as usual, hardly stirred.

Laura put her books down on the dresser, then switched the dial of the radio to "off" with a hard, vicious twist of her fingers. Crossing the room she opened the closet, hung up her coat, and slammed the door hard, thinking, "So what if it wakes her? I hope it does!" But it didn't.

On the way to the rear of the apartment she glanced briefly at her mother. In the wheel chair Anna slumped like an abandoned rag doll. Her peroxide hair, showing gray and brown at the roots where it was parted, fell over her forehead. Her chin was on her breast, and from one corner of her mouth a trickle of spittle trailed to the collar of the shabby brown dress. The green sweater

211

she wore was open; it hung about her thin shoulders in rumpled folds, and from its sleeves her skinny wrists and the fingers tipped with bright red nails protruded like claws of a chicken, clutching the worn arms of the chair. Passing her, Laura repressed an exclamation of contempt.

In the kitchen Laura poured herself a glass of milk and stood drinking it by the drain. When she had finished, she rinsed the glass under the tap. It fell from her hand and shattered against the floor.

"Is that you, Laura?" Anna called.

"Yeah."

"Come here. I want you to do something for me."

Laura sighed. "O.K. As soon as I clean up this mess."

She dried her hands and walked into the front room. "What is it?" she asked.

Anna motioned with her head. "Over there, on the dresser," she said. "The check from the relief came. I wrote out the store order. You can stop on your way back and give the janitor the rent."

"All right," Laura said wearily. She took her coat from the closet. At the door to the hall she paused and turned to face Anna, who was already fumbling with the radio dial. "Anything else?" she asked, playing out their bimonthly game.

Anna smiled. "Yes," she said. "I didn't put it on the store list, but if they have some of those chocolate-covered caramels I like ..."

Laura nodded and closed the door. Music from the radio chased her downstairs.

When she returned, laden with packages, she stopped in the bedroom only momentarily to turn down the volume of the radio. "The least you can do is play it quietly," she muttered. "I could hear it a block away."

In the kitchen, still wearing her coat, she disposed of the groceries.

"Did you get everything, Laura?" Anna called.

"Yeah."

"Pay the rent?"

"Uh-huh."

"Did they have any of those caramels?"

This time Laura didn't answer. Somewhere, deep inside, the low-burning flame of hate flickered to a new height.

"Laura!" Anna called.

"What d'you want?" the girl shouted angrily.

"I asked if you got my candy."

About to reply, Laura's gaze fell to the remaining package on the porcelain-topped kitchen table. It seemed to hypnotize her, holding her eyes fast and drawing her hand toward its curled neck. Slowly her fingers untwisted the bag and plunged inside. When they emerged, they carried two squares of candy to her mouth. Without tasting, she chewed and swallowed rapidly.

Behind her Laura heard the shuffle of wheels. She turned to find Anna crossing the threshold of the bedroom. Snatching up the bag, the girl hurried into the dining room and faced her mother across the oval table.

"D'you have the candy?" Anna asked.

Laura nodded and held up the sack.

"Give it here," Anna said, extending her hand.

Laura shook her head and put the hand with the paper bag behind her back. Puzzled, Anna sent her chair around the table toward the girl, who waited until her mother came near, then moved quickly to the opposite side, placing the table between them again.

"What kind of nonsense is this?" Anna asked. In reply, Laura put another piece of candy in her mouth.

"Laura!" Anna demanded. "Give me my candy!" She gripped the wheels of her chair and spun them forward. It raced around the table after the girl, who skipped lightly before it. Three times Anna circled the table, chasing the elusive figure that regarded her with narrowed eyes. Exhausted, finally, she stopped. Across from her, Laura stuffed more candy into her mouth and chewed violently.

"Laura," Anna panted, "what's got into you? Why are you doing this?"

Laura took the bag from behind her back and held it temptingly over the table. "If you want it so bad," she said, breathing hard, "come and get it." She shook the bag triumphantly. "See," she said, "it's almost all gone. You'd better hurry."

Inside, at the very core of her being, the flame was leaping. A warm glow of exultation swept through her, filling her body with a sense of power and setting her nerves on fire. She felt like laughing, like screaming, like dancing madly. In her mouth the taste of chocolate was intoxicating.

Her mother whimpered. "Give me the candy ... Please, Laura."

Laura held the bag high. "Come and get it!" she screamed, and backed away slowly toward the front room.

Anna spun her chair in pursuit. By the time she reached the bedroom, Laura was at the door. She waited until her mother's chair came close, then she whirled and ran through, pulling the door behind her with a loud crash.

Leaning against the banister, Laura listened to the thud of Anna's fists against the wood and her sobs of angry frustration. The wild exhilaration mounted. Hardly conscious of her actions, she crammed the remaining candies into her mouth. Then, from deep in her body, a wave of laughter surged upward. She tried to stop it, but it broke through in a crazy tide of hilarity. The sound of this joyless mirth rebounded from the stair well and echoed from the ceiling of the narrow hallway — as it was to echo, thereafter, along with the sound of footsteps and falling rain, in her dreams ..." (pp.97-102)

I have quoted at length the description of this scene of hate not only because the narrative constitutes a rare accomplishment by a psychoanalyst with superb writing talent, but because Laura's wish to compete with her mother (by taking away the candy — the object of her mother's wish) clarifies the source of her bulimia and is paradigmatic of the passion in the sexual E4. In appropriating or introjecting mother's right to have the satisfaction of her candy, Laura not only takes revenge on her but steals away her pleasure in what amounted to an orgy of pleasure-hate.

The weeks following the crucial hours just described were very difficult ones for Laura. As she worked the guilt-laden memories now released from repression, her self-regard, never at any time very high, fell lower and lower. Bitterly, she told the ugly rosary of her pathetic past, not sparing herself (or me) the slightest detail. In a confessional mood, she recited all her faults of behavior — throughout the years. Under the influence of newly acquired but undigested insights the pattern of her sessions with me changed. No longer did she find it necessary to pour out the acid of her hate and contempt, to vilify and condemn me and the world for our lack of love for her. Now she swung the pendulum to the other side: everyone had been too nice to her, too tolerant; she didn't deserve anyone's good opinion, particularly mine.

In keeping with her new mood, Laura also changed the style of her life. She became rigidly ascetic in her dress, adopted a strict diet, gave up smoking, drinking, cosmetics, dancing and all other ordinary amusements. The decision to surrender the novel joys of sex with her lover, Ben, was hard to make, but, tight-lipped and grim with determination, she declared her intention to him and stuck by her word." (pp. 102-103)

To her acquaintances, Laura seemed so much better that Lindner's reputation in Baltimore "soared to new heights."

Because she no longer disrupted their gatherings with demonstrations of her well-known "bitchiness," because she no longer thrust her problems on them or called for their help in times of distress, they felt relieved in their consciences about her. In brief, without laboring the point, so long as Laura disturbed no one else and kept her misery to herself; and so long as she represented to her associates the passive surrender to the mass ideal each one of them desperately but fruitlessly sought, just so long were they impressed by the "new look" that Laura wore. (p. 104)

To her therapist, however, only the style of Laura's neurosis had changed. In light of protoanalysis we can say that she had shifted from the

215

sexual position (hate) toward that of the social (self-recrimination) and self-preservation (self-discipline and atonement). According to Lindner's report, he was quite deliberate in influencing Laura to let go of her "defensive mask of self-abnegation." At some point he felt the time had come to call a halt "to Laura's daily mea culpa, to put a stop to the marathon of confession she had entered at the beginning of the second year with me."

> Try as she might I knew she could never salve her conscience by the penitential acts and renunciations she invented, and I feared the outcome of a prolongued contest between contrition and atonement: it could only lead to the further debility of her ego, to a progressive lowering of self-esteem which might wind up at a point I dared not think about. (p. 104)

In Lindner's eyes, Laura's self-reproach provided for her "precisely the same kind of neurotic satisfaction she had been securing all along by her old techniques. The martyrdom she now suffered by her own hand was equivalent to the self-pity formerly induced by the rejection she had unconsciously arranged to obtain from others." And, in a more personal mode, he reveals: "To tell the truth, I became tired of the 'new' Laura, weary of her pious pretenses, and a trifle nauseated with the holier-than-thou manner she assumed." (p. 104) It is in connection with this personal reaction that Lindner holds himself chiefly responsible "for the almost fatal error in timing I committed when I finally acted on an otherwise carefully weighed decision to eject my patient from the analytic rut in which she was, literally, wallowing." (p. 105)

He now proceeds to tell of the session that took place on a day prior to his leaving for a meeting in New York. Laura was his last patient on that day. She complained about the fact that he would miss an upcoming session on occasion of his project: "it is just that I feel this is the wrong time for you to be going away." (p. 106) Then, she reprimanded him for smoking and went on to speak about how she herself had quit (just as she had quit sex) in an effort to make amends for how she used to be. Now he retorted: "And you think giving up smoking and so on will make you a better person?" This was only ten minutes before the end of the session which could not be prolonged since he had a train to catch. Laura's body had become rigid, and she was beginning to feel that there was no use to any of her trying. "I tried to do what is right — but I never can. I think I am working it all out — but I am not. I am just getting in deeper and deeper. It is too much for me, too much ... " (p.107)

Laura slashed her wrists, and succeeded in bringing her analyst back from New York for her hour on Saturday — this time at the hospital. Two pages later we read that "the episode provided her with genuine and useful insights, not the least of which were those that led her to abandon her false asceticism and to stop playing the paragon of a well analyzed adjusted person among her friends." (p. 109)

The suicidal gesture of Laura stimulated a deeper understanding of her attitudes, particularly in the transference situation and "the burden of distrust she had born for so long became lighter and lighter." (p. 112) Yet, one day she failed to show up for the appointment, and when later in the evening her therapist picked up the telephone, he heard an animal-like voice producing meaningless bubbles, "urgent in tone, but unidentifiable. It was Laura in the middle of an eating binge." And once more Lindner broke the analytic neutrality, fully knowing how his colleagues "would be appalled by such a breach of orthodoxy." (p. 114)

I quote the tail end of his report:

By the entrance I found the switch and pressed it. As the light went on, Laura covered her face and shrank against the wall. I went over to her, extending my hands.

"Come," I said. "Stand up."

She shook her head violently. I bent down and lifted her to her feet. When she stood up, her fingers still hid her face. As gently as I could, I pulled them away. Then I stepped back and looked at Laura. What I saw, I will never forget.

The worst of it was her face. It was like a ceremonial mask on which some inspired maniac had depicted every corruption of the flesh. Vice was there, and gluttony; lust also, and greed. Depravity and abomination seemed to ooze from great pores that the puffed tautness of skin revealed.

I closed my eyes momentarily against this apparition of incarnate degradation. When I opened them, I saw the tears welling from holes where her eyes should have been. Hypnotized, I watched them course in thin streams down the bloated cheeks and fall on her nightgown. And then, for the first time, I saw it!

Laura was wearing a night robe of some sheer stuff that fell loosely from straps at her shoulders. Originally white, it was now soiled and stained with the evidences of her orgy. But my brain hardly registered the begrimed garment, except where it bulged below her middle in a sweeping arc, ballooning outward from her body as if she were pregnant.

I gasped with disbelief — and my hand went out automatically to touch the place where her nightgown swelled. My fingers encountered a softness that yielded to their pressure. Questioning, I raised my eyes to that caricature of a human face. It twisted into what I took for a smile. The mouth opened and closed to form a word that it labored to pronounce.

"Ba-by," Laura said.

"Ba-by?" I repeated. "Whose baby?"

"Lau-ra's ba-by.... Lo-ok."

She bent forward drunkenly and grasped her gown by the hem. Slowly she raised the garment, lifting it until her hands were high above her head. I stared at her exposed body. There, where my fingers had probed, a pillow was strapped to her skin with long bands of adhesive.

Laura let the nightgown fall. Swaying, she smoothed it where it bulged.

"See?" she said. "Looks — real — this way."

Her hands went up to cover her face again. Now great sobs shook her, and tears poured through her fingers as she cried. I led her to the bed and sat on its edge with her, trying to order the turmoil of my thoughts while she wept. Soon the crying ceased, and she bared her face again. Once more the lost mouth worked to make words.

"I — want — a — baby," she said, and fell over on the bed — asleep ....

I covered Laura with a blanket and went into the other room, where I remembered seeing a telephone. There, I called a practical nurse who had worked with me previously and whom I knew would be available. Within a half-hour, she arrived. I briefed her quickly: the apartment was to be cleaned and aired: when Laura awakened, the doctor who lived downstairs was to be called to examine her and advise on treatment and diet: she was to report to me regularly, and in two days she was to bring Laura to my office. Then I left.

Although the night was cold I lowered the top on my car. I drove slowly, breathing deeply of the clean air.

Two days later, while her nurse sat in the outer room, Laura and I began to put together the final pieces in the puzzle of her neurosis. As always, she had only a vague, confused memory of events during her seizure, recollecting them hazily through a fog of total intoxication. Until I recounted the episode, she had no clear remembrance of my visit and thought she had dreamed my presence in her rooms. Of the portion that concerned her pitiful imitation of pregnancy, not the slightest memorial trace remained.

It was clear that Laura's compelling desire was to have a child, that her feelings of emptiness arose from this desire and that her convulsions of ravenous appetite were unconsciously designed to produce its illusory satisfaction. What was not immediately apparent, however, was why this natural feminine wish underwent such extravagant distortion in Laura's case, why it had become so intense, and why it had to express itself in a manner at once monstrous, occult and self-destructive.

My patient herself provided the clue to these focal enigmas when, in reconstructing the episode I had witnessed, she made a slip of the tongue so obvious in view of the facts that it hardly required interpretation.

It was about a week after the incident I have recorded. Laura and I were reviewing it again, looking for further clues. I was intrigued by the contrivance she wore that night to simulate the appearance of a pregnant woman, and asked for details about its construction. Laura could supply none. Apparently, she said, she had fashioned it in an advanced stage of her intoxication from food.

"Was this the first time you made anything like that?" I asked.

"I don't know," she said, somewhat hesitantly. "I can't be sure. Maybe I did and destroyed the thing before I came out of the fog. It seems to me I remember finding something like you describe a couple of years ago after an attack, but I didn't know — or didn't want to know — what it was, so I just took it apart and forgot about it."

"You'd better look around the apartment carefully," I said, half joking. "Perhaps there's a spare hidden away someplace."

"I doubt it," she replied in the same mood. "I guess I have to mike a new baby every ..." Her hand went over her mouth. "My God!" she exclaimed. "Did you hear what I just said?"

Mike was her father's name; and of course it was his baby she wanted. It was for this impossible fulfillment that Laura hungered — and now was starved no more .... (pp. 116-118)

Though this was a therapy in which we may believe Lindner, as he tells us that there was gradual improvement and a characterological shift through an abundance of insight, he unfortunately does not tell us much about Laura in her healthy state. After having documented, well enough, the change from this hateful sexual E4 pattern to the overly well-inventioned and controlled self-preservation E4 style, he goes on to tell us that she did make real improvement. But we would like to know more about Laura after her insight into her envious incest wish. The sentence "and now was starved no more" surely indicates the end of her bulimia — but what happened to her love life? Earlier in her therapy she had started to open up to sexual love, then this was interrupted by the activation of a sadistic father image (the counterpart of her victim position in identification with mother). Now that she has come to the awareness of her sexual desire toward her father, we can imagine that she will be able to let go of her view of him as sadistic. She came in contact with something forbidden to her, and the power of this insight was a function of her daring to confess her forbidden impulses. Though I can imagine that this marked a transition to a greater psychological freedom, I am intrigued that Lindner ends his account, as he does, without a clarification as to whether this was the last time he met

Laura, and whether the expression of Laura's "starving no more" (which sounds like an end of excessive envy) in her life reflects only her experience at the moment, or is a stable achievement.

Before closing this chapter, let me bring up one final consideration. Though I never met Dr. Lindner, and I don't know the story of his life, I would be surprised that he were anything other than an E8. A certain toughness seems ideal for a prison-psychotherapist, which he was, and two other segments in his book, *Fifty Minute Hour*, show how his self-confidence, courage and healthy aggressiveness make him particularly able to help aggressive tough ones.

The suspicion that he could be an E8 is reinforced, if not confirmed, through his counter-transference vis-à-vis Laura's "poor me" game. It is evident that he dislikes dependency and sees through it, and that both his confrontation of Laura in her martyr role (along with his clear-eyed poise before her aggression) have been effective in bringing her to a striking personality shift.

Here, however, we may conjecture that Lindner's aversion to masochism might have been modulated by a consideration that emerges from the various reports in this book and, I think, psychotherapy in light of protoanalysis more generally: that it is part of the healing process that the extremes of certain traits (here extra-punitive/intra-punitive, demanding/self-demanding) in the instinct-related subtypes become more balanced, and that it is necessary for the "recessive" sub-personality to emerge before an integration between the conflicting tendencies may take place.

I would characterize the E8/E4 coupling in therapy as explosive. The sadistic style of the E8 therapist can "dynamite" masochismn, as long as it is not destructive to the client through the therapist's unawareness or insufficient personal development.

CHANGING THE PAST
INTO WHAT IT TRULY WAS

Here is the transcript of a session with someone who was new to therapy, having practically walked off the street into one of my workshops. "Modesto's" problem was shame, and this had been manifesting in a bizarre manner, not in terms of intensity alone, but in terms of his lack of perspective on his symptom.

Much was accomplished in this session. Modesto broke through to an understanding of the origins of his situation in his early relationship with his father. Furthermore, being able to re-live and express his early anger allowed Modesto to understand his father's real past situation and to feel empathy toward him for the first time. After the session Modesto's subtle foreign accent ceased to be of any concern to him, yet he became interested in further psychological and spiritual practice. Today he teaches a movement class of his own conception, emphasizing spontaneity.

Modesto: It's an issue that I have again been feeling since a little while ago, but it is very old. I've been dragging it along. Now I've given it a word and it's, "the lack of self-esteem." Watching a person who was talking about his problems I identified myself with him. It's a little diffuse. I know that there is something there that keeps me from flowing and feeling secure and such things. Now it's mitigated a bit, but in these last years I have felt very rejected. I was living in another city, and this matter of being a foreigner brought me to a point where I no longer spoke.

Claudio: Foreigner from where?

M: I'm not Spanish and I was living in Barcelona and they would make me notice a lot that I wasn't from there and I began to feel very bad.

C: [*Ironically.*] It would be a *reasonable* reason to feel bad.

M: On top of that I was Argentinian.

C: Oh! On top of it. Of course, that is really too much!

M: I made efforts and I even came to hate Argentinians. I left Barcelona because I was fed up with that; and when I arrived here, I had the same problem again, but over time it passed. But no, there is something here, isn't there? I know that I also came with other issues, because there are other people who are Argentinians — who are foreigners — and they own up to it.

C: They don't feel so inferior because they are Argentinian. On the contrary, they are rather famous for it.

M: It was a huge complex, but I have seen ...

C: Not even the example of the other Argentinians helped you. I think this is a good issue to work on — the bad image you have of yourself.

M: But it's added on to others.

C: Let's see ...

M: But then this becomes a little harder for me.

C: We're in one of the most intimate groups in Madrid. (It's a bit like a Turkish bath where everyone strips.)

M: I would have to go back to when I left Argentina. I was very shy. I have always been shy. I had insecurity problems. I lived for three years in Paris and [the shyness] went away; I could be myself. But then everything came back again in Barcelona.

C: I would propose that you work on this issue of feeling very small, feeling bad, feeling rejected. All of this goes along with a feeling of shyness, shame perhaps. Is that the issue? Do you feel like that now?

M: No, what I do feel is a fear of showing all that lies behind that.

C: That's it.

M: I've come thus far okay, I've laid it out very well and ... it's that at some point I have to go into that and I have to ...

C: I have the impression that you have a few confessions to make and that's where we could work — on you feeling good about who you are without the need to hide yourself, without the need to manipulate your image in order to sustain that you are decent and therefore acceptable.

M: Confessions.

C: Give us a few telegraphic affirmations. Concerning all that.

M: Not accepting myself as I am and I would like to be different. It's like I'm ashamed to say it: "I'm not handsome, I've always had complexes."

C: Go on like that. "I'd like to be different, I'm not like this, I should be like that ..."

M: I would like to be different; I would like not to be a foreigner; I would like to go home and not have to prove anything ...

C: "I would like to not be how I am." Stay with that a little more. See what else comes up.

M: I'd like to not be how I am. I don't know how I would want to be.

C: You started with being ashamed of how you are. Try staying more with, "I'm ashamed of being how I am." That is the theme of our work: shame of yourself connected to timidity, with not wanting to be rejected, etc. ...

M: [*head down*] I'm ashamed of being how I am.

C: Get in touch with all that that means to you. Feel it here. Feel all the things that you are ashamed of. Filled with shame.

M: I'm ashamed that I don't do things well. I become ashamed. I feel bad because things are not harmonious. I don't achieve the things that I set out to do.

C: Can you be more concrete?

M: I'm ashamed of not being me; I'm ashamed of being ashamed.

C: That's it, go on. "I'm ashamed of not being me." "I'm ashamed of being ashamed to be me," maybe?

M: I'm ashamed of being ashamed to be me ... I'm ashamed of being ashamed to be me ...

C: The shame of betraying your own self, in view of the great shame of exposing yourself as you are.

M: I'm ashamed of exposing how I am.

C: Could you dare to expose a little of that disgusting being that you seem to think you are?

M: Yes. I feel that I am a manipulator. In order to get things, affection, I manipulate things. I don't know how to be more concrete.

C: It might have consequences. It makes you very ashamed to concretize it. Could it be that the irrational shame is a complete fantasy, and you go around placing blame on whatever you are doing?

M: I feel lost now.

C: All right. We'll stick with the shame of being a foreigner which is big enough.

M: Okay.

C: You might not have any other shame bigger than that. You give so much credibility to absolutely foreign values, different from you.

M: I know about that one. I definitely experience that and I've been experiencing it during recent years.

C: What do you think about that? A person who is ashamed of not being from Barcelona? Or when in Madrid, is ashamed of not being from Madrid. What do you think of the human being who has that ailment, who thinks like that, who torments himself because he's not from there?

M: I don't know what I think, but I would like to slip by unnoticed. I don't like to stand out. I have a different accent that people remind me about: for example, they say that Argentinians are like … are shit. As if I have to prove that I'm not like that and so then I betray myself.

C: Can you visualize your internal being with the image of that person who you hold painfully in your memory? And can you personify the "voice of Barcelona," the feeling of Barcelona … That you are a shitty Argentinian, a manipulator. What else? Give the accuser a voice.

M: We don't want you. Why are you here? Why don't you go back to your country? Because you are all alike. We don't trust you because we trusted you, and you have lost our trust. You lied. I know a ton of people [from Argentina] and you're all the same. It's better if you leave. We don't want you.

C: Do you recognize that as your own voice? Do you feel that you are saying that to your own self?

M: No, I feel it's something like this … [*He makes a gesture with his hands like something from outside that surrounds him and throws itself at him.*]

C: Like something separate from you. It was *"Barcelona"* that felt this way. It's not the case that you reject yourself for being how you are and for not being like the people from Barcelona …

M: I feel that I can have those problems but I can also feel other things or be like them; and the only thing that makes me different is the way of speaking which gives me away.

C: Does it seem unfair to you, that feeling of how they experience you, how they are toward you?

M: It bothers me. I would like to be one of the crowd, to be the same as everyone else. I would like to return to my neighborhood where I knew everyone and that [criticism] didn't exist. I didn't even know how I talked and I didn't even know that I was a foreigner.

C: It bothers you. Often during Gestalt sessions I have told a joke that no one ever appreciates. In Chile it's called the story of Machuca. There are two electricians repairing an installation up a pole. They work as a team — one on top who is soddering with melted lead. And the melted lead drips on the back of the one who is bent over. They have been brought before the judge, for the one on the bottom has been detained by a policeman for saying a word intolerable for a public place. He says to the judge: "But your honor, I promise you that when the melted lead dripped on me I only said to him: 'Machuca, be more careful; be more careful, Machuca, the melted lead is dripping on my back.' I promise your honor that I didn't say anything else."
It only "bothers me"? They treat you like a shitty Argentinian because you don't speak with the same accent and it "bothers" you? Of course! Okay, what alternative could there be?

M: Mine was to leave Barcelona.

C: Look for another one. A response that is less developed in you and that you need to develop.

M: One thing that I never did was to tell them things: that I also felt that *they* were stingy; that they thought about bucks, money.

C: You were thinking that and you would tell them that. Take advantage of that memory to dramatize it as if you were doing it right now.

227

M: You cut down all the Argentinians ... Ta-ta-ta ... [*He stutters.*]

C: Do you notice how much you stutter? You can't hardly say it.

M: I feel like they're not the ones to blame.

C: What do you feel when you say that, that they are not the ones to blame? That you are being unfair to dump the blame on them when they're only invalidating you?

M: Yes, I make them right. They have an opinion of Argentinians which makes sense.

C: You're right about being despicable. Are you? Just a moment ago you denied it. Which one will it be? Do you agree or don't you agree?

M: That I'm despicable ...

C: I think that you cannot accuse them of treating you like that because you feel despicable. That's your real problem.

What have I said? What have I wanted to communicate to you? I think that you need someone to tell you that you feel unworthy, that you are causing this yourself. It's not only that you feel rejected by someone outside yourself but that you are so totally vulnerable that you reject yourself. You couldn't reproach anyone who called you disgusting because you are saying it to yourself.

So, I think that to exorcise that you would have to give yourself permission to expose the feeling of self-disgust, allow yourself to feel disgusting. Declare yourself disgusting here. Get into that problem. We might be able to do an emotional *reductio ad absurdum* if you get into that emotion.

M: [*head down*] I feel like a piece of shit. I feel like I'm a shit. I feel inferior.

C: Allow yourself to get into it, don't worry about your image.

M: I feel that something is going wrong with me because ... I don't know ... I put out so much hatred and irritation. Deep down I feel I am a fucking shit, an idiot.

C: You softened it. What is like being a "fucking shit"? What is it?

M: I'm a fucking shit.

C: What's it like to be that? Would it be pure stupidity or could it have something to do with that hatred which you mentioned just a moment ago?

M: Now I'm ashamed to treat myself like that.

C: Sure, but let yourself do it a little more.

M: I'm ... [*He stutters.*]

C: It's easier for you to feel rejectable, get the feeling of that idea; or better yet, get face to face [*with it*]. Imagine that you are talking to yourself, face to face.

M: You're a disaster. (He's a person who doesn't move straight.) You're not honest. You're a manipulator full of fears.

C: And what do you feel facing him? In the presence of his fears, his manipulations. Express with gestures what you feel before him. Develop it. Amplify it. Give it words or speak in gibberish.

M: What?

C: That's words without meaning.

M: [*He speaks in gibberish.*] "Note, totetote ... pi, chu ..." [*He makes gestures as if to push him away.*]

C: Okay, give it words with the same tone [of voice].

M: Leave! Get out! Get out! Get out!

C: Now answer that.

M: As the other one?

C: You just heard his accusation ... You've told yourself to fuck off.

M: Okay, let's see ... Why do you want me to go? You are going to need me.

C: What are you doing there acting like that? You're reasoning [with him], aren't you? He tells you: "Leave, leave, leave!"

M: I say to him: "Listen, think about it, because you are going to need me, when you have problems you are going to need that part of your life.

C: What does he offer to you so that he won't be rejected?

M: Yeah, that he can make good use of me. You wouldn't get a bad deal with me, having me there, in a corner.

C: Okay. So, if you now look at what we have done and the different ways in which you have approached the aggression and rejection, what is missing? Or if you look at yourself being in that way, do you have any comment?

M: I don't know, a reconciliation ...

C: You'd have to reconcile yourself, yes. Tell me ...

M: It doesn't look so bad to me anyway. He's not as destructive as he thinks. [*minimizing*]

C: "He's not as destructive as he thinks." It seems disproportionate to me [given] the degree to which you suffer from this, the degree to which you have this symptom of feeling unhappy, or that others reject you because of absurdities; and I would say that it's not that "he's not destructive." What you are saying is quite destructive; it's like you're swindling yourself out of its importance.

M: Hiding its importance.

C: Like saying, "Nothing's wrong, nothing's going on," "Everything is okay."

M: Yeah.

C: Because it's a little embarrassing to show your dirty laundry.

M: I don't know if it's that.

C: Is it painful to do this type of work?

M: No, up until now I don't think it's been heart-breaking.

C: For me one thing is missing ... You either sell out to the aggressor and just say to him "think about it"; or you get the urge to go back, to go far away from here to Argentina; or you feel terribly bad, that feeling they're completely right: "I'm disgusting." Do you imagine what other people would feel in your place?

M: Other people ... ?

C: People who in a place like that are rejected. Isn't there another alternative? It seems to me that self-affirmation is missing. It would be normal to get angry when you get kicked around. Could it be that your real problem is that of letting yourself get kicked around which is underneath all that?

M: No. Generally I get away, I camouflage myself, I try to be like them.

C: When you kick animals, they kick back. I think that healthy human beings also have an aggression that comes from being at least animal-like. A human can also transcend the animal but ... it's as if in you something is missing. Don't you think? Don't you have a perspective about yourself as if there's an organ missing there?

M: Yes. With what I know about myself, these things for example, I have that same aggression in other things. I have it with my mate or with people who don't have that problem ... and I express my ill will there.

C: Does anyone have any inspiration of how ...?

Participant: Why don't you speak in Argentinian? With our "s's"? Don't speak like a Spaniard. Speak the way you speak.

M: I feel like I speak like an Argentinian. [*Laughter from everyone.*]

C: It seems ridiculous.

Participant: You're forcing it; it's like you're holding something back in your mouth all the time.

M: It's that I spent ten years trying to speak Argentinian.

C: But not enough. It's been ten years that you've been trying to speak Argentinian?

M: No, Spanish.

C: You can tell that you have made a big effort to camouflage yourself.

M: On the other hand, when a person says to me, "What part of Argentina are you from?" he's kicked me. They've discovered me!

C: They've discovered that you're a thief, like an Argentinian.

M: No, that's not what it's about. It's stupid, isn't it?

C: I'd say it is.

M: But I've suffered a lot from it.

C: You can't tell.

M: You can't tell?

C: You take it with a lot of stoicism. You lick your wounds all alone, showing the world a good face.

M: I don't know. I suppose that I lacked ...

C: What's missing for me is tragedy. I sense that you're living a tragic life but that you don't allow yourself to feel the tragedy in this moment, when you speak, when you share.

M: I don't know, I'm going to try it because ...

C: Okay, begin anywhere.

M: Let's see ... Why the fuck do they do all this to me? Because I'm Argentinian. If I weren't Argentinian I wouldn't have all this hassle, they wouldn't have hit me, or accused me of all these things. You're all a fucking piece of shit because you take advantage of the fact that I'm Argentinian. The first thing they asked for were [my official] documents, what documents did I have. When they saw that I was Argentinian they accused me of everything. You're all a bunch of sons of bitches. You're a fucking piece of shit.

C: Don't constrict the pain.

M: No. Son of a bitch, son of a bitch! You're all a bunch of sons of a bitch! With Spanish papers they wouldn't have done that to me. Just because of a shitty piece of paper! They don't look at anything, not anything that's inside a person. It's only the paper that matters. Go to hell! You're all nothing but garbage! Because you can't do that.

C: You've become human with the invitation to tragedy. Keep talking from there, with that felt sense of tragedy.

M: And another thing, you're cowards and you've beaten me. But why? Because if I hadn't had those papers I would have been scared shitless, but there they get away with anything, anything. Now I'm afraid to be an Argentinian; it scares me to be a foreigner. I don't have friends, so you can do all this to me. I feel that I am in danger because any day they can do the same thing to me all over again. It can be unfair. And it doesn't do me any good to speak up. I'm a person. Why should someone be hit just for being Argentinian? [*He cries.*]

C: Now [speak] the same, [but] with anger.

M: Why, you sons of a bitch? Why? Go to mother fucking Hell. Damn! You're a bunch of God damned ..., you're unjust, you take advantage of [your] authority, you take advantage of everything. You don't have any humanity. Get out of here, get out of here, get out of here! Fuck! Go and be together with your people.

C: To what previous situation in your life does all this apply? When did you feel similarly rejected?

M: With my father.

C: Say the same things to your father.

M: Why do you hit me? Why do you hit me? [*He cries.*] Don't hit me, I love you, Daddy, don't hit me ... Don't hit me.

C: Give free rein to your weeping; stronger.

M: Don't hit me anymore, Daddy.

C: Let yourself have it, let yourself scream.

M: Don't hit me, Daddy. Son of a bitch! You're a son of a bitch, you're a son of a bitch. Fucker!

C: With more aggression.

M: Fucker! Son of a bitch! Why don't you hit someone your same size? I was a small person and even more, your son. Bad! You're bad, Daddy. Fucker! I love you. [*He cries unconsolably.*]

C: [*He gets up and hands M. a pillow.*] Don't make yourself the good little boy buying his love. Develop what was missing; what was missing then.

M: Son of a bitch! I would kill you! I would kill you! I'd beat you and I'd kill you if I were as big as you. Son of a bitch! I would kill you!

C: Now kill him, he's right there in front of you.

M: [*beating the pillow*] Fucker! Son of a bitch! Why do you hit me? Why?

C: Give your childhood rage free rein without having to justify yourself.

M: [*He hits the pillow.*] Take that! Take that! Take that! Miserable! Beast!

C: Isn't there something in particular missing? Some situation?

M: I don't understand.

C: Accuse him of something specific.

M: Why did you beat Mom? Why did you beat me? Why aren't you happy? Why? Why do you spoil everyone else's life? Idiot! You're so stupid!

C: Keep accusing him but going over the issues.

M: [*He cries, and he covers his face and shrinks.*] Why ...? Why did you act like that with us? Why didn't you play? Why the fuck are you bitter? Why, Daddy?

C: Take a step beyond asking him why. Move into accusatory rage, for this ... and that ... Insult him for specific things.

M: Son of a bitch! You were brutal with all of us.

C: Transform it into aggression, into insults. You were ...

M: A pig. A disgusting pig.

C: He was the disgusting one.

M: Yes, he treated us like idiots.

C: I have the impression that you are swallowing the poison again. You got out a little, but then you stopped accusing him too quickly ... What's happening?

M: [*He cries.*] It's that I'm ashamed. He loved me a lot and suddenly he changed. I was his favorite son and he had a lot of fun with me; and then he changed. I loved my father a lot, but he changed.

C: And you didn't lose hope.

M: I don't know. He changed a lot.

C: Tell him how he changed and how he is different for you.

M: Daddy you changed. Before you loved me a lot and you would play with me a lot. You would push me in my stroller and you would do a ton of things with me. Then you started to hit me and to hate everyone. I know that they did things to you. You would try to destroy me. Why did you want to destroy me? I would have liked you to be how you were before.

C: It seems to me that there are people who tend to get stuck on mommy's lap. It's easier to get out of that when one can feel free to get angry. You must have felt a great frustration; you must have felt, at the animal level, the desire to kill him as you did just a moment ago. It's like you were doing it very well but you cut yourself off. I propose that you do a little more ... or have you had enough for today?

M: I don't understand. Kill!

C: [*Playing dumb.*] Now I've forgotten what it was about. We were talking about your parents?

M: Do you want me to do it?

C: Do what?

M: I understood that you wanted me to express my rage against him.

C: It was a recommendation. It seemed to me that you were doing very well, you were more alive. This is so deeply forbidden, that if you don't call him disgusting you swallow all the poison and you call yourself disgusting. So, "undo the retroflexion," * as they say in these circles. Tell him: "Stupid, disgusting," all the things you can; inspiring yourself with all the innumerable scenes you lived through with him after he changed.

M: Idiot! You're stupid! Idiot that you are! You're an idiot! Asshole! Son of a bitch!

C: Remind him of some instances, some examples.

M: Remember when you would compare me to Victor and then for any little thing you'd smack me. Imbecile! How can a grown up person hit a child like that? You're abusive, you're sick; you're screwed up. Crazy!

C: Say it with more contempt.

M: [*with contempt*] Crazy! Screwed! Shithead! You're a fucking piece of shit! You're disgusting! Stupid idiot!

C: Keep talking while feeling your disgust for him.

M: You repulse me! It's disgusting! Guys like you should have to go to war to embitter your life like that ... Oh! Look, I despise you. Get out, get out, get out. Go to Hell! You're a shit and a turd. Get out! Leave!

C: Okay, let's imagine that he heard you. Imagine how he is now ... Now you're in his internal world, in that imaginary situation in which you spoke to him in a way you didn't in your childhood. How would that alternative past be where you dared to tell him the truth, what you felt, what you saw ...? What does he feel deep down?

M: Him?

C: Yes, upon hearing that.

M: What does he feel after what I have said to him?

C: Yes. What does he feel after ... ?

M: [*He thinks ... He speaks for his father.*] I don't know, I didn't want to hit him. They used to hit me.

C: They would hit you?

M: [*for his father*] They would beat me ...

C: Who?

M: [*as father*] People, work. They would humiliate me. I would get up very early and I would work many hours.

C: Imagine that you, your father, is explaining how he would come home beaten. How life beat him down.

M: Imagine ...

C: I'm proposing that you *be* your father, answering yourself. You were saying ...

M: Yes, what my father would say.

C: If he would have said what he really felt ... We are imagining if there had been communication.

M: [*Father*:] I would have liked it if you, my son, would have learned a profession; if you were a doctor, if you were someone important.

C: But does he convince you that he didn't want to hurt you at any time? That everything was with good intentions? It's like you're erasing with one stroke the fact that he rejected you.

M: I feel it like that.

C: Yes, you feel it like that. If you imagine how your father felt, do you feel that your father didn't want anything bad for you, already! He didn't know, he couldn't help it. How was it? Now you're him explaining himself. Him making himself heard to his son.

M: [*Father crying.*] I was fed up and I didn't know what I was doing. I did not want my life to be like this. They would humiliate me at work and I would come home very tired and I would drink and I'd get into a bad mood, and I didn't know; but I never wanted to hurt you. I was working only for you. I did it for you.

C: So now, you're experiencing your father in a very different way. You are understanding him in a way you couldn't then. Give your father an imaginary hug. Go back to the past and experience that moment of understanding.

M: [*He hugs himself, cries and speaks quietly with his father.*]

C: Do you want to say anything more? It seems that you have been projecting all of that in the world — Barcelona and the rest of the world. An aggression that was a childhood ghost that you created because you couldn't see, you couldn't understand what was happening to your father. In the panic of the situation you didn't have ... or with your child's mind you couldn't imagine. Isn't it like that? You felt too kicked around to have more empathy. A lot of empathy, a little empathy. How do you feel now?

M: Fine.

C: Only fine?

M: Fine.

C: It looks like you are breathing more deeply.

M: Yes, I feel different.

C: As if your body had more substance.

M: I feel myself breathe.

C: What else do you feel? Let us zoom in on what's happening.

M: I don't know, it's like it did me good to cry. Something has happened. My body feels as if it's run a lot.

C: I'd like to see you look around because you are still very connected to a very private world. Allow yourself to feel whatever you feel, but in the presence of the gaze of others. Good.

Participant: I felt identified with you. I came from Cuba at the age of ten and I also had to change my accent, my language. When you connected with your father I remembered that my father hit me when I was ten and had thrown the hatred at the world, something that had to do with my father also, and I have felt like I really resonated with you.

M: I hadn't realized that until now. I had never gotten to these things.

C: Then you discovered many things.

M: Yes, above all something very important. [*He smiles.*]

This was a remarkable achievement after the strikingly limited insight manifested during the first part of the session, where the denial is so pervasive and he is not even in touch with his embarrassment at showing his "dirty laundry."

What is it that he means when he says that he has discovered something specially important? I believe that the answer is his father's love. He has discovered the buried past of his original relationship with his father before it was damaged, and in reaction to painful events it became a phantasmatic relation with an unconscious and distorted father *imago*.

Up to the point at which I say: "What's missing for me is tragedy" (see page 233), I feel that I did quite well as a therapist, yet not well enough for the needs of the present client. Nothing worked really, in spite of my clever interventions, until I said "I am missing tragedy." My invitation to Modesto to adopt a tragic attitude was the turning point in the session.

One who is acquainted with the Hoffman Quadrinity Process will appreciate how the essence of that therapeutic approach is here condensed into a single session. Once he was in touch with his feelings, it was easy to trace them back to their source in childhood, and in the end he accomplishes not only the recovery of childhood pain and the expression of what anger he could not express as a child, but ultimately the reinterpretation of his past, and the change in his father image from a punitive phantom to the reality of a well-intentioned person who was himself the victim of his limitations and his environment. Though the word *forgiveness* was not uttered, I understand it as the essence of the alleviation he experienced after the session.

At first I thought of calling this section "Changing the Past," for I associated the healing that was obtained here to that elicited by Milton Erikson through the implantation of alternative memories to the ones elicited in the course of hypnotic regression. On second thought, however, it seemed clear that the situation was different — this was not a case of a "memory implant," but of a shift from a fantasized bad object to an original love-bond that had been traumatically severed and forgotten.

5

ENNEATYPE 5

In response to the guide's call to the great pilgrimage in Attar's allegory, the owl came forward with a bewildered air and said:

> I have chosen for my dwelling a ruined and tumbledown house. I was born among the ruins and there I take my delight—but not in drinking wine. I know hundreds of habited places, but some are in a state of confusion and others in a state of hatred. He who wishes to live in peace must go to the ruins, as the madmen do. If I mope among them it is because of hidden treasure. The love of treasure draws me there, for it is to be found among the ruins.[1]

That "ruins" may be taken metaphorically, and that the treasure sought by the miser is not necessarily material will be conveyed by Chaucer's description of the cleric among the Canterbury pilgrims:

> An Oxford Cleric, still a student though,
> One who had taken logic long ago,
> Was there; his horse was thinner than a rake,
> And he was not too fat, I undertake,
> But had a hollow look, a sober stare;
> The thread upon his overcoat was bare.
> He had found no preferment in the church
> And he was too unworldly to make search
> For secular employment. By his bed
> He preferred having twenty books in red
> And black, of Aristotle's philosophy,
> To having fine clothes, fiddle or psaltery.

> Though a philosopher, as I have told,
> He has not found the stone for making gold.[2]

As in the symbol of the owl, love of knowledge is coupled here to love of money, and both (the material and the intellectual) are what is left to one whose main characteristic is non-involvement in relations, in life and even in ongoing experience. Thus, more than "love of gold" is involved in avarice. Indeed, the pursuit of wealth is better illustrated by E8, E1 and other characters than by E5, who is excessively otherworldly and intellectual. The essential issue is rather one of non-giving, lack of generosity and holding-on.

If, in conformity with Ichazo's protoanalysis, we seek the cognitive mistake which underlies the motivational aspect of the ego, we must ask, "What is the world view that supports retentiveness?" "Why do some people 'specialize' in holding back?" And, we may answer: because they do not look forward to contact with others as enriching, and therefore anticipate being depleted. They are constantly threatened by the specter of poverty or impoverishment. By giving the little they feel is theirs they feel that they will be left with nothing at all.

Since one unwilling to give can expect little from others in a world of give-and-take, an E5 seeks to reduce all his or her needs, and learns to live with very little. Of course, this is not only a pathology, for austerity is sometimes pursued as an ideal (as for Hermann Hesse's *Siddhartha*, who says: "I can think, I can wait, I can fast"). As in any character, the soundness or unsoundness of a trait will depend on context more than early history.

E5 is the type of person who knows how to refrain from bothering others with his needs, who anticipates that complaining or invasiveness will only make things worse. He has learned early in life that whatever he did was bound to fail; that he could not achieve anything by either force or seduction. Perhaps because there was no responsiveness in the early environment, there was nothing to do but to live with privation, holding on to his meager resources. Since he cannot go out to the world to claim what he needs or to charm it out of others, he can only hoard; thus, the solution of distancing—of availing oneself of a good wall in order to protect one's intimacy. The expression "ivory tower" conveys that this isolation involves the accumulation of values.

While Shakespeare's Shylock is *not* an E5, and Moliere's *Avare*, beyond caricaturing a secret passion for riches, hardly describes a character, we find masterful observations of E5 in Moliere's *Misanthrope*—who wants no association with corrupt humanity; believes all expression of affection to be hypocrisy; prays, and yet treats people badly.

The vulnerability and impotence involved by an exaggeratedly passive and unexpressive or unfeeling disposition is the theme of many of Kafka's works. Though he does not describe character as much as situations, what is most typical in them is an experience of feeling persecuted in a world where no appeal is possible, and in which it is even impossible to find the pertinent authorities.

An E5 character has already received attention in the psychological literature: Meursault—the protagonist of Camus's *The Stranger*. A paper by Nathan Leites, under the title of "Trends in Affectlessness" (in a book by Murray and Kluckhohn, who comment that Leites takes Camus's novel as "a protocol of the ethos of our time"), elaborates brilliantly on the character's detachment and indifference.[3] I quote below a selection of passages from Leites's work:

> The novel [The Stranger, by Albert Camus] contains only a few explicit indications—almost entirely overlooked even by the sophisticated critics—about the hero's past. But these few are quite significant. As to his father, "I never set eyes on him." As to his mother, "For years she'd never had a word to say to me and I could see she was moping with no one to talk to." "… neither Mother nor I expected much from one another." "As a student I'd had plenty of ambition … But, when I had to drop my studies, I very soon realized all that was pretty futile." The child and the adolescent is thus shown as reacting with withdrawal of conscious affect in intrapersonal relations (that is, the relations between the various components of the self) and in interpersonal relations. He is thus reacting to the guilty rage induced by the severe deprivations which were imposed by an absent father, an indifferent mother, and a withholding wider environment.
>
> It is this characteristic defense which the hero perpetuates

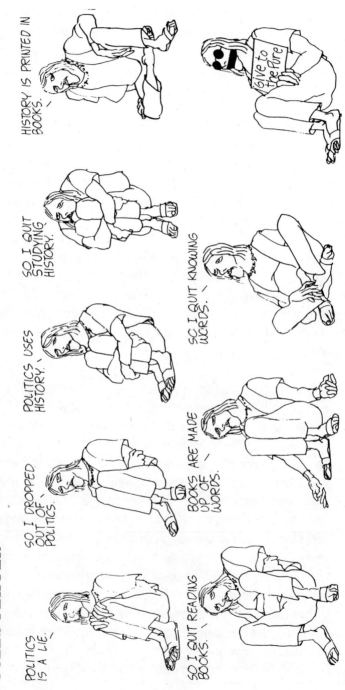

and elaborates in his adult life, and which gives his personality—conveyed in a style appropriate to this dominant trait—its particular aura. I shall now discuss the various major manifestations of the hero's affectlessness.

Firstly, and most obviously, the hero is usually rather clearly aware of the *absence or weakness of affects in response to intrapersonal and interpersonal stimuli*. This is in sharp contrast to the intensity of his reactions to external nonpersonal stimuli—to the colors, smells, tactile values, and sounds of cityscape and landscape. These he knows to be his "surest humblest pleasures." The hero is also presented as feeling a persistently strong and unbrokenly euphoric sexual attraction towards his girl friend—almost the only point in which I would question his plausibility. Perhaps the author, so free from many illusions, is here still presenting a derivative of the Western myth on the transcendent position of "love" in human nature. "I could truthfully say I'd been quite fond of mother—but really, that didn't mean much." His affects appear to him as *questionable* rather than as inevitable and valid: "I came to feel that this aversion [against talking about certain things —N.L.] had no real substance." He is much *aware of the almost total dependence of his affective on his somatic state* conforming (though in extreme fashion) to what is probably a contemporary trend.

While the hero is acutely aware of his atypicality as a "stranger" to the world, he *spontaneously subsumes most of his few near-affective experiences in interpersonal relations under general categories*. When his lawyer asks him whether he had loved his mother, he replies, "yes, like everybody else." When his girl friend asks him, "Suppose another girl had asked you to marry her—I mean a girl you liked in the same way as you like me—would you have said 'Yes' to her, too?" the hero does not find such a hypothesis inconceivable and his emotions towards Marie unique. He answers, apparently effortlessly: "Naturally." In this, he presumably manifests a widely diffused trend in the quality of Western "love" experiences in this century.

It may be surmised that such "generalizing" procedures are in part a defense against the unconscious threat of overwhelming affect. When the hero learns of his mother's death, he arranges for keeping "the *usual* vigil" beside the body. The owner of his habitual restaurant affirms "there's no one like *a* mother" and lends him a black tie and mourning band procured for the occasion of an uncle's death...

The hero shows *a high degree of detachment towards decisive impacts of his environment on him*. During most of his trial he feels as if somebody else is about to be condemned to death. "... He ['one of my policeman'—N.L.] asked me if I was feeling nervous. I said 'No,' and that the prospect of witnessing a trial rather interested me." When danger mounts, "the *futility* of what was happening seemed to take me by the throat."

All value judgments have ceased to be self-evident, as they have in some variants of contemporary empiricist epistemology. There is a *tabula rasa* where the traditional ethical postulates stood.

The hero *abstains from morally reacting to others* as much as to himself. His incapacity for moral indignation is again related to certain contemporary trends.

What are the behavioral counterparts to the hero's valuelessness? His tendency is to *minimize overt action*, symbolic as well as motor. He tends to react with silence to communications of others, perpetuating the wordlessness of his relations with his mother. He shows a preference for the *maintenance of his personal status quo*, at any given moment and with reference to his overall mode of life. When an evening conversation imposed on him is prolonged, he feels that "I wanted to be in bed, only it was such an effort making a move." When his employer offers him a Paris job, "I saw no reason for 'changing my life.'" Getting out of bed requires an intense effort.

Whenever he contemplates *alternative courses of action*, he becomes convinced that they lead to an *identical result*. Thus, nothing is a "serious matter." When his boss offers him a Paris job, "really I didn't care much one way or the other." When he is present at a tense underworld encounter which may instantly develop into shooting, "it crossed my mind that one might fire or not fire—and it would come to absolutely the same thing." (pp. 619-621.)

In the domain of short stories we find a superb and realistic description of an E5 in Melville's *Bartleby*—in whom a refusal to offer what is asked of him coexists with the passion for an isolated niche.[4] Bartleby, the Scrivener, is most laconic, in the forty pages or so of the tale where he hardly says anything other than "I would prefer not to." Yet we know about him indirectly. The fictional narrator tells us how he hired Bartleby thinking that his sedate character would operate beneficially both upon the flighty temper of one of his employees, and the fiery one of another. Then he tells us how, "At first Bartleby did an extraordinary quantity of writing. As if long famishing for something to copy, he seemed to gorge himself on my documents. There was no pause for digestion. He ran a day and night line, copying by sun-light and by candle-light. I should have been quite delighted with his application, had he been cheerfully industrious. But he wrote on silently, palely, mechanically." (p. 102) But, the job of being a scrivener used to involve not only writing, but verification; and when first summoned to collaborate with his employer in the examination of a document, Bartleby for the first time replied, "I would prefer not to." So strange was his uttered refusal, after several entreaties, that his employer simply gave up.

> I looked at him steadfastly. His face was leanly composed; his grey eyes dimly calm. Not a wrinkle of agitation rippled him. Had there been the least uneasiness, anger, impatience or impertinence in his manner; in other words, had there been anything ordinarily human about him, doubtless I should have violently dismissed him from the premises. But as it was, I should have as soon thought of turning my pale plaster-of-paris bust of Cicero out of doors. (p. 103)

I quote further, from a later passage:

I observed that he never went to dinner; indeed, that he never went anywhere. As yet I had never, of my personal knowledge, known him to be outside of my office. He was a perpetual sentry in the corner. At about eleven o'clock though, in the morning, I noticed that Ginger Nut would advance toward the opening in Bartleby's screen, as if silently beckoned thither by a gesture invisible to me where I sat. The boy would then leave the office, jingling a few pence, and reappear with a handful of ginger-nuts, which he delivered in the hermitage, receiving two of the cakes for his trouble.

He lives, then, on ginger-nuts, thought I; never eats a dinner, properly speaking; he must be a vegetarian, then; but no; he never eats vegetables, he eats nothing but ginger-nuts. My mind then ran on in reveries concerning the probable effects upon the human constitution of living entirely on ginger-nuts. (pp. 105-106)

While in Bartleby a self-shrinking is apparent to the outer world as an extremely constricted life, this gives a one-sided view of E5, inspired in the self-preservation subtype. To complete the picture, here are some paragraphs from the script of Ingmar Bergman's "Wild Strawberries" (a social E5).[5] Here Isak Bork is a retreating person, but also an outstanding one. Early in the script he explains that rather than being guilty of errors, exaggerations and even tremendous lies he prefers to remain silent. As a result he has found himself alone in his old age.

This is not a regret but a statement of fact. All I ask of life is to be left alone and to have the opportunity to devote myself to the few things which continue to interest me, however superficial they may be. For example, I derive pleasure from keeping up with the steady progress made in my profession (I once taught bacteriology), I find relaxation in a game of golf, and now and then I read some memoirs or a good detective story. (pp. 169-170)

In an early scene in the movie he drives with his daughter-in-law, and as the following dialogue begins he is speaking about his son:

Isak: Evald and I are very much alike. We have our principles.
Marianne: You don't have to tell me.
Isak: This *loan* for example. Evald got a loan from me with which to complete his studies. He was to have paid it back when he became a lecturer at the university. It became a matter of honor for him to pay it back at the rate of five thousand per year. Although I realize that it's difficult for him, a bargain is a bargain.
Marianne: For us it means that we can never have a holiday together and that your son works himself to death.
Isak: You have an income of your own.
Marianne: ... Especially when you're stinking rich and have no need for the money.
Isak: A bargain is a bargain, my dear Marianne. And I know that Evald understands and respects me.
Marianne: That may be true, but he also hates you.

✝✝✝

Isak: Evald and I have never coddled each other.
Marianne: I believe you.

✝✝✝

Marianne: You are an old egotist, Father. You are completely inconsiderate and you have never listened to anyone but yourself. All this is well hidden behind your mask of old-fashioned charm and your friendliness. But you are hard as nails, even though everyone depicts you as a great humanitarian. We who have seen you at close range, we know what you really are. You can't fool us. For instance, do you remember when I came to you a month ago? I had some idiotic idea that you would help Evald and me. So I asked to stay with you for a few weeks. Do you remember what you said?

Isak: I told you that you were most cordially welcome.

Marianne: This is what you really said, but I'm sure you've forgotten: Don't try to pull me into your marital problems because I don't give a damn about them, and everyone has his own troubles.

Isak: Did I say that?

Marianne: You said more than that.

Isak: That was the worst, I hope.

Marianne: This is what you said, word for word: I have no respect for suffering of the soul, so don't come to me and complain. But if you need spiritual masturbation, I can make an appointment for you with some good quack, or perhaps with a minister, it's so popular these days.

Isak: Did I say that?

Marianne: You have rather inflexible opinions, Father. It would be terrible to have to depend on you in any way.

Isak: Is that so. Now, if I am honest, I must say that I've enjoyed having you around the house.

Marianne: Like a cat.

Isak: Like a cat, or a human being, it's the same thing. You are a fine young woman and I'm sorry that you dislike me.

Marianne: I don't dislike you.

Isak: Oh.

Marianne: I feel sorry for you. (pp. 178-180)

The E5 character seems an exaggeratedly fixed form of what William Sheldon described, in the forties, as the "cerebrotonic" temperament—withdrawn and oriented to perception rather than action or emotional expression.[6]

E5 people are usually silent, and when they speak they tend to talk in general or abstract terms. There are people who, when speaking of the basic material of a descriptive case, make us see with their own eyes and allow us to listen through their descriptions; we know what is being said and who is saying it, like good novelists do in portraying a situation. On the contrary, there are people who make an obscure report. Their report is a summary, or a filtered experience, which has already been interpreted, while the particulars remain hidden. More generally, there is an atmosphere of concealment in the E5 people. They do not show themselves directly, and they are the most hidden people of all.

E6s are afraid, but do not hide so much. And because they do not hide so much, they are more in touch with fear. E5s, because they hide, do not connect with their fear. E5s do not feel afraid, they *avoid* situations that would awaken their fear.

Of course, they can say "I don't dare to talk to my father," or "I don't dare to talk to my boss," or "I don't dare to ask for a raise," or "Oh, I don't dare!" But this is not *feeling* afraid, it is fantasizing about what would make them feel afraid. Often people of this type have this anticipation of fear. When they are pushed by somebody else, they realize that they are *not* afraid. Therefore, if they did not avoid things, they would realize that they are not as afraid as they imagined themselves to be. It can be an unfelt anxiety.

Not feeling and not doing, but being an observer of life, naturally leads to a feeling of not living, and this may stimulate a desire for experience. Out of the clash between the fear of and the desire for experience, there results a thirst for knowledge—a desire to be with life without moving into it. This is commented upon by Elias Canetti, in his book *Earwitness: Fifty Characters*, in his description of "The Narrow-smeller"--character who would dance constantly with people, though separated from them.[7] I quote his complete caricature in view of its extraordinary psychological richness.

> The narrow-smeller shrinks away from smells and avoids them. She opens doors cautiously before she crosses a threshold. Half-averted, she stands there for a while, to smell with one nostril and spare the other. She sticks one finger into the unknown space and brings it to her nose. Then, with that finger, she holds one nostril shut and sniffs with the other. If she does not lose consciousness immediately, she waits a bit. Then she puts one leg sideways across the threshold, but leaves the other foot outside. It would not take much more for her to dare it, but she hits upon a final test in time. She gets up on her tiptoes and sniffs again. If the smell

does not change now, she fears no surprises and risks the other leg as well. She is standing inside. The door, through which she could save herself, remains open.

The narrow-smeller seems isolated wherever she may be, she has a layer of caution about her; other people watch out for their clothes when they sit down, but she watches out for her isolation layer. She fears vehement sentences that might pierce through, she addresses people softly and awaits answers just as softly. She does not come halfway to anyone; in the aloofness in which she remains, she follows the movements of other people: it is as though, separated from them, she were constantly dancing with them. The distance remains the same, she knows how to ward off any approach and certainly any touch.

So long as it is winter, the narrow-smeller feels best out of doors. She worries about the spring. The blossoms and fragrances will begin and she will suffer unbearable torments. She prudently avoids certain bushes, she goes her own, intricate ways. When she sees an insensitive person sticking his nose in lilacs far away, she becomes ill. Unfortunately, she is attractive and gets pursued with roses, she can save herself from them only with quick faints. People find this exaggerated, and while she dreams about distilled water, her admirers put their foul-reeking heads together and try to figure out to which flower scents they could convert her.

The narrow-smeller is regarded as noble because she avoids any touch. She is at her wits' end with marriage proposals. She has already threatened to hang herself. But she will not do it, she cannot bear the thought of possibly having to smell the savior who cuts her down. (pp. 17-18)

We may speak of "depression" as a description of the impoverished emotional life of E5 people, yet it is not a damp but a dry depression. They do not cry so easily, they feel apathetic. It is exceptional for them to cry easily, but there is always a depression—with a loss of energy and an inner atmosphere like a desert.

Every type has its own hell, yet E5's hell is rather like a limbo where nothing ever happens. Type 4 are dramatic, type 5 are apathetic. Yet, affective relationships may be very intense, because E5s are distant from everybody, except themselves.

While there are people who are everybody's friends, E5s have a very limited social circle. They keep at a distance from most people; but since, being human, they have a need for relations, they need to place everything in one or two friends. Because of this there arises a great need for trust, a need for confiding in these elected people with intensity.

This can easily be illustrated with historical examples. In most people belonging to type 5 the following prevails: the more they suffer, the more numb and cold they become. However, more developed E5 people are more in touch with their sensitive sides. A typical case is that of Chopin. He was, perhaps, the most romantic among Romantics in the history of music. Yet his was the romanticism of a shy man. A somewhat aristocratic person, with an aloof feeling of personal distinction and humor, but little "outpouring of the heart" (in his own words). Yet in his music he expressed an exquisite tenderness and also the rage of a revolutionary.

Every instance of character pathology involves a caricaturesque deformation of a healthy quality, and just as in E1 an appreciation of perfection becomes perfectionism, and in E2 freedom becomes willfulness and licentiousness, in E5 there is neurotic detachment instead of true spiritual non-attachment.

In Hinduism, as in the Oriental traditions in general, there is an ideal of non-attachment. This is expressed in the *Bhagavad Gita* as one of "being the same in pleasure and in pain." This does not mean that there is no pleasure, but there is a center that does not move beyond the polarities involved in experience; there is something incorruptible, a stability of the mind, allowing experience to be what it is. On the contrary, neurotic non-attachment, which culminates in type 5, involves a loss of contact. It is not truly non-attachment, but an avoidance of contact and a very strong attachment to inner states; and thus, an intolerance of the experiences that would be generated through contact.

It is easy to understand that non-involvement is suitable to the scientific endeavor, which calls for lack of bias; and since an E5 treasures knowledge, the association between the character and scientific occupations resembles the association between E4 and aesthetic pursuits.

Reviewing the E5 persons of whom biographies have been written, however, I find not only illustrious scientists (including Newton and Darwin), but many important philosophers; and I think that some observations of Lytton Strachey on Hume will make apparent why:

In what resides the most characteristic virtue of humanity? In good works? Possibly. In the creation of beautiful objects? Perhaps. But some would look in a different direction, and find it in detachment. To all such David Hume must be a great saint in the calendar; for no mortal being was ever more completely divested of the trammels of the personal and the particular, none ever practiced with a more consummate success the divine art of impartiality. And certainly to have no axe to grind is something very noble and very rare.[8]

Another thinker who substantially influenced the history of culture and whose accomplishment rested in an open-minded impartiality was Erasmus. A contemporary of Luther, Erasmus is regarded as the father of humanism; he was the undisputed intellectual authority of his age. Here are some passages about him that I have found in a biography of Luther by a Spanish Jesuit:

Who was Erasmus, this man who, without noise or arms dominated Europe like a despot? ... writing is throwing the stone and hiding the hand ... nothing is worse in Erasmus' eyes than religious "formalism," insincerity, the many legal prescriptions, intransigence and other abuses of the church at the time.

... the independent Dutch is far from letting himself be swept into the orbit of the *Wittenberg Theology* ... he will place himself at a safe distance.

... a fragile frame, pale ... shut in among silent books and parchment ... always shivering ... Appreciative of Luther yet unwilling to turn against the pope, it fell on Erasmus to attempt a reconciling position between them, and he was criticized by both: Luther wanted him to fight by his side; the catholic world would attack him as a carrier of the "Lutheran plague."[9]

In his biography of Erasmus, Stefan Zweig reflects:

This position of Erasmus', this indecision, or rather, this will not to decide was all too simply interpreted by his contemporaries as cowardice ...

He prudently bent away from the situation; he gallantly oscillated like a reed to the left and the right, only to avoid being broken by the wind and always rise again. He did not carry his declaration of independence—his *nulli concedo*—proudly before him, like a banner, but under his mantle, like a thief carries his lantern; he temporarily crouched and hid and used pretexts during the barbarous collisions of collective madness; but, more importantly, he safeguarded and kept intact his spiritual jewel—his faith in humanity—and from his flame Spinoza, Lessing and Voltaire (and all future Europeans) were able to light their own.[10]

We are all trying to be in one way or another, and E5 looks inward. Theirs is an unbalanced search, just as that of E8 who seeks to feel alive through intense encounters, and E3 people who try to get in touch with themselves through the eyes of others. In the case of type 5 the illusion is that outside there is nothing good ... Because of this assumption they are afraid of being "eaten up." Laing, who wrote *The Divided Self*, introduced the term "engulfment." "Fear of engulfment." And this is also related to the question of not being able to say no. E5s are "good" children who do not know how to establish limits. They have such a desire for life that, if they are given something, they feel tempted to surrender themselves entirely. Thus, this fear of engulfment is, in some ways, realistic. Type 5 are misers who strikingly don't know how to be miserly; that is to say, their holding on is a meager compensation for the fact that they are excessively available to demands, excessively obedient and accommodating. Detachment and engulfment-proneness has existed as a polarity of counterbalancing tendencies among which an integration is missing. For instance, they are misers who do not know how to ask for money, because the taboo of avarice is very strong. They have a great need for privacy, but do not dare to close their doors, feeling too shy to say to somebody: "I don't want you to come in."

The types at the bottom of the enneagram, E4 and E5, are the ones who suffer the most. In general, the people at the top suffer less. Type 9 are thick-skinned, psychologically speaking. Theirs is an elephantine psychology, a pachydermatous psychology. They have learned to bear their burden, they have learned to carry it and not to complain. This is a different feeling from that of type 5. Type 5 resign themselves, but although they make no demands they experience a feeling of deep dissatisfaction. Types 4 and 5 suffer from depression, although in different ways.

Any neurosis always involves an alienation of one's deepest self, but this is even more striking in type 5, where one could apply the word "alienation" in a more restricted sense. It is a social alienation, a social distance, not so much self-alienation. On the contrary, these people are not alienated from their own depth. They are the types academic psychology calls "schizoid." They are very much in touch with their own inwardness—though at the cost of losing touch with others. The extreme manifestation of the E5 pattern may be found in what psychiatry calls "catatonia" - a form of schizophrenia in which there may be total loss, not only of action, but also of movement. The person becomes paralyzed and there is a feeling of not wanting to belong to the world.

KOVEL'S "RICH GIRL"

I am sure that Kernberg would agree with Kovel's diagnosis of Sarah as a person with a "narcissistic personality." In the language of protoanalysis, Kovel's story is that of a social E5 whose "totemic" self-ideal* has been built in response to (an E3) mother's values. After de-idealization of her mother and giving up on her mother's love, her totem fell into obsoleteness, and she into a limbo of meaninglessness.

It fell on Kovel to assist Sarah in the transition from a no-man's-land to a life truly of her own. I reproduce below the beginning of the chapter, entitled "Rich Girl," in his book *The Age of Desire*.

For a long time Sarah could not work. She would lie about dully, alternately staring at the green paisley wallpaper or the television, and eating sunflower seeds, carefully cracking the shells between her molars and then expertly shifting the debris to the front of her mouth, where her tongue and incisors, acting in concert, winnowed the nut and ejected the fragments of shell. Sometimes she would not get out of bed until the pile of shells had grown so large that it could no longer be ordered in a neat mound and would spill uncomfortably under the bedclothes. She would rise scratching, stumble about the apartment until the means of cleaning up the shells were gathered, and then sink down again, either onto the bed or the toilet, where she could sit for an hour at a time, poring over *The New Yorker* and waiting for something to happen.

On better days she would rouse herself to go to dance class. There she could forget her troubles. Sarah regretted not having stayed with ballet, as her parents and childhood teachers had so often urged. Even now, with so little practice and being out of condition, her tall, slender body retained its grace and suppleness. No matter how infrequently Sarah went, she was the pick of the class. She reveled in the envy of the others and delighted in the praise of the instructors. In response to their encouragement, she even considered dancing professionally. After all, there was still time, and the way she was floundering, what was there to lose? Sarah would muse this way, actually growing excited, until she recalled the precipice she had stood upon long ago. She was thirteen and radiant in her new lavender outfit. There was Mme. Deschamps at the piano, looking eagerly at her, and there behind her, rank upon rank of eyes, their gaze (adoring, she could feel it) merging with the school footlights. The music swelled and she swelled with it, swelled with a joy that turned into frenzy, and then panic, paralysis, a silence of movement and tears of mortification. Her mother was most understanding, and even her father showed no disapproval, but it would be ten years before Sarah would again step onto a dance floor.

Upon reflection Sarah decided that there was a lot to lose just then. There had always been a lot to lose; and now, as she headed toward her thirtieth year, there seemed to be more and more. True, her limbs flexed as of old; but the long hours Sarah spent staring at the mirror confirmed with all the violence of the eye that the invisible elastic cords that had knit her body wondrously together for so many years were snapping one by one. Entropy was overtaking Sarah. She could see the sagging beginning to set in; tiny wrinkle by tiny wrinkle, a droop there where once a fine tense arc had held sway. Her train to balletic glory had left years ago; what she faced now was watching the younger, confident women step aboard while she awaited the inevitability of physical injury. Sarah felt like the proverbial athlete dying young, one, moreover, whose real triumph was strictly in the imagination. She had had so much. Only her mother really knew; and her mother was the only person in the world from whom Sarah would turn away at that final, triumphant adoration her imagination was preparing for her.

Sarah's mother had once been a champion swimmer. Even now, in late middle age, time, abetted by the skill of plastic surgeons and the carefully screened rays of southern suns, had been kind to her. Sarah despised her mother's coarse cultivation of youthful beauty no less than she loathed her own helpless imitation of the older woman's values. Yet, the disgust she felt for her mother when the latter periodically sailed through the door like an armada was never without an admixture of envy. This great whale of a woman, with belted muscles running across her upper back (the product of decades of smashing tennis balls no less than the backstroke) and narrow Tartar eyes, this foolish, fond, empty, powerful woman never failed to excite awe in her daughter. And for all of the amused contempt with which she treated her mother, the truest feeling Sarah held for her was terror, which was why months passed without a visit.

"Sally! Look at this mess! What have you done with the allowance we sent you? I told you to get a cleaning woman with it. Even though you're too depressed to work right now, dear, the least you can do is to maintain appearances. It's the best therapy, after all. Dr. Rhapsode was saying so himself just the other day. Why don't you answer me, dear?"

"I would prefer not to."

"Prefer not to? What kind of talk is that?"

"You wouldn't understand. It's from a novella, *Bartleby*, about a man who wouldn't work. Sometimes I feel that way ... about everything!"

"Sarah, darling, you read too much. Your father was saying so himself just the other night. 'She's too sensitive, that's all'; that's just what he said. He thinks, too, that you're going to make it. We believe in you, Sally, just remember that. No matter what the world does to you, just remember that you'll always be Number One with Daddy and me. Of course, we love Martha, too. But you were the first, and somehow, I know you hate it when I talk this way, but give your old mother the satisfaction just once, you know we hardly ever see each other, though goodness knows, it's not *my* fault. Where was I? Oh, yes, somehow, Sarah, you were special right from the start, the way you looked at us from the crib. Forgive me, dear, I'm getting maudlin again. By the way, you know how I hate to ask you these things dear, you're so touchy about them, but how is that new doctor coming along? You know, the one with the funny name?"

Sarah was the firstborn of her generation. Both sets of grandparents had come over from Eastern Europe to escape pogroms and the tsar's conscription, and to make their fortune in the West. Many who undertook this exodus failed or returned to the Old World; but her grandparents held on and held together. On her mother's side, Sarah's grandfather started with a pushcart, then gradually accumulated sufficient funds to buy a small clothing store. He never became wealthy; but he did well enough to end his days in Florida and to watch his only child rise in the world, first through her athletic prowess, then by a marriage whose material fortunes he was pleased to have helped launch with a little capital. Sarah's paternal grandfather stitched the clothes from whose sale the modest dowry arose, and remained an ardent anarcho-syndicalist to the end of his long days, an end likewise passed in a Florida retirement community, where he argued fiercely with ancient Communist adversaries by the side of the pool. Sarah's father was the youngest of three children and the only one who ever amounted to anything. His success as a salesman alienated him somewhat from his brothers; and after his marriage and first auto dealership, he managed to have less and less to do with them. The old man lived with his successful son for a while around the time of Sarah's birth. But when Sarah's father acquired the Mercedes dealership, long-smoldering tensions erupted between the two. Claiming he would not live off the profits of Nazi capital, grandfather took his ever-docile wife with him and moved South, where the union pension fund provided him with a dignified end. All this took place before Sarah was three. Of her paternal grand-parents nothing remained but a dim recollection of shouting. Nor does Sarah know what anarcho-syndicalism is, despite seventeen years of an education more elaborate than that offered real princesses.

Sarah could pick her head up at two weeks of age. She sat at three months, walked at nine, said her first words at eleven. She began swimming lessons at six months of age and had her first exercise class at a year and a half. By three she was picking words out of a dictionary and had begun violin lessons for toddlers. Tested before entering kindergarten, she scored off the scale in all categories, and so was moved immediately into an enriched pro-gram at school. The principal told her mother that the tests were designed to select the winners right from the start. It was the post-Sputnik era. America was going unabashedly toward a meri-tocracy, and Sarah was to have heaped on her all the resources the most potent economic organization in the history of the world could bring to bear on the cultivation of an individual.

By age five Sarah had begun to suffer from the piercing headaches that would afflict her for the next decade and then dis-appear as mysteriously as they arrived. All test results were normal or inconclusive. Her case kept a lot of suburban doctors busy for a long time, and its ramifications extended for miles into metropol-itan medical centers as well. Sarah's father used to say, half-boast-ingly, that he had to sell a Mercedes 300 each week just to keep the doctors going.

After a few years of this, it was decided that the case was psy-chosomatic, and Sarah was packed off to a child analyst, Dr. Freestone. By then it was apparent that something was definitely troubling the child and that the headaches were, in the words of the school counselor, a "cry for help." On Sarah's first visit, Dr.

Freestone found a sulky, whiny girl clinging to a mother who anxiously watched every move for signs of disorder. While the doctor tried to play with Sarah, her mother kept up a steady patter of supposedly helpful descriptive comments, alternately calling attention to the child's brilliance and warning her against breaking the toys. Once when Sarah paused in the middle of doll play her mother anxiously interjected, "Sally, I know that look in your eye. You're going to have a headache. Here, take one of your pills."

After several sessions, Dr. Freestone took the parents aside and gave them her opinion. "Sarah's headaches aren't only a cry for help," she said. "They are also a protest against everything that is being jammed into her head. I think I can help her, with your cooperation. But if we don't all work together, she'll not make any progress. And to cooperate means that you must learn to stop pressuring that child. Certainly she's gifted. But she's beginning to believe that nothing she does is for herself. She's under incredible pressure, which is just not healthy for a seven year old — or for anybody else. Now, it's been my experience that often when parents put so much pressure on a child, it's their way of dealing with their own problems. So, I'd like to ask you a little about yourselves; and if it's necessary, I'll refer you to a colleague of mine who will see you as a couple."

It proved necessary; and in summarizing the case to her colleague, Dr. Menschlik, the family therapist, this is what Dr. Freestone said:

These people have not differentiated themselves from each other, and they're trying to hold the child in a symbiotic tie to keep their own dependency needs met. Without her they'd either tear each other apart or the marriage would dissolve. Sarah pays the price by being made into part of each of them. The mother is a markedly hysterical individual with strong phallic needs and tremendous repressed hostility. She's a typical combination of colossal egocentricity and vanity, on the one hand, and a mortifying self-abnegation, on the other. That's one of the sources of the hostility: the frustration of feeling so great yet living a life in which everything she does is for husband and daughter. Of course, the hostility goes deeper than that. I couldn't help feeling anxious just sitting with her; imagine how Sarah feels! Her mouth reminds me of a piranha. As you might imagine, the husband degrades her terribly. He has a tremendous castration fear, which he handles as would a typical male: counterphobic ... macho ... the supersalesman. Meanwhile, he keeps the wife down and avoids her, for fear (accurate, I suppose, if he's reading her unconscious) she'll bite his penis off; and he enormously overindulges the girl, both to show what a big man he is and to make his wife jealous. At the same time, she overprotects Sarah, wanting to make her into the penis she herself can't have, and by the same token, needing to guard her against her own jealous hostility. And the worst of it is that the parents don't really talk to each other but through, around, or by each other. And inconsistent! The father is indulgent one minute, then harsh and punitive the next. In addition, he's away a great deal. I don't think he knows who he is, really. He told me his own father was strictly from the old school, had rigid values and all that, but that he himself wanted to be different, which is why he became a salesman, where the puritan ethic, so to speak, doesn't belong. And because he found himself successful at it, he drifted further from his father's way, thereby feeling empty and impoverished. Then there was some kind of break between them. Needless to add, there's a lot of that punitive old man embedded in his superego, but of course it's not integrated with the ego, so he's inconsistent. And his wife's even more so. She's fluttery and like a little girl one minute, stern and demanding the next, and the third, turns into a howling banshee. It took some time to extract from her the fact that she has a temper, so concerned is she to maintain appearances. Evidently, it's a dilly and must really terrorize the little girl, especially as the rages usually come out without any warning. Apparently, she never hits Sarah, but I doubt whether that would make any difference; it's the mental abuse that counts. And for all that the mother is constantly on the child, watching every breath and every movement, I get the feeling that she's never really there, that she never sees Sarah as Sarah, that she's *really only looking at herself.*

The sessions with Dr. Menschlik lasted six weeks. It was the father who withdrew, then dropped out. This is usually the pattern in family therapy, though Dr. Menschlik was not misled into seeing the matter as one-sided. He noticed from the beginning how Sarah's mother subtly set her husband up as the villain; how she made herself — or allowed him to make her — into the frustrated, put-down, all-faithful and all-suffering wife; and how this made him guilty, an emotion he never revealed except through a mounting evasiveness. Such was the result when Dr. Menschlik tried to get them to talk openly with and to each other. Evidently, they needed their distance and found authenticity an intolerable threat to the intactness of their marriage. Sarah's parents, for all their means, were of the common type who can neither live with nor without each other. Solitude was unbearable to them; and it was impossible to distinguish whether their world was constructed for the positive material benefits it afforded or as a buffer against facing reality alone.

Sarah's sessions lasted almost a year. Dr. Freestone made her feel a little safer; and after an initial period of resistance to going, it was hard to keep her away. Then she went away to summer camp, and the headaches disappeared. In September the parents suddenly found Dr. Freestone very expensive and decided not to resume the sessions. Sarah pined a little, then appeared to forget the entire experience. She was doing brilliantly in school and had made a few new friends. The headaches came back periodically until they finally withered away in adolescence. Meanwhile, better days seemed to have set in. Sarah's gifts were acknowledged in school; and the satisfaction this afforded her parents kept their intricate personal system in a state of balance. Even the incident at the ballet recital hardly seemed to matter, so accomplished was Sarah, so able to recoup gratification from other achievements. Mr. Dichter, the able and demanding literature teacher at the Lorelei School, was positively awestruck by her poetry and openly called her "the next Sylvia Plath." Communications Coordinator Elaine

Dirndle, on the other hand, was even more taken with Sarah's capacities in the performing arts, and in the end, her influence held sway. Lorelei was one of those schools favored by the fortunes of prosperous alumni and had, among other riches, its own television studio. By her junior year, Sarah was writing, directing, and producing shows of exceptional promise. And applying to college was just like shopping at Saks Fifth Avenue with Daddy's credit card. She even had the extra pleasure of turning down scholarships.

True, she was aloof and had by then already shown a knack for becoming unhappily involved in brief, savage romances; yet, in all, one could not have found a young woman of eighteen more poised on the edge of a fair future than Sarah. This is why it was so baffling to her doting parents when she refused to get out of bed one Sunday morning and, in a dry, strangled voice that her mother could scarcely recognize, said that all her achievements — from the merit scholarship to the tennis trophy to the laudatory inscription chiseled into the school library plaque — gave her no sense of who she was and what she wanted, and that she was indeed the most unhappy person she knew. And could not her parents help?

Not since the ballet recital had Mr. and Mrs. M had such a shock. But they were prudent people; and after satisfying themselves that they could not prove to Sarah the fallaciousness of her reasoning, they set about trying to help. A call to the local rabbi yielded the name of Dr. Brisket, a psychologist counselor well enough known to reassure the Ms that he was capable of handling their daughter. "Just remember, dear," Mr. M told Sarah before the first visit, "that you have nothing to hide. In fact, he should be paying you for the privilege of listening to what you have to say." And with that benediction Sarah set off for therapy.

Sarah was first surprised and then irritated that Dr. Brisket spent so much time listening without ever acknowledging the cleverness or profundity of her insights into herself. Nonetheless, she was beginning to like the man when, in the middle of the sixth session he abruptly interrupted her train of thought with the observation that he could no longer be of help to her alone. Instead, she would have to be seen with her parents. "You see," Dr. Brisket later explained to the three of them, "this is a knot that will have to be untied at the level of the family." The situation had not changed fundamentally since the time of therapy with Dr. Freestone. Sarah was finding it psychologically impossible to differentiate herself from her parents; and they were equally reluctant to let her go, undoubtedly because of what they feared would be stirred up if they had to deal with each other directly instead of living off Sarah's accomplishments. As for these achievements, it was no wonder Sarah took so little pleasure in them. "Nothing Sarah does can be felt as her own," Dr. Brisket pointed out, "since it is all done for praise, and as this is the glue of the family's sickness, the greater her achievement, the less free she can feel."

Dr. Brisket could be very persuasive when he wanted to be; and because there was nothing in the world the Ms desired so much as the happiness of their daughter, before long he had the three coming together to the handsome office over his garage. At first they tried talking — the doctor, much more active now than when he saw Sarah alone, frequently interrupting with observations of the various tricks they were playing on each other, and how no one spoke directly to anyone else or made any real demands. This seemed to go quite well, but after a month, Dr. Brisket, ever sensitive to people's resistances, began to realize that it was going *too* well: the Ms, talented and well-intentioned, had figured out the rules of this game and were now succeeding in being good, dutiful, even creative patients without making the slightest real change in their relations, which had always been characterized by a veneer of perfect correctness. They had learned to survive Doctors Freestone and Menshlik, and they were going to learn to survive Dr. Brisket as well. "Too much intellectual bullshit here," snorted the doctor, and he set about to vary his tactics. First he enjoined them from reaching any conclusion or commenting with any insight about their mutual condition. Instead, he assigned them tasks that were to turn their old ways topsy-turvy. Sarah, for example, was made to stop writing poetry and to do the dishes, while Mrs. M had to take up painting, and her husband, who could scarcely recall the color of his wife's eyes, was told to spend an hour a day waiting on her hand and foot. There was some grumbling about the new regimen, which encouraged Dr. Brisket for a while, but the grumbling itself was so good-natured and the tasks carried out too dutifully for his taste. Once again the family seemed headed for a well-oiled and intelligent nonresolution of their problem.

"Stop the music!" Dr. Brisket cried out one day in the fifth month of treatment. "You people are so afraid of change that I could send you all to different planets and your relations would remain the same. I think we have to go much deeper." Stroking his goatee, he explained that unlike his colleagues, he was not satisfied with the therapeutic status quo. In his restless search for a therapy that would break through emotional barriers, he had come upon the teachings of a new, ethological school. According to this doctrine, man's behavior is rooted in deep set, instinctual animal rhythms. Any therapy that did not touch this profound biological core was like a prescription of gargling for throat cancer. Brisket was not holding to the Freudian doctrine about instincts, which regarded sex and aggression as animal forces within an individual that limited his growth. No, the instincts were *social* and *life giving*: one had to get in touch with them in a setting with other people. Thus, family therapy was still the treatment of choice, but it had to be a deep, biological family treatment. Only by touching her rootedness with her parents could Sarah gain the strength needed for her full development into the wonderful person she was. But they had to go deeper than words or role playing; they had to go all the way back.

Accordingly, when the Ms appeared the following Tuesday, they changed into simple body suits before the session ("to break down the cues without stirring up too much excitement," explained the doctor). The consultation room was dimmed, and in place of the rather severe Danish chairs upon which they had been used to sitting they found mattresses and cushions. Now they were on the floor and, with the doctor hovering above them, formed a ring joined hand to shoulder. And instead of talking, they had to stare at each other. The gaze was the thing. It was eye and body contact, according to Dr. Brisket, that formed the earliest unity of the human bond, and this could be broken into right here and now. The new regimen went as follows: two of them would stare uninterruptedly for twenty minutes at each other, while the third endured his or her separation. Then they would switch roles, so that each family member experienced his or her bondedness as well as separateness in any given hour. All the while they had to breathe deeply and slowly, with particular attention to expiration. The doctor's job was to keep this going — no easy task, considering the massive anxieties stirred up by the novel procedure. But once the giggling stopped and the exasperation wore away, the Ms got down to business and things began to happen.

As Sarah later described it:

Sometime in the third session I began having this woozy feeling. There was a tingling in my fingertips and then my mother's face began to get mushy, you know, as if the features were no longer distinct from each other. I began to feel excited and then mushy myself, looking into her eyes, not knowing whether to cry or to be blissful. Then maybe my mom couldn't take it any more, what was happening, and she began to say something, in that grating, whining way she has, something like, "Why do you look at me like that, dear?" and it wasn't so much the question itself as the way she ended it by calling me "dear" that flipped me. I suddenly felt I could never get anything from her, that I couldn't stand being with her one single instant longer and something awful was going to happen. I started to get up and the doctor tried to stop me and my dad said, with his phony manner, like he was trying to sell me something, "Wait, Sally dear, we're just trying to help you." There it was, the "dear" again, and the fact that it was me who needed help and they were all there just as before, just as complacent and remote and full of shit as ever. The next thing I knew, I was being pulled off my mother. Her glasses had broken and the pocket on her blouse had been ripped, but she wasn't hurt otherwise. My mother's quite a bozo, but I don't know what would have happened to her if they hadn't stopped me. But they only stopped me from killing her physically; I was still besides myself and for the next half-hour went on and on denouncing them however I could for their bullshit values and ways, the box at the opera where they could pretend they were cultured; driving the Mercedes to the synagogue, where they pretended they were religious; and the five-thousand-dollar burglar alarm at the house, where they pretended they were safe and free. I really let them have it. It felt great, and after I got it all out there was even a glow of warmth in me for the first time, a wish that we could hug, bathe ourselves in tears, and make up. The doctor was real pleased, too, and said we were finally getting down to brass tacks. But I could see how hurt they were, even when we tried hugging at the end of the session. The next week my father suddenly managed to have a pressing business engagement the day of the appointment, and my mom and I could hardly go through the motions. Two weeks later my folks pulled out. To tell the truth, I wasn't half sorry to see them do it. Funny thing, I felt a little easier with them from that time on until I left for college. But slowly, over the years, a kind of coldness has set in; and now, except for my mother's occasional visits, I hardly ever see them. I don't know why; there seems to be nothing there for me except pain. They would like me to be close, but I can't handle it.

After a distinguished career as an art major in college, Sarah decided to try her luck in the great world of creative media. She worked in television awhile, then at a family magazine that was inserted as a supplement to the Sunday newspapers of middle-sized cities nation-wide. When she grew discouraged at the thought that her work was appearing anonymously in one or another Springfield, she left the magazine to find something more expressive of her individuality. But all she could locate was a job in an advertising agency. Sarah was learning the unpleasant truth that this world is full of brilliant young women like herself, and that the path to advancement is by and large open only to those who are both rapacious of their fellows and sexually complaisant to the men in command. This discovery was a great blow to Sarah, who until then had expected that her gifts alone would act as a lodestar, drawing recognition and reward her way. To learn that she was not complete in herself was crushing. A certain integrity prevented her from adapting to the ways of mundane success; at the same time, however, a kind of quiet despair set in, which she experienced as a depletion of what had always seemed to her an endless fount of creativity.

Sarah felt hemmed in. Her inward horizon was narrowing while her outward prospects had shrunk to a narrow cubicle in an advertising agency. When she gazed out the window all Sarah could see were other young women engaged in similar work in the glass box across the street; and when she looked down at her desk, all she could see was the fantasy image of fulfilled, exuberant young femininity she was helping to engineer for a cigarette ad. There was a beautiful and exotic tropical tree in the lobby of the agency. One day it was gone, and Sarah noticed how the room had been architecturally crafted to contain a well for the placement of just such a tree, one that would maximally enhance its wild and lush character. The next day another gorgeous tree had been put in its place.

So she quit, and tried love. She had a trust fund from her father and doles under the table sufficient to keep her from invading it. After a series of desultory and/or excruciatingly painful relationships, Sarah met a professor of established family, a man much older than she and a world authority on Romance languages. Despite, or perhaps because, of the fact that he reminded her of Mr. Casaubon, the desiccated pedant of *Middlemarch*, Sarah decided to turn all her charms to the end of marrying him. By this time she wanted nothing so much as the security of a genteel life that would allow her to circulate amiably among the intelligentsia of a large university; and her experience with sexuality made the prospect of a celibate marriage as reassuring as bodily rapture had once been enticing. When, however, this illusion faded, too, and her marriage turned to dust, empty formality, and eventually cold separation, Sarah began taking to her bed again, as she had not since the age of eighteen. And it was this turn of events that brought her to me.[11]

Kovel has done a fine job of reporting on Sarah's life and psychopathology until the time of her coming to see him, and he also does a fine job of reporting how Sarah related as a patient to him, or, in other words, her *transference*:

A session with Sarah seems like a week in the Arctic. There is winter in her soul, and a cold dry wind blows from the couch to my chair. If, as analyst, I must empty myself out to become a vessel for the reception of Sarah's desire, then in working with her I experience myself as empty, too, save for that wind.

I am writing of transference, for the description of that metaphor is a necessary recourse. Transference is known intersubjectively, with the analyst in the role of Other to the patient's self. It is what emerges once one listens long enough to allow desire to break down the screen of ordinary language into more elementary particles; and these particles serve to refract desire into the configuration specific to each individual. Sarah's transference is not the particulars of any utterance, nor in any remembrances. It is rather, as Freud described, the past *repeated*, not holistically or exactly, but as evoked by the conditions of the present, i.e., the analytic relationship. When Sarah looks straight through me at the beginning and end of a session; when her voice takes on the quality of a listless monotone, so different from its usual musicality; when my ostensibly helpful interventions meet with scorn and derision; when I feel myself so often alone in the room or talking to a masked dummy; when Sarah goes to sleep or falls silent for twenty minutes at a time; or when, in general, she talks *at* me, as though I were a thing, or at best a mirror to her, and not *to* me, the way one does to another person, then transference is happening to us.

Transference is layered, and what we are observing here is

only the surface of Sarah's Other, that which is immediately behind the socially presented self. It is the first inner line of subjectivity and the contour of Sarah's defensive organization, protecting her from the more malign, murderous, deeper Other, which we have reconstructed as a composite of mother's invading phallus and Sarah's own ravening condition of emptiness. And to her eyes the cold hollowness is also a defense for me, a means of keeping me away from the malignity inside her lest I, too, upon whom she is coming to depend, succumb to it. (pp. 105-106)

Kovel's further commentary in the rest of "Rich Girl" essentially points out his diagnosis—of "narcissistic personality"—and his contention that to suffer from a narcissistic personality is to suffer from a life led in late-capitalistic society. In beginning my own commentary to "Rich Girl" I originally wrote: "though I agree with his diagnosis (equivalent to that of 'social E5' and appreciate his comment to the effect that 'pathological narcissism is a leading candidate for the archetype emotional disorder of late capitalism,' I don't see that his brand of Marxist Freudianism helps his patients better than classic psychoanalysis (except at the hands of those whose ripeness and wisdom is a blessing whatever the medium)."

In Sarah's case, I missed a therapeutic intent by Kovel of re-connecting his schizoid patient with the life of interpersonal feelings. Though Dr. Brisket had succeeded many years ago in bringing Sarah to experience and express her rage toward her invasive-possessive ("phallic") mother, this had been only a brief explosion, and I was under the impression that by allowing Sarah to sink back into emotional disconnection and failing to support the integration of her childhood anger into her adult psyche, Kovel had been of little help.

Deeming Kovel's chapter a case of therapeutic failure, and wishing to append a document reflecting therapeutic success, I contemplated the inclusion of one case in Mira Rothenberg's *Children with Emerald Eyes*. Her remarkable results in the cure of the autistic child would serve to emphasize the relational aspect of psychotherapy—without which the usefulness of theory and technique is very limited; and would expose the sterility of this kind of intellectual insight, that in psychoanalysis often becomes a substitute for the wisdom of transformation. Yet, to my great satisfaction,

I discovered that I was wrong about Kovel's failure. Once more I picked up his book (as I turned my attention to the writing of the preface to his case) and, scanning its pages, I discovered (toward the end) a chapter that I never read and had not even noticed: "The Mending of Sarah."

Here Kovel continues what we now see was only an incomplete narrative, and shares with us a glimpse of the breakthrough that prompted him to write his book on the need to combine psychoanalysis with "Marxist praxis." What he theorizes as Marxist practice, however, I would simply call honest and compassionate human engagement. I quote him again:

> "I had another dream. You were in it and you had one breast in the middle of your stomach. I don't remember the rest of the dream, but it left me feeling low."
>
> "Low?"
>
> "I don't know why. You were so deformed ... pathetic. I hardly ever feel sorry for you but I did a little, in the dream. I don't now. I was just thinking how you would interpret this dream."
>
> "You want to save me the trouble?"
>
> "No, it's just such a bore. Why should I tell you what the dream means? You'll just make some intellectual game of it, then we'll talk some more — or, rather, I'll talk into a vacuum — and then the session will be over. I think of the time spent here, drifting, floating, without any sense of direction ... then those awful words of yours, 'We have to stop.' Why do we have to stop? This is where I want to be even if I hate it. Why stop? If you cared, you'd extend the session. So what if I don't make use of it. I pay for it, don't I? So I can pay you some more and stay some more, no? No. What's wrong with it? My husband's policy doesn't care. He gets nice insurance benefits so we can get shrunk. I think they figure it keeps us quiet, makes us better citizens. I bet that pisses you off, you with your socialist ideas. Well, it's true. We're all parasites. You feed off me, I feed off him, he feeds off his family just as I did off mine, and our families feed off the people from whom they get their dough in the first place. Back to you again, Doctor. So if we're all parasites, why not enjoy it?"
>
> "Sucking off my one breast, right over my stomach."

"Which is halfway down to your crotch. This week, I can see, is going to be devoted to the penis, just as last week was to the breast."

"Your dream is trying to draw an equivalence between them, saying that I have both ... and neither. And the same goes for your image of yourself."

"What am I supposed to do with that? What good is it to me?"

"You know, I just imagined then that I did have a breast and that I tried to feed you with it, and you bit it, real hard. Nothing is good enough for you because you hate yourself so badly."

"I never believed my mother, no matter how hard she tried. And with Alan it was the same way. He was always doting on me, before and after the marriage. He adored me, gave me everything, but nothing was good enough. So we soured on each other. With him, I think it was my fault. But my mother was bad."

"Yet you recall nothing except her excessive devotion. Was the excessiveness the badness itself, the fact you each had nowhere to go?"

"Simply being close to someone is intolerable. Yet I can't bear being alone. Closeness is worse. I'd rather have roaches crawling on my belly or claw my body to ribbons. So good to look at, so rotten inside. No one is to touch me ...."

"You are silent so long."

"I remembered something else about mother. The 'touching' brought it back. She gave me enemas. Not too many but I recall them well now. She hated my insides. Assaulted me, too ... like with a big prick. To be trapped with her ... and now with you."

"You have to present yourself as hideous to keep me away. Yet you keep closed, holding back, as you must have with her, trying to get me to intervene. And when I do you treat it as though it were an enema to be expelled."

"That's the way I feel about what you just said. Except it's like forcing shit up inside me. Well, I won't give in. I'll stay here forever or until you kick me out. The trouble with this analysis is that it's too real. What happens here is just like what went on with Mother. It only reconfirms my suspicions and self-loathing. For me there are no metaphors."

"I think you would like to be close. You think, though, that this means yielding to me, and fear that I would penetrate and rape you if you did. And that would mean your dissolution."

"Why must you always criticize me? Never anything good to say to me."

"I don't know that you can accept anything good I have to say. Never once have you told me that anything good was happening here."

"Well, why should I? You want me to be honest, and that's how I honestly feel. Anyhow, you're criticizing me again."

"But here's how I honestly feel. I do try to make some kind of emotional contact with you, to touch you somehow, but I despair sometimes of ever getting through."

For the first time in the several years I had been working with her something softer crept into Sarah's voice.

"Please don't feel too bad. I don't want you to give up on me. You're all I have right now."

Appropriation

It would be fatuous to claim that this moment constituted a "breakthrough" for Sarah. I don't believe in the breakthrough concept, which seems to me to cheapen immeasurably the complexities of human discourse. But there was a change in Sarah — or, rather, us — after this session, so that it was impossible to think so hopelessly about her as before. We both knew that she would somehow "make it" without knowing exactly what "making it" meant. One thing it must have meant was that Sarah seemed to be a different person to me. I found myself unable to apply the diagnostic appellation "narcissistic character" to her afterwards, although it had seemed exceedingly lucid beforehand by all the canons of psychoanalytic reasoning. And this was perfectly reasonable, since one defines a narcissistic character by the type of relationship formed in analysis, and that relationship had in fact changed decisively from this moment forwards.

But if we can diagnose people by the type of relationship they form to others — and this, it seems to me, is a much sounder way of understanding them than by the dissection of a conjured-up mental essence — then it follows from this example that all diagnoses are forever provisional and will remain so until all historical possibilities are exhausted. If anyone seemed stubborn and intransigent, it was Sarah; month after month she proved herself a fixed, cold, "narcissistic character," and then, quite swiftly and effortlessly, became something else — without, to be sure, ceasing to be Sarah. So a diagnosis is like a negative piece of history. It is not an entity fixed in space and time but a piece of history waiting to happen. Lest we get carried away on a wave of therapeutic optimism, we should recall that most history does not happen, and what happens often turns out wrong.

But what happened to Sarah and me was historical. After a long and obdurate struggle, during which we behaved like two enemy states balefully watching each other across a swathe of contested territory, we began to get along. And what had made it possible was a twofold motion that can be understood only as the consummation of the protracted and agonizing praxis that went before it: my opening myself to her by confessing my frustration; and Sarah's forgiveness of me for it. And this had to be spoken to be made explicit.

There is no reducing this event or analyzing it away. It is totality; and it happens, after which a new historical totality arises. It could not have happened without my frustration to confess, and this could not have happened without months of beating my head against her narcissistic carapace. Beforehand, Sarah and I are the narcissistic pair: strangers to each other. In the real event, a kind of contact occurs; we are each different and remain so afterwards because this event henceforth reacts with everything within and between us. I do not think we can contain this totality in the notion of "insight," although the kind of subjective enlightenment called insight is one of its concurrences; and I do not think we can account for it in terms of the past, by claiming, for example, that I provided her with "good mothering," though it must have been the case that her mother, larded with complacency and self-righteousness, could never have admitted to any human weakness, and that this quality in her contributed to Sarah's own inaccessibility. No, all these matters are real enough but none accounts for the decisiveness of my opening myself to her when I did, and her forgiveness. Sarah cannot be mended by any number of analytically correct insights: something definite and real has to happen between us (although it has to happen in a psychoanalytic way). If "insight" is the crux of psychoanalytic work, then it must be a material event, not just the play of ideas. Psychoanalysis is not a matter of breaking something down "analytically" into component parts the way a chemist approaches a problematic substance. Rather, it is the finding of differentiation within a totality without losing the sense of that totality, which always includes the individual's relation to history. What is differentiated is not lost but finds a new relation of individuation to the totality of which it remains an element. In other words, individuation is predicated upon a point of real contact being established within the analytic situation. There has to be such a point — which for Sarah is constituted as forgiveness — if change is to occur. Only then could her proud heart yield.

Weakness is the great danger for narcissism. If the narcissist is to grow, she/he must forgive not sin but weakness. At its root, forgiveness means the renunciation of hatred toward some object; and since loculated hatred is a defining feature of neurosis, it may be that a moment of forgiveness goes beyond Sarah's case to be a decisively healing event. Each must forgive as she/he was bent, and no two moments are alike. Sarah's moment of forgiveness — which was also, I think, a "moment of truth" — was hers alone; to be more exact, hers and mine alone together, for she had to forgive me in order to forgive herself, to renew contact with the social world and to reconcile herself with her own history. I am confounded by the uniqueness of this moment, which was, after all, predicated upon years of very painstaking work between two very definite individuals ... confounded, too, by the contrast between this uniqueness and Marcuse's notion of "one-dimensionality", which describes a state of being that has passed beyond richly articulated individuality to become the atomized, homogenized, and shallow personages to whom we apply the term "narcissistic person of our time." Marcuse and those in his tracks were not wrong. Sarah was that kind of person, yet she became otherwise. A person is correctly seen as a member of a faceless mass because of lack of concrete relatedness to others in a historical project. It is not a matter of any in-dwelling essence or of an externally imposed condition, but of a real loss in consciously chosen praxis. From this standpoint Sarah was, in fact, a complete grain of sand, not because of any "ego defect" but because of the way she was locked into the total relationship between her and the world. Her lack of sociation, of participation and affirmation, was, I must admit, shocking to me. Yet for all the reality of her narcissistic desociation, it remained historically open to future praxis. Her analysis became a praxis of this kind, which restored through her forgiveness a real human tie and opened her onto history. Her power, we may say, was immanent and awaited its moment in such a praxis. And what is specific about the praxis called psychoanalysis is its austere and painstaking respect for and reconstruction of desire. It puts enough consciousness to bear on a neurotically trapped desire to create the condition for the forgiveness of desire's hatred. For this alone it must be credited for standing against the barbarism of its age.

I feel more hopeful about Sarah and psychoanalysis now. We should not delude ourselves, however. She still has to return to the entire reality for which coldness and a false self are nicely tuned mechanisms, and where aloneness has become a social imperative. Against that reality the gains of analysis may seem slender indeed.

Psychoanalysis does not do more, really, than allow a kind of "true speech" to take place. I do not mean this in a purely intellectual way. For speech to become true, it must connect itself with the material realities of life — the realities of the body, of desire, and of the actual relationship with the analyst. All this occurred in Sarah's moment of forgiveness, which was a precondition for the further development of true speech. Speech is but discourse, however; it is material and concerns objects, but it does not presume or include mastery of the object. And the therapy has not yet been invented that includes control of the object along with exploration of the subject. Given the alienation of subjectivity in capitalist society we can do no more at present than dream of such a therapy, which would, indeed, be better called some species of revolution.

But good therapy or analysis is not merely subjective, either. Because it is material, true speech is alive to historical possibility even if it does not conquer history. It is not passive contemplation, nor is it a matter of "adjusting" the person to fit the situation. This may be what the employer wants when he foots an insurance bill, but it does not have to be what he gets. The insurance policy that covers part of the treatment is itself part of the reality of the treatment and subject to confrontation by true speech. Sarah and I have begun discussing this usefully, too, along with the rest of the conditions of her life. To the extent that she can speak truly about them she is that much less alienated. The rest, however, is up to her, for the analysis is not located in her world but removed from it by the abstract exchanging power of the money that is her wage and my fee. This leads us somewhat closer to real historical alienation but cannot take us there, for the "there" must always be defined sensuously, and the only sensuous presentations with which we work are those of the analytic situation itself.

Am I influencing Sarah here, in violation of the canon of analytic mutuality? This is a tricky issue and cannot easily be put to rest. No doubt I do not lecture to her on my theory of society, nor do I take any definite position on what she should do with her life. But it would be utterly hypocritical to deny that I influence Sarah, even if this be done, so to speak, quietly. The "shock" that I felt over her lack of social participation was a real one; and even if I kept it to myself, it was bound to influence my response to her.

And my preoccupation with the question of whether therapy helps one adjust to a crazed world is bound to induce me to "steer" Sarah in one way or another, again, only if quietly and by selecting from her own responses rather than by forcing my own solutions upon her. Beyond this there lies the nest of values that are transmitted silently, whether through unconscious and habitual reactions of speech or through the choice of magazines for the waiting room. Indeed, wherever the issue of "reality" intrudes, whether it is the reality of the analytic setting itself or the reality to which her discourse refers, I cannot help influencing Sarah. When she mentions her attitudes toward, say, work, or refers to her mother in a way that discloses some element of social class, I must respond through the categories of my own experience.

Once we push it to this level, however, it is obvious that the question of influence in analysis takes on a different aspect, for it is not a matter of whether one influences patients but of how. Since it is impossible — not to mention undesirable — to eliminate influence from any human situation, the problem becomes one of specifying it and bringing it under conscious control. Recall that therapy is a ritual, a rite of passage from the family to something else. Specifying influence means the determination of what kind of family is to be left behind and what kind of "something else" is to be set ahead. Are we to eliminate the family and turn individuals over to the state, as Plato suggested long ago and as certain therapies do now, albeit in disguised fashion? Or are we to allow individuals to overcome what is archaic and murderously destructive in family existence, that which has been instilled in the grotesque family setting of capitalist society, and at the same time to retain the moment of intimacy vouchsafed by the consolatory function of that same family? And, similarly, do we hold out a vision of reality that is at least lucid, if not transcendent, to the individual who is in our care? Must we accept the value, numbly espoused by the great body of psychotherapists, that the world to which the patient returns is both transparent — and therefore not in need of demystification — and neutral, and hence implicitly benign? More, need we flaccidly continue to endorse the prevailing "health ethics" by means of which one abolishes the moral complexities of living in a world where the unfree labor of the many permits the thought (and therapy) of the few and joins in with the clear and softly fascistic narcissism of the so-called new age, that narcissism of "healthy sexual performance" and the "how-to-live" technical manuals? One thing only is clear, even if it has become something of a cliché: we always take a position, even when we do not take a position.

Analysis has always chosen. Here, then, is another choice, not so different perhaps from what many have done implicitly all along but refreshed with the waters of emancipatory socialism that have flowed alongside for more than a century. There should be, after all, a unity of theory and praxis. A praxis, therefore, that is alive to the contradictory complexities of family existence, that regards reality as unfree and in need of demystification, and that lives with moral subtleties, i.e., that shows a concern for human freedom in an unfree reality. Is not such a praxis both psychoanalytic and dialectical? And if dialectical, must it not strive toward universality? Must not psychoanalysis appropriate Marx if it is to be itself?

Psychoanalytic theory is the metadiscourse of desire. Now, it may be established that psychoanalytic practice is the praxis of desire, its discourse itself. Desire is what emerges out of its historically material setting, the analytic situation. By fixing the time and opening ourselves up to the patient, we create a sensuous reality in which time becomes unbound and desire flows like maple sap in early spring. Desire is that with which we "work." Through our relationship together we find words for the brute things of existence and so arrive asymptotically at a true speech, or at least a truer one. And in so doing — if we do it well — we undo something too — that ancient lesion set going when capital severed production from the home and left the one to grow cold and the other to fester.

I think I was wrong before: there is love in our work, and something to be guarded in dark times. It is not trivial to open a person somewhat further onto history. I have grown more content with incremental and nonabsolute gains. Put dialectically, one deals with determinate negations. Each little bit helps and leads somewhere. The real good of the world can occur silently and inhere in countless small advances. Each one, as Blake would have it, is a particle of infinity and eternity. (pp. 219-227)

I always appreciated the art with which the narrator in the *Arabian Nights* and other Eastern books inserts literary jewels in the necklace of his narration—an art in which coherence doesn't turn into the compulsion to make everything explicitly relevant to the theme. How could I then resist the pleasure of granting Kovel the occasion to share his vision of a Marxist psychoanalysis? His inspiration, undoubtedly, is the elaboration of his experience as a therapist who understands the difference between the mere talking and the participation in an active encounter, and we may conjecture (through the present chapter) that the case of Sarah was the most decisive, and because it is this text which explains the title of his book: *The Age of Desire*. Sarah, after all, is one cut off from desiring, and her coming out of the neurotic limbo may be broadly spoken of as a return to desiring; therefore, it is appropriate of Kovel to say, as a psychoanalyst: "Desire is that with which we work."

From here Kovel goes on to say that "Psychoanalytic theory is the meta discourses of desire," and that "Psychoanalytic practice is the praxis of desire." Yet, the love of life, self and others that are intrinsic to mental health are so radically different from the deficiency motivation of neurotic needs that in *Character and Neurosis* I have proposed a distinction between eros and libido—love and desire.[12] In line with that, I would prefer to speak of a "praxis of love" along with a "theory of libido."

RECONSIDERING A SECRET PACT WITH THE DEVIL

Pepita is a self-preservation E5. She attended a workshop of mine in which she reported (after a therapeutic exercise with a group companion) a vague but scary intuition of carrying a monster inside her. Because she had scarcely opened her mouth during the group sessions and I felt that I had given her insufficient personal attention, and also because a skill-fully conducted gestalt session might afford the best opportunity for fol-lowing up on her exploration of the "monster within," I approached the group of three (in which she was about to be assisted by her peers), and took over for most of the session below.

Pepita: I feel scared. Last night I was in a hammock and I thought I would stay there during the whole night, and I was very cold but I didn't mind; and suddenly the dogs started to pass by, and I started feeling afraid, panic rather, and I started to tremble, and then one of the dogs started to run around me and bark, and I was even too scared to leave, because I didn't know how big the dog was. So I stayed there without moving for about three hours; I don't know how long it was.

Claudio: And what do you feel as you are telling this?

P: This is something that happens to me often: I become tense, and inside I don't feel a thing, I abandon myself.

C: Okay, and are you feeling like that now?

P: Not now; what I feel now is what is happening to me: I cannot connect to the monster, nor to anything.

C: Okay, I would like you now to exaggerate that attitude of recoiling as you were describing from yesterday. Can you do that?

P: Yes.

C: So, become paralyzed.

P: Uh huh.

C: So, you don't feel a thing?

P: No.

C: You seem to be turning into a stone.

P: Uh huh. I don't even want to breathe.

C: Now continue speaking as if you were a stone. Petrified. Describe your-self as this stony being. What it is like that you want to be like that?

P: I don't want to move, there is a lot of pain too. It pains me to move.

C: You truly imagine that moving would cause you pain? What about now?

P: No, I don't know. I don't know what is going on inside.

C: So there is nothing going on. Okay, so we have the stone and we have the monster. If you could be between these extremes you would be perfect, you would be human. If there would be something between the two, or if you had both alternatives. So let us see whether it is possible to bring these two extremes together somehow. What could that be like. How can the monster and the stone relate?

P: I believe that I am neither of them. If I look with detachment, I am not the monster and I am not the catatonic person, either, all the time.

C: Not catatonic, but isn't it that you don't have the freedom to do what is appropriate in the situation?

P: Yes, I don't feel free.

C: You don't feel free.

P: I was saying last night, after the exercise, that I felt that the monster had me trapped, and I told my partner a fantasy: when I was seven years old I made love to the devil, and I made a pact with the devil to only be loyal to him, to only give myself to him.

C: And what is the connection with that pact? Is it that you identify the devil with the monster?

P: Yes.

C: What do you think of that pact, according to which you have been living [it seems]? Is it valid for you still? Do you want to continue to abide by this pact?

P: No.

C: Then I think it would be important to reconsider the matter.

P: I think that I am not living in any way. That is to say, I am something that doesn't really exist. And I want to begin to say what I want. [*Birds begin to sing beautifully at this moment.*]

C: So, you want to be human. You want to liberate yourself from the devil, be free from the devil so you can be yourself?

P: Yes, yes.

C: Well, I think you need to have a conversation with the devil. Imagine that he is here. He is always here.

P: "I don't want to continue serving you. I want you to teach me ... "

C: Careful! It is not necessary that you ask anything of him. Do you want to maintain this relationship? Do you want to be a disciple of the devil now? You have to choose between two alternatives, and I think it is more likely that you want to be independent, and you were conveying that you want your independence.

P: Well, I don't know whether I want to let go. I don't know if I want him to leave.

C: Ah, this is interesting. You have to become clear first, then, as to whether you want to let go or not, or whether there is an alternative, and the devil might be of help in a different way. Is there any other alternative?

P: To tell him that I don't want him. "Leave me free, so I can be and I can do what I want to do!"

C: [*playing the devil*] "Yes, I won't give you anything but your own creativity and your own reason ... what you have ... what is yours." Now ask the devil to teach you something.

P: "For my sake, yes, let me be, let me exist, I ..."

Participant intervenes and says: Will you be able to defend yourself alone?

C: Don't you need a strong protector?

P: Yes, yes. I thought about that last night; that the devil was my security. I even thought: the devil is here, near to me, so the dogs will not bite me.

C: Yes, he is your customary protector. I think it will be very advisable that you take a step toward independence, and find another protector. Or, get used to an alternative protector. There are people who can relate to God through fantasy, just like you did to the devil; and it is not just fantasy, because fantasy is a means of contact with something that is beyond, and it works. But I don't know what the best image may be for you. Anybody who has existed, anybody whose spirit you feel you could connect to.

P: The only time when I have felt a guidance was a fantasy of a man in a desert. He was walking in the sand, in armor.

C: That was the image of an inner guide to you?

P: Yes, it is always when I feel very bad. I turn on Ravel's "Bolero," and the image I get is of this man who walks along the desert.

C: It seems to me that this may be your own inner guidance manifesting this way, and you could seek further relation to it through this image. We all have the potential of contact with a transcendent principle that we might call an angel. Now, could it be that what you are calling a devil may be an angel, and yet you have misrepresented it?

P: I suddenly think that I chose the devil because I felt better protected.

C: There are people who, when they feel unprotected, seek a guardian angel. If you prefer the devil, what is the advantage to you?

P: More power.

C: Ah, he is more powerful—of course.

P: Yes, and he gives me much pleasure.

C: Ah, I see: so he permitted justified aggression.

P: Yes, he was my accomplice.

C: And could you imagine that God might also approve of your aggression? That God might also want that you liberate the animal within? Even bees, which are such low creatures and are socially more perfect than us, have a sting. Nature has given them that perfection.

P: I don't know.

C: So, it doesn't seem to you that heaven may allow you to get annoyed?

P: I feel that there is something that doesn't allow me. Right now, that you talk to me about God ...

C: It seems you have an objection? Is it that you cannot believe in God's power?

P: I feel that God abandoned me.

C: Abandoned you, left you?

P: Yes.

C: Ah! You felt like appealing to the devil because God didn't respond. And now, do you think that this was true, or could it have been your fantasy as a child?

P: No, I believe so.

C: You feel it is so?

P: Yes, I feel it. And I remember a scene, a specific scene. I used to go to the cemetery, as a child. I was visiting the dead, and suddenly when I moved to another country, I felt very unprotected. I have always felt in danger, but as a child I felt that God did protect me, and suddenly he ...

C: Let me see, I want to understand this better. When was the moment when you felt abandoned? And of what do you reproach God concretely? In what form wasn't he there for you? How did he fail?

P: Well, in my adolescence, from the age of nine, I felt very much alone, but very, very much alone. I always felt alone, but from the age of nine onward I had nobody; aside from loneliness, I didn't have anybody.

C: You digested this experience badly, and we have to do a little work involving the reliving of this loneliness, so you can once more reproach God, explicitly, getting angry with him ...

P: Just like that?

C: Instead of abandoning him, give him your accusation.

P: Concrete accusations?

C: Yes, as if you were a nine-year-old girl, telling him about your life.

289

P: [*to God*] "I think that you took my mother from me, and my father too. The little I had with them, you took it away, and you took away paradise, my place at the Bahamas where I had secret places, my hidden places where I could hide, where I went to feel good; and suddenly I am somewhere else ..."

C: He took away your nest ...

P: Yes. Everybody is different; the language, and everything ...

C: Imagine that God tells you: "Spoiled girl, I want to mobilize you a little bit, so you don't become so attached to things that they have to be always the same. I want to make you a woman, to throw you in the world ... "

P: No; he tells me, "Manage as you can." And it is as if God remained in the Bahamas.

C: And God tells you: "You don't want to understand me, I wanted you to not be so passive, to not be so much a little girl; it was now time to understand life better, not be so over-sensitive and spoiled."

P: Spoiled?

C: Yes, everything has to be like the Bahamas, with its nest and private places, which gave you a sense of over-protection.
P: Yes, I had my field, my very protected places, and I felt they were mine.

C: And wouldn't you say that you were too attached to those places?

P: Yes, very attached.

C: You know how the self-preservation 5 is over-attached to the nest, the sanctuary, the cave.

P: Well, as a child I was very much like that, but later as a grown-up, well, not my room, but the apartment, nobody could come into my apartment ...

C: Not even God.

P: No.

C: Specially not.

P: Yes; specially not.

C: There you were alone with your protector?

P: Yes, and I sought ... and that is what I was talking to S. about: I sought the assassin. Because I always dreamed about a murderer, all my life; and always when I came to my house I searched the closets and everywhere to see whether he (the murderer) wasn't hidden there. But there is an emotion that I feel ... that there is something that excites me.

C: Let me see, you were beginning to complain to God of his abandonment, and I would like you to come back to that, being more concerned with the feeling than the content. Get in touch with your reproach, with what you might have said before moving away from him; like, "I'll abandon you, God; I am not going to choose you."

P: That is my problem. I feel that I have never the right to reproach.

C: You leave, instead.

P: Yes, because he didn't have to give me anything, he just was.

C: Of course, God has no obligation.

P: *Ha, han*. So, when you tell me: "Complain to him," I find it difficult.

C: Yes, how could you complain before God; but the little girl that you were didn't feel that way. To leave is equivalent to complaining. To leave is a form of complaining, but for you it was more comfortable. So I think that you need to earn some freedom for yourself in that regard. If you can be more free to complain to God, you will have more freedom with everybody. You will find that alternative to turning into a stone or into a monster.

P: [*speaking to God*] "You were the only being there for whenever I wanted, and I came to the cemetery with you, and you were always there, and suddenly you left, suddenly you were not there anymore."

C: I think you have made a good beginning, and now what you need is to get the feeling out, and I leave you with Mario, who is very good at doing this. Let us see whether you can let your resentment to God come out.

Mario: Once more, begin to talk, and put movement into it; move your body.

P: "You were the only person there when I needed you; when I needed to be with somebody, you protected me, and suddenly you left, you disappeared, you didn't say why or when, or where I could find you, nothing; you didn't leave any signal. But I also think that it was myself who left."

M: That was your way of expressing your aggression. Now get more upright, and instead of moving away, move toward him, come toward him, as if you were falling toward him, come against him, put him there. Now open your eyes, and know that he is there, put God there, instead of withdrawing, which is your usual way. Tell him with your gaze and your body, with your teeth, with your mouth that you are there. Not away in your sanctuary ... Breathe, you know how to breathe. Breathe in, absorb strength. Feel the right to be there face to face.

P: [*moves*]

M: Breathe more — more presence, more air, more strength; feel it in your breast, in your arms, in your face, your jaw.

P: "You took away from me everything I had. You took the only thing I had."

M: What did you have, without fear?

P: "I want to kill you!"

M: Let it out.

P: "I want to kill you!"

M: [Say it] to him ... forward ... to him ...

P: "Why did you leave me, why did you abandon me?"

M: Breathe ...

[*She breathes heavily, then moans.*]

M: Now with all your strength. Feel it.

P: "You took away my space, you took away my force!" My hands are full of electricity.

M: Former violence. Don't paralyze yourself, don't let fear paralyze you. Move.

P: "You took away all my energy, all my strength, everything, my person! I don't know where I am."

M: You are here, you are in your body.

P: No, no, I don't know where I am.

P: You irritate me. I don't know where you are.

[*She makes noises. Spits.*]

M: Here you are spitting.

P: "Son of a bitch. You ... why did you take everything away? Why did you take away from me where I am, and my body, my space, my energy. I don't know where I am. You son of a bitch."

M: Come back to childhood. There you are before him. Breathing. In your body. Bring your body, your awareness. An angry body, a violent body.

[*She screams furiously, madly.*]

M: With your pelvis too, with your teeth. Good.

[*continues screaming*]

M: That is good, with all your body, your pelvis, your breast.

P: "Son of a bitch. Come. I am here you son of a bitch. I am fed up with you."

M: [*coaching her*] "And here I am ... Complete ..."

P: [*She moans.*] ... "You hide. You always hide. You go away. Where are you hiding! I will find you, anywhere, in my body. And I will abuse you in every possible way, so you come back. You come back somewhere in my body."

[*She screams, spits, and pounds.*]

P: "I want to rape you, kill you!" [*very loud*]. But I always feel that he abandons me. Suddenly disappears, and I am left without energy.

M: It is you who leaves. See what more you need.
[*She makes a gesture of knifing him, and tearing him up, persecuting him where he hides.*]

M: Let your monster out and face him. Kill him. There he is. Seek him. Kill him.

P: "I am going to find you."

M: You found him, here he is.

P: "I am going to find you, and I will kill you! I don't love you! I hate you! I will kill you!"

M: Take some time to catch up with your breath, and tell us, what do you see before you?

P: It is all torn up, but no blood. It is green.

M: Is there something that you want to do, still? Something more in order to empty yourself? Any rage left in you? Any revenge?

P: Yes, I want to say that I want to live.

M: Say it. Do you feel that you got enough of your anger out? Is that part of you satisfied?

P: No, but I feel empty, as if it is gone.

M: Okay, stay with the emptiness ... in contact with your emptiness ... this space that is left.

P: "I needed you without knowing that it was you. I don't know whether I can follow you, but I am open to attempt it. I want you to take care of me; that you be there when I am afraid."

Other companion, playing God: "I am always present. You only need to look to find me."

P: "But I need your help to become stronger, because I don't feel strong."

Companion: "You don't have to be strong, you are strong enough; you only believed you are not."

As seen, I left Pepita at the point when it seemed that what was missing was mostly additional catharsis, and I trusted that this could be carried out by her peers.

Pepita was thrust into the big world and then she felt lost. How is one not to feel lost in a world without a place of safety? And how is she not to lose herself in a world where she has to be on guard? She illustrates the characteristic fragility of the self-preservation E5, a neighbor to the avoidant E6 who shares with her an extreme difficulty in the expression of anger.

The theme at the beginning of the session, when she is scared of barking dogs, suggests to me that her half-paralyzed way of being is mostly a reaction in the face of such aggression as is part of an adult's environment.

Of course, the uncommon feature of this life history is the seeking refuge in the devil. In her imagination the devil can be a strong protector that compensates for her frailty and impotence in face of the world. The story of a pact with the devil—a pact that was real and lay nearly forgotten in her mind as a purely fictitious event—may be taken as the expression of the fact that, out of despair, she chose destructiveness. She cannot express aggression with her body, but her mind has accepted its intent.

In view of this, of course, it seems paramount that she reowned her ability to get angry; and because getting angry at God seemed to be the utmost taboo for her, it seemed important to exorcise her turning away from heaven in her childhood. Moreover, this was important in view of the fact that her greatest pain—that of abandonment by God—seemed to be sustained by her turning away from the divine—itself the outcome of her inability to experience conscious anger in face of her early frustration.

It is striking how E5 takes revenge by severing contact; like killing the other, but in a bloodless way. It is particularly significant that even when she kills God in an apparently "bloody" way, Pepita finds that there is no blood there; not even the color red is there, but green.

6

ENNEATYPE 6

With E6, more than in the other enneatypes, it is more difficult to speak of a single character. To begin with, there is the counterphobic variety in which the visible character could hardly be called "fearful." In this case, the individual has learned to defend himself or herself in the face of paranoid fantasies through intimidation, in such a way that aggression and fear come to constitute a vicious circle. The more disturbed instances of this counterphobic and pugnacious variety of the suspicious disposition are diagnosed today as instances of "paranoid personality disturbance" according to the DSM-IV. (See cartoon by Gahan Wilson, next page.)

Yet, in contrast to this eminently "strong" and overtly aggressive character stands that variety of the suspicious disposition in which fear manifests directly as a weakness (as is the case in the dependent and the avoidant personalities in DSM-IV). Such expression of cowardliness is caricatured by Feiffer in his cartoon of a woman at the edge of a dark cleft in the ground. In the first scene she says: "I can't"; in the second, she turns around saying, "I won't"; in the third, once more she faces the abyss and tells herself, "I must"; the next caption reads, "I'll die, if I try"; while in the following, her body faces one way and her face the other, as she tells herself, "I'll die if I don't try"; after this we see her preparing to jump as she says, "I will!"; then, arriving on the farthest side, she exultantly proffers, "I did." In the final scene, however, it is not the cleft that is painted black, but the adjoining terrain, on which she stands as she tortures herself with, "What have I done?"

In addition to the counterphobic sexual subtype and the insecure self-preservation subtype of E6, the theory presented by Ichazo acknowledged a social subtype. In this case it is not fear that is turned into an opposite (as in the counterphobia of the sexual subtype), but doubting. The person in this case is either too sure of things, too intolerant of ambiguity, too much of a true-believer in this or that, i.e., a fanatic; or else too concerned with making sure through an obsessive reliance on reason and precision. A caricature of this obsessive-like subtype is Dr. Strangelove, whose one-sided devotion to science amounts to unconscious brutality.

Whether fear or doubt are conscious and apparent to an outside observer or not, they are present in the E6 person's inner life. Terror prompts Macbeth's murderous initiatives (after he has killed his predecessor), just as anxiety about not knowing what to do or how to live drives people to become "true-believers" in this or that ideology. Regardless of whether the style is combative, rigid or insecure, the core motivation of the E6 character is anxiety — or rather, escaping from it.

Some escape this anxiety through seeking the security of protection and become dependent on others; not trusting themselves enough, they feel alone and incapable without outside support. In a world of danger, they seek alliances, and for this they endeavor to be, not inimical but friendly, trustworthy and supportive — as allies are supposed to be. The taboo on aggression that results from the needs of dependency weakens them in the face of aggression, and contributes to their insecurity and also to their need for external support.

Yet the vicious circle and interdependent origination of fear and aggression is as true in the insecure as in the violent paranoid style — the psychological situation aptly described by Quino's caricature of a "rat-man" who, in his analysis, reports a dream reflecting a cat-identity. (See a variation by Draco which follows on the next page.)

While anxiety, in a counterphobic, is allayed by skill and readiness in attack, another variety of E6 seeks to soothe anxiety through protection; and in the third (social) subtype of E6 (who lacks trust either in self or another), abstract reason or ideology are relied upon as an impersonal frame of reference. While some shy away from danger and others see their greater safety in strength, and flee forward rather than backwards (as if their assumption were "there is no better defense than attacking"), those in this

third category are neither too shy nor too bold, but rigid, obsessive and cold.

Since the psychoanalytic theory of neurosis most widely in vogue is that of neurotic behavior being anxiety-motivated, we may say that, on the whole, there is nobody to whom psychoanalytic interpretation is more appropriate than to an E6. I take the Freudian "id" — a sort of monster in the basement, incompatible with civilization — as a 6 construct. Just as for nobody is the experience of an accusing super-ego so much in the foreground as for the E6; so nobody can identify better than an E6 with the Oedipal child who hates his father and wants his mother for himself; and nobody so much fears or has succumbed to castration. Freud's formulations, of course, were theories based on personal introspection and self-analysis, and Freud was not only a genius but a counterphobic, for whom it was particularly therapeutic to discover his own rivalry with his father and his fear of castration.

In *Character and Neurosis: An Integrative View* I have claimed that the core of E6 — its fixation, in other words — is self-accusation.[1] Self-accusation and guilt are two faces of the same coin, of course. According to the subtype, self-accusation or accusation of others may be in the foreground — and they are dynamically linked through the mechanisms of projection and identification with the aggressor. Basic extensions of these are distrust of others and insecurity. Whichever is on the surface (distrust of others and self-accusation or guilt and insecurity), however, both apply: E6 finds it difficult to trust the world, to trust authority, to trust his or her senses, to trust his judgement and ability to discern what he needs to do moment after moment.

The more distrust, the more need to make up for it through reliable authority — the greater the need for an authority admirable enough to be trusted. This need may lead to the creation of idols, a tendency to hero-worship, a construction of personal dreams (as in Don Quixote, who does not follow a person or a party, but the knight errant in his imagination), other supports, points of reference or guides.

Because the E6 psyche is one in which the issue of authority is prominent we may call it an authoritarian character. Though only a component in what psychological literature calls the authoritarian personality (and some E6 people are low scores in the questionnarie designed for its measurement), I would say that it was mainly E6 people who contributed to the statisical results obtained with this test (the F-scale); and E6 people, likewise, whom the famous research team had in mind in formulating the classic authoritarian personality syndrome of: authoritarian aggression, authoritarian submission, superstition and stereotype, rigid super-ego, and alienated id.

Whether the surface behavior towards authority be an excessive obedience to certain individuals, an excessive orientation to rules or a passion to be in command, there is typically ambivalence to authority — a coexistence of impulses to submit and to rebel. This, in turn, is only a particular expression of a broader trait of ambivalence that is inseparable from the experience of doubting and the concomitant anxiety. An exception to this overt ambivalence may be — as was pointed out — the social subtype in which an intolerance to ambiguity and an obsessive search for precision and adherence to norms may cover it up.

Just as the extreme of the E5 behavior pattern is to be seen in catatonic psychosis, the extreme of E6 is conveyed by paranoid psychotic conditions. The two ingredients in these are delusions of persecution and of grandiosity, which may also be regarded as complementary conditions: hostile self-aggrandizement breeds insecurity, which, in turn, supports compensatory grandiosity. In paranoid character, too, a sense of danger and vulnerability coexists with manifest or unconscious grandiosity. Here, a need to feel powerful and great is a compensation for the sense of powerlessness and vulnerability; and it is toward the satisfaction of this need that a powerful other — a powerful father figure — becomes important.

In *Ennea-type Structures* I caricatured the E6 psyche as that of a persecuted persecutor, for regardless of whether the persecution of others or the sense of being persecuted stands in the foreground, the two are interdependent.[2] In the insecure (self-preservation type), self-persecution is most ostensive, and the taboo in being aggressive toward others perpetuates an all-too-vulnerable position that sustains the need for protection. Yet, the "persecuted persecutor" concept applies to the case of the counterphobic as well, as was made clear from a consideration of Macbeth or the bull-dog cartoon already shown.

That the concept of the authoritarian personality arose from an attempt to understand German anti-Semitism was no coincidence, since E6 has been particularly prominent in Germany. The situation in the late thirties and forties, in particular, involved a mass of people who were willing to follow a leader, and had a great desire to believe. E6 people have a tendency to believe those who use strong words, those who are "certain" of things, and those who speak in the name of high ideals. The problem for E6 is precisely that of choosing wrong authority. Instead of believing in the person who is right, they tend to believe in people who speak *as if* they were right, and who have the special gift of making themselves believed. They are easily seduced by mystification, by grandiosity; they are attracted by idols, all too idealistic, and gravitate toward the sublime. Both the coward and the counterphobic chide themselves for being frail persons, and hate their own weakness. They worship strength, attracted by the strength of others, and subordinate themselves to strength. The case of Don Quixote — who lives in a fantastical world in which he sees giants where there are only windmills — contains an important insight, showing how paranoia (seeing villains where there are none) serves grandiosity: many times in his adventure Don Quixote believes that he is carrying out good deeds, when actually he is only expressing his need to be a hero.

Perhaps the richest source of observations on E6 in the realm of fiction are those from Dostoyevsky — who, like Freud, harvested his data from his own experience. In his novels we find, in particular, variations on the weak-dependent husband and on the idealistic and ruthless fanatic; while in his treatment of Ivan Karamazov he deals not only with self-accusation, ambivalence and other traits, but with the Oedipal situation and parricide.

To complete this account with a literary illustration, I will take Raskolnikov — the central character of *Crime and Punishment* who is neither a weakling nor a fanatical obsessive, but a counterphobic — who may serve to point out how much the counterphobic may differ from the "paranoid" as it stands in DSM-IV.[3] There is neither jealousy nor concern about betrayal in Raskolnikov — and yet a paranoid-accusatory view of the whole world; and a violent response to this view is the theme of the book's argument. Early in the book Raskolnikov, for a moment, questions his implicit paranoid and accusatory disposition vis-à-vis the world:

> And what if I am wrong?" he cried suddenly after a moment's thought. "What if man is not really a scoundrel, man in general, I mean, the whole race of mankind — then all the rest is prejudice, simply artificial terrors ... (p. 24)

To read this novel is to be immersed, through empathy, in Raskolnikov's anxiety — a symptom, so intense, that makes him feverish and causes him to appear to his friends at the edge of madness.

We meet him walking slowly "as though in hesitation" after he has "successfully avoided his landlady on the staircase." We are told that each time he passed her kitchen, on the way to the street, he "had a sick frightened feeling, which made him scowl and feel ashamed" — for he was in debt. Dostoyevsky hastens to explain that this "was not because he was cowardly and abject, quite the contrary; but for some time past, he had been in an over-strained, irritable condition." He has become isolated and given up attending to practical matters. On reaching the street "he became acutely aware of his fears."

The source of Raskolnikov's anxiety is in a project that is forming in his mind. He despises himself for being frightened about something trivial when he is considering "a thing like that." Little by little we are given to understand what "that" is about. He has been thinking of Jack, the Giant Killer, lately. But will he be capable of that? And we follow him to the place of the crime that is taking shape in his fantasy. At this point, in his mind, it is not a crime so much as a test of courage and greatness: to kill the old money-lender who exploits his poverty is truly justified and trivial; and, if he were a great man he would not be so concerned with the opinion of the world.

At a time before the Russian revolution Dostoyevsky was describing a kind of fanatic that was to become common, yet there is no borrowed ideology in Raskolnikov; only a personal conviction of right and wrong that clashes with public opinion and sensitivity alike. He is not insensitive like a Dr. Strangelove. On the contrary, he is capable of love and is moved more by protectiveness than self-interest. We will see him give all his money away to a poor family, and fall in love with a prostitute who becomes to him the model of Christian virtue, in her sacrifice to support her mother. He is adamant about not wanting to accept the sacrifice of his sister — his mother wants her to marry a well-to-do gentleman so that Raskolnikov will be able to pursue his studies. Paradoxically, this criminal that Dostoyevsky presents to us can just as well be described as an intensely good and very idealistic young man. Just as the shy and avoidant E6 is too inclined to seek protection, the strong counterphobic is too paternalistic; too inclined to offer it.

Not only will Raskolnikov kill an old woman because he believes he should not be poor and that it is okay that he steals her money (nor is it just in view of his sense that her life is of no value); but also, he will kill her to prove his ability to rise above ordinary humanity and its prejudices.

At first Raskolnikov has only harbored fantasies of daring recklessness. Dostoyevsky explains, already on page 3: "in spite of the monologues in which he jeered at his own impotence and indecision, he had involuntarily come to regard this 'hideous' dream as an exploit to be attempted, although he still did not realize this himself."

And then we follow Raskolnikov on the way to a "rehearsal" of his project. Immediately after the visit to the old lady, we see him torn by the psychological conflict — for what part of him has regarded right, now seems loathsome. He thinks: "and how could such an atrocious thing come into my head, what filthy things my heart is capable of." In the insecurity of his self-loathing and his alternating perspective, we see the difference between a violent E6 and the psychopathic E8.

In the third chapter, Raskolnikov receives a letter from his mother concerning his sister's intended marriage. While he reads it, his face is wet with tears, but when he finishes, "his face was pale and distorted, and the bitter, wrathful and malignant smile was in his lips." When we next see him in the street, some passers-by take him to be drunk. He feels adamant about not letting his sister enter a marriage of convenience for his sake, and he asks himself how he will prevent it. He is keenly aware that he is living upon his mother and his sister, who are borrowing money to support him. He feels it is not the time "to suffer passively, worrying himself over unsolved questions." He must *do* something. And then, what had been a mere dream takes on a new meaning ...

As he walks along he sees a drunken young woman on a bench. A scene follows in which Raskolnikov intervenes so as to defend the girl before the advances of a fat dandy. He rages with moral indignation, just as he has raged before his mother's plan of marrying off his sister; and his protectiveness towards the unknown girl matches the one he has felt for his sister and also for Sonya, whose misery has forced her into prostitution. Though the mood is dramatic rather than comic, we are before the same syndrome familiar from Don Quixote, who makes the peasant Dulcinea into a princess in his imagination, and sets out to defend the innocent sex from the world's villains.

In chapter five Raskolnikov reports a dream of a man in a fury who is beating his horse to death. Raskolnikov next asks himself, "Can it be that I shall really take an axe, that I shall strike her on the head, split her skull open ... " He shakes like a leaf. His reason tells him one thing, his feeling another — and he tortures himself, just as much for hesitating as for persisting in his idea.

Chapter six gives us some antecedents on his acquaintance with the old woman and her half-sister, Lizaveta. We are made witnesses of a conversation between Raskolnikov and an officer in a bar, weeks before, in which Raskolnikov says, "I could kill the damned old woman and make off with her money, I assure you, without the faintest conscience-prick." He then pretended to be joking, but conjectures that "a hundred thousand good deeds could be done and helped, on that old woman's money." And he asks, "What do you think, would not one tiny crime be wiped out by thousands of good deeds?" To the officer's comment that while she does not deserve to live, still "there it is, it's nature," Raskolnikov replies: "but we have to correct and direct nature, and, but for that, we should drown in an ocean of prejudice. But for that, there would never have been a single great man. They talk of duty, conscience — I don't want to say anything against duty and conscience; — but the point is, what do we mean by them?"

Then comes the long description of the crime — complicated in that the arrival of the old woman's half-sister makes it a double crime. Raskolnikov had been very afraid in the presence of the old woman, but after the deed, and especially after the second unexpected murder, "fear gains more and more mastery over him. And loathing, which grew stronger every minute."

From then on in the novel, his persecution anxiety runs parallel to his temptation to give himself away, which in the end he does; and Dostoyevsky reflects on how the compulsion to confess serves the guilty one's thirst for attonement. And in atonement the book ends, when Raskolnikov is sent to prison, and we understand that his acceptance of responsibility and punishment turn him into a different man.

Dostoyevsky would return to the theme of transformation through atonement in his ultimate masterpiece *The Brothers Karamazov* — and we know how this reflected his own experience as a prisoner in Siberia. Yet the pugnacious Raskolnikov is more a projection of a sub-self in Dostoyevsky's mind than a reflection of his outer personality. Though an E6 and one with radical ideas, Dostoyevsky was not outwardly aggressive, but mild, patient and warm; and not expansive but withdrawn. It has been pointed out that instead of the sweeping landscapes of Tolstoy, Dostoyevsky's novels create an almost intolerable sense of confinement, and his biographer E.H. Carr points out that a statement by one of his characters might well be a motto to some of his works: "in a confined room even thought becomes confined."[4]

Dostoyevsky lacked playmates in his childhood, and even though he was brought up with six brothers and sisters in a three-room flat, his was an isolated family; he never developed ordinary social intercourse beyond the intimate relations of the family hearth. "In such relationships, when they were forced on him, Dostoyevsky throughout was "jealous, exacting, hypersensitive; he both gave and expected too much."

"A friend must be a brother or more" wrote Dostoyevsky, and Carr observes: "No lesser tie was tolerable to him." Carr also tells us that in all Dostoyevsky's dealings as a young man before Siberia, he was "pursued by the uneasy, nervous temperament which seated beneath his awkward and unprepossessing exterior. If we consider that, in addition, he was a hypochondriac and that 'he belonged to the unhappy race of men who perceive the depths of their folly even at the moment of committing it and whose remorse is almost simultaneous with the action to which it relates.' "

We recognize in Dostoyevsky the phobic and most explicitly guilt-ridden self-preservation variety of E6. His conception of love emphasized a willingness to suffer that has been ... masochistic, but also revealed much courage, just as the inhibition of violence had been the outcome of enormous self-control.

❦

Dostoyevsky's nonviolent courage is reminiscent of Gandhi's, another instance of a sweet and delicate E6 in whom nonaggression was an achievement rather than a simple inhibition. "A Soldier of non-violence," a biographer called Gandhi, who claimed the courage of being willing to die without killing, and indicated that violence was better than fleeing. "I would rather see India take up arms to defend herself than remaining a cowardly witness of its dishonor."[5] If in Dostoyevsky it is the warmth of brotherly love and self giving in the context of family and loyalty that are most striking, in Gandhi it is the sense of duty.

Gandhi as a child was very shy and withdrawn, and he recounts in his autobiography that his books and lessons were his only companions.[6] After school hours he ran back home because he could not bear to talk to anybody. When at the age of thirteen he was married to an assertively independent girl, it shamed and infuriated him that she showed no fear of the dark; whereas he could not bear to sleep in an unlighted room.

Then there was a striking change: shyness vanished when Gandhi dared to fight to serve his fellow-beings.

Early in adolescence, after doubting the existence of God, Gandhi decided to leave, for a later time, his metaphysical questions and turn to a certainty that "morality is the basis of things and ... truth the substance of all morality."

One event, more than anything else, contributed to turn Gandhi from a devoted and obedient son to a man of striking austerity. It happened at the time when his father was sick; when every evening, young Gandhi usually stayed by his father's bedside massaging his legs and reading to him. One evening, however, at a time when he was feeling bothered by the sacrifice expected of him, he allowed his brother to replace him, and returned earlier than usual to his own room and pregnant wife. He made love to her, and a knock was heard on the door: his father was dead.

A guilt-prone E6, Gandhi upbraided himself for having allowed himself to be "blinded by animal passion" and writes in his autobiography that this was a blot he was never able to efface or forget.

How hard Gandhi tried, we all know; though we may not remember that he came to be, indisputably, the most public figure in the world of his day.

RYCROFT'S "MISS Y."

Dr. Charles Berg, a contemporary of Freud, was the analyst of my analyst's analyst, and his account of a successful therapy in his book *Deep Analysis* would have surely constituted my first choice of a case report to illustrate the evolution of an E6 individual through psychotherapy if it were not for the fact that my memory of having read Berg's *Deep Analysis* in the 1950s was blurry enough that I was under the impression that the patient in it was a schizoid E5.[7]

My actual first choice of a case history illustrating some success in the treatment of an avoidant E6 was one of the forty-nine accounts of psychoanalytic and supportive/expressive psychotherapy that are the subject matter of Wallerstein's book *Forty-Two Lives in Treatment/Processes of Psychoanalysis and Expressive Psychotherapy*, identified there as that of the "English Professor."[8]

It is presented as the case of a compliant obsessive-compulsive suffering from phobic and anxiety attacks, and is discussed in a section of the book entitled "Varieties of the Transference Neurosis." It brings to our attention the dangers of a so-called *insoluble transference neurosis* "leading to a stalemated treatment in certain classes of passively dependent or masochistic individuals." The author points out how this has been well known to psychoanalytic literature since it was focused upon and given a name by Alexander and his co-workers, who precisely on account of it propose innovations in psychoanalysis. It is explained that some of the patients who are the subject of this book were treated in a way specially designed to not indulge in the patient's neurotic dependency need to avoid the risk of such stalemate, and the present report on "The English Professor" is noteworthy for the extent to which the issue is taken into account.

That the "English Professor" is not an E1 is also apparent from his "tremendous inhibition of affect and impulse," typical of E6 and most typical of its timid phobic variety. Also, "his willingness to suffer" that Wallerstein, et al., call masochistic, is clearly recognizable as an E6 phenomenon not shared by E1 (rather than being the "masochism" of E4, who suffers in order to attract love through pain, in the self-preservation E6 "masochism" is secondary to intra-punitiveness). The passion for warmth is another matter. The emphasis is in harmlessness. A person who cannot defend himself becomes "dependent" on a non-threatening environment and protection.

The results of five years of psychoanalysis and some more of psychoanalytic therapy were satisfactory to Wallerstein in that the patient achieved "full sexual development" and "orgastic potency," and even contracted marriage. They are less impressive when we consider the words of the patient who reflects that he has gained the ability to say to himself something like, "I am a law abiding citizen and if my bladder is full I have the right to excuse myself to you and go," and who also sees in retrospect that he had expected too much from psychoanalysis.

Since Dr. Wallerstein's publisher has not granted permission to quote the case I had originally selected to illustrate E6, I am choosing, instead, Rycroft's "Miss Y." — an illustration of the counterphobic variety of E6 in psychotherapy.

The *Handbook of Character Studies*, published by de Vries and Perzow in 1991, begins with Freud's more relevant papers, and samples of the writings of psychoanalysis from Abraham, Reich and Fenichel to Kernberg.[9] It ends with a case report by Charles Rycroft: "The Analysis of a Paranoid Personality" that spans twenty-six pages.[10] I quote in full the first half of Rycroft's report, which contains an interesting description of a near-psychotic sexual (counterphobic) E6.

I

Recently, on rereading my paper on the "Function of Words in Psycho-Analytical Treatment" (1958), I noticed for the first time that almost all my clinical examples were taken from one patient, a woman whom I had in analysis from 1948 to 1952. In this present paper I shall give some account of this patient and describe certain aspects of her analysis.

There are, of course, certain disadvantages in reporting a case six years after the end of treatment, but these will, I hope, be compensated for by my having in the meantime acquired sufficient distance to be able to present both her and my contribution to the analytical relationship with reasonable detachment. As Miss Y. was a person who tended to evoke very strong reactions in everyone who had dealings with her, the detachment given by the passage of time is perhaps of particular value in the present instance. I have, however, made no attempt to conceal my own emotional reactions, as I believe that by including them I shall give a truer account of the dynamics of the analytical process than I should were I to present myself as having been a detached observer throughout.

II

The story of Miss Y.'s analysis begins two years before she came to me for treatment. She was at that time in her midthirties, an unsuccessful actress living an insecure and Bohemian existence. Quite suddenly she became depressed and withdrew completely from her previously very sociable life. During her "breakdown," as she called it, she experienced various peculiar changes in her moods and perception of reality. These she observed and recorded, using them as the material for a self-analysis which she conducted for the next year. As her only guides she relied on the only two books on psychoanalysis she had ever read, Theodore Reik's *Ritual* (1946) and Wilhelm Reich's *Character Analysis* (1949). She also occasionally talked on the telephone with two doctors whom she had known when they were medical students and who both had shown a passing interest in psychoanalysis. On the basis of her introspective findings, and armed with what we should consider somewhat inadequate theoretical support, she undertook not only an independent self-analysis but also the construction of a new system of psychopathology. Unfortunately, she never put down on paper any definitive statement of her system, but during the first few months of her analysis with me I came to know it intimately. So far as I could see, it was entirely logical and self-consistent and, apart from its not being true, I could find only three flaws in it. First, it was based on only one case. Second, it attached no significance to any experiences after the age of three months. Third, it took no cognizance of guilt. In all other respects it conformed to the usual pattern of recognized psychopathological theories and took account of both internal and external reality, of stages of libidinal development, and of libidinal fixations and the transformation of infantile libidinal drives into nonsexual social and artistic activities. Her three stages of libidinal development were (1) uterine, in which the relation to the mother was mediated by auditory, tactile, and postural channels; (2) birth, which was a "traumatic" stage leading to "paranoid" anxieties particularly associated with visual and thermal sensations; and (3) oral, in which the relation to the mother was mediated by the mouth and all other bodily organs with the exception of the genitals. The phenomenon of love was associated with this third stage, and under ideal conditions of development played no further part in human relations after this stage was passed. This, to her mind, was her one really original contribution to psychoanalysis, the discovery that all love is "infantilistic," as she put it. In her view, really mature sexual relationships contained no trace of love, and in her own sexual relations forepleasure was only permissible as a regrettable concession to the immaturity from which her partners, all unfortunately unanalyzed, inevitably suffered. Sexual relations were, however, not purely sensual acts — sensuality was, indeed, in her view masturbatory — but were experiences of "transcendental harmony" produced by the interchange of electrical energy. It would, I think, be a mistake to dismiss these ideas of hers as nonsense. Once one has cut one's way through the semantic confusion centering round her use of the word *love*, one can see that she was struggling to formulate an insight about the qualitative difference between genital and pregenital love. Her theories had extensive ramifications, but for the moment I shall give only two other details. First, she held that all sublimations have their origin in some specific aspect of one or other of her three stages, music, for instance, being derived from the primary pleasure of listening to the pulsations of the umbilical cord. Second, she had discovered the existence of psychically real internal figures; these she called "effigies" for reasons which will become apparent later. Miss Y. had absolute conviction of the essential truth of her system, and this conviction had exactly the same bias as has ours in *our* analytical theories; her experiences during her own personal analysis.

After about a year Miss Y. came out of her depression and decided to have treatment with a psychoanalyst. She knew that analysts, like all other bourgeois professional people, charged exorbitant fees for their services, so she set to work to save money and to get a well-paid job acting, with a view to seeing an analyst during the middle of the day, when, she surmised, they probably have difficulty in filling their vacancies. After a year she had saved about £150 and had got a part for which she was paid £25 a week in a show that promised to have a long run. She then got into touch with one of the doctors I mentioned earlier, who referred her to me with a diagnosis of phobia.

Her conscious reason for seeking analytical treatment was not that she had realized she was seriously ill. On the contrary, she believed that she had much more to give analysis than analysis had to give her. The reasons she gave during the first few weeks of analysis were:

First, she wished to become a child analyst, believing that the insights she had obtained during her self-analysis would enable her to make original contributions to the theory and practice of child analysis.

Second, she intended to become physically immortal. She had discovered that physical illness and aging were caused by the "paranoia" engendered by a traumatizing and hostile infantile environment, and she therefore concluded that thorough analysis of her reactive sadism and conflicts would eliminate the otherwise inevitable tendency to decay and death. She rather reluctantly admitted her inability to carry out unaided the complete analysis necessary to ensure immortality, so she decided to enlist the help of a classically trained analyst, fully realizing, of course, that *his* limitations would have to be made good by what *she* taught *him*. Since the ultimate goal was physical immortality, she could afford to envisage an almost interminable analysis. However long it lasted, it would be short in comparison with the ultimate reward of life eternal — for analyst as well as herself. She had never encountered anyone who was prepared to take these ideas of hers seriously, but she did not herself consider them particularly outrageous or original. She thought she was merely drawing an obvious logical conclusion which conventional analysts, with typical bourgeois cowardice, had been too frightened to face. So far as I know, she was unacquainted with the notion of the death instinct; the pathogenic factor which she hoped to eliminate by complete analysis was the paranoia induced by the sadism of the infantile environment.

Third, she wished to be relieved of a pain she experienced during sexual intercourse. This pain was unilateral and occurred only with deep penetration. She had already been informed by a competent surgeon that it was indubitably of organic origin and that it could be relieved by a lower abdominal operation. She was not, however, prepared to accept this, the whole idea of surgery being anathema to her.

Miss Y. did not mention her ideas about physical immortality during her initial consultation, quite consciously withholding them until she felt I was fully committed to continuing her treatment. At the time I accepted the referring physician's opinion that she was a suitable case for psychoanalytical treatment without question. My first impressions of her were of her determination to have analysis, her tremendous tenseness, and her bewilderingly complex mode of speech, which last I shall describe in detail later.

III

Two details of the initial consultation proved later to have contributed significantly to the dynamics of the analytical relationship, even though at the time they passed unnoticed by me.

When we came to discuss fees she told me about the money she had saved and that she was at present earning £25 a week. I then asked her how long she expected the show to last and how much of the year she usually spent "resting," thereby using the common stage euphemism for "unemployed." She said perhaps six months a year, so I suggested we discuss fees on the assumption that she earned £12 not £25 a week. I had correctly guessed that £25 a week was considerably more than she was accustomed to earn, but I entirely failed to realize that I had confronted her with an attitude toward money which ran counter to all her preconceptions about professional people. She had assumed without question that analysts were ruthless in their pursuit of fees, and that I would fix hers without any regard to her circumstances. The fact that I enquired carefully into them and took account of them when deciding on the fee I should charge had, therefore, the effect of undercutting one of her most cherished grievances.

I became aware of another significant feature of the initial consultation when I found it necessary to investigate my own countertransference. I then realized that Miss Y. had very effectively dared me into undertaking her analysis. By presenting herself as a difficult case and as having made strenuous exertions to make treatment possible from her side, she had appealed both to my sporting instincts — a phrase, incidentally, she would have found highly offensive — and to that counterphobic tendency which makes one determined to undertake a task just because it has been presented as difficult. I learnt later that games of daring had been carried to hair-raising lengths in her childhood and that she had retained into adult life an exceptional capacity to accept physical risks. At one time she had earned her living in a circus riding on the pillion of the motor-cycle that circles the Wall of Death. By daring me in this way she evoked a determination to penetrate her

defenses which, in alliance with her own determination to be analyzed at whatever cost, helped to overcome her equally great
determination *not* to abandon any of her defenses. The importance of this lies in the fact that her analysis turned out to belong
to the not uncommon category which raises the question of why
the analyst commits himself to the treatment of a patient from
whom he cannot expect the usual economic reward.

IV

Miss Y. was small and slight, but her marked presence made her
appear taller than she was. She was strikingly good-looking,
though the effect was marred by her tense expression and posture.
She spoke in a low, harsh, or husky voice. Her clothes were either
untidy to the point of sluttishness — my receptionist nicknamed
her the Gypsy — or exotic to the point of being bizarre. She was
intensely interested in her effect on other people, but made no
attempt to appear smart or fashionable.

At first I often had considerable difficulty in understanding her
highly individual mode of speech, and I had therefore to analyze it
in some detail. It contained the following five peculiarities: (1) She
made her own choice of prefixes and suffixes, always, for instance,
saying "comatic," not "comatose." (2) She gave words private
meanings that were remote from and yet obviously somehow
related to their accepted meaning. "Comatic," for instance, meant
lethargic, intellectually lazy, unawakened. (3) She had a number of
favorite words which she used in unusual or old-fashioned senses.
One of these was "reactionary," which meant sensitive or respon-
sive. (4) She had invented new words and appropriated a number
of already existing words to signify various intrapsychic phenomena she had encountered during her self-analysis and for which she
had had no words in her pre-breakdown vocabulary. The most
striking example of this was the word *effigy* to describe an internal
object. (5) She preferred abstract to concrete modes of expression

and avoided metaphor, preferring to restrict her vocabulary to words which have lost all apparent connection with any concrete object or activity. This was the crucial disturbance, and its cause became clear in the light of her reactions to the use of metaphor by myself. It then became obvious that she had difficulty in distinguishing between the literal and metaphorical meanings of words, and between words and the concrete objects they signify. If, for instance, I used the phrase "getting something off one's chest," this evoked the sensation of something on her chest weighing her down, not the idea of unburdening herself. My use of this phrase was taken as a sadistic attack, a deliberate attempt to make her feel a weight on her chest. I am not sure to what extent this difficulty existed in her everyday life or how much it was exacerbated by regression during the analytical session.

She herself tried to maintain that the difficulties in verbal communication that sometimes arose between us were due to her American upbringing and that she was unfamiliar with idiomatic English. This was quite untrue, as for various reasons I insisted confidently from the beginning, and I later learned that all the significant figures in her childhood had been brought up in England and had all clung militantly to their English middle-class accents despite long residence abroad. The real reason for her conviction that she could not understand English and that I could not understand her expatriate speech was her unconscious belief that there had been an irreparable break in the channels of affective communication between herself and mother-figures which no words, not even those of her mother tongue, could ever bridge.

Although I became in time familiar with the idiosyncrasies of her speech and knew, for instance, that "reactionary men have no sense of structure" had nothing to do with politics but meant that sensitive men are incapable of lasting personal relationships, I deliberately refrained from making more than the minimum amount of accommodation to them for fear of becoming involved in a linguistic folie à deux which might make it harder for her to work through her hostility to the uncomprehending mother-imago. I am not altogether sure that I was right in adopting this policy.

Some of her neologisms were amusing, but quite unintentionally so. A lowerarchy was a hierarchy viewed from above — those of us who are not at the top of course usually view hierarchies from below. She once, again quite seriously, said: "Annoyed? I was paranoid." I have, of course, been describing an early stage in a schizoid thought disorder, the result of a regressive disturbance in symbolic thinking and of the confusion created by her attempt to master unaided the disordered perceptions of her breakdown. This thought disorder cleared up completely during the analysis. During the period of recovery she used to make up jokes based on metaphor being taken literally. Some of them were used as captions for a volume of humorous drawings made by a friend of hers.

In line with her belief in her capacity to analyze herself without external aid was her faith in her own untrained creative powers. At the age of ten she had decided to become the female Shakespeare; at the same age she also decided to become a ventriloquist. At seventeen she wrote a poem identical with one by Verlaine and a melody identical with one by Rachmaninov. At the age of thirty she had been told, so she said, by a ballet teacher that with a few weeks' practice she could reach the standard of a ballerina. She also claimed telepathic powers. The only artistic gifts to which she made no pretensions were painting and drawing. It is not surprising that one of her reports at Dramatic School — acting was the only art for which she had any formal training — described her as exceptionally talented but quite incapable of learning from anyone. A dream she had in the first year of analysis depicted the omnipotent character of her belief in her genius. It also shows her failure to deny *completely* her need for external support.

Dream I. She was demonstrating to a group of stuffy bourgeois professors her ability to dance without touching the ground. She had, however, to keep one finger touching a round tea-table in the middle of the room.

Her determination to deny any need to be dependent on others was also shown in her attitude to external dangers and difficulties. Not only was she physically fearless but she also seemed without social anxiety. She was never shy or overawed by anyone and was quite incapable of accepting any offers of patronage that might have helped her professionally. She also denied any anxiety about the economic insecurity in which she habitually lived. During a phase of the analysis in which she was penniless she refused unemployment relief and tried to persuade herself that hunger pains were psychogenic. Nor did she admit that any dangers attach to sexual promiscuity.

She would not have used the word *promiscuous* about herself, but it would be hard to find another word to describe the bewilderingly rapid series of transient encounters that made up her sexual life. In her view it was a search for an ideal partner with whom she could experience complete sexual harmony uncontaminated by either love or sensuality. Occasionally, or so she said, her search was successful, when she found a "reactionary" man, but then, alas, they always proved to have no "sense of structure." The others always proved "comatic." Rather inconsistently, I thought, she referred to her sexual partners as lovers.

It will already have become obvious that Miss Y. was counterphobic rather than phobic, and that in many ways her character was paranoid. In the last section of his paper on Schreber, Freud observes that the familiar principal forms of paranoia can all be represented as contradictions of the single proposition "I (a man) love him (a man)," and goes on to show that projection cannot be the essential mechanism in paranoia. Although Miss Y. certainly used the mechanism of projection extensively her defensive personality seemed to be based on a massive contradiction of her unconscious wishes and fears rather than on denial and projection. Her heterosexual promiscuity contradicted her underlying attachment to the mother and her fear and hatred of men. Her pretensions to genius, an example of what Freud called sexual overestimation of the ego, contradicted her unconscious need for object love, this being reinforced by her ideological rejection of love as infantile. Her imagined discovery of a means by which death could be eliminated was a contradiction not a denial of death. Similarly her conviction that almost everyone other than herself was sadistic was as much a contradiction of her need for love as a projection of her own sadism. This was shown by the fact that it was just those classes of persons whose occupation it is to care for others and whose care she needed that were in her view most sadistic. She considered all doctors, especially women doctors and psychiatrists, to be sadists. In principle psychoanalysts were not, though during the first year of analysis most of my interpretations were considered to be deliberate sadistic attacks. In charitable moods she attributed my sadism to the contamination I had suffered while acquiring a medical qualification. All mothers she met were scrutinized closely and any mistakes or awkwardnesses they showed were attributed to sadism; when possible she interpreted this to them.

Her need to love and feel loved had, however, found one outlet. She kept cats — several of them, which she had saved from being put down. She was devoted to them and fondly believed that they were dependent on her. Fortunately, she decided early in the analysis that I too was fond of cats. That cats were part of an external reality about which she had normal emotions and in which her usual omnipotent defenses did not operate was shown by the fact that the first open, naive expression of anxiety in the analytical situation occurred in relation to one. One day the housekeeper's cat went to sleep under the analytic couch, from which it emerged during the middle of the session. When Miss Y. suddenly noticed it stalking towards the door, she leapt off the couch on the opposite side. I remained seated. I am convinced that if a man, not a cat, had emerged, she would not have batted an eyelid.

Another feature of her personality, which was, I think, manic rather than paranoid, was that her appearance and whole demeanour could alter so much that it was hard to believe the different characters presented to one were in fact aspects of the same person. In one character she was hard, aggressive, querulous, and argumentative, and usually sluttishly dressed. In another she was transfigured and radiant, absolutely confident in her ability to charm everyone she encountered. In such moods everyone in the street stared at her appreciatively as she passed and complete strangers came up and talked to her. It was an important step in the analysis when she compared this to the way passersby will stop to talk to a happy baby and, though still flattered, recognized it to be an intrusion on her privacy. These changes in mood at first occurred independently of the analysis and were remarked upon by others than myself; later they became associated with changes in the transference.

In describing Miss Y.'s character I have already used the terms *counterphobic*, *paranoid*, and *manic*, and the question arises, I think, whether she was, *psychiatrically* speaking, psychotic. She certainly displayed incongruity of affect. This was well described by one of her lovers who once remarked to her: "It's the glorious irrelevance of you. You look at the sugar-bowl with intense hatred and talk of the weather with an expression of ecstasy." I am fairly sure that at first she was terrified that I would decide she was mad and was more than relieved that I never in any way treated her as such.

Since Miss Y. often behaved and spoke in a way that in every-day life one might be inclined to dismiss as pretentious, absurd, and bizarre, I must mention explicitly that very early on I decided that she was in fact a very gifted, though profoundly disturbed, person, and, in particular, that she had an unerring aesthetic sense. It would be hard to justify such an impression by citing examples that would be generally convincing, and I shall only say that her sensibility often manifested itself negatively. No one could have hated Rembrandt as passionately as she did without a profound though denied insight into his understanding of aging and death.

So far I have presented Miss Y.'s character and ideas without relating them in any way to the childhood experiences which alone make them comprehensible. My reason for having done this is that during her analysis I had to learn to feel at home with the defensive personality she presented to the world before I could learn the bare facts of her childhood, let alone acquire any imaginative understanding of it.

V

Miss Y. was the youngest child of the only English-speaking family living in a small village in America, both her parents having emigrated from England. They were converts to Catholicism, and five children followed each other in rapid succession, first a boy and then four girls. The whole family's life was overshadowed by a series of deaths which occurred before Miss Y. was ten years old. Her mother died when she was just over two. An aunt then came to keep house and care for the children; she died when Miss Y. was four-and-a-half. The children next had a governess who was committed to a mental hospital when Miss Y. was ten and who died there soon after admission. Miss Y. had some recollection of all three deaths. In her early teens her father remarried. Her stepmother found Miss Y. unmanageable and both parents became very strict in their attempts to control her adolescent interest in boys. She reacted by becoming more and more defiant. In her late teens she was put for a while into a reformatory run by nuns and later, after failing to hold down a number of office jobs, she was shipped back to England to live with some distant relations in a small provincial town. She soon found the aspidistras and antimacassars unendurable and before she was twenty-one she ran away and got a job with a circus. From then onwards she lived a precarious, unsettled, and nomadic existence, her only contacts with her family being very occasional letters to her sisters and appeals for financial help to her brother. Under these circumstances no confirmatory external evidence about her childhood was available, while her own description of her treatment by her father and stepmother bore all the hallmarks of paranoid distortion. The idea she had at the beginning of her analysis that both her father and brother had attempted to abuse her sexually was, fairly certainly, a delusion. I suspect that her father was a moody and difficult man who was often at his wits' end as to how to handle five motherless children. They ran wild and much of their hostility and resentment was worked out on each other in bullying and spitefulness, with my patient, as the youngest, bearing the brunt of a lot of it. I think, too, that to begin with she was her father's favorite child. She owed to him her interest in poetry and acting and was the only one of the children to be infected by his passion for Shakespeare. His getting rid of her, first to a reformatory and then to England, was, I suspect, the action of a man bitterly disillusioned in his idealized favorite daughter rather than that of a crude disciplinarian. What her precise misdemeanors were I never discovered. The other children have all made conventional adjustments to the American way of life.

Although these facts about her childhood are very scanty, they are enough to make her unconscious longing for the mother, her conscious hatred of her father, and her fear of death, all imaginatively comprehensible. They offer, however, no explanation of the paranoid twist to her personality, of the fact that her infantile traumata led not to repression, impoverishment of the ego, and symptom formation, but to the development of an ego itself based on active contradiction of her pathological, unconscious impulses. One consequence of the fact that she emerged from her childhood not with a psychoneurosis but with a paranoid, manic character was that energy which in a neurotic is dissipated in symptom formation or held in leash by repression was available to her organized ego, though at the price of a partial break with reality. This was the basis of the forcefulness of personality which was one of her most striking characteristics.

VI

Miss Y.'s analysis lasted for rather over four years. I shall not attempt to describe its course fully, but shall confine myself to giving a general picture of the three phases into which the analysis fell and to describing in more detail a number of crucial episodes. Miss Y. was a prolific dreamer of remarkably undisguised dreams, which I shall use extensively as illustrative material without reporting her associations, which were in general more confusing than illuminating.

The three phases into which the analysis fell were:

1. A phase of resistance, in which Miss Y. fought to prevent disintegration of her omnipotent and narcissistic defenses.

2. A phase of regression, in which she reexperienced the despair and depression that had necessitated construction of these defenses, and

3. A phase of recovery, in which she acquired sublimations and reconstructed her defenses on a less omnipotent and narcissistic basis.

Since the phase of regression had a rapid onset and ended suddenly during one of my holidays, this division into three phases corresponds closely to the clinical facts and is not a theoretical construct introduced to facilitate exposition. The phase of regression was, however, foreshadowed more than once during the phase of resistance, and I shall describe one instance of this in some detail.[11]

The account above reports on a case of therapeutic success, yet I am of the opinion that improvement occurred mostly as a result of a gradual building of trust and the corrective emotional experience allowed by the therapist's willingness to charge the insolvent patient little and then nothing, and only negligibly as a result of the sophisticated psychoanalytic interpretations offered. I quote below only a selection of passages from the rest of Rycroft's report.

The phase of resistance lasted for just under two years. The preceding sections of this paper have in the main been based on impressions and information acquired during the first phase. It was characterized by long periods of intense hostility toward me, alternating with short periods of complete harmony. During the hostile periods she attacked me on almost every possible account. I was held to be sadistic, insensitive, stupid, and ununderstanding, and to be a legitimate target for her hatred of all things English — English conventions, English snobbery, English doctors, English food, English cooking, and English weather. All attempts to interpret this hostility were taken as indicating my approval of what she was attacking and therefore as further proof of my insensitivity and stupidity. Alternatively I was thought to be deliberately provoking her by affecting to approve the obviously intolerable conditions by which she was daily traumatized. Now although most of this hostility was undoubtedly transferred, the accusation that I was being ununderstanding did at times and in certain respects have some validity. There were two reasons for this, one unavoidable, the other the result of a failure in discrimination on my part.

The unavoidable reason was the confusion created by her highly individual habits of speech. (p. 570)

The avoidable reason was that I failed to discriminate sensitively enough between different types and sources of aggression. Evidence of penis envy and oral frustration was only too obvious in her attacks on doctors and on English food and weather, and it was true that she envied me for being a man and felt frustrated by the mother country which gave her neither food nor warmth, but her dreams — as I only realized much later on when I had reason to abstract them from my notes — suggested that her envy and aggression were not primary and instinctual but were part of her defense. Her repudiation of her need for love and her attachment to internal objects from whom she derived her sense of omnipotence had imprisoned her in her internal world and her fundamental demand on me was that I should help her take the risk of abandoning her self-sufficiency and trust an external object. Having made this demand on me, having instated me as someone by whom she could hope to be rescued, her anxiety compelled her to hate and fear me. Just because I was the person she had chosen to liberate her from her internal objects I inevitably became the person who threatened to destroy her sense of omnipotence. Just because I was the person she had put into a position in which I could prove myself trustworthy and make her aware of her need for love I became the person it was most necessary to prove hateful, insensitive, and ununderstanding. Furthermore, she had to test out that I could continue to be benevolent, however venomous she might be.

I have already mentioned that the phase of regression was foreshadowed on more than one occasion during this first phase of resistance. The most impressive of these occurred near the end of the first year of analysis and was precipitated by circumstances external to it. She had been persuaded, partly by myself, to have a surgical operation for her dyspareunia and went into hospital during one of my holidays. The operation was planned to take place three days before I returned to work. I was therefore surprised and disturbed when she telephoned to tell me that she would be coming to her session despite having had the operation only three days previously. When she arrived she walked straight to the couch without looking at me or greeting me in any way. She lay down and went completely limp, in striking contrast to her usual very tense posture. She remained silent and uncannily motionless. I assumed, rightly, that she had discharged herself from hospital almost immediately after the operation, and knowing that she had had a lower abdominal operation feared that she might have had a hemorrhage. Her absence of color did nothing to reassure me, and I remember entertaining for a moment the idea that she had come to die on the couch. I was therefore more relieved than distressed when I noticed that she was weeping silently. After a while she tried to speak but failed, and I helped her off the couch onto a chair. She then told me what had happened. She had had the operation with much less pain and distress than she had feared and had been coping successfully with the barbarous conditions in an English hospital until a small child had been admitted to the ward. This child had cried all night and she had been as much

upset by the indifference of the nursing staff as she was by the crying itself. Next morning she could endure it no longer and after a
row with the ward sister and house physician had discharged herself from hospital. I hardly needed to point out that she was reex-
periencing her own desolation after the deaths in her own childhood and that her indignation on the child's behalf was born of
her own need for consolation.

VIII

During the months following this episode she began to change.
She stopped being promiscuous and became preoccupied with
her memories of a young Frenchman, half her own age, with
whom she had had a short affair. She lost her job after a quarrel
with the producer and then sabotaged every audition she went to
by her unaccommodating attitude. Her savings were nearly
exhausted. She became increasingly aware of her dependence on
me and stopped attacking me incessantly. She began to have anxiety dreams in which I featured as a benevolent and protecting figure. (pp. 573-574)

The emotional atmosphere of this phase is even harder to
convey. This is partly because it contained two elements which are
logically incompatible and which yet coexisted without apparent
contradiction. One was a feeling that I was bored, tired, ill and
indifferent, while she was listless, despairing, and overcome with a
sense of futility; it was as though she was reenacting a
mother-infant relationship from which all life had been withdrawn.
The other was her belief that I could be trusted to see her through,
could be a support until she succeeded in gaining access to her
own sources of vitality. At times the only evidence of hopefulness
in her was the regularity and punctuality with which she attended
sessions. She paid no fees during this period, living entirely on
borrowed money. However, despite her helplessness and absorp-
tion in the analysis, her dependence on me and surrender to me

as an introjectible good object never became fully explicit, largely, I think, owing to her fear of the destructive implications of her incorporative phantasies, her fear that she might turn me into an effigy. As a result she never asked me to lend her money and deflected some of her longings onto the Frenchman who by living abroad remained out of range of her aggression and could do nothing to disillusion her. (p. 575)

I do not intend to describe in any detail this last phase of recovery. Much of it consisted in working over again material I have already presented, but with the difference that she was capable of operating the normal split in the ego which enables psychoneurotic patients to observe and reflect upon the material they present instead of becoming totally immersed in it. There were also periods in which development seemed to be occurring spontaneously and in which my function was confined to providing a setting in which insight could increase and to being ready to intervene when she seemed to be losing her way. I have no doubt that in view of the emotional insecurity of her childhood and the social insecurity of her adult life the mere continuity of the analytical relationship had a therapeutic effect. I think too that the sudden emergence of a sublimation and, with it, of a firmer grasp of reality indicates that a normal, nondefensive ego organization must have already been present when treatment began, however overshadowed it may have been by her highly defensive "personality." The last phase of her analysis was a phase of recovery, not only in the sense that she recovered from her regression, but also in the sense that she recovered certain faculties and potentialities which had previously been dissociated and therefore inaccessible. In the last resort this was based on recovery of the belief in the possibility of affective communication, a belief which had been shattered by the traumatic experiences of her childhood. The most obvious example of her becoming more in touch with, more at home in outer reality was her changed habit of speech — I remember being amazed when she first came out with such an ordinary word as *flirt* — but much more than this was, of course, involved.

In April 1951 Miss Y. received a telegram telling her that her father had died. After unsuccessful attempts to find a friend to stay with her, she rang up and asked me to come and see her. The sense of urgency was obvious in her voice and I went at once. When I arrived, almost the first thing she said was that in a sense I needn't have come at all, all she had needed was the certain knowledge that I had appreciated the urgency of her call and that I was willing to come, though of course, she added, the only way I could show this was by actually coming. What she needed was that her grief should be recognized, otherwise she was in danger of denying it. Miss Y. had realized this danger herself, hence her call to me. After talking about this for a little while she gave me a cup of tea and I returned home. My reason for reporting this incident — the only occasion on which I stepped out of the analytical role — is to give an example of the sensitivity and perceptiveness which she had kept hidden behind her narcissistic defenses, a perceptiveness which made her realize how easy it would have been to recall only the grievances of her adolescence and to maintain that she had always hated her father and recognize immediately how urgently she needed a witness for her grief. It did not, of course, require much imagination on my part to appreciate that someone who had lost three mothers in her childhood and who as an adult had had to fabricate theories denying the inevitability of death, needed endorsement of her threatened insight when confronted with the fact of her father's death. (p. 578-579)

A few days later she expressed concern on my behalf for the first time. She was worried, she said, about the aggression I must have to put up with from my other patients. During the same hour she said she had just realized how much she always wanted to be the center of attention and how hard she found it to tolerate the idea that it was unrealistic of her to expect me always to be able to understand immediately what she was getting at.

Her earlier sexual promiscuity had been homosexual in the sense that her idea of eliminating love from sex involved denial of specifically masculine and feminine emotions. She now began to express quite simple feminine anxieties. She complained of her compulsion to flirt. She admitted to being frightened when walking alone through dark streets at night. She dreamt that a man tore open her blouse and then broke one of her vases. When she set up house with a man she was appalled at her tendency to nag him. (p. 580)

Unlike the actual surgical operation she had, which was an outstanding success, her analysis was only partially successful. Although she became a much softer person, she remained in many ways narcissistic and schizoid, and there was, I think, a manic element in the partial recovery she made.

Although Miss Y.'s analysis ended prematurely, she had a proper last session. During it she said: "Well, I see it all now. It wasn't their fault and it wasn't mine either," and then turning round to look at me she added, "though why in hell didn't you say so at the very beginning?" This was meant half-humorously, but perhaps she had a point. (p. 581)

DARING TO GET YOUR MOTHER OFF YOUR BACK

Vincent: I want to work on a dream. I am in a country home with some friends. I go out for a walk, and I'm already going along a highway filled with cars; that is, there's a traffic jam. I'm walking along the side of the road on the shoulder — a very big and steep embankment made of sand. Every now and then there are some darker areas (I suppose it's because water goes through there); then ... I jump over these patches, until I come to one that has a little streamlet ... with a little water. I try to jump over it and I don't reach the bank. I slide in the sand. At the beginning I try to struggle to make it all the way up and I see that I can't: that each time I struggle I fall further. In the end it doesn't matter to me and I fall into the water. The water is cold, but I am comfortable in the cold water and I let myself be pulled along until there comes a moment when I think that if I keep letting myself be pulled along I'm going to reach a river which I surely won't be able to get [out of] and I will drown. Then there comes a moment in the river where it becomes a backwater. And there is like a building, or something like that — but in the river, in the backwater. The walls are inlaid with Arab tiles and it's difficult to climb up. I struggle a lot but I make it and inside there is like a pool ... with large fish. They could be barbels [river fish] or something like that. I look at them, but no; it's as if they are already too big to be caught. Behind, there is a much bigger pond; there are some nets on one side. I am looking at them and I trip and I fall on my back.

Oh! Well, before that I get the feeling that there are people near-by ... and a different kind of fish. And then there comes a big squid ... an octopus, up from behind and it constricts my throat. It begins to squeeze me and the only thing I do is to wait for someone to arrive who can help me, as if those people up there were going to appear or ... and then I wake up.

C: Well, there are many images in this sequence. My suggestion would be for you to repeat the events, but now adding body movement to your narrative. Please return again to the sequence in the dream: you come upon the streams, etc., turning this space into your stage.

V: Well, I leave the house ... to take a walk ... and then I'm walking along the sidewalk ... every now and then a dark stain appears, and I'm jumping over them because they are small, until I come to one that has water in it ... I try to jump over it and I see that I'm sinking and I fall into the water ... There comes a moment where if I go on like that I will drown ...

C: Prolong and intensify that situation, and understand it as a metaphor of your life; like a message from the dream about something that is happening in your day-to-day reality. It's going to be worse later, when that river becomes the other. There you really will ...

V: Yes, now ...

C: That's good, now are you anticipating what will happen.

331

V: I have to get out of here; if I don't, I won't be able to.

C: Instead of continuing with the dream, elaborate further. You are in the water? On the edge of the water?

V: The wall? No.

C: In the water?

V: Part in and part out. I am tired but happy. I have done it. I have been able to climb the wall. Now the current isn't taking me. How curious it is to know where I am. This place is in the middle of the mountains ... of the ocean ... there is water.

C: You are going along the upper part of a wall in the middle of the water?

V: Yes, it leaves like a pool.

C: Is there water on both sides?

V: When I climb the wall, no. But later, yes.

C: Does the water flow?

V: A little. It's very tranquil and clear.

C: And there are fish.

V: Yes. Where I pay most attention is to the small one; to the big one, no.

C: Where do you pay most attention?

V: On the small one.

C: On the small lagoon?

V: The small lagoon ... and I see the fish well. I know there are some in the other [lagoon], but I don't see them. Then I fall again. I go on falling, my head is sinking, then ...

C: Are you falling through the water or through the air?

V: No, no, through the water. I am already below the surface.

C: Okay, okay.

V: Then I see that there are windows.

C: And you're falling and you see windows ...

V: It's curious, no? ...

C: What do you feel is curious?

V: It's salty. And then comes the squid. No ... I can ... take off...

C: Now begin to experience it as a metaphor of your existence in this moment.

V: [*Murmurs*] ... Tricks ...

C: Who does it remind you of?

V: The squid? Of my mother ...

C: Mother ...

V: Mother, mother, of my mother, because she's a widow and she squeezes me.

C: Your mother squeezing your neck ...

V: I can't get her off of me.

C: Let's see, continue the dream there; let's see what you find with this squid. Instead of waking up.

V: I try to take it up to the surface. Fear. My strength fails me. Something like ... if I take it to the surface, it will suffocate and I will have to let go. It's late. The people have gone ...

C: You wouldn't be so responsible if it died of ...

V: No.

C: So then you have the option to let yourself be strangled or kill the squid.

V: What I want is for it to let go of me; it should let go of me. That is, not kill it myself, not directly, or indirectly.

C: Let's see if your wanting it to let go of you can [stand up to] your squid, so that it will let go of you.

V: No, the squid won't let go of me.

C: It's not enough that you want it. Okay, there are two options: which one do you want? There's nothing more. There's not a third now, we are in an Aristotelian world. I would advise you to try the first. Perhaps it may be easier. Either continuation of the dream is possible. Both of them would be interesting to try ...

V: It continues to coming down ...

C: In the dream you could even die, isn't that true? That is, you could try it. The squid won't let go of you in the dream, there you wake up?

V: Yes, as soon as it grabs me I can't get it off of me.

C: The alternative is to put an end to it. I think that that's where you find yourself. And to continue means to continue to dream. Take some path. Decide.

V: I throw it off, or what should I do?

C: No, you can take it home. No, I'm joking. I think that you have here the best opportunity for more attention to the issue, and the best stimulus.

V: It's as if it almost had taken off my head ... the head and the body.

C: It seems like the moment you accepted it, it no longer scared you.

V: Dying?

C: Yes.

V: Not if my body remained below and I were to go somewhere else ...

C: Yeah.

V: Left the body below.

C: And how does it seem to you to spend the rest of your existence in that condition?

V: I was like a ghost, not able to do, existing ...

C: Does it sound familiar to you, this state?

V: Yes.

C: Speak a little more about what this ghost-like existence is like.

V: A feeling of impotence, of not being able, as if my body were blocked, not able to move. My desire was becoming more ... to follow my body to what I want, obligation.

C: Can you describe it a little more?

V: Yes. My body is dead, paralyzed ...

C: Obligation?

V: Yes, my obligation to behave with people ...

C: That is like having a dead body.

V: Not being able.

C: Not being able to do what you want ...

V: Yes, I won't be able to do it.

C: Not be able to do what?

V: To express my aggression, and come off compulsive smiling.

C: Not be able to come forth out of obligation, you're saying.

V: Not respond to that obligation, the body. And the body has to obey.

C: The body has to obey, and that ...? Oh! It should obey and it doesn't respond. Impotence ...

V: I feel like I'm pulling on my body, with my will alone.

C: Okay. Good, then one of the alternatives for a dream continuation is to remain not being able to get yourself out of this strangulation, not being able to do anything ...

V: No, the strangulation goes away once I'm dead.

C: It leads to the state of not doing anything, of not doing anything ... the body. It's as if from the seed of not getting the squid off of you, this condition of impotence remains. This is the result.

V: It's like the squid wants me down below.

C: It wants you down below. Okay, let's go then to the other side. We'll take the squid off you and see whether that is not a happier solution.

V: To breath again and rise above [the surface], that is, without any effort ... just take the squid off of me, take off the weight.

C: The tension has left your face. Intensify.

V: At least now the air enters.

C: Give it further attention and keep on developing that state. Be master of yourself?

V: More like having life, or strength, or freedom.

C: Move from that place and express it so that you can intensify that experience which is so ...

V: I'm moving ... The guilt about the squid remains with me.

C: The guilt still takes away a little freedom from you.

V: I should have found a way for both of us to live.

C: You *should* have ... Poor squid, you should have seen a way to arrange it. I suggest that you get rid of that guilt on your back, that you also throw it away from yourself. Imagine that ...

V: It's as if a part of it were stuck to me ...

C: Yes, yes. What sensation do you have, the part that sticks? Specify it. You do it. Imagine that you get your mother off your back. See what happens. Fuse it with what preceeded, fuse the image with the idea of ... taking your freedom, getting her off your back.

V: How uncomfortable my back is! I can't move. You weigh so much.

C: What comes out is complaint. Will you continue complaining? Will you be able to get out from under her with complaints?

V: No! She'll stick more.

C: Hum?

V: She'll stick more.

C: Make it produce more of a demand. It's still only a simple scientific statement.

V: Of love.

C: She's sticky but she's useful.

V: Sticky ...

C: I would tell you to cast her out from you.

V: LEAVE ME!

C: From the emotion that arises.

V: SHIT!

C: What's happening?

V: I love you, Mom.

C: Okay, we want to let you stay in the rage still. We'll leave that ["I love you, Mom"] for later. Yes, she is scared because your freedom is making tiny explosions, you are becoming free of her. Small explosions, but you cut them off very fast.

V: Nothing more comes out of me.

C: Continue, give yourself more continuity in getting her off your back. Strength. "Go away, go away!" Or whatever comes out for you. "Leave me alone, don't stick to me!" Whatever content that makes sense in your real life.

V: I'm fed up! I don't want you anymore!

C: It seems that now you are feeling it deeply, without leaving and negating that conclusion. You'll have to kill her.

Participant: You'll be living a long time for your mother ...

C: Well, we'll leave the thing there, the part that wants to put on the brakes. "Living a long time" to put on the brakes. C'mon, let's see, go for it, give it more pressure. Do you think that you can give words to that part of yourself that wants this to end, that doesn't want you to mistreat your mother, that ...?

V: She's not a bad person.

C: She's not a bad person and you are a good boy, what do you think?

V: "Don't do that to me, how can you say that ... "

C: Who says that?

V: My mother.

C: Your mother says to you, "How can you do that to me?"

V: "Your mother who has taken care of you. I love you. I've done so many things for you."

C: Of course! How do you receive that attitude?

V: You are asphyxiating me. I'm suffocating.

C: Now put yourself in her role and exaggerate that asphyxiating manipulation ... with guilt and ...

V: "I love you very much and you know that I've spent my whole life at home, caring for you all."

C: What does she feel when she tells you that? What does she feel deep down?

V: Abandonment. "I understand you."

C: "I understand you," she says.

V: "Don't leave me, you can do what you want ... "

C: "You can do what you want, only let me asphyxiate you ... Do it for me."

V: "Suppress your aggression."

C: You are telling yourself ... I don't know. What are you telling yourself?

V: Endure it, not this.

C: Are you saying to yourself, "Quiet down"?

V: Don't get excited.

C: "Don't get excited," do you recognize it?

V: Control yourself.

C: Control yourself, don't get angry at your mother ...

V: Yes.

C: Do you recognize it as a psychological problem?

V: I don't know.

C: If you don't know, I don't have an opinion. You don't know whether you want to work on liberating your aggression, your capacity to stand up to your mother, so then it's better that I decide it ...

V: I prefer to work.

C: Hum, do you want to?

V: It scares me.

C: Who could help us here, to bring out .... With the help of a cushion and a towel I think that now the next stage is promising. Would you like to? Have you ever worked with Pedro? I think I would recommend it to you; what do you think? Follow his instructions a little.

V: Who is the cushion for?

Pedro: I'm not your mother. Your mother is the cushion. Here is Mommy, hum? What? Do you want to give Mommy a little kiss? Go on, Mommy ... Give Mommy a little kiss, a little kiss for Mommy. Go on, hurry, go. She has done so much for you. You're going to do something bad to me? What are you going to do to Mom? Let's go, c'mon. What's going on? What? What do you want to do to Mom? Give her a little kiss, c'mon go ahead, hurry up. What do you want to do with her? What are you going to do here, right now, with Mom? What are you going to do with Mom now? Say it. What do you want to do? Let's go.

341

V: I'm inflating and I'm controlling it.

P: Well c'mon, go on controlling yourself. Do it, do it, do it. No, not me, do it to Mom.

V: It doesn't matter to me.

P: C'mon, it's your Mommy, not me, it's Mom, fuck!

V: It's a cushion.

P: It's a cushion, it's a cushion ... It's a Mom cushion, nice and soft to rest your little head there. C'mon, cuddle up. Is Mom chubby?

V: No.

P: What's she like?

V: Thin, she feels very weak, you can't harm her.

P: Would you be able to? Well okay then, c'mon, take her in your arms and give her little caresses. Hurry up, c'mon, little caresses here for Mom. Like that, Mama's little boy, c'mon, tell her how much you love her, for every-thing she has done to you, for how she's made your back, c'mon guy, get on with it. What? Do you like her?

V: Yes.

C: No one would say that you have the intention of bringing out your aggression.

P: What? Are you very comfortable here? C'mon.

C: You no longer remember your purpose.

P: C'mon, c'mon, get it out, it's only a cushion, fuck! C'mon, risk it!

Precisely because it is only a cushion. C'mon, c'mon bring it out against the cushion!

V: [*screaming*]

P: Go on, harder, c'mon!

V: [*screaming*]

P: Let's go, dare to do it, fuck! C'mon, don't cut it off. Breathe here. Let's go, c'mon, c'mon powerfully.

V: [*screaming*]

P: Let's go, more!

V: [*keeps on screaming*]

P: Go on, go on. More, more, more! C'mon, get it out, c'mon out, out!

P: What's going on? Is it Mom or is it a cushion? Where are we? You're going to grab the cushion here by the corner, the other hand on the other corner, c'mon. And bash it. It's taking the shit that you have inside here from Mom. You're not doing anything to Mom except dump all the shit that you've received from her and leave it behind here.

V: [*screaming*]

P: That's it, let's go.

V: [*screaming*]

P: That's it, dump out all the harm she did you.

V: [*screaming*]

P: Let's go, more.

V: [*screaming*]

P: Even more. Get on your knees, bring it out from here, from here.

V: [*screaming more deeply and continually*]

P: Let's go, to the max!

V: [*screaming*]

P: C'mon, let's go, until you're left clean.

V: [*beginning to slow down*]

P: Don't let yourself be beaten by weakness.

V: [*screaming again*]

P: C'mon, more, louder and harder, faster, faster, more, more! Let's go get everything you have in here out. Let's go; c'mon to the max.

V: [*He screams and begins to calm down.*]

C: Now you look as if you are contemplating something new.

V: As if I had expelled something.

C: As if you had managed to get her off your back.

V: Yes, I'm left with the doubt about whether all of her or part, a lot or a little.

C: Okay, to consolidate it, it would be good for you to imagine her in front of you and say something to her, from this new freedom, from this capacity to be direct and not suppress your aggression. One phrase.

V: It's a feeling; it's as if I were seeing her very clearly, but without words.

C: Say something to her out of that feeling.

V: Mom, I love you. Images come to me ... her ... behind me ... now I can ...

C: Good ...

I am convinced that the turning point in this session was not the help of the person in the group in whom I had delegated coaching him (and who alternated between caricaturing his softness and stimulating him with insulting words and a loud voice). What did it — I am sure, because I remember well the patient's expression — was my reminding him of his purpose and his motivation: to act consistently with his understanding that in order to heal he needed to gain the right of getting angry at his mother.

The transcript can hardly convey how impressive his transformation was, for the most clear indication was in his demeanor, that turned into one completely different from what it had been at the outset of the session: he looked as if he had suddenly matured, and as a person who is not asking permission to be; as one whose symbolic act of courage was a turning point in his life. As he sat in the group during the sessions of other participants, his serious and poised expression persisted, and he seemed to radiate a quality of "being there."

7

ENNEATYPE 7

No character is better represented among the Canterbury pilgrims than E7 (just as it is the case in Boccaccio's *Decameron* and, more generally, in the picaresque romance genre). Here is the picture that Chaucer gives us of the Friar:

> There was a *Friar*, a wanton one and merry,
> A Limiter, a very festive fellow.
> In all Four Orders there was none so mellow
> So glib with gallant phrase and well-turned speech
> He'd fixed up many a marriage, giving each
> Of his young women what he could afford her.
> He was a noble pillar to his Order.
> Highly beloved and intimate was he
> With County folk within his boundary,
> And city dames of honour and possessions;
> For he was qualified to hear confessions,
> Or so he said, with more than priestly scope;
> He had a special license from the Pope.
> Sweetly he heard his penitents at shrift
> With pleasant absolution, for a gift.
> He was an easy man in penance-giving
> Where he could hope to make a decent living;
> It's sure sign whenever gifts are given
> To a poor Order that a man's well shriven,

And should he give enough he knew in verity
The penitent repented in sincerity.
For many a fellow is so hard of heart
He cannot weep, for all his inward smart.
Therefore instead of weeping and of prayer
One should give silver for a poor Friar's care.
He kept his tippet stuffed with pins for curls,
And pocket-knives, to give to pretty girls.
And certainly his voice was gay and sturdy,
For he sang well and played the hurdy-gurdy.
At sing-songs he was champion of the hour.
His neck was whiter than a lily-flower
Bur strong enough to butt a bruiser down.
He knew the taverns well in every town
And every innkeeper and barmaid too
Better than lepers, beggars and the crew,
For in so eminent a man as he
It was not fitting with the dignity
Of his position, dealing with a scum
Of wretched lepers; nothing good can come
Of dealings with the slum-and-gutter dwellers,
But only with the rich and victual-sellers.
But anywhere a profit might accrue
Courteous he was and lowly of service too.
Natural gifts like his were hard to match.
He was the finest beggar of his batch,
And, for his begging-district, payed a rent;
His brethren did no poaching where he went.
For though a widow mightn't have a shoe,
So pleasant was his holy how-d'ye-do
He got his farthing from her just the same
Before he left, and so his income came
To more that he laid out. And how he romped,
Just like a puppy! He was ever prompt
To arbitrate disputes on settling days
(For a small fee) in many helpful ways,

Not even appearing as your cloistered scholar
With threadbare habit hardly worth a dollar,
But much more like a Doctor or a Pope.[1]

For E7, Ichazo used the word "ego-plan," in reference to an excessive tendency to substitute plans or projects for action; to think rather than do. True as it may be that sometimes the E7 individual can be described as a dreamer, this is certainly not the case in all, and even then it falls short as a description.

More than a dreamer, for instance, Chaucer's Friar is a charmer — who seeks and offers sweetness, and sometimes an E7 is a charmed charmer. The inclination to the fantasy of a dreamer seems secondary to something more basic: a striving for pleasure or comfort.

The character of an E7 can often be described as that of a schemer — i.e., one who defends himself or herself through intelligence. Just as type 6 needs intelligence to know what to do, as an antidote to fear, and as a means of neutralizing inner doubt, E7 persons use their intelligence to explain and manipulate, to elicit admiration and get people to love them. They have a remarkable capacity for convincing others, being not only explainers but persuaders. This trait, too, is humorously addressed by Chaucer as he presents the Friar's reasoning that, for those who cannot weep it is best to "give silver for a poor Friar's care."

Though "ego-plan" is the term Ichazo used in the United States, the first time I heard him present protoanalysis in Chile, he used the word "charlatan." At first I couldn't understand why he resorted to this term, nor what gluttony had to do with charlatanism, but in time I have found it to be a very evocative word. A charlatan certainly uses words a great deal, and as Karl Abraham says of the oral-receptive personality:

We find in them, besides a permanent longing to obtain everything, a constant need to communicate themselves orally to other people. This results in an obstinate urge to talk, connected in most cases of being overflowing. Persons of this kind have the impression that their fund of thought is inexhaustible, and they ascribe a special power or some unusual value to what they say.[2]

But E7 is not just one with verbal facility, even more pertinent is the fact that the word "charlatan" has a connotation of fraudulence, and Chaucer subtly lets us know that his Friar is a trickster, who managed to be regarded as "a noble pillar of his Order" in spite of a not so noble self-interest: had claimed ("or so he said") to have a special license from the Pope to hear confessions, and had cleverly made people's remorse into his business ("It's a sure sign whenever gifts are given / to a poor Order that a man's well shriven"). Even the pins for curls and pocket-knives that he kept for pretty girls smack of a trickster's approach to seduction — though he was handsome and had cultivated his voice.

A charlatan is typically one who talks about what he does not really know, and he may even trick himself into knowing what he does not. We associate charlatanism with the kind of quack found at fairs, selling an old Egyptian snake ointment, or the like, for illness. In Madame Bovary, Flaubert has left us a memorable description of E7 in the figure of Monsieur Hommes, the pharmacist, who convinces the all-too-accomodating and insecure Dr. Bovary (an E9) to perform surgery on a poor servant — with all-too-tragic consequences.

> Ah! You'll have to fight many a prejudice, Monsieur Bovary; every day your scientific efforts will be thwarted by the peasant's stubborn adherence to his old ways. Plenty of our people still have recourse to novenas and relics and the priest, instead of doing the natural thing and coming to the doctor or the pharmacist. To tell the truth, however, the climate isn't at all bad: we even have a few nonagenarians. The thermometer — this I can tell you from personal observation — goes down in winter to four degrees, and in the hottest season touches twenty-five or thirty degrees Centigrade at the most — that is, twenty-four degrees Reaumur at a maximum, or, in other words, fifty-four degrees Fahrenheit, to use the English scale — not more! You see, we're sheltered from the north winds by the Argueil forest on the one side and from the west winds by the bluffs of Saint-Jean on the other. However, this warmth, which because of the dampness given off by the river and the number of cattle in the pastures, which themselves exhale, as you know, a great deal of ammonia, that is nitrogen, hydrogen,

and oxygen (no, just nitrogen and hydrogen), and which, sucking up the humus from the soil, mixing all these different emanations together — making a package of them, so to speak — and combining also with the electricity in the atmosphere when there is any, could in the long run result in noxious miasmas, as in tropical countries; this warmth, I was saying, is actually moderated from the direction from which it comes, or rather the direction from which it could come, namely, the south, by southeast winds, which being of course cool themselves as a result of crossing the Seine sometimes burst on us all of a sudden like arctic air form Russia![3]

Flaubert's charlatan has a keen interest in inventions, new discoveries and being at the forefront of knowledge, which illustrates a tendency in E7 people to become somewhat bizarre intellectuals, with an exaggerated drive to invent or discover new things — ranging from reasonable designs to harness the energy of oceans and tides, to such impossible ones as perpetual motion. I have in mind people who devote a great deal of effort to getting unusual patents, for instance. Such exaggeration of character is, in turn, emblematic of a more widespread use of intelligence to be extraordinary, to produce a remarkable product, and thus to have something to give. But since often the drive for glory surpasses the person's capacity to support it, the result can be machines that do not work or ointments that do not cure. The pretense of great knowledge is of course a function of a desire and pretense of intellectual greatness, but it is more exact to say that there is, within the psyche, a polarity (or even a split) of big and small. Outwardly they are gentle and not arrogant, but seemingly modest, and we may sense that in their "humility" they want others to become aware of their greatness — and even the special virtue of their modesty. They do not claim any glory, but they want their ideas to be successful.

The quack, who typically peddles remedies, manifests another generalized tendency in E7: to adopt the role of a helper, and to be concerned with the alleviation of pain. The conjunction of traits may sometimes find an outlet in a medical vocation. Particularly in the social subtype, where there is the inclination to be of service. But E7 is often generous and hospitable — the kind of person who will say: "I am at your service," "Get in touch with me whenever you want," "Here's my phone number." And this may be either unconscious seduction or a conscious idea of an exchange: the opportunistic expectation that by putting somebody into their debt they can expect reciprocity.

It is neither the evasion of concreteness nor helpfulness that stand out as dominant traits of Chaucer's Friar, but a combination of love of pleasure and self-interest that is typical of the self-preservation subtype. And while every E7 individual can identify with the three subtypes (since they exist in his psyche as sub-personalities), these are, in some ways, opposite. Notably, there is a polarity between idealism and the lack of it, between gullibility and cynical distrust, between being too much of a dreamer and being all too "materialistic."

A modern description of the sensous, earthy and unidealistic kind of E7 follows, taken from the first paragraph of a detective story — "McNally's Secret" by Lawrence Sanders.

I poured a few drops of an '87 Mondavi Chardonnay into her navel and leaned down to slurp it out. Jennifer's eyes closed and she purred. "Do you like that?" she breathed.

"Of course," I said. "'87 was an excellent year."

Her eyes popped open. "Stinker," she said. "Can't you ever be serious?"

"No," I said, "I cannot."

That, at least, was the truth. In my going-on 37 years I had lived through dire warnings of nuclear catastrophe, global warming, ozone depletion, universal extinction via cholesterol, and the invasion of killer bees. After a while I realized I was bored with all these screeched predictions of Armageddon. It hadn't happened yet, had it? The old world tottered along, and I was content to totter along with it. I am an amiable, sunnily tempered chap (and something of an ass, my father would undoubtedly add), and I see no need to concern myself with disasters that may never happen.

I could have explained all this to Jennifer, but didn't. She might think I was serious about it, and I wasn't even serious about not being serious, if you follow me.[4]

Here are widespread traits depicting a hedonistic "playboy" style, with its cheerfulness and amiability. Beyond a reference to a light-hearted lack of seriousness, the passage reflects the schizoid underground (E5) of the enjoyer (E7); not only a matter of pleasure-seeking avoidance of heavy thoughts, but a disconnection from feeling. Our character confirms this a couple of pages later, when he reveals "my devotion to triviality as a way of life had taught me to shun strong feelings." (p. 9)

A fundamental trait of E7 is permissiveness or indulgence which I take as the essence of gluttony. And, since it would be impossible to be self-indulgent and at the same time super-ego driven or sub-servient to authority, the character is rebellious — though sometimes sweetly or diplomatically so. E7 people are apparently gentle, sweet, kind, friendly people, yet they do not pay very much attention to authority and they implicitly assume authority to be bad. They are not engaged in a struggle against authority, like E6, or E8. They simply do not heed it; they do not need it; as if they had lost their faith in authority. Thus, they do not believe in limiting their own desires, and they allow themselves a great deal of freedom, just as they allow it to others. Their motto is "live and let live."

Another trait of E7 is as important, i.e., rebelliousness — which is not confrontative or direct, but sly, and typically manifests as an opposition to the conventional. This rebelliousness is dynamically linked to the indulgence of desires, of course; gluttony could not live without an opposition to the social constraints that militate against its interest. Rebelliousness is also linked to the search for utopian or remote alternatives to the conventional and ordinary. More importantly, an unconscious rebellion prevents E7 people from enjoyment of the ordinary, and enslaves them to the pursuit of the remote, in the name of freedom.

In *Ennea-type Structures* I characterized the E7 stance as one of "idealistic opportunism," and in relation to the more down-to-earth variety of the character, "*pseudo*-idealistic" might be more exact. Whether the opportunistic or the idealistic aspect is in the foreground, however, the masking of self-interest behind some form of fellow feeling is reminiscent of reaction formation, as in Moliere's *Tartufe*, who is a parasite under the guise of a saint.[5] The cartoon on the following page makes a similar point.

"*Let me add, my name is Martin. And the lobsters you have chosen are Jerry and Agatha, respectively.*"

What is funny about this joke? Only the excess involved in addressing lobsters by name? I think not. Rather, that the friendly equalitarianism involved in intimate address (here over-done in its extension to lobster) is in the context of restaurant policy and in the interest of attracting clients.

In his book of the seventies, *The Greening of America*, Charles Reich speaks of three successive forms of American consciousness, and it is easy to recognize in his first two descriptions the early dominance of the New England puritan style and the achievement oriented E3. While he understands the cultural shift of the sixties only in terms of evolution, anyone familiar with the character styles can easily see that the "New Age" was heralded by an E7 spirit, and continues to bear this personality imprint.

Consider the following, that I quote from an unpublished Italian humorist:

These New Age musicians never get angry! Nor do they get depressed. How unlike the passional impulses of Beethoven or Mozart's morbid sadness — to say nothing of the torturous Chopin! The New Age musician is an ocean of peace, cosmic serenity, radiant light in his heart and creative mind. But it is useless to speak of one who may be only grasped through the sublime life of spirit: take, for instance, the famous "Oceanic light of the bright soul."

I don't think I need to review any further the wonder of the New Age. They are to be experienced rather than talked about. Think of the ineffable sensation of the "energy" felt through the visualizations proposed in New Age workshops. Fellini and Visconti are dilettantes when you think of the fantasies presented in this shop-new-age-work. I only have to think of how my friend Ernestino, after reliving the drama of emerging from the womb saw in a violet vortex a cascade of green stars turning orange — evident symbol of a harmonization between the heart and the sexual chakra ...

Obviously, the cultural shift away from authoritarianism and the recent psycho-spiritual revival entail a promise, yet the many jokes about the new spiritual market and new narcissism are inspired by a new social pathology that echoes the personality pattern of the individual charlatan ... dreamer ... opportunist.

As a biographical illustration of E7 let me point to Columbus, who was animated by the exploratory drive characteristic of the type, and was the first to put navigation by the stars in practice. Columbus had a dream, though he was not the kind of person who lived in the clouds, being a man of action rather than a thinker. Yet, his interpretation of what he did was fantastic — not only that he believed he had reached the coast of Asia, but, more strikingly, that he apparently had no problem in making slaves of the Indians, whom he sincerely wanted to make into Christians.

Not only among *The Canterbury Tales*, but among Nasrudin* jokes I find E7 better represented than any other personality style. And among jokes in general: either E7 is more funny, or he originates more jokes. It is fitting, then, that I end this section with one. I heard it in Rio de Janeiro, where the local character is precisely E7. The gist of the joke is the E7 trait of "not making problems" and insisting that "everything is okay" — a comfortable position that derives from the avoidance of psychological pain.

A woman goes to her husband in a rage and tells him that she has just found out that their maid is pregnant. The husband replies: "That's *her* problem." The woman insists: "But *you're* the one who got her pregnant!" The husband retorts: "That's *my* problem!" And then the wife asks: "And do you think this means nothing to me? What do you want me to do with my feelings?" The husband calmly replies: "That's *your* problem!"

A very comfortable attitude! E7 people are very friendly and very helpful, but tend to avoid binding commitments, and don't want to be inconvenienced.

PACO PEÑARRUBIA ON HIS PSYCHO-SPIRITUAL PROCESS

Not finding a published report good enough to illustrate E7, I requested one from one of the most distinguished Gestalt therapists in

Europe, and I am pleased to say that it gives evidence that he has "done his homework." The report is rich in that self-understanding which Gestalt therapists have come to value more than theory and technique.

The account is also rich in observations and deep in confessional material. Concerning the transformation process, it is interesting to see how he depicts that "bouncing point" that individuals sometimes come to in life, where the despair of having become intolerable to oneself leads to the gateway of self-acceptance.

Rather than a case-report in psychoanalysis or existential-humanistic therapy, as the other reports in this volume, Peñarrubia's account brings into the book the experience of one whose main help came from being exposed to my intervention, which included the specific development of Ichazo's program of protoanalysis, the development of the virtues and contemplation of the Holy Ideas.

1. In a Place in La Mancha

I was born in a Manchego town to a family of farmers (my father) and merchants (my mother). All the life of my home revolved around the commerce of overseas articles (where a bit of everything was sold: food, cloth, tools, perfumes ...) managed by my parents, although the one who really held the reins of the business was my mother. She was a social-3 who was raised since childhood in the store among her father and her brothers, completely identified with the family business — which she later inherited — and with a markedly mercantile vision of the world ("buy well to sell better") where she and what she sold were inseparable.

My father is a sexual-7, tender and charming, who contributed his seductive arts to a business which he never considered entirely his own. He is a weak man, dedicated body and soul to the veneration of my mother, who he has always idealized so much that he needed other women to covertly rebel against his goddess.

I was the Benjamin, after three girls (even though the second one was born dead), and my birth was difficult. My mother almost died and I came out suffocated and slow to react after they submerged me alternately in cold and hot water.

357

I always was made to feel a little ambivalent about my arrival in this world: on the one hand I knew myself to be wanted, above all because I was a boy, and on the other, I heard hidden recriminations: "I was never the same after the last birth," my mother would say, or "We would have had more children if the last birth hadn't been so dangerous," my father would say. Around the time I was seven years old my mother became sick and had to be operated on in the capital; they never explained her illness to me, but I remember my father's consternation and a few comments about how it was scars from my birth.

I remember my childhood as happy, raised by a girl (my nanny, Josephine) who I see more often than my mother in my earliest memories. I didn't have illnesses, I grew healthy and happy, more involved in the house than out, playing with the sister that preceded me and with my cousins; and it's not until school age that I have memories of the outdoors where I would escape to play with my friends. Before that, the world was made up of two spaces: one that was domestic and secure — the patios and attics in my house and the homes of my grandparents and aunts and uncles; and the other, my parents' business, the public domain where one couldn't play, but rather a serious and problematic place (conflicts always came about on this side). Although for me it was a fascinatingly abundant place: everything was there; it was like Ali Baba's cave, and even to this day I can close my eyes and revive in an instant the smells of the spices, pickled fish, shoes, bags of legumes and salt ...

Only, that horn of plenty deprived us of our parents, and my brothers just as much as myself developed a kind of aversion to the store and all it implied. Among the priorities at home, the business was always first and that deprived us of greater attention, in exchange for freedom (actually I did whatever I wanted to do), and of having the rest of our needs met.

I think that I was, if not a spoiled child, then at least a coddled child because I was the youngest and the boy in a world basically of women. From my father I remember his explosions of anger (he tolerates frustration badly), and a few frightening beatings of my oldest sister when she began to go out with boys. I made myself into a good and submissive child, desirous of fulfilling my mother's expectations, but incapable of renouncing my desires and likes, like my father. I also learned very early the laws of negotiation: be amiable, the customer is always right, they must leave content but carrying what you want to sell them, no one should leave the store without buying (if you don't have what they're looking for, you sell them something else), etc. My mother taught me from a very young age all about this opportunistic use of relationships.

At eleven years of age they placed me in a seminary. To this day I don't know how much religious vocation there was on my part and how much of it was my mother's wish. All of my adolescence unfolded in this ambiance. I even went through the novitiate (from age fifteen to eighteen) and I made vows of poverty, chastity and obedience until the age of twenty when I enter the university to study philosophy. There I begin to abandon religious ideals which are transmuted into political and social ideals. I leave the Order (a French congregation of Paulist priests) and I go to Madrid to study psychology.

From my time as an aspiring priest I glean, above all, an excellent humanistic education; team sports where I lost my fear of physical violence; and I developed a certain capacity for leadership, a love of the Greco-Latinate classics, the study of the Bible, sensitivity to music and the beauty of the liturgy, the examination of conscience and inquiry into the texts of the Spanish mystics of the Counter Reformation.

The rules of poverty were not hard for me (we didn't own anything of our own), nor those of chastity (over the years I overcame my compulsive masturbation); but I had a lot of difficulty with obedience: having to ask permission for everything was something that was really insufferable for me and the touchstone for my successive spiritual directors.

My university years are dark: the subjects of study don't interest me, the political environment is oppressive. I travel through Europe during the vacation months, working, doing anything to pay for my winters; England ... France ... Sweden ... are synonymous with fresh air and sexual freedom. In between, Madrid is like being in exile.

I was at the point of not finishing my psychology degree. During the last semester, and while I was very depressed, I meet Ignacio Martin Poyo, who runs encounter groups using humanistic techniques. I begin to work with him. I come to know Gestalt and my life begins to change. Simultaneously, I fall in love and I decide to live with the woman who is today my wife and companion.

There are years of maturation both personal and professional. I become a good Gestalt psychotherapist, economic prosperity even develops. At the age of thirty I direct a psychotherapeutic center, I have a good team of colleagues and I begin to be recognized as a trainer for Gestaltists. Everything seems to smile on me.

During that time, my wife's pregnancy fails, once we had decided to be parents. The same day that she miscarries I meet Claudio Naranjo. I cannot but feel the synchronicity of this loss and of this discovery, like the beginning of another cycle in my life which will lead me through many hells and many heavens. Above all it will help me to integrate my emotional and spiritual worlds, which was from the beginning the engine of my search, although I tarried and erred many times along the way.

2. The Best Aggression: Being Good

When I was small I wanted to be a saint. It's difficult for me to understand these ideals in a country child, where the values were clearly other (my friends wanted to be warriors, bull-fighters, adventure heroes ...), unless they were some other version of glory. And glory, or fame, or celebrity, has always been the carrot behind which I have run: my mother.

All of my life is the quest for my mother's love, and I must have learned early that being good would work best for me in this enterprise.

My next older sister was the "bad one," the naughty one, the big fat one around the house, the troublemaker and the cause of scandals. I adopted the opposite role: submissive, conformist, affectionate, adaptable; all the feminine values that I thought my mother liked. Thinking that in that way she would like me, I negated the double message, in that later I have discovered that my mother, deep down, liked transgressors — like her brother, an uncle of mine, who I think was a sexual-8, and who was another parental figure for me until he went away (fled?) out of the country. This style of man fascinated and terrified her at the same time. It was in this way that my feeling was always that I let myself be colonized being good, and simultaneously, a lack of love or enmity was subtly transmitted to me: she despised me for being soft. Wanting me to be a saint she assaulted me, and by being good I attack.

In therapy I didn't manage to become conscious of this complexity until I did the Fischer-Hoffman Process with Claudio, one of the pieces of work that most deeply healed me, while at that same time cleaning out many of my relationship conflicts. I had no idea to what degree I had "eaten" my mother. I developed a paradoxical character: externally submissive, rebellious inside; amiable and not creating problems, but deeply resentful. I rescued myself from this schizophrenia primarily with intellectual pirouettes: my intelligence has helped me to explain everything to myself and to arrange my experiences so that they wouldn't hurt me. I am an expert in making over the bothersome and unpleasant [experiences] of life, and also in disguising my aggression with tolerance and servility. Underneath I carry a terrorist who demands: "Why is it that by being good I have not gotten what it is I was promised? If I have fulfilled my part, why don't they give me the ration of love that I deserve?" And on top of it all, I have the feeling that there couldn't be a love that would satiate me, that it's never enough because I have an intrinsic difficulty in receiving; I only know how to gobble and cause indigestion.

The experience of this hunger is the most insufferable that I know, and congruent with my progressive seeing of it more nakedly, it has become more insufferable and, curiously, more acceptable. My attention was always taken with the title of Fritz Perls's first book, *Ego, Hunger and Aggression*, because that simple formulation pertained to me.

During one of my first sessions with Claudio I was sucking my thumb, but I had the urge to bite myself; I went to him to tell him about my fear of self-mutilation [self-injury]. Claudio said to me: "How hungry!" And I began to understand my life.

3. The Best Revenge: Being Happy

I have always put myself above the negativities of this world, negating them in multiple ways, but there was a common denominator: if I carry it off well, if I am happy, if I enjoy myself and obtain pleasure ... that will mean that they didn't get the best of me. Or that my strategy was not erroneous. Or that I am not deluded.

If I have a good project, I am safeguarded from routine and boredom. If I understand things quickly, if I explain them to myself instantly, I am saved from them skipping over me, injuring me, defrauding me, or hurting me. With my head I can create a dissuasive space wherein I can protect my "sensitive" heart. Later, I have discovered that I don't have a heart because of so much atrophy of the pain muscles.

A great part of my life I have lived with this illusion of happiness, of pleasure; deep down, a profound dehumanization although I feigned precisely the contrary. Later, all this has fallen away, to the extent that I have dissolved my rebellion.

Against what/who do I rebel? To a large degree I have reacted against my mother's conventionalism, against her rigidity, her control and her unflinching ways of being. But what I have mostly rebelled against is the mediocrity of my father, who is a 7 like me. I always perceived his authority as weak, wounded to impotence in the face of my mother's strength. And along with her authority I always sensed the smell of falsehood; that things aren't so much good or bad but adequate or not depending on who is present to them, depending on the values of the audience. It's as if I had discovered very young that the world of adults was a compromise, a stage set without much solidity, and that what was important was to learn the language; it wasn't necessary to profess the creed. The best [thing to do], therefore, is not to take it seriously, commit yourself only to the possibility of happiness, and, if things go badly, change the scene (real or imaginary); because in the end, the one who sets the stage badly does so because they want to. I didn't know that this was rebellion. I thought that it was optimism, idealism, positive character ... I never would have put into question my enthusiasm and my cheerfulness (because they were my blind spots) without the work with the Enneagram which was definitive, possibly the most powerful tool, along with Gestalt therapy, in my inner process.

Before my knowing that I was a glutton, Claudio was already having me work from that angle. In the first group that I did with him, at mealtime I was arguing with a colleague, defending a hedonist posture against the other's Apollonian position. I asked Claudio his opinion, and he answered me with a saying from his country: "In Chile we say that too benevolent a surgeon allows the wounds to rot." I didn't understand the meaning, but it hit me deeply — one of those impacts that one doesn't forget, which are like turning the consciousness upside down, and which one understands deeply with the passing of time.

When I finally knew my sin, I understood that gluttony was nothing less than my permanent anxiety and that my conception of the world was a string of rationalizations, of self-explaining justifications, of charlatanry in the end.

All this took me some time and the most pervasive feeling was that of seeing myself and the world for the first time, with the aggravation that I didn't like what I was seeing.

Now it turned out that underneath that insulting enthusiasm there was a pessimist who didn't believe in authority, nor anyone else, nor love ... a vindictive skepticism which I had identified with my small happiness: save myself through pleasure, with a total lack of consideration for the world for which I had apparently "sacrificed myself so much."

And I encountered guilt, that old illness against which I had thought myself immunized.

4. The Best Purgatory: Conscious Suffering[6]

My work during the last ten years, with Claudio as a permanent reference, has been a coming and going from the most infirm to the most saintly and vice versa. I had thought health was also linear, that one went along getting over internal difficulties, becoming ever better, without there being room for regressions or growing worse. In this also have I been greatly deluded and I have had to learn from exhaustion and discouragement.

With the Gestalt work I had glimpsed my fear of conflict and I had discovered my denial of pain: I was able to rescue my feelings of abandonment during my adolescence (my family falling apart, my being away at boarding school, my panic about the discipline ...) and recover the tears that I had blocked since I was fourteen years old.

With the Enneagram work my perspective changed radically: I was my worst enemy and that was hard for me to digest. First came the resistances (forgetting, simplification, pseudo-understanding), then mistrust and the civil war (persecute myself, hyper-vigilance ... a lot of disgust toward myself and much desolation because I didn't see a way out; it seemed impossible to me to beat the machine). Then conscious suffering, which was really the alchemy that transmuted something deep inside [me]. But let's go step by step.

This whole process cannot be separated from my experience of SAT* over four years, including the ten day solitary retreat, and the gradual synthesis of the therapeutic tools that Claudio has distilled over the years: meditation, bodywork, self-observation, group processes, etc.

Without the bombardment from various flanks, I don't think that I would have been able to submerge myself and touch bottom, because another of the things that I began to see was that I am like a cork that always comes out floating, and in SAT that changed: the most ecstatic experiences were nothing but preparation to drop down a little more into hell.

One of these first hells was recognizing my limitations: I was "greener" than I thought, I had dreamed the process more than I had lived it. I found myself to be very poor in resources, very insecure as a man, much more insensitive than I wanted to recognize, very superficial as a therapist.

Fragment from my diary: *During the session I speak to Claudio about my doubts about so much love as I feel [which] seems to me more proper of a mother, not of a man. I connect with anxiety, with the "passive-feminine" which he explained in Bilbao about my character. I ask him: "What man am I if I feel all this like a woman?" Claudio indicates to me: "I don't think that this puts your sexual orientation on trial (I think that this was my actual terror, although I kept it quiet), but rather that each of us has those two parts, masculine-feminine, inside of us." It's like a revelation, something that I've been explaining to my Gestalt students for years, and that I have now understood for the first time.* (November, '85)

The next hell was my guilt. I was a trickster and all my life was a fraud: I asked for love when all that interested me was recognition, I believed that I surrendered and it was no more than a strategy for my mate to change and not give me problems, I accepted Claudio's authority and underneath I hoped for prestige and to "make a guru curriculum" at his side. In my professionnal life I discovered how much seduction there was, how I "dreamed" of my patients' advances without committing myself to their most central conflicts ... And all of that made me feel deeply unworthy and a liar.

Fragment from my diary: *Disgust at my fear. Early fissure in my self-esteem before the falseness of presenting a mask that's not true, or better said, of not showing my face [at all], and escaping so that my cowardice wouldn't be seen, but with the inner awareness of this lie that doesn't fool me. This doubt is the same as the fissure that I was talking about: I fear retroflexion as much as*

self-complacency, and the confusion that this generates in me has
always been my internal war, my lack of inner peace. (October,
'85)

After came a crisis in faith like the one that led me to abandon
my religious studies. I didn't believe in God, [He] was more like a
colleague, someone from my family, whose obligation it was to
protect me, but [I had] no confidence at all that [He] would do it,
like my father.

Claudio spoke at SAT about how our earthly parents are doors
to the eternal, and I had had that experience: resting on Claudio's
chest I had felt myself transported to another world of light, to a
deep experience of the divine. But I still had a lot of rebelliousness
and difficulty in surrendering.

Fragment from my diary: *Claudio has cited the book of Kings:*
Yahweh says to Elijah, 'Be silent and know that I am God.'
Remain still and open yourself to divine experience. How I wish
that this would happen, and how difficult to encounter myself.
(August, '88)

I couldn't consider God as my father because I couldn't feel
myself to be a son of God; not even a son (surrendering myself),
nor worthy, nor good.

The most important thing that happened during that time is
that Claudio spoke to me about conscious suffering. I don't
remember in what context, but I imagine in relation to the des-
peration that all of this was producing in me. He explained this formulation from Gurdjieff* to me and how Fritz [Perls]* worked in
the same direction through pain. For me it was something very
revealing. I had never given myself that opportunity to suffer without fighting myself, without evasion, respecting for myself those
legitimate feelings. I call it purgatory because that's how I experienced it literally: a coming to know my own juices, a purging of
myself like the snail that corks its own shell and survives feeding
on its own mucous. I think that it's this experience that has most

deeply humanized me. It taught me compassion. It gave me a lot of strength to break unhealthy bonds (with colleagues at work, above all) and to work without fear. At SAT '91 I still felt like a mangy dog, to whom, notwithstanding, the gods had treated to a vision of ecstasy. Claudio synthesized it for me: "You came here like a mangy dog and you leave like a sainted mangy dog."

I want to allude to the Retreat experience because of its significance in all that I'm speaking about.

It was in the summer of 1990 and I had conceived of it as a challenge: survive ten days alone, without smoking, meditating ... The first days I got depressed like never before, and without the familiar crutches with which I had always entertained myself: go do something else, dream, plan ...

The most discouraging [thing] was feeling that God didn't listen to me. And then to begin to see that God's silence was proportional to my noise. There was a subtle guilt and a sticky narcissism that didn't let me implore, ask without pride, need without shame.

"Praying has been 'making space,' 'making silence' so that God could (hear me) speak to me. I was far too occupied with discovering things, understanding matters in my life, that I couldn't hear God: I had been supplanting Him, that is 'finding fault with God.' Claudio pulled me out of it, he gave me the noon prayers." (1990)

To pray, to ask for mercy, to implore [God] for forgiveness of my sins "including the ones of which one is not conscious." [It] became light, an old, recognizable faith returned. I knew that I had broken this link in my adolescence, not forgiving having been expelled from home, not forgiving when at fifteen I broke my arm which was never as good again and I could no longer play basketball like before. I had asked God with so much intensity for my arm to recuperate!

Little by little I began to discover an inner joy which in no way resembled my euphorias, and I understood the deep meaning of a few Christian maxims which had always touched me: "Truth will set you free"... "In your hands I entrust my spirit"... "Make me according to your will"...

5. Conclusion (As Provisional As Definite)

I know that in this work any conclusion is nothing more than provisional before setting out for another day's march along the path. Even so, I don't refuse to define what has been traveled.

In all this time I have matured and I feel more and more like a human being. To use an animal simile, I have stopped playing the monkey; running from here to there and entertaining myself with superficial imitations. At one time I connected with the frog, centered in my belly, croaking from my intestines, rooted in my center of gravity.* From that position life is seen in another way.

My way of working has changed a lot: I am more sober, less excessive, I listen better and my intuition is more fine-tuned. I am also more of a fighter and confrontative. My professional life is really the conductive thread of my inner work, that's why I am so grateful to it because "giving" therapy is the occasion to work with myself.

In the last SAT ('92) all of the instructions around "not doing" were for me very illuminating. And really every day I do less (in the sense of activity) and I am more. I was saying there, about my work, that my feeling is one of being "a transmitter, like a kind of looking glass, and my only task is to keep the glass clean so that the thing passes through to others. So that others can work. But I need to pay attention to keeping the glass clean, that it not tarnish."

Also, I have more patience and more humor. I close with a reflection written after last summer's work:

Sometimes I elevate, sometimes I feel a profound weight at the base of my trunk: pure earth, forget flying. I try to bring together what's above with what's below: I put myself in my heart. Here I barely feel anything: I relax. I am a child sitting at the door of the heart. I wait with patience, without anxiety. It can open at any moment. I know that God goes down my street from time to time.

I wait tranquilly, in case He comes. (August, '92)

CONCLUDING REMARKS

I hope that at this point the reader will surely appreciate what I had in mind in announcing that here is a document rich in observations. Peñarrubia's insight into enthusiasm and gladness as expressions of blindness, for instance, are so thoroughly nurtured in his own insight that they are sure to open the eyes of others with a hypomaniac disposition. The understanding of enjoyment as rebellion and revenge, I think, is a particularly valuable psychodynamic observation that I had never seen formulated elsewhere.

All-in-all, I find a rather heroic achievement reflected in this account, as the author has been so open to the undermining of his self-image; and typically, his maturation has involved the sober discipline of contacting such guilt and unpleasantness as the glutton compulsively avoids.

CHARMED CHARMER

The following session is with a sexual E7, where the dominant issue is the polarity between deep-seated rebellion and superficial charm. Usually, persons with this character are out of touch with their anger and displace their rebellion from their original situation (in connection with their parents) to abstract issues in the world. In view of this, the present session is quite exceptional. Danny knows very well, from the outset, that he had trouble getting angry with his father because his father was very charming; yet he follows my directions effectively, and the symbolic act of chopping off his father's head in the dramatization of an early dream seems to have brought about a real step in his liberation process. He emerges with a better grasp of his present situation, and says that he now has a more realistic perception of his father.

Danny: My issue is apparently generic, maybe one without much drama.

Claudio: We'll take that into account.

D: It has to do with my father; more than with my father ... with fathering, with my relationship with him and my relationship with fatherhood. This issue, over the years, has never really interested me, but since I turned thirty-six it's something that has seeped into my life.

C: And how old are you?

D: Thirty-nine. At thirty-six I became a father. I had twins and it was a shock. I had always rejected having children, and suddenly a very strong love and obsession were born in me. I'm sometimes even a little rigid with regard to them and their schedules.

C: Which of the two problems seems to you to be most interesting as a starting point? That of you being the son of your father or of the father, or that of being the father of the child?

D: I have a dream that I had at three or four years of age and that I've always remembered. This year it has started to surprise me ...

C: You had that dream when you were three or four years of age?

D: Yes, and it was that they were chopping off my father's head and my grandfather was watering the sea with a hose. I got up, went to my father's bed and began to touch his neck because I was scared that they would have cut his head off.

C: That happens to parents.

D: It's as if I were just able to assimilate this dream now. To have accepted that in some way I escaped the norm or what my father wanted in some way for us to be, and I feel maybe ... For example, I feel that in the family I'm not enough of a father, although I love my daughters a lot; but I feel that I lack depth.

C: And could that be because you're still too much of a son?

D: I've been very much the son, now I don't know anymore.

C: Not so much anymore but ... Could it be related? You are not father enough because you are too much of a son?

D: Yes. Then my wife also has problems. She hates her father. I feel that at home, suddenly the father is missing and ...

C: I think we have the information already. Let's get into the issue in some way. I imagine that in your Gestalt therapy experience you must have chopped off you father's head in the most explicit way and with all the corresponding emotion, or have you not?

D: I don't know, I don't think so.

C: There's still work to do.

D: That's a pending issue. Maybe I've worked on the mother issue more. I feel that I worked on it in therapy, some two years ago.

C: From what you're saying I believe that that would be a very good place to begin working, to get into the part of them in which you chop off his father's head. That is, get into the experience of that dream which is so old but is still alive in you, which you are beginning to recognize at this time. It's as if it is very strong in the structure of that time ... The little boy, that boy, if you could be that boy that dreams that he chops off his father's head. And we already know enough psychology to know that it's the boy himself, a part of the boy himself who chops off the head. He is creating that dream, he is projecting.

See if you could state, even if in fantasy, what that little boy's experience is like. What's going on with him? Why does he feel that anger toward his father? Why even wishing him dead? What fury exists there?

D: It's that at this point I have to say something. It's that the problem I have is that my father is very seductive.

C: That is a very big problem: to chop off the head of a charming father.

D: I've always had a burden of guilt with this issue.

C: That's why you haven't worked on it enough.

D: To think that my father loves me and it's as if I always do the opposite. It's been years that we haven't lived together, so there's not so much of a problem. I've always felt that I'm going against the current despite ... And that has been one of my greatest problems in the end.

C: Of course, the problem is the guilt-laden patricide. It's the desire to chop the loving father's head off; a father whom you more or less believe to love you; therefore, it's the worst possible thing you could ever do in your life.

D: If I had to chop off my mother's head I wouldn't have the same kind of remorse, I'm sure. From that place, it's always been very difficult for me to become angry at my father. Instead, I've been very, very angry at teachers.

C: Sure, it gives you an escape valve.

D: I've been against everything that had to do with rules. I've set up a life in which no one can tell me anything.

C: You've heard about how 7s have the father issue ... They express it with hatred toward patriarchal culture and toward civilization. And [a desire for] the utopia of a better world.

D: I sensed that it was something along those lines. There was something strange in all of that. I think that this is my problem — a core problem.

C: Even more central, I think, is the problem of not [allowing yourself] to get into this emotion, staying [on the level] of talking about it with a lot of interesting facts that promise much — maybe even getting to the bottom of it some day.

D: Can I say I'm angry?

C: Even if it's with your imagination. But the anger of that boy, who already at that time, at three years of age, chopped off his father's head ... there can be a lot of reasons for that. What pressures are you under? What's hurting you? What is it that is making you angry in order to have generated that dream?

D: There's a kind of perfection that he tries to transmit that bothers me. I'll say it: "The kind of perfection, cleanliness and balance that you try to transmit [transmitir — exude] bothers me because I don't feel perfect or balanced, and I feel dirty."

C: He makes you [feel like] shit. His perfectionism puts you in a very filthy position, very unworthy.

D: Yes, it's the feeling that he is God and I'm hell, or something like that.

C: And if you leave out the "something like that" how would it be?

D: Well, hell.

C: Now, I would propose that you express the same thing more in a child's words. That you would be telling your father how you feel in the face of his demand which is so ...

D: I don't know; I would say ... "It's hard ... You infuriate me!"

C: You infuriate me? That term is already more grown up.

373

D: He makes me throw a temper tantrum. [He makes me lose my temper.] When I was little I would have tantrums.

C: Get into the spirit of the tantrum as you say it.

D: And my father would stick me in a cold shower to make my tantrum go away.

C: Imagine yourself. You are there in the cold shower and you're telling him this.

D: "Fuck it, man! Leave me alone! Let me have my tantrum. Let me express my aggression, my feeling so fucked up."

C: It seems like you need to respect those temper tantrums, integrate them. As if, if you were to make a hybrid of your everyday personality and the temper tantrums, it would be perfect. Does the proposition seem effective to you? If you could put the two together, you wouldn't have a father problem anymore. But let's continue with the tantrum. Talk to him from that place. Talk to him from a space of emotional freedom and complaint.

D: "Well, leave me alone. Why can't I express my anger? Why can't I express my aggression?"

C: There you went over into the adult again: "Why can't I ...", instead of: "Leave me alone." Throw him into the shit. Get angry at concrete things.

D: "Fuck it, man! You're dirty too, and you're dark too, and you are unbalanced and don't come selling me a story about how you are ... About how there's nothing going on here."

C: Look, he wasn't as clean as he pretended to be, so perfect. He is not a God, he acts like a God. He acts perfect.

D: He acts like God probably.

C: Is his perfection hypocritical?

D: Yes, in fact my father is partly racist.

C: It seems like there was a feeling of injustice in what you succeeded in saying as a child. As if he were playing a trick [on you] with that perfection.

D: Yes. He wanted things to be some way that they weren't. In my childhood I lived ... I looked at my father's perfectionism from a distance or at the whole thing of looking good for other people ["caer bien a la gente"]. And out of nowhere someone would say to me: "And you're Dancourt's son? Well, it doesn't seem like it."
　　　And then [in] my world of a child and of my neighbor friends, where suddenly I would realize that my neighbor friend wasn't his father's son but the maid's son ... there was a dark world that they never expressed; that they never talked about.

C: So then it was like a super-dignified, hypocritical posture from which he looked down on you from up above.

D: It was an image, a fantasy that everything is clean, perfect and "don't say anything rude."

C: I think you felt that very clearly even as a very little one and now I'd like you to give words to the little boy who didn't yet have words; to throw it in his face.

D: I would say to him: "Dad, I have tantrums, probably you do too." The only thing that comes to mind is: "Dad, what do you do with Mom?"

C: That "do" would be too much. It's as if he were human, but he pretends to be above sex.

D: Yes, my father plays too much at being a "father." He always played a "father." Seen now from [the perspective of] adulthood it was something suspect. But I never saw it. I always got hooked into the idea that I was the misguided one. My father would ask himself: "Is my son bad?"

C: I suppose that intellectually it would be clear to you that you have to turn that perception around. It is necessary that you grant yourself the dignity that he has been monopolizing and even if you see that you are misguided, that you undo the deception you need to throw more in his face.

Let's see, how can it be done? Addressing yourself to the father of your childhood or that all too fatherly role of his ...

D: "The father principle," the fatherhood.

C: Really confront the "father principle." Chop off the head of the "father-of-the-fatherland."

D: Chop off the "father principle's" head? ... "You're not so elevated. You're not in the heavens, or the heavens aren't ... The earth is. You are not so far away. You can't be so far away."

C: C'mon, put a little more vehemence into it, a little more protest. You have to free yourself from him.

D: "Well, you're not so far because one day you can fall down and give yourself a good whack."

C: It seems that it doesn't stimulate much, that invitation to talk to the "father principle," even though you said it was such an important issue ... But just like that, all of a sudden, talking to him doesn't work. Could the other one work better, the one from your childhood? To follow the lead of the dream?

D: Yes.

C: I think so, because it's a temptation to evade the father with the "father principle."

D: It's that the "father principle" doesn't do anything for me.

C: Yeah, that's not where it's at.

D: I say "fatherliness," well, because ...

C: To elude your father. Let's see then. That little boy, that you were, dreamed that his father's head was chopped off. What was it that chopped off his head? You dreamed that you chopped off your father's head.

D: One day I told this dream to a friend and she said to me: "So you have lived with so little head." As if I also chopped off my own head.

C: Sure, you lost control of your own guiding principle; it seems to me that you left your ship without a rudder. And that's because it caused you great anger and great pain, I suppose, with your father. As if there was nothing left to do but chop off his head. It was like the force of a kicking fit. You need to get into it emotionally, I don't know how. If maybe you could imagine yourself in the dream, be the one in your own dream who was chopping off your father's head, and [feel] what he felt at that moment of chopping it off.

D: Man, now the image of Teseo chopping off Gogona's head is coming up a little, with monsters and things coming out of them. But what are you saying? That I should get into the image of me chopping off his head?

C: In as much as we have arrived at the conclusion that you're the one at guilt, that you should reintegrate that projection, that you should be that boy from your own dream, a boy three years of age who chops off his father's head.

D: I suppose I would feel a lot of fear.

C: A lot of fear, but a great desire to chop off his head. Inspire yourself with the memory of the tantrum. Remember yourself in the energy of the fit. What anger is there? The anger of being right there, in that moment. Which father's head are you chopping off? The perfect one's, [the one that belongs] to that pressure, the one that makes you feel like shit.

D: I feel freedom.

C: Now you imagined it with pleasure.

D: It lifted a burden for me.

C: I ask you to relive it one more time, but now do it with the gesture, with the movement of chopping off his head.

D: [*makes the gesture*] Ah!

C: How do you feel now?

D: Half good, half desolate.

C: He loved you so much!

D: He loves me.

C: He loves you with his head chopped off, halfway chopped off?

D: [thoughtful]

C: What do you feel? That you have to do it even though you end up alone, or that you have to abstain from experiencing that emotion so as to maintain that confluence with him?

D: I think it is doing it even though I end up alone. I've ended up alone. It's not real for me to say that I don't chop it off, actually I've gone ten years without seeing him. I've distanced myself from him and, well, I'd rather chop off his head. I don't know, I may even go home and feel a profound liberation.

C: But for now you feel a faith in that you have done the right thing by chopping off his head; that it was time already for you to chop off his head, for you to take responsibility.

D: I feel that all the anger, all of the struggle, and all of the aggression that I am feeling these days has to do with that.

C: Now we will imagine that there is still one who is fearful that he has done wrong. "Let's see if we can undo this chopping off of the head, to forget." Is there something like that? The temptation to recover the father? To return?

D: It would be the temptation to have an unconditional support, but it's not ...

C: It seems clear that you don't feel that that's where it goes — to go along at the cost of the fiction, of an inauthenticity that makes you neurotic.

D: I don't want him close. There was a period when I began to draw images of fathers and suddenly my father called. My father lives in Venezuela now.

C: You have begun an act of greater separation, it seems like it's been very real. What's left is that this be fleshed out more. Your father lives in Venezuela and what would you need to tell him now to bring yourself up to date with him? From this position of the son who has already triumphed, oedipally, by chopping off his head?

D: What would I say to him? "Well, I would have liked to have known more about you; more real things. I would have liked to have known your real life."

C: But don't get ahead of yourself; tell him that you chopped off his head. Begin there: "I chopped the head off of my idealized image of you and that's a little bit like saying good-bye."

D: "I've chopped the head off of my idealized image of you and now I can speak to you more directly."

C: That's it! You have a few things pending ...

D: "What shit! ... "

C: It's going well, the melody was going well.

D: "Why the fuck is there so much heirarchy in your relationship with [me and] my siblings? Why the fuck does my older brother drive and you never invite me to drive your car? Why, if you now say that I'm your favorite son, don't you come to see me in Spain?"

C: You say it with a nice attitude.

D: "Fuck it! Why haven't you come to see me in Spain instead of traveling to Peru so much?"

C: Let's see, make yourself a little more lordly; a person with poise, self-possessed.

D: "Why the fuck haven't you come to visit me?"

C: Try saying: "It has hurt me ..."

D: "It has hurt me that for as long as I have been here (fifteen, sixteen years) you haven't come to visit me and you have always gone to see my older brother."

C: "That distances me from you."

D: "That distances me from you and it distances me from everyone. When my older brother doesn't even write you a single fucking letter, doesn't call you; and every month I'm calling you on the phone and writing letters to you and thinking what things I could bring to you that might please you."

C: Would you say that you are saying good-bye to him, that you are driving him out of your inner life like a boy that has him enclosed in there, as the father, in a childish way?

D: That is my wish.

C: You take away his authority; you chop off his head as far as authority over you goes.

D: Yes, now it seems to me that he wasn't such a good father. "Why, I don't even understand why my twin brother still lives with you."

C: Develop that more, the "You haven't been a good father."

D: "You haven't been a good father. You've wanted to be a good father; you've played out the image of a good father."

C: Be severe.

D: "You've been a stupid father."

C: I'm struck by the laconic quality, by the little you say about what a bad father he was to you.

D: I have very deep in my heart the image that separated me: first thinking that I wasn't a good son, that if I were bad ..., as if the bad were bad. "When I was finally an adolescent, and you would say to me that I was a cold-hearted boy that I didn't want to be at home..." not even with his family. Well, I'm not surprised.

C: I'm interested in knowing where you feel you are with regard to what we have done up to now. Has something real happened in your situation in the face of "fatherliness" and your father?

D: Yes, well, what's real is that I've let myself see him more realistically ... perceive him, feel him in a more realistic way ... without a feeling of guilt. I don't have a guilty feeling and I free myself from a lie, from a fantasy.

C: Tell us all what that fantasy is like that you have liberated yourself from.

D: That my father was God or that he was perfect or that he was good.

C: You have maintained the deeply needed ["de tanta necesidad"] father illusion that you had.

D: Yes, probably, although he was affectionate. I feel this, but I also feel that he was an affectionate father.

C: So, affectionate and a bad father.

D: Yes, affectionate but ... And a bad father? Okay!

C: And you were confusing that if he was affectionate it must mean that he was a good father.

D: I feel good with my father at a skin level, when I give him a hug.

C: Maybe the father you had was a seductive father, one who made you feel, through his expressions of affection, that he was a good father. He was tricking you. He was a bad father that made you feel so taken in because of his expression ...

D: Couldn't I be doing that with my daughters?

C: Good question. That would be another problem. Let's see, what do you think?

D: Man! I'm very affectionate with them.

C: How is the question transformed into a statement?

D: I am doing that with my daughters because I am affectionate but underneath I don't feel secure. I fantasize that they are not going to care about me.

C: You want to make up for that by promoting yourself.

D: On the other hand, my wife is more direct and more aggressive; more dramatic and more stubborn. And my wife comes along and they go off after her. They ignore me completely; and here I am trying to create the beautiful world that my father created.

C: You're passing on to your children the world of fatherly affection. Let's see ... I wanted ... even if we don't get into it completely, a little bit of accusation of yourself as a bad father. If you are seducing them, it's because you have that insecurity that more than likely you aren't doing it well. Give your perceptions a voice.

D: Well probably ... No, not probably. I feel that I'm covering something up with the affection [I give] my daughters. Man! Do I feel affection! But ...

C: C'mon, get more into that "something." "I am covering up ... " in another way.

D: I'm covering up insecurity. Man! Until I reached thirty-six I practically didn't have any big responsibility with regard to people and all of a sudden I saw myself with two little girls and I think that in the face of that problem I reacted by seducing.

C: For fear that you don't have enough to give you have to seduce?

D: I don't have a father image. I was surprised once when I asked my father about his father and he told me that he was a person that went from party to party: "A carouser." My father's father was a partier. It bothered me a lot for him to tell me "a carouser" because I, in the face of such a father, well, I thought that behind that there was something marvelous. It turned out not so; it was his mother and not his father.

C: And you? How did you get to your grandfather all of a sudden? You were talking about yourself, how you are with your daughters.

D: Well, because ... And me? Well ... And me in relation to my daughters?

C: Well, first we started with your daughters, that maybe you weren't such a good father in view of the [fact] that you had to seduce them; and then, in some way, we ended up talking about your carousing grandfather. I ask myself, is there something to think about — in that you, in the face of your daughters, are not enough for yourself ... ?

D: I don't have the feeling ... I don't feel like a solid individual.

C: Is there anything else? You were saying that your father made you feel dirty.

D: Yes, I think: "Yuck! If my daughters were to see me!"

C: A dirty father.

D: I'm not a man of breeding. I am not an exemplary man.

C: You are not a man like your father. Explain to your daughters that you are not a man like your father.

D: "Well, my daughters ... " [*laughter from the people*]

C: What happened?

D: Well ... [*silence*] "I'm messy. I can't teach you order."

C: See what it would sound like to tell them: "Because I'm messy I can't teach you order, I feel inadequate and I seduce you; I become especially affectionate."

D: "Daughters, I love you but I am perhaps a bit fragile. Sometimes I feel like nothing; I feel bad to have set up a life for myself [to suit] my standard and my comfort. How can I teach you will, strength or order when I'm always looking to be comfortable, to be at ease? How can I expect you to get good grades when I was a disaster?"

C: "Because I feel that deficiency I treat you especially affectionately to compensate."

D: "Because I feel totally deficient in image ... Because I don't feel [have a sense of] my father, well, I try to compensate. I try to invent a father for myself."

C: Invent a father for them maybe.

D: Invent a father for them and invent myself — I'm a father, and I also have that.

C: On the contrary, I see now how these two things are tied together: How feeling small before your father, this complication that you have to fill up with the same myth about the father. But that would be another chapter.

D: It's very clear.

C: Anything else? Do you feel satisfied?

D: Yes.

Frequently, awareness of their parent's personality brings people to understand their own; yet here the converse may be said to be true: D.'s motivation to consider his relation with his father has been stimulated by the fact that he has become the father of two daughters.

8

ENNEATYPE 8

Though E8 characters abound in *The Canterbury Tales*, I begin this time with one from Canetti's *EarWitness: Fifty Characters* —"The Granite-cultivator."

The granite-cultivator is a woman who does not care for excuses. Murderers try to excuse themselves too and they talk and talk until people forget that there is a corpse. If *he* could talk, then the whole thing would look altogether different. Not that she feels sorry for the victims, for how can a person possibly let himself be murdered? But then again, it is good that there are murder victims so that the murderers may be punished.

The granite-cultivator has her children pray at night: "Charity begins at home!" When they fight, she goads them on until they resort to violence. The thing she likes best is seeing them box; she cares little for harmless sports. Of course, she does not object when the boys swim. But it is more important for them to learn how to box.

They are to get rich and know how to make millions. But they are to feel no pity for the suckers who let themselves be cheated. There are two kinds of people: cheaters and cheated, weak and strong. The strong are like granite, no one can get anything out of them, you can squeeze all you like. It is best never to give anything. The granite-cultivator could have struck it rich, but then the children came. Now let the children get rich. Work is bad for the mind, she tells them everyday. If you're smart, you let other people work for you. The granite-cultivator sleeps well because she knows that she gives nothing.

Her door stays shut. No man crosses her threshold. Men hang you up with kids and then forget to pay. And they're not very capable either, otherwise they wouldn't keep trying. If a man who has really made it were to come, she would certainly recognize him. But a man like that has no time and so he never comes. The loafers, they'd like to come.

The granite-cultivator has never wept. When her husband went to the dogs, she couldn't forgive him. She has held it against him for eight years now, and when the children ask about him, she says: "Father was stupid. A moron like him goes to the dogs." The granite-cultivator does not view herself as a widow. Her husband, who was such a moron, does not count in her eyes, that is why she is not a widow. Men are totally useless anyway. They feel sorry for people and let others put one over on them. She does not give anything, no one takes anything from her, men could learn by her example.

The granite-cultivator does not like to read, but she has harsh homilies. When something harsh is said to her, she hears it immediately and adds it to her harsh homilies.[1]

Ichazo called this character an ego-venge — to underline vindictiveness. This requires an explanation, for many E8 people are so quick to respond in kind that the word "revenge" seems to be out of place. For we associate revenge with a delayed reaction, and to the extent that this is true, the immediate revenge of those particularly prompt to get even may be better described as extra-punitiveness, or simply, violence. E8 people don't harbor resentment for long, and other people — notably E4 and E6 — can be more vindictive, in the sense of holding on to resentment and a persistent motivation to repay injuries.

Yet, in a particular sense, E8 is vindictive, and significantly enough to justify the association of this word to the character: the E8 personality itself constitutes a "getting even" with the world in response to painful childhood experience. Typically, the person acts today in a way that compensates for his or her helplessness in the face of perceived injustice he or she was treated to during childhood. We may say that they have to take justice in their own hands; and power, in the name of justice. Paradoxically, this is the core of what today is called the "anti-social personality disturbance." Just as they were hurt *then*, they set out to hurt others *now*. Just as they felt impotent *then*, they decided (implicitly, and at a very early age), to avoid weakness at all costs, and seek to be in control. Because the world failed them and they felt alone, they have decided to go it alone, to be self-reliant and strong.

The problem of the E8 is an over-development of aggression that amounts to an under-development of tenderness, and a repression of the need for affect. E8 people, therefore, need to develop tenderness and their sensitive side. A serious case of type 8 is an excessively rough person — a certain animalization has taken place, leading to an over-aggressive manner of being. This would seem a more instinctive manner of being, as in the Freudian conception of an id-centered character, but this is not exactly the case. Rather, it is that of an ego that *sides* with instinct, not one that is open to self-regulation. The situation may be likened to that of a person who, instead of repressing, becomes an enemy of the repressor. And enmity toward the mind's repressive side is not spontaneity. I call it counter-repression; and it contributes to the rigidity of this personality style, notwithstanding its intolerance of constraints.

Instead of being inhibited, instead of standing in the way of the fulfillment of their desires, instead of feeling that their sexuality is prohibited, instead of repressing, E8 people do the opposite thing: they side with their desires, they defend them. More than id-driven, they stand against their super-ego, their internal censor and society's representative. This attitude of being against the super-ego is not an animal's spontaneity, however, but a super-ego turned upside down. The result is not true naturalness, but a roughness that is defensive, reactive.

E8 is the most rebellious of types — the person who does not believe in authority, who learned very early to be independent of authority. We can say that they have become power-oriented in defiance. They have learned to oppose the power of established authority through means of forcefulness, intimidation and great autonomy. In their psyches, not to depend on others is in service of a readiness to make war, as is also being strong and fearless. To succeed in the struggle for existence, they have learned to defy intimidation and confront danger. Those who are afraid do not risk; E8s, repressing fear, develop a special taste for risk.

The E8 strategy is that of not expecting to be given anything. They go ahead and take what they need; so much so that, if they are given something, they do not enjoy it as much as if they had seized it themselves. E8 is an exploitative personality of one who pushes for advantage. If E7 is a fox, E8 is a shark.

Alternatively, we may understand their psychological situation through that of rape. A rapist is not satisfied when given love; that makes him feel weak, and he perceives affection as weakness in the other. The rapist feels more inclined to seize, to conquer; something easy does not interest him so much. He gets more pleasure out of getting something by force, for this involves his experiencing power. (I am using rape as a metaphor, just as I used cosmetics as a metaphor for E3. It does not mean that E8s are literally rapists. Some rapists belong to type 8; probably the majority, but not all, of course. Driven to challenges, they are the most challenging.)

E8 may be strikingly sadistic. In response to early frustration the E8 has learned to get hold of things even at the cost of another person's suffering. And especially so in delayed revenge. They grow used to the frustration of others that is entailed by their own satisfaction and this pain has ended up becoming a sadistic pleasure. First they needed to attack in order to get satisfaction, but in time, psychological predation has become a pleasure in itself. Part of their pleasure is feeling the other person's pain, which is also a sign of E8's own power, an affirmation and a love substitute (prove your love by suffering me).

They are also very cunning. Both types 7 and 8 are cunning, but E8 combines slyness with violence. Because they are cunning, they believe that everybody else is also cunning: theirs is a very cynical view of life.

Wilhelm Reich was the first scientist to describe this character in depth, calling it "phallic-narcissistic." In man, the E8 is an over-masculine macho; among women it is less frequent, and may come across as masculine, or just as strong, direct and sexual. E8 is lusty because their "I want" is significantly expressed through sex, because they are in touch with their desires, do not accept conventional limits and they invalidate the voice of conventional authority. Theirs is a revolutionary spirit. Social movements rely heavily on type 8, who are the rebellious, active and courageous people. E8 people are direct in their speech and in saying what they think. They may seem healthier than the rest, but this is only an appearance, because their neurosis is like the negative of the more common pattern of inhibition and guilt in regard to sex and aggression. In actual fact, they are neither better nor worse, simply different. They seem not to avoid anything, they do not escape, and that impresses us as a strength; yet their weakness is that they cannot tolerate dissatisfaction. They have to obtain satisfaction at any price, and thus their passion for intensity: wanting more, more and more. They are full of initiative, they do not keep still. They are the opposite of the passive character: they are adventurous; they enjoy getting around and proving to themselves that they are stronger than the dangers they face. And, mostly, they repress "femininity" and dependency, and turn a deaf ear on their super-ego — repressing guilt, feelings of inadequacy and other forms of psychological pain.

The E8 pattern is that of an anti-social personality in today's language. They are the "evil-doers" from a certain point of view; but they are not worse than others. Whatever the appearances, all neurotic styles are morally equivalent.

In the title I gave the E8 chapter in *Ennea-type Structures* I emphasized the trait of "coming on strong" — which is to say over-powering and over-whelming.[2] Quino has given a funny illustration of this trait in a comic strip showing two men seated on a train as it approaches a station. The bigger fellow calmly — as a matter of course — removes the shoelace from one of the shoes of his frail and shy-looking companion. The big fellow, who until then has been reading, places the shoelace in his book to mark his place as he closes it, and then gets up to leave.

Or, consider the manifestation of "coming on strong," in the cartoon by Gahan Wilson, which follows.

Among the world-famous, Stalin illustrates the more sadistic kind of E8. It is said that the people of Tiflis have been fun-loving and brutal, and a biographer of Stalin observes that, as a child he absorbed the "cynicism of the rabble."[3] Stalin was not a good student — he preferred excursions. Then he became a kinto ("lord of taverns and bazaars, a half-poet and half-thief"). During this time he developed physical strength, an unscrupulous

"Where the hell's that kid got to?"

personality and a readiness "to mock life or death." Eventually Lenin would write in his last will that Stalin was "too brutal and rude to be leader of the Communist Party." (p. 19)

Obviously Stalin's brutal dominance coupled with the high level of power that he had already reached and his fame as a revolutionary allowed him to seize the leadership after Lenin's death. This dominance had established itself from the time when his father sent him to the seminary where he was exposed to anti-Czarist ideas by religious socialists. He soon became an agitator among the workers, though he also used to spend the night reading Marxist books.

Already in his revolutionary beginnings Stalin betrayed the cause he enthusiastically espoused: when he was discovered by the authorities, he gave the names of all his peers who had been attending anti-Czarist meetings. He explained it later: this was a way of saving them from the bourgeoisie and giving the Party a good bunch of able revolutionaries.

I will not undertake to summarize Stalin's life beyond remarking that it echoed his adopted name — meaning "iron man." His identification with class war and war on the intellectuals gave outlet to such violence in him, that many of those near him could not bear to endure ... at the cost of their lives. Not even Stalin's daughter could any longer approve in silence what she saw, once she came to de-idealize her father enough to recognize his executions as monstrosities. She chose to take her own life rather than turn impotently against him and lose her life as others had.

However true that being a revolutionary, in some, is mostly a symptom of an intensely rebellious personality, it is also true that revolution is an antidote to the destructive *status quo* of social attitudes and institutions, and that revolutionaries, like Garibaldi or Marx, are moved more by love than hate.

Here is a personality portrait of Marx by Paul Annenkow:

> ... his personality was characterized by energy, assertiveness and unbreakable security ... He gave the impression of being a man who has in his hands the right and the power to demand attention ... clumsy movements though firm and resolute. His manner, strikingly opposite to social norms, was proud and slightly disdainful; his sharp voice, hard as metal, fit perfectly well with his radical

judgements about people and situations. He speaks always in an imperative tone which cuts off any attempt to oppose him and impregnated all and each of his words, constituting an almost painful physical stimulus. His way of expressing himself conveyed a conviction rooted in his deepest being to the effect that his mission was to dominate and prescribe to others the rules of behavior. In front of me I had the living incarnation of a dictator ...[4]

During his student years, Marx was part of a forbidden student organization and became one of its presidents. He was once imprisoned for drunkenness and tumult, was accused of carrying arms and denounced more than once for not paying his debts. However anti-social all this may seem, and however true that he looked down on the expression of feelings as "sentimental," Marx was in many ways a very loving man.

In Tania Rosal's book on Marx's love life, she reports that as a young man he aspired to an egalitarian relationship based on mutual respect.[5] In his books, *The Holy Family* and *Critique of Critical Critique*, Marx speaks of this communion of man and woman through the joint discovery of their being through love. He felt deep love for his wife Jenny and also for his children.

> ... Marx loved his children deeply. He wasn't just tender and capable of being for hours a child himself while with them, but also he felt magnetically attracted toward other kids, specially the miserable and abandoned ones who crossed his path ...(Rosal, p. 61)

Practicing psychotherapy with a friend of mine who is a type 8, I understood something I had never seen in a more external acquaintance with these people: behind the invasive attitude of plunging ahead and seizing, was his difficulty in receiving. A cynical view of others contributes to this in E8, along with the repression of neediness and the sense of being an evil person. But they cover up all this with the rationalization that evil is not evil. From a conventional point of view they would be regarded bad, but they do not believe in conventional values. So they adopt a different set of values: good people are hypocrites, and evil those who are really right. But this is a superficial construction, and behind lingers a poor self-concept, the self-image of being an undeserving person. However much they go ahead and seize what they want, love cannot be seized; love can only be received. Thus, they substitute more tangible things for the ineffable that cannot be seized. And, while one can possess somebody, and make another do whatever one wants, deep down this is not fulfilling because one knows that one is manipulating ... dominating. Thus, E8s are somehow condemned to dissatisfaction, and the passion of lust is ever kindled by this underlying dissatisfaction. However much they try to fill themselves, they are not filling themselves with what they need. Their relationship with themselves is sado-masochistic and self-punitive. They also have an implacable sense of justice.

The image of Henry VIII seems to me as good a caricature of "taking justice in one's hands" as a literal portrait can be. Nor can I think of a clearer instance of aggressively-biased justice than this lusty king who used his power to put his wives into the grave. Henry VIII was atypical in one regard, however: contrasting with the general picture of an E8, he was a theologian, while most phallic-narcissists (and this is my favorite term in the extant psychological vocabulary) are cynical skeptics, not only iconoclasts.

The outer image of an E8 is not so much the elegant king, but the Mexican "macho" — tough and dominant, animalistic, sexually assaulting, violent and gross. There is a very strong E8 quality to Mexican culture — which inherited its character from the tough *conquistadores* and from the combative Indians at the same time. That E8 is gross rather than refined is underlined by Theophrastus, who names one of his characters "A Friend of the Rabble." Vulgarity is also emphasized, along with dishonesty, by Chaucer in his description of the miller in *The Canterbury Tales*.

> The *Miller* was a chap of sixteen stone,
> A great stout fellow big in brawn and bone.
> He did well out of them, for he could go
> And win the ram at any wrestling show.
> Broad, knotty and short-shouldered, he could boast
> He could heave any door off hinge and post,
> Or take a run and break it with his head.
> His beard, like any sow or fox, was red

And broad as well, as though it were a spade;
And, its very tip, his nose displayed
A wart on which there stood a tuft of hair
Red as the bristles in an old sow's ear.
His nostrils were as black as they were wide.
He had a sword and buckler at his side.
His mighty mouth was like a furnace door.
A wrangler and buffoon, he had a store
Of tavern stories, filthy in the main.
His was a master-hand at stealing grain.
He felt it with his thumb and thus he knew
Its quality and took three times his due —
A thumb of gold, by God, to gauge an oat!
He wore a hood of blue and a white coat.
He liked to play his bagpipes up and down
And that was how he brought us out of town.[6]

Also, Chaucer's summoner, "hot and lecherous as a sparrow," illustrates the lusty E8.

Garlic he loved, and onions too, and leeks,
And drinking strong wine till all was hazy.
Then he would shout and jabber as if crazy.

In this case it is exploitative self-interest that is emphasized:

He would allow — just for a quart of wine —
Any good lad to keep a concubine
A twelvemonth and dispense it altogether!
Yet he could pluck a finch to leave no feather:
And if he found some rascal with a maid
He would instruct him not to be afraid
In such a case of the Archdeacon's curse
(Unless the rascal's soul were in his purse)
For in his purse the punishment should be.
"Purse is the good Archdeacon's Hell," said he.

But well I know he lied in what he said;
A curse should put a guilty man in dread,
For curses kill, as shriving brings, salvation.
We should beware of excommunication.
Thus, as he pleased, the man could bring duress
On any young fellow in the diocese.
He knew their secrets, they did what he said. (p. 34)

I have argued in *Character and Neurosis* that the most distinctive
defense mechanism in E8 is a form of negation that affects the perception
of both psychological and physical pain — a desensitization in service of
dominance and aggression. Such desensitization permits the E8 to turn
anxiety into excitement to the point that a life without risk becomes too
much boring. I have already pointed out how there is repression of the
need for affection and a relative anesthesia to guilt, shame and general discomfort that would arise from the clash between impulses and socially
shared conscience.

I find a good illustration of the skill of Mexican toughies in raising
their pain threshold in a joke about a man who has been stabbed and lies
in a pool of blood with the knife still in his chest. Somebody comes along
by dawn, sees him there under a street lamp, and asks with great concern:
"Does it hurt a lot, brother?" And there comes as answer: "No, only when I
laugh!"

A possible trait of E8 is punishing the fraudulent, i.e., cheating the
cheaters, stealing from the undeserving — as in that legendary champion of
the underdog, Robin Hood. They have great contempt for the weak and for
the naive — but contemptuousness itself is a trait of theirs beyond content.
Intensity I have already mentioned. The most intense characters are E8 and
E4, the sadists and the masochists. Still another trait (suggested by Reich's
appellation of "phallic-narcissist") is arrogance. Such is the case of the
miller in Chaucer's tale of the Reeve:

There was a miller lived there many a day
As proud as any peacock and as gay;
He could play bag-pipes too, fish, mend his gear,
And turn a lathe, and wrestle, and poach deer.

397

And at his belt he carried a long blade,
Trenchant it was as any sword that's made,
And in his pouch a jolly little knife.
No one dared touch him, peril of his life.
He had a Sheffield dagger in his hose.
Round was his face and puggish was his nose;
And he was bald as a monkey; to speak fully,
He was a thorough-going market bully
Whom none dared lay a hand on or come near
Without him swearing that they'd buy it dear.
He was a thief as well of corn and meal,
And sly at that; his habit was to steal.
Simpkin the Swagger he was called in scorn.

Among the traits of this cunning miller is that of being anti-intellectual — also typical of the E8 syndrome.

The greatest scholar is not the wisest man
As the wolf said in answer to the mare.
Them and their precious learning! Much I care. (p. 123)

I had intended to end with several pages about the familiar character Rhett Butler in *Gone with the Wind*. While in the well-known movie his personality is softened, the novel protrays him as cynical, not concerned with people's judgments — or, rather, defiant and materialistic. Since permission to quote was not granted by the publishers, I will, instead, illustrate the chartacter with two passages from Balzac concerning his Vantrin in *Old Goriot.*

He was the kind of man people call a jolly fellow. He had broad shoulders, a well developed chest, muscular arms, and heavy square hands with a vigorous growth of fiery red hair on the fingers. His prematurely wrinkled faced showed signs of a harshness which was contradicted by his affable easy manner. His bass voice was by no means unpleasing and his great jovial laugh seemed in keeping with it. He was obliging and genial.

If a lock stuck, he soon had it taken to pieces, mended, oiled, filed and put together again with the remark, "It's all in my line." Nothing seemed too out of his province, moreover. He knew all about ships, the sea, France, foreign parts, vistas, men, events, the law, great houses and prisons. If anyone grumbled unduly, he would immediately offer his services.[7]

He obviously is a practical person, well-connected to the outer world and with a keen eye for everything, and with information that, far from being erudition, is the know-how of one who seeks mastery. Though he had lent money to the pension owner and other lodgers, these repaid him promptly because of "a certain look of his, penetrating and full of determination, which inspired fear in spite of his good humored air." (p. 40)

We sense that he is one who likes to have others in his debt and whose generosity is far from being a self-sacrificing, empathetic disposition. "The very way in which he spat, showed an imperturbable sang froid which proclaimed him to be a man who would not shirk at committing a crime if it offered a way out of a dubious position." His look of determination and the cold-bloodedness conveyed by his way of spitting may be said to betray lack of fear and lack of care about the feelings of others: a readiness for anything and freedom from social expectations. "His eyes, like a stern judge's, seem to pierce to the heart of all questions, to probe all consciences, and examine every feeling." (p. 40)

COME OVER, RED ROVER

Most appropriately, Lindner (in his book *The Fifty Minute Hour*) begins his account of his patient Mac with the first encounter — which did not take place across a desk but over the heads of an audience at a meeting.[8] Before the description of this event, however, we learn from Lindner that he himself is politically involved:

> For many years I have been active politically in a small way out of
> a conviction that the psychoanalyst belongs in the world, among
> men, and should participate in the life of his community. I have
> felt that he has a public responsibility which cannot be discharged
> by living the anchorite existence most analysts live, limiting their
> purview to the dim caves in which they practice their art like orac-
> ular recluses surrounded by the esoteric symbols of a mystic craft.
> Because of this belief I have, from time to time, joined movements
> and societies of a progressive cast, and have loaned my name — for
> whatever its value — to causes I've considered worthy." (p. 48)

Lindner also makes known to us that he is a radical who doesn't
mind collaborating with Communists when a convergence in goals makes it
desirable, though he is critical of the Communist Party and of the motives
of some who profess themselves Communists. Because he is interested in
elucidating Communism as a neurotic symptom, he accepted Mac at a time
of overcommitment and at an uncommonly low fee, he explains later. I
quote further:

> All of this is by way of explaining my presence at a public meeting
> where the audience included a number of Communists, among
> whom was Mac. And it is not strange that I should illustrate my
> digression by writing of segregation, for this is the issue on which
> we clashed at our first meeting. At that time a debate on socialized
> medicine was being planned by the organization of which I was
> nominally the chairman, and the topic we were considering relat-
> ed to the choice of members for a panel which would discuss the
> points raised by the debaters when they had finished their pre-
> sentation. I remember that, as I was reading aloud a list of the
> names that had been proposed for this panel, an angry voice from
> the rear of the room interrupted me. Someone called, "Are there
> any Negroes on that list?"
> I replied that I didn't know, and asked the secretary, who
> shook his head in negation. As I turned again to face the audience,

the same voice cried out, "I demand to know why Negroes have been deliberately excluded from that panel!"

I answered that I was sure the exclusion had not been deliberate, the list had been composed from names submitted to the committee, the final selection made on the basis of an individual's qualifications to discuss such an issue and on nothing else. Then, believing this answer would satisfy whomever it was had interrupted, I proceeded with the business at hand. But I had no sooner begun than the voice called out again.

"We're not satisfied with that answer," it shouted. "We demand that the Negro people be represented on that panel!"

The belligerence of the voice and the presumption of the "we" were challenging. I asked the speaker to stand up and identify himself. There was a stir at the rear of the room, and then a tall figure detached itself from the group and rose. It was Mac: six feet and three inches, pock-marked face, crown of sandy hair, sport coat, turtle-neck sweater and G.I. fatigue pants.

"My name has nothing to do with it," he said in a quieter voice in which a small quaver indicated that he was less sure on his feet and alone than seated in a crowd. "The point is that there should be a Negro on that panel."

"The committee will be glad to consider any names you care to submit to it," I said. "If you want to suggest someone qualified to be a member of the panel, no one's going to ask the color of his skin."

Mac stirred uncomfortably. Gruffly, he said, "That's not enough. That panel has to have a Negro on it."

"Why?" I asked.

"Because there should be a Negro on the platform of every public meeting sponsored by a democratic organization, which this is supposed to be."

"Why?" I asked again.

"To represent the interests of the Negro people of this community," he answered.

"Don't you trust the other members of the panel to represent those interests?"

"That's not the point, whether I trust them or not. A Negro should be up there, that's all!"

"But suppose we can't find anyone qualified to participate on the panel? Isn't it better to have the interests of all the people well represented than to have any particular group poorly represented?" I asked.

"I'm not arguing that point,' he said. "All I think is that a Negro should sit on that platform."

"Just as an exhibit?" I asked.

Now Mac was angry. "Even if he just sits there and don't open his mouth, it will still show how we stand on the Negro question," he said.

"It seems to me," I said, "that if you put anyone on that platform merely to exhibit him and not because he's qualified to take part in the discussion, you're exposing him to ridicule. Frankly, I question your motives."

Spurred by whispered encouragement from his neighbors, Mac shook his head. "You can question all you like," he said. "Anyhow, you're not the only member of this organization. I put my question in the form of a motion instructing the committee to place a Negro on the panel." He sat down amid cries of "Second!" from various parts of the room. There was some brief discussion, the question was called, a vote taken and the motion carried.

I at once confessed to him that I had forgotten his name — possibly in retaliation for my defeat in the balloting that night at the meeting — and therefore hadn't recognized him over the telephone. He acknowledged the apology with a wave of his hand and sank into the chair near my desk, his big frame collapsing as if it were falling apart at all its joints. He closed his eyes in weariness for a moment, then opened them and looked around — at the books, the couch, the framed etching of Freud at his desk, the African and New Guinea sculpture in the room.

"This is a nice place," he said. "Quiet. Away from the world."

He reached for the cigarettes on the desk, lit one, filled his lungs and then fixated the glowing end as he spoke.

"A big guy like me. I've been all over, done everything. Now I gotta come here and lie on a couch and cry off to you." He shook his head with a grimace of disgust. "But I can't do it any more by myself. The harder I try the worse it gets.

"If the Party knew I was here, I'd be in for a rough time," he continued. "They don't like psychoanalysis — or psychoanalysts. Especially guys like you. They call you a Social Democrat. D'you know that?" For the first time he looked directly at me.

"I know it," I said. "Psychoanalysis is a bourgeois science: psychoanalysts are the lackeys of the capitalistic class. I'm an unstable Social Democrat. So what are you doing here?"

"The Party's position on psychoanalysis —" Mac began. But I interrupted him. "I know the lecture," I said. "That's not why you came to see me."

Mac stamped out his cigarette with a stained thumb. "No it isn't," he said: then he smiled, "I'm just trying to put it off a little."

"Everyone does," I said. "What's it all about?"

I have already shared my impression (see Enneatype 4) that Lindner is an E8 individual, and the passage above shows his willingness and ability to challenge a challenger. The same may be said of his first individual conversation with Mac, which happened during the coffee-break immediately following the meeting, where Lindner once more shows himself as one not easily intimidated:

Coffee was served when the meeting had ended and the crowd broke up into small groups. Later, when I went up for a second cup, I found myself standing in line behind Mac. He waited for me after he'd been served and we took our drinks to a quiet corner of the room. For a few minutes we drank in silence. I could feel his eyes on me and, slipping into the clinical attitude of relative detachment which my years of psychoanalytic practice have taught me is a necessary protection against the personal discomfort of having yourself scrutinized for your weaknesses, I allowed him enough time for his examination. When he had finished, I offered him a cigarette. He lit his with a Zippo on the surface of which was scratched a legend, partly obscured by his large hand.

"So," I said, "you're a seaman, an ex-G.I, you were in the landing at Salerno, and you're married and you're a Party member. What's your name?"

"Name's Mac," he said, "but you're wrong almost all across the board. I was in the Merchant Marines, I work in a canning factory, I got the lighter from a buddy who was at Salerno, I used to wear a wedding ring but my wife is divorcing me."

"And the C.P.?" I asked.

"That's where you're right, Mr.Holmes," he said.

We laughed, and then I could feel his eyes searchingly on me again. (pp. 49-51)

Months later, Mac called to make an appointment with Lindner. I now turn to the passage describing this first professional interview.

"It's me," Mac said. "It must be. Everything's shot to hell. I've got no feeling for anything. I feel like what's happening to me somehow isn't happening — like I'm an observer. Sometimes I even think of myself as if I'm a scientist or something, looking down on a bug struggling on a slide under a microscope. You poke it with something: it moves. You put some acid on it: it wriggles. That bug's me, and so's the scientist.

"My wife left me three months ago," he continued. "She threatened before but she never did it. Now she's gone and done it. She's suing for a divorce and I don't even care. It's just a thing that's happened. Once, if anything like this happened I'd have been ripped open inside. Now she's away somewhere with the two kids and it's like I don't even give a damn... And it's the same everywhere. In the Party I once thought I could be something. I cared what was happening. I was a good worker. Now it's a sort of dream. It goes on, like everything else. But it's not important. I go to meetings, distribute literature, do what I'm told — like a machine, because it's the only thing I know how to do."

"But you care enough to come to see me," I said, "and you're certainly not very calm or detached now."

"Now's different," Mac answered. "But usually I'm dead, rot-

404

ten inside, decaying, shriveling up like a piece of fruit you leave on the shelf."

"Tell me more about your wife leaving you," I asked. "Why was that?"

"This is the part that hurts," Mac replied as he reached for the cigarettes again. "I'm no good to her, haven't been for a long time. You know what I mean. Even my pecker hangs dead." He bent to the light I held and drew deeply. "I haven't been a man in maybe two years. She's tried everything and so have I. Even other women. But it's no good. Sometimes I get a little feeling in me like it's going to be all right. Once, about two months ago, I was on a party and there was a dame there made passes at me. I grabbed her off as quick as I could and took her to a hotel..." Here Mac caricatured a laugh.

"It even sounds funny to me," he continued, "but it was a hell of a night. I tried until I thought my guts would drain out. Just with trying it would get half erect and we'd hurry to make a score; but it was no soap."

"And yet," he went on after a brief pause, "There's something queer about that too. Because I have a discharge every time."

"You mean you ejaculate without an erection?" I asked.

"Yeah. I don't get excited, you understand, and I don't feel anything; but the semen just comes out at a certain time as if it was the real thing."

Anticipating my question, he continued, "After this happened a few times I went to a doctor and he sent me to a urologist. The urologist couldn't find anything wrong. He said it was psychic and I should see a psychiatrist."

"And did you?" I asked.

Mac shook his head. "No," he said. "I knew that this was only a little bit of the problem and I didn't want anyone probing around in my head."

"And yet you came to see me."

"I came to see you for two reasons," Mac said as he ground out the butt. "The first is that it's gotten so bad now I gotta have help. The second is you're the only one in this town I can trust."

405

"Does ____ know you came to see me?" I asked, mentioning the name of the local chief Party functionary.

"Hell, no!" Mac almost shouted. "He'd have ten fits if he found out. Whenever he hears your name he breathes hard anyhow. Plus the fact that there's a kind of unwritten Party ban on going to a psychoanalyst."

"It can't be a very effective one," I said. "I've already analyzed two people from your 'cell' and a couple more from outside of Baltimore."

"I know that," Mac said. "One of the guys you analyzed quit the Party and the other isn't going to last too long I'd say. That's one of the main gripes against you guys, you know. People who get analyzed don't seem to stay with the Party. Or if they do, they can't be counted on."

"Counted on for what?" I asked.

"Counted on to follow Party discipline," Mac answered. "And that's important — to me at least."

"Why?"

"Because no matter what happens," Mac said deliberately and with emphasis, "I want to stay in the Party. I've got to!"

"Why?"

"Because the Party is my life," Mac answered. "Because the Party is right. Because the Party is the only way to build a new world."

"You're sure of that?"

"I am. It's the one thing I am sure of," Mac said. "Look. I've been all over the world, Doc. I've seen the kind of misery no one would believe. The Party's got the only answer for the way out. I've been a Communist for years. I read all the literature before I became one, too. With me it's not like I hear you guys say — because I hated my old man or got pushed around by my sister or something fancy like that. I'm a Communist out of conviction, real conviction, from the neck up, even though I feel it in my intestines."

"*There's* something you feel," I observed.

"I can still get hot by what I see all around me and what's happening," Mac said. "It's not the same kind of hot like it used to be, because then I'd be in there pitching for what I believe. Now all I do is —"

I interrupted Mac here. "So what does this mean?" I asked.

"It means," Mac said, "that if getting analyzed means I have to quit the Party, it's not for me."

"You'd rather go on being detached, impotent, miserable and (I gather) ineffective in everything you do?" I asked.

"If I have to," Mac said, "yes. I'm in the Party to stay. Look." Mac held out his hands. "If I thought it would bring Socialism a minute faster than it's coming I'd nail these hands to the cross myself!"

"Interesting you should use just that figure of speech," I observed. "But isn't it true that your even coming to see me is a breach of Party discipline?"

"I'd have my ass eaten out but good if anyone knew about it," Mac agreed. "But I'm doing it because I think that if I can get straight on my personal problems, I'll be a better Communist."

"Why pick on me to do it?"

"Because I think I can trust you not to try to influence me against the Party. Is that true?"

I shrugged. "A psychoanalyst doesn't *influence* for or against anything," I said. "But a patient, an analysand, has to be willing to subject all of his beliefs and opinions to the analysis. Are you?"

"I think I am," Mac said. "I want to shake this thing. I want to feel human again." Now there was a note of pleading in his speech.

"But not at the expense of the Party."

"That's right." The edge was back in his voice. "Not if it means giving up the Party. But does it have to? That's what I want to know."

"I can't answer that," I said. "I'd be lying to you if I told you one way or the other. I know analysts who would tell you you'd be a better Catholic or Jehovah's Witness or Communist or whatever after an analysis. But I just don't know. I've analyzed Communists before and, as you said, some stay with the Party, some leave it. What'll happen to you is something I can't predict."

Mac thought awhile. Then, as if he had come to a decision, he said, "I feel sure enough of my convictions as far as the Party goes not to have to worry about that. I think my beliefs will stand up under any kind of questioning."

"It's a gamble," I commented.

"Not with me it isn't," Mac countered quickly. Then, "What d'you say? Will you take me on?"

I thought rapidly. My schedule was overful already. I had promised myself to cut down rather than increase my hours. If I took Mac as a patient, it would be for a long and stubborn analysis. Not only were his symptoms among the most difficult to treat — as I had learned from bitter experience before with impotence and depersonalization — but he showed a rigidity of personality, an uncompromising mental structure, that would stand in the way of my best efforts and his best intentions. And as for his being a Communist, here too I knew what could be expected: the moment any of his cherished formulas were questioned there would be hell to pay: his analysis would be hung up for many hours while he did battle with his Marxist conscience: factors that would ordinarily have little or no place in an analysis would be introduced: there would be delays and canceled appointments. Finally, without his having to tell me, I knew that Mac could not afford my fees, and already half my patients were paying reduced fees while I placated myself with the rationalization that I was treating them because they were "interesting" cases.

But the chance to analyze yet another Communist! The chance to test once more my ideas about the breed of men who become militant socialists! I had already, while stationed in a Federal prison, analyzed a high official of the Party and an officer of a trade union was also a Communist. Then I had treated a social worker, an engineer, a student and a teacher who were all card-holders in the Party. Mac would be the first worker-Communist on my growing list, my first real "proletarian." The temptation was not to be resisted. I found myself already manipulating my schedule and framing excuse-arguments to give my wife when I told her I would be taking another patient for three or four hours a week at a small fee. (pp. 53-57)

After he has answered in the affirmative, Lindner still wants to know, "Will you tell them at Party headquarters that you're coming to me?"

Yet Mac's anticipation was not correct: before the end of his analysis he was to quit the Party.

After remarking that he has seldom had a more enthusiastic patient than Mac during his first months of analysis, Lindner proceeds to introduce us to the outlines of Mac's history:

Mac had been born thirty-four years before we met. The place of his birth was a farm in western Ohio where his parents lived with his father's people. The model of a Conestoga wagon on a shelf in my study reminded him of his family origins. Stolid, imperturbable and determined Dutch settlers, they had pushed their way westward in one of the first migrations from the East Coast, coming to rest, characteristically, in a place that reminded them of the home they had left in Europe. Mac's grandfather, who was a very old man when Mac was born, had staked out a large tract of land. As his three sons came of age he parceled it among them, reserving for himself and his second, much younger wife a few acres in the exact middle of the family holdings. White-bearded and with clear blue eyes that remained undimmed to the hour of his death, tall and as strong as one of his work horses, this paternal grandfather was destined to play a major role in the formation of Mac's personality. So was the patriarch's wife, a half-breed illegitimate girl who had been maid of all work on the farm until her mistress died and she was taken to wife as a matter of course.

The youngest of the three sons was Mac's father. He was the old man's favorite, alike to his father in features as an image in a mirror. A vast silence surrounded him. Indeed Mac recalled no word his father had ever spoken. But his manner was kind and his uncommunicativeness more than made up for by a soothing, peaceful presence. His wife, Mac's mother, died in the moment Mac was born. A faded daguerreotype, its cracked pieces glued to a strip of cardboard, was all that Mac ever knew of her. In her place was a conglomerate fiction composed by the boy over the years from his grandfather's reminiscences and the memory of two brief visits paid the half-orphan by his mother's parents. They were, he remembers, big people with heavy hands and huge feet. As they sat in the kitchen and spoke of their daughter's death, they filled the room with the smell of earth, and their low, hoarse voices blended with the snapping wood in the fire and the simmering bubble of the water kettle to become fixed for a lifetime as the sense-scenery of Mac's dreams.

A wet-nurse tended Mac the first three years of his life. Actually, she ministered to him only part time, and for the remainder deputized the oldest daughter of her large brood to act as cook, housekeeper and milkmaid for Mac's father and the distant cousin who worked as hired man. The ample-bosomed nurse was like a general who regularly visits the front. Every morning, while it was still dark, she drove up in a rickety buckboard. It was she who would take Mac from his bed, suckle him, clean and dress him, then turn him over to her daughter with a list of instructions for his day's welfare and activity. A wet smack on his cheek and she was off, to return again after supper with a milk-full breast, a sponging and a final kiss administered while she folded the warm quilt around him. Between the dawn and dusk of her brisk visit there was the sugar-tit, prepared by this natural pediatrician from a lump of honey knotted in a rag and moistened with milk. It was in his mouth all day and most of the night and its taste, recaptured during the early part of his psychoanalysis more than thirty years later, was an assurance of peace and an allayer of fears.

Soon after Mac had turned three he was taken to live in his grandfather's house. Now he came under the dominion of his dour step-grandmother, whom he learned to call "Ma," and the idyll of perfect freedom in which he had lived heretofore was shattered. Ma was a soured woman, intolerant of small boys and dirt, embittered for life by her illegitimacy, and fierce in all her compensations for early experiences as the offspring of an Indian woman and a westbound hunter hungry for the feel of human flesh. In contrast with the large affections of the wet-nurse who stood in his mother's place, Ma was as sterile in her feelings as in her womb. In her scheme there was no place for this two-legged animal with its wants, its needs, its stinks, its inability to comprehend what was expected of it. The first thing to go was the sugar-tit, and the next a rough wooden horse carved by his father, now smooth and sticky with the love of small, hot hands. From Ma, for the first time, Mac heard the words "bad" and "naughty." They applied to everything he did; but mainly to the contents of his pants and to the twig of flesh that hung between his legs and made his belly turn over with vibrations of secret pleasure when he touched it, when he rubbed the flank of a cow a certain way, or when thunder broke from the sky.

Pa — Grandpa — was different. He was as big as a giant and when he stepped on to the porch the house shook. It almost scared you even to look at him, but beneath his brusque and boom there was a tenderness, and when his huge hand held yours you could feel as safe as if you were held by God. Grandpa looked like God, too, whose picture was on the front of the Bible from which the old man read every night. And Grandpa acted like God, too, dispensing a swift justice to the animals on his farm, to his sons, his hands, his wife and Mac. From Grandpa, Mac learned anger and the indignation that were later to make him want the kind of world where Grandpa's justice would be a matter of course, a society founded on the fairness that was Grandpa's rule of life. For Grandpa saw things directly and simply, black and white, and his fundamentalist faith could as little be shaken as the hills that fringed the horizons of the land where Mac spent his childhood.

The first of the World Wars claimed the life of Mac's father. He was crushed by the carriage of a big gun that fell on him in an accident in training camp. At the time his death meant little to Mac; only as the years piled on each other did the space left by the quiet one's going get bigger and come to matter. Meanwhile, there were the farm chores, the animals, the few brief months of school each year, the river that coiled through bottom land, the woods. There were hunting with the uncles, fishing with Pa, preserving with Ma, and all else that makes life in the country busy. At twelve there

411

were more intimate and secret delights whose forbiddenness came home to him with stabbings of guilt in the evenings when, with the sick fascination of fears of discovery, Mac watched the slow movement across the page of Pa's great forefinger and heard the glottal sonorities of the old man's voice as he read of the wages of sin from the Book. And always there was Ma, fussing behind him, nagging, critical, sharp in her words and tone, forever unsatisfied and bitter-resentful.

When Mac was fourteen, the old man fell on the ice and broke his hip. He was then almost ninety, and with this fall his spirits also fell. When he took to his bed he seemed to shrivel and dry as if his juices were draining through a hidden tap on his body. For six months he lay on his bed, dying a little every day. During this time, Mac was with him constantly. Out of an urge to talk, perhaps to make a pattern of his life, he told his grandson the tales that made up his history. In snatches, and in a sequence that was the old man's alone, dictated by a curious internal logic, there emerged stories of poverty and persecution, the sea voyage to new lands, the heartbreak in the port city and the scrounging for silver to buy the gear for the westward march; the yard by yard struggle across the hills and rivers, the fighting with outraged men and angry Nature to clear and hold the land, the tearing down and the building; the great joys and the great sorrows of ninety victorious years. In Mac it made a brew of memories, both bitter and sweet; and when the old man at last closed his eyes, unknowingly Mac had distilled from these six months the essence of Pa, and drunk of it so deeply that it was to flow forever with his own blood

The old man's death changed the world for Mac. The restlessness that had always been in him, but anchored first by his wetnurse and then by Pa, broke free. He could not abide Ma and her ways, and the war the two had been waging since the day Mac moved into her house now flared into open combat. So on a certain night, in traditional fashion with a bundle over his shoulder, Mac left.

He went to Chicago and there began the Odyssey that terminated on the couch in my study. The list of jobs he held is a long

412

one. Always he worked with his hands and earned his money in sweat. Never did any one job last very long, chiefly because of the nature of the times, but also because of his restlessness, his querulousness and his inability to take orders. He knew poverty, not only of the slow kind on the margin of existing, but the absolute kind, with the threat of starvation and death, the shame of beggary, the humiliation of picking over the contents of waste cans and garbage dumps like an animal, loathing oneself and disgusted but sharp in the eye for a bit of molding bread. And he knew idleness; not the leisurely kind, but the sort that fouls the mind and drugs the spirit; the listless, dragging, debilitating kind that shuffles in long lines at soup kitchens, huddles against the night-cold in musty mission rooms behind windows where

    JESUS
    A
    V
    E
    S

in harsh electric light glares against the sky.

Then one day, with the farm now many years behind him, Mac stumbled upon his destiny. He had been out of work for weeks, living in a Hooverville among other castoffs. A car drove up to the ramshackle picket fence someone had made around the encampment to caricature the community of the undamned, and from it stepped a man with a well-fed look on his face. He asked who wanted work. Some of the older hands apparently knew him and turned their backs. But Mac had hunger in his belly and an itch in his muscles, so with a few others he piled into the truck that followed the man's car. They were driven to a big shed by the docks, where a hot stew and coffee were served. Then the man gave each one a rough club and told them to line up and follow one of his assistants.

They walked to a pier by which strikers were parading in a thin picket line. When the strikers saw them coming, the shout of "Scabs!" went up as they closed their ranks to make room for others who came running from behind a shed. At a command, the crew Mac was with charged. After a brief battle, most of them broke through and reached the end of the pier where a freighter was moored beside huge crates of machinery and piles of scrap iron. These they began to load into the hold of the ship. Mac worked eagerly, glad to be feeling the blood flow again through his arms and legs. That night the strikebreakers were fed from the ship's galley and bedded on blankets below deck. From outside, restrained from attacking the scabs by a detachment of police, the strikers taunted and cursed at them, but with little effect, for these were work- and food-starved men.

On the third day the job was done, the scabs paid off, and a truck came to carry them back to Hooverville. Mac and a buddy left the truck as it passed the railroad yards. They caught a south-bound freight. As the train highballed out of the city, through the slats of the cattle car they saw the ship they had just loaded swinging into the current.

"That was a stinkin', lousy thing to do," said Mac's buddy, "and I wouldn'a done it but for hunger."

"What was so stinkin' about it?" Mac asked.

His buddy told him; and out of the telling came hours in libraries with fat books and a dime dictionary, came listening and talking, came hearing with new ears and speaking with a new tongue, came sitting on cane-bottomed chairs in union halls and weary marching round and round on picket lines, came *Solidarity Forever* and *Joe Hill*, came the Party's little booklet with a place for stamps, came new words, new thoughts, new deeds. And in the late thirties, came a visit one night to a doctor's office in New York, a job on a tramp for Marseilles; then a long, cold night of walking, running, lying breathless in the snow of a Pyrenees' pass, and in the morning a ride on a truck, and in the evening a dole of dungarees and cap; then marching and a wooden gun and *Link, Zwei, Drei, Vier*; then, at last, the trenches and the splintering brick walls of the University outside Madrid, a real gun and the red blood of a Moor on his bayonet and the sweet smell of rotting facist corpses pasted for always to the inside of his nostrils.

When the war in Spain ended, Mac returned to the States. He

joined the Merchant Marine and was assigned by the Party to union activity. He roved the world during the next years, carrying out Party tasks with efficiency and will. This work took him to strange places, and he did strange things for a farmer boy from the western reaches of Ohio. The internal politics of the Party never interested him, and despite its changes of course, its upsets and veerings, he hewed strongly to the line. When war was declared against Germany and Japan, he wanted to enlist but was told that because of his record as a fighter in Spain he would be marked in the United States Army and hence of little value to the Party. Disappointed but ungrudging, he remained a merchant seaman; but when the Soviet Union joined the Allies and the underground everywhere came alive as if touched by a magician's wand, Mac found his place as a courier and contact man among resistance groups and between national Party units. The work was exciting, dangerous, and the pitch of his life was passionate.

In the last year of the war Mac married a comrade from New York whom he had made pregnant. This was no shabby affair: it had nothing to do with the malicious fictions of the press and the yellow journals about free love among the Reds. The girl was Jewish, of strong moral character, and a virgin when Mac met her. They had been in love for more than a year but had postponed marriage because of the death of the girl's brother in the air over Germany and her respect for the tradition of her people. But in the seventh month of their love, and on the first night of sexual intercourse, there was an accident of contraception. As soon as her year of mourning was over, they were married. The twins were born in the summer of 1945 when the war ended.

With the coming of peace Mac was no longer important to the Party in the Merchant Marine. He was transferred to heavy industry, where he was assigned to organize certain craft workers. At this task he failed miserably, whereupon he was tried in a succession of assignments in New Jersey and Pennsylvania. Finally, he was instructed to move with his family to a place near Baltimore and to place himself at the disposal of the Party officials there. They reviewed his record and ordered him to work in a canning factory where the cleaners and packers were unorganized. On Sundays he had a delivery route for the *Sunday Worker*. This is what Mac was doing when he came to psychoanalysis...

While the analysis was concerned, in its opening stages, with a recounting of the superficial history that has been sketched, it was a veritable honeymoon for both Mac and myself. Long-forgotten experiences and incidents were recovered, and a rough pattern of Mac's basic personality was worked out. He recognized, very soon after he began, that he had romanticized his family origins; that he had stood in awed admiration of his grandfather even though the old man, because of his great size and imposing personality, had terrorized him; that he had hated violently his step-grandmother but — according to a well-tested analytic dictum that a child identifies with the frustrating parent on the principle of the defensive, "if you can't lick 'em, join 'em" — that he had acquired and absorbed many of her traits. He realized, too, that he had been made exceptionally dependent by his wet-nurse, and that the greater part of his restlessness throughout his life came from an inner compulsion to seek situations that could be equated in his unconscious with that happy condition of total surrender to someone or something in utter faith. He achieved, also, some striking insights about his sexual life: for example, that his grandmother's curt disposal of the sugar-tit which was in his mouth constantly was a symbolic castration (the honeyed lump representing to him, by upward transposition, his penis), and that in sexual activities during adult life he was always made anxious by a remote but heretofore never comprehended fear of trusting his sexual organ to a woman. Thus he would never allow his wife, or other women he had been with, to handle or fondle his genitals and, despite the pleasure he had had in intercourse, was always somewhat relieved when he was able to withdraw. In this connection he recognized that a habit to which he had never given a passing thought — that of going to the bathroom and urinating the moment intercourse had been accomplished — was in reality a practice he had established in order to permit an examination of his organ to obtain assurance that it was still there, intact and unharmed. And the reverse of this was also an unconscious fact with Mac: that the penis could not only be harmed but was in itself an instrument of harm. He recalled how his step-grandmother had regarded it as something foul, dirty, and an object of shame to be loathed. In his innermost thought he, too, had such an opinion of it; but he also used it to punish his step-grandmother, and his chronic condition of dampness well beyond his eighth year was due not only to the indulgence of his wet-nurse, the laxity of the daughter who substituted for her and inarticulate expression of the child's wish for attention, but also as a challenge to and aggression against the woman he had to call Ma.

The recovery of so many memories and the working through of them in the weeks that followed enabled Mac, with my assistance, to arrive at a better understanding of himself and his motives. He began, then, to see himself in a new light. The masks he had been wearing for his own and the world's benefit one by one fell away from him. Beneath all the poses he had assumed to hide his true face there emerged the portrait of an adult with the psychology of a child, of a man equipped for manhood but starving for the diet of an infant. And as he recognized his dependent core and the aggression beneath the skin, the dam of his internal rage broke, and for the first time in years he began to feel again.

Mac began to feel, acutely and deeply. In the first flush of the return of feeling he became as one who has been blind many years and who, by a miracle, recovers his sight. He looked about him and everywhere there were only bright colors. His senses responded to life. At night he walked the streets of the city, smelling its odors, gazing into its lights and rejoicing at its sounds. At his work he became lively, full of verve. In the analysis, day after day, he vented what he had so long repressed. On the heads of those who were long dead or until now forgotten, he poured a vitriol of passion, ventilating much of his vagrant, but unexpressed fury. In the permissive privacy of my study he relieved himself of the top layers of his hatred for everyone who had ever given him slight or insult or hurt, from his step-grandmother through his employers to the Communist stereotypes Party propaganda provided for him.

Meanwhile, he observed himself carefully and with a new vision in his daily life. He saw the little evidences of his yearning for dependency, how he forced people to put him into a dependent relation with them, how he was avid for the infant-security he got when, in the smallest affairs, he could surrender himself to the care of another.

Only in his sexual life did Mac, at this period, remain frustrated and disturbed. At the height of his enthusiasm with the results of the analysis so far, he twice attempted intercourse with girl friends. On the first occasion he reported sexual stirrings, but on neither venture did he experience even the semblance of potency: both episodes were total failures. But were it not for this, Mac would have been satisfied with his progress and have brought his therapy to a premature ending. I, of course, understood what was happening as a "transference-cure," and awaited the day when the flimsy structure he was building would collapse. I knew that he had only scratched at the surface of his neurosis; that what had until now been accomplished was the effect of relieving pressure through ventilation, minute and superficial insight, and the shifting of all of the burdens he bore onto me and the process of analysis. In me he found a new receptacle into which he could pour, and onto whom he could project, the stuff and substance of his life. During this period our relations were more than cordial — at least so far as Mac was concerned; but I, having been through this process many times before, could detect what was hidden in it, and the internal barometer of my previous experience with many patients warned me of a storm over the horizon.

It came; and when it struck, it was with fury. (pp. 58-67)

Perhaps it is not fair for Dr. Lindner to say that until this point a "mere transference cure" has taken place. Psychotherapy, like relations in real life, often proceeds to an early honeymoon during which some progress is gained, and then leads to a more difficult period, in which early hopes are frustrated, and positive feelings towards the therapist give way to the negative and critical. Speaking of "just a transference cure" fails to take into account benefits that go beyond and are not contingent on the patient's feelings towards his therapist, and certainly are more than a false happiness predicated on hope.

I cannot doubt that Mac came to analysis as someone quite unaware of his self; but with a little self-knowledge, in the situation of freedom and openness afforded him by the therapeutic situation, he came to understand his life better and to feel what had been his repressed feelings. Only because he made a connection with his experience was he able to see more brilliant colors in his surroundings. But his symptom remains. Let us return to the case.

Lindner has told us of his expecting "a storm over the horizon."

One day, in the course of a session, Mac mentioned that he had a dream that he considered foolish and not worth recounting.

> "I am walking along Charles Street (in Baltimore) towards Mount Vernon Place. There is no traffic on the street and I seem to be alone. There is no one behind me but I hear footsteps. This scares me and I open my mouth to scream, but when I do my tongue falls out on the ground. This doesn't surprise me: I just pick it up and put it in my pocket and go on walking.
>
> "Ahead of me I see the monument (The George Washington Monument at Mount Vernon Place in Baltimore). Now I notice that the side of the street I'm on is in very bright sunlight, but the other side is dark, pitch-black almost. Then I see the man who is behind me, but he's on the other side of the street, the black side. He seems to be paying no attention to me but I somehow feel that he is really watching me very carefully. I walk on a little way — begin to feel very tired. It gets so I can hardly lift my legs and Mount Vernon Place seems miles away. I become worried that I'll never make it to the monument, I'm so tired. I try to call the man to help me, but I have no tongue and can't make a sound. I reach into my

pocket to get it but it's gone. I search for it frantically and awake in terror with the blankets all tangled up."

When he had finished relating this dream Mac disparaged it as foolish and asked me if I really thought it worth taking time to analyze. I remained silent, and for a few minutes Mac stirred uncomfortably on the couch. Then, gruffly, he said the dream meant nothing to him; it was nonsense and he had no associations to it. I suggested that at least a part of the symbolism in the dream was quite obvious, that he might do well to consider its significance for the analysis. Mac countered with a curse and said he was a fool ever to have gone in for this stupid business. All right! So losing his tongue in the dream meant he wasn't talking... So what? It was all a lot of crap anyhow. What good was it doing him? No wonder the Party had proscribed psychoanalysis! In any case, how could anyone ever get well just by talking? He had been talking, talking, talking for months and he was still as far from his goal as ever; and he was tired of it, sick and tired of the whole thing! At this, I pointed out that he was now actually paraphrasing a part of the dream, that part where he was growing weary and hopeless about attaining his destination. He answered that the monument certainly was an apt representation of his analytic goal: it is shaped like an erect phallus; in Baltimore, perhaps because of this, the park at its base has become a hangout for homosexuals and prostitutes. He passes it everytime he has to go to Party Headquarters, about two or three times each week.

"Obviously, then," I said, "in order to get to the erect phallus, or potency, you have to talk."

"Don't be so smug," Mac answered. "I knew that before I told you the dream. But there's more to talking than you think."

"In the dream," I said, "you lost your tongue when you thought you were being followed. Who was following you?"

"You, of course," Mac snorted. "You follow every word I say."

"But you weren't surprised when your tongue fell out."

"No, I wasn't.' Mac sighed. I've known all along that I'd have to clam up at some point in this analysis — when it became necessary to talk about the Party."

"So you choose silence, and therefore impotence, rather than talk about the Party," I commented. "But why did you search so frantically for your tongue in the second part of the dream?"

Mac's agitation became obvious. He lit a cigarette with trembling hands; sweat glistened on his forehead. Slowly, he said, "The dream shows that my sickness and the Party are mixed up together. I guess I've known it all along and I've been afraid of it. From what you say I gather that the tongue falling out business means more than just being unwilling to talk: it means castrating myself."

I interrupted him here. "The first day I spoke with you," I said, "you told me you'd be willing to crucify yourself if it would bring socialism a minute nearer. What you're saying now is that you'd castrate yourself for the same reason."

"I would."

"You are."

Mac turned on the couch and looked at me. I could see the pain and torment in his eyes. "You're a hard guy," he said. He turned away and continued, "But I guess you have to be." He was calmer now as he summed the dream to this point. "Let's see. The Party and potency are tied up in my mind... how I don't know. But I gather that in order to solve the potency problem I have to talk about the Party. By not talking about the Party I'm castrating myself — or deliberately choosing castration, as you say. All right, now where do we go from here?"

"To the monument," I answered.

"It would be a lot easier to get there," he said, "if you were a Communist. I could talk to you then."

"You mean if I came over to your side?" I asked.

Now the entire dream fell into place and a flood of associations followed. I (the analyst, man in the dream) am walking in darkness. A not-so-unconscious purpose of Mac's analysis is to get me to come over on his side, i.e. to join the Party. This would not only benefit me; it would help him. He needs help in reaching the monument (potency) but fears that to obtain this help he will have to analyze his relationship to the Party and to disclose Party secrets. If the analyst would only see the light and come over to his side, he (Mac) could talk freely and be assisted toward potency. The prospect of continued impotence is a frightening one, but even if he wants to, he can't tell everything that is on his mind. There are secrets, confidences no one outside of the Party can be trusted with. These are perilous times for the Party. Often, while on the couch, he has to suppress a thought, a street address, a name, or something else that crosses his mind. When he does this, the associative chains break; so he will never get well. He is a fool ever to have attempted this business. Maybe he should just go and have his penis amputated, have done with the whole mess; or maybe he should quit the analysis, forget about being impotent. As things stand, he is always afraid of a leak, afraid that something he has been entrusted with will slip out. I (the analyst) am too clever. He has been warned against me. I know how to put two and two together. I'm not to be trusted. How did he know? — maybe I'm an undercover agent for the F.B.I. He knows I worked in a prison once, a federal prison, too. There's rumor going around that in Los Angeles and New York, federal agents are posing as psychoanalysts and abstracting political secrets from people. And he knows, also, that I practice hypnosis. What if I hypnotized him someday and got him to spill all the stuff he had to suppress in the interests of the Party?

Following the analysis of the significant dream, Mac became intensely resistive. The negative, transference, latent until now, betrayed itself by his silence, his curt manner with me, and his rudeness. Hour after hour sped by while Mac fought an eternal tug of war over whether he could trust me sufficiently to do the thing he knew he had to do: associate freely without regard to content. Interpretation availed little. When I established the connection between his present attitude toward me and his former attitude toward his stepgrandmother about the secrets of his masturbation and sex play with the farm animals, he merely shrugged. When I related his present silence to the silence his father practiced in his brief life, and showed how it was tied to a sense of having sinned against his grandfather, he accused me of being fanciful.

Then his resistance took a new turn. Instead of remaining silent, he began to talk. To an untrained observer, his production now would have seemed like free association. It had every semblance of an unimpeded flow of ideas, thoughts and experiences. He related incidents from his glamorous career as a courier in the underground, described the personalities he had encountered and some of his lurid sexual adventures. Along with this, he began to make me presents of Communist literature. At each visit he brought me a gift of a book or pamphlet, and he would begin his hours by discussing a point raised in some brochure or article he had given me the hour before.

Both of us knew that Mac, during this phase, was using every device possible to avoid the issue. His counterfeiting of the process of free association was designed as a fence-straddling procedure to satisfy his desire to solve his problems without tackling their core. His gifts were aimed to convert me to militant socialism, and at the same time to bribe me. His attempts to convert his hours to a forum for the discussion of Marxism were really intended to convince himself of his own sincerity as much as they were planned for my benefit. But, at last, an hour came when Mac could no longer fool himself, and realized he hadn't at all fooled me.

I remember that a snowstorm was raging outside on the evening Mac's analysis reached a climactic point. He appeared very weary as he stretched out on the couch, lit a cigarette, and began in a monotone that I sensed he was using to disguise an inner excitement.

"They're giving me the business again," he began. "I just came from Party headquarters. From the way they talk it's just a matter of time until they replace me at the cannery. They say they're looking around for a spot where I'll fit in better, be more effective."

"Have you really failed?" I asked.

Mac shrugged. "I guess so. What with the analysis and everything I guess I haven't given the job what it needs. But, Christ! I hate to be pushed around like this. If I had my way I'd..."

"You'd what?" I encouraged him.

Mac ground out his cigarette. "Nothing," he said. Then, after a moment of silence, "Look, Doc. This analysis is a frost, isn't it?"

423

"Why do you ask?"

"Because I'm thinking of chucking it and moving on. I guess I can peddle pamphlets somewhere else; it doesn't have to be Baltimore."

"Why do you think the analysis is a frost?" I asked.

"Because I'm not getting anywhere," he replied. "Look. I had a girl out last night and all I did was dribble all over her. And now they tell me I'm even a failure in my work. And I know I've been a failure here. What more proof d'you want?" He held up his hand. "Wait," he said. "I know what you're going to say. But I can't do it, that's all. I just can't do free association and I know that's the only way out."

"And why can't you?" I asked.

"Because I'm afraid of a leak, that's why. Because if I ever let out what's in my head I'd be punished, that's why. Because as much as I trust you, I don't trust you enough. I've got dynamite in me: Party secrets, names, addresses. These keep crossing my mind. If I open my mouth once I'll spill all over the place. I can't do it, that's all... I just can't do it!"

Now I asked Mac to associate to the word "leak," which had appeared more frequently than any other in discussions we had had about this resistance to the analysis and in connection with the Party. He did: the word was idiomatic and vulgar for urination; urination is a function of the penis; the other function of the penis is to transport semen —. At this Mac jumped from the couch and turned to me in bewilderment and consternation.

"Holy Christ!" he exclaimed. "You don't mean to say...?"

"You've been unconsciously giving away Party secrets all the time," I finished for him.

He began to pace the room, more agitated than I had ever seen him, muttering to himself, over and over, words which I took to be "semen, Party secrets, leak, dribble..." Then he stopped before my chair and looked piercingly at me, while I did my best to appear calm despite my exhilaration over the knowledge that this hour would see the analysis brought to a head.

"Let me get this straight," he said. "Somehow it seems I've got

424

semen and secrets mixed up in my head. So when I try to lay a girl and dribble out semen, it means I'm unconsciously giving away Party secrets." I opened my mouth to interrupt, but he held out one restraining hand and covered his eyes with the other.

"Wait! Wait!" he commanded. "It's beginning to fall into place. I really want to give away these secrets but can't do it with my mouth. So I let them dribble out through my penis. Why my penis? Because somewhere that's tied up with the Party like semen's tied up with secrets. Now if I could tell these secrets, with my mouth, I mean, maybe I could have a real ejaculation!" He paused, and his perplexity was plain. "But why should I want to give away Party secrets? Because they're too much of a burden to me? How is that? There're plenty of guys who know a lot more than I do. Why should it affect me this way?"

This time it was obvious that he was asking for an answer.

"To find out the answer to that," I said, "We'll probably have to go deeper into your early sex life. But offhand I would guess that your desire to disclose Party secrets means that you have an aggression against the Party, and maybe this has to do with the equation of Party with Grandmother."

Mac returned to the couch and threw himself down on it. "A few months ago," he mused, "I would have laughed in your face if you said that. Now I'm not so sure." And for the remainder of that hour he did little more than express his amazement at what had gone before. When he left that evening, he was in a very different mood.

At his appointment two days later, Mac reported the first successful sexual experience he had had in many years. He had achieved and maintained a strong erection, and the experience of ejaculation had been intensely pleasurable. His enthusiasm knew no bounds. He was going to send for his wife, they would resume their former life, they would...Here I checked him.

"Do you think," I asked, "that your problems are solved?"

This sobered him. He sighed. "I guess not," he answered. "But is it really necessary to go on with this? After all, I know what's behind it now."

"But do you really?" I said. "It seems to me you have little more than a formula, a series of equations founded on a few good guesses. I'd say there's still a long way to go." So Mac went on.

At this hour, and for some weeks thereafter, the truth of my last statement was brought home to Mac. For there now opened before us the vast panorama of his childhood sexuality and the intensity of his early feelings against his grandmother. Between these and the manner in which both related to the Party, the analysis wove like a shuttle on a loom, back and forth, back and forth. From him poured a seemingly endless series of memories, told with much of their original passion, of a child who was blocked in his expression at every turn, whose every action was called "bad"; of a longing for love and acceptance, the security of a kind word or gesture, and of the hot hatred that eventually came to take their place. Then, in a rush of memories, came what had been hidden, even from Mac, of the first ripples of that sexual tide that was to sweep him later to the edge of destruction. At first, what he had to relate was no more than the usual history of the vicissitudes of the developing sex urge; but with Mac, after his removal to his grand-father's farm, a pathological twist was given to it. From being an instrument for the reception and communication of pleasure as well as the prime organ for reproduction, his penis took on a new significance as the child he was saw how it and its behavior affected Ma. In short, it became a weapon, a tool for revenge; and in the life he lived in fantasy he regarded it — all unknowingly, of course — as a veritable arsenal of destruction; and with it, upon his grandmother — and, later, upon everyone who stood in his way — he wreaked a vengeance in imagination which hardly ever, until the microscope of analysis was trained upon it, reached the level of awareness. And this had a curious result: Mac became afraid of his penis, of the destructive possibilities which he and he alone had given it; and, hence, when his neurosis in adult life formed a tidal crest, he had to inhibit it, to curb its fancied noxious potential.

But where, in all of this, did the Communist Party fit? Another dream supplied the missing links.

"I am early for my appointment and when I enter your

study you're not there. Thinking to occupy myself until you arrive, I go to the bookcase and select a volume from the shelves on the left side of the window. I start to read. Just then I hear you enter. I become confused. For some reason I don't want you to know I've been reading your books. I try to hide the book on me but it won't go into any of my pockets. Suddenly I thrust it into my mouth and it seems to go down my throat. But when I say hello to you, the book flies out of my mouth and hits you in the forehead. You fall down and I'm afraid I've killed you."

Mac's immediate association to the book was education. Correctly, he stated that the Party had given him an education he could not otherwise have obtained. As a child he thought his grandpa was God because he knew so much; sometimes he finds himself thinking the same way about me. But on second thought I (the analyst) don't really know so much. My knowledge runs all over the place. Outside of psychoanalysis I have no framework for what I know — no coherent, consistent, logical, correct way to order my thinking. He, Mac, is really a better-educated man than I am. In the days when he was on the bum, in Public Libraries between here and the West Coast he read everything printed in English on socialism and dialectical materialism — Marx, Engels, Lenin, Stalin, even Hegel and Fuerbach. He knows socialist theory better than — or at least as well as —anyone he has ever met in the Party. No; that isn't quite true. There's one fellow, a leader of the Baltimore faction, who is really hot stuff. He's a Ph.D. He really knows his Marxism, knows it the way I (the analyst) know my Freud. But personally this Party philosopher is a pompous ass, a twisted neurotic if he (Mac) ever saw one... Married to a dame, a former socialite or something, who is just as screwed up. Christ! How he hates them! Hardly a worker in the lot. If it ever comes to the barricades —

Here I interrupted him. "Then the dream doesn't refer to me," I said. "It refers to your Party philosopher. How do you account for this?"

Mac produced the day remnant, the bricks form his extra-analytic life of which the dream was built. On the previous evening he had gone to Party headquarters for a meeting scheduled to be held around the decision to change his assignment. Mac was the first one to arrive. He read from a book on a table until the others came. The next arrival was B, the Party philosopher and local leader. After greeting Mac, he (B) commented knowingly on the volume Mac had in his hands.

"I felt like throwing it at him," Mac said. "The snide bastard's always showing off his education."

"You hate him, you said."

"I do."

"That's why in the dream you killed him."

By now Mac's anger was out in the open; but it was more than anger; it was pure, primitive rage.

"I hate every last one of them," Mac cried. "And what's more, I hate the Party too, and everything it stands for. I've hated it deep down inside of me from the minute I was recruited." His voice rose almost to a scream. "I hate it! I hate it! I hate it! I'd kill the lot of them if I could. I'd shove this goddam Party so far down their throats it'd come outa their asses! I hate it and I hate them and I hate you and I hate me for being such a chicken son-of-a-bitch that I have to lay here telling you about it!"

In a few more moments the rage had spent itself and Mac closed his eyes, exhausted by his furious outburst. Now, more calmly, he said, "So it's out at last. Now that I've said it I've said everything, I guess. I carried that around in me like a stone in my guts for years. I suppose I should be glad I got rid of it after all this time. I guess that's the bottom of the barrel, Doc. What else can there be?" (pp. 67-76)

If the fine quality of Lindner's writing has distracted us from appreciating his excellence as a psychotherapist, the passage above will surely remind us of his excellence as an interpreter of dreams and desires. Under his skillful guidance — through which he can guide Mac to the perception of how his dream was being enacted in the here and now — his patient brings through a new layer of resistance, and comes by a different view of his life. His allegiance to the Party, which seemed his savior, now seems a straightjacket; and surrender to it the inverse of instinctual freedom.

Not only insight and feeling awareness have been gained: for the first time after the ambiguity of the word "leak" (applicable to reserved communication and to urination, and by extension, to ejaculation), the measure of liberation from the Party expressed itself in sexual satisfaction. The process will deepen still until the Party is de-idealized in his mind, and he allows himself to recover his manhood vis-a-vis this collective projection of bad parental authority.

Next (after the discovery in catharsis of the rage toward the Party), was an intellectual understanding of why, hating the Party as he did, Mac had stayed for so many years.

We spent the next weeks answering the question I posed that night. Briefly, this is that answer:

At sixteen Mac had run away from home, after Grandpa had at last closed his piercing eyes in death. Between the time the old man died and the night he ran away the boy lived in fear of his own aggression. His hostility toward his grandmother was not just an ordinary resentment, it was a living hate that threatened to engulf both of them in tragedy. Unconsciously, Mac knew that if he stayed, he'd kill the woman; and so he ran from her presence to protect them both. But his experiences in the world only increased his hate and aggression, and provided him with new targets, for as an unskilled, untutored farmer lad, he was at the mercy of every economic breeze, unwanted and without a place. His embitterment during the years of wandering knew no bounds. When his destiny, in the shape of a buddy in a cattle car southbound from the scene of a strike caught up with him, he was ripe for the taking.

It is true that the Party made a rational appeal to Mac, that he was attracted to its doctrines intellectually and as a result of his reading and observation of the world. This appeal was enhanced by the fact that it presented answers — in a simple and easily digested form — to questions he had been asking himself and others through his formative years, especially when he was exposed to the paradoxes of American society in the late 'twenties and early 'thirties. Nor can it be denied that the cheap education he received on his way to, and later within, the Party was a major factor in his allegiance. It compensated for the inferiority he felt as an unlearned farmer boy. Indeed, it even permitted him to feel superior to every man — from Einstein to his analyst — who did not possess his ready formulations and the guidance of a simple set of maxims to meet every situation or problem. But beneath all of these, and of such basic importance that it alone really mattered, the Party provided Mac with an adjustment. Within the Party, Mac could give vent to his hatred and aggression — originally directed against Ma and later the world — with almost unlimited freedom. It not only permitted him to express these qualities, but directed them upon a broad segment of society, channelized them toward a plentitude of objects, gave him the words and even the techniques to implement them. More than this, while making his hatred and aggression acceptable, it also served to contain them. Therefore, at one and the same time the Party gave Mac permission to indulge in aggression, yet saw to it that this aggression was sufficiently controlled that he need not fear its getting out of hand as it once almost did with his grandmother. So, in essence, for Mac the Party was a way of adjusting, of compromising, of containing a negative rebellion that might have destroyed him had he not found his way into it. In the Party's ranks he discovered a solution to the problem of how to be hostile without suffering the effects of hostility, of how to gain acceptance for his aggressiveness and to hold on to it without being treated as a mad dog and destroyed for it. The Party, then, was Mac's neurosis — a neurotic solution he deliberately chose as a lesser evil than the madness to which his hate was leading him. (pp. 76-77)

Here the results of the analysis of this patient illuminate the case of many other E8 individuals who, like Mac, found in revolutionary activity a socially acceptable channel for their aggression and their thirst for justice. Yet, in spite of improvement in his self-concept and the satisfaction of a non-destructive indulgence of his aggressive lust, this didn't make Mac into a full person.

But like all solutions that men under pressure to adjust improvise for their perplexities and conflicts, the Party did not work. It offered no real answer; it could not, because it was nothing more than a symptom of Mac's difficulty, a stopgap "adjustment" doomed to failure from the outset as every "adjustment" has to fail.

The price Mac had to pay for what the Party did for him was in the coin of discipline and at the exorbitant rate of human cipherdom. The discipline demanded by the Communist Party is almost incomprehensible to those who have not met it first-hand. It is absolute, rigorous, uncompromising. It holds every member strictly accountable for his smallest acts, it permits of no slightest deviation or breach. It calls for the continuous criticism of behavior and thought by the self and others and, like Party policy, discipline veers and shifts with the prevailing currents of the time. Its impermanence in all save the proposition that under every circumstance the Party is correct requires an unusual kind of plasticity among those whom it affects. For a time Mac could follow it and be goverened by it without strain — so long, that is, as his neurotic needs were being met by the permissive framework the Party provided for his aggression and hostility. He was therefore compliant to the discipline during the years of industrial strife and war years, but following them — in the halcyon days when for a time there was no one to hate or fight — he began to chafe under it. It became burdensome and nagging, resembling the regime of his grandmother. So in unconscious ways he flaunted and tried to defeat it. Borrowing from childhood, he symbolically betrayed its secrets. In other and smaller ways too numerous to catalogue he also tried to undermine it, and as the analysis progressed Mac was amazed to see how extensively he had been working against this discipline which, on the surface, he had for so many years taken for granted and complied with.

The reduction to cipherdom, to simple cog-ship in the grand

wheel of the Party's ambition, was also at first unprotestingly —
and, indeed, with relief — accepted by Mac. Recall that he was,
underneath all, a wholly dependent type whose primary longing
was forever to be a kind of suckling as he once was to his wet-
nurse. After the homeless, friendless years he spent in the world,
when the Party bared its bosom to him at recruitment, he nestled
to it in gratitude as he did long ago to the breast of the wet-nurse.
But he overestimated its ampleness and plenitude, and in a short
while he had drained it dry. While policy demanded and gave lati-
tude to his hate, agression and hostility, even Mac's voracious
appetites were satisfied; but, in the middle 'forties, as the weather
vane of policy turned, for Mac the bosom he had counted on to
replace the one he had lost, the breast he had believed a fountain
that would nourish him for all time, shriveled in his mouth. In
anger and frustration, then, he turned upon it, prepared to rend it
with the teeth of his basic hatred.

So this is the story of the psychoanalysis of Mac. It has told
how and why he became a member of the Communist Party in the
United States. He joined in an attempt to make an adjustment to
the contrasts and conflicts within him that were destroying him,
and would likely have destroyed others. He joined, not primarily
out of belief or conviction in the aims and goals of the Party, nor
as a missionary to mankind, nor even as a rebel against injustice:
he joined as one would voluntarily enter a prison in anticipation of
crimes, as a preventive against becoming criminal and, because by
joining, he could — or felt he could — remain a dependent infant.

In the course of his analysis Mac learned that the Party was his
neurosis. When he concluded his analysis, it went with his symptoms. About six months after we had terminated, Mac quit the
Party. He no longer needed it ... (pp. 77-78)

A TANTRIC* DAYDREAM

Tristan: The dream is the following: I'm with a group going up a mountain, and suddenly, some legionnaires with weapons appear and I sense that they are going to kill me. They are going to kill the whole group. We all take off running and I realize that if I go with them they'll kill me, that they will kill the whole group if it stays together. I go in another direction and, suddenly, I feel that they are pursuing me, and I feel an excitement like this ... "Oh fuck! They are going to kill me!" I keep feeling the excitement of danger and it gives me pleasure to be between life and death.

They continue pursuing me and I am realizing that I am alone and that there are two of them following me, but I don't know if they are the ones that are carrying weapons. All at once I look behind me and I am blind. I cannot see behind me. I realize that I only have the sense of feeling, and my feelings are trusting them, but my head is telling me: "Look out!" And I say: "Well, even if they kill me, I'll go with them because I trust my feelings."

I go on ahead with these two people behind me and I go to the town which is nearby. And in the town I begin to perceive that they are rejecting us again, the inhabitants in general. And I begin to ask myself: "What the fuck is happening to me that I am being rejected? Why are they rejecting me when there is no reason to? I am running away!"

I am in a labyrinth. There are two exits. At one of the exits stands the one who has the weapon and I can't attack him because if I so much as get close to him he'll kill me with the weapon; if I had anything at all I would go after him. On the other side there was a kind of military authority, but that one doesn't have a weapon and I say: "I can handle this one because he doesn't have a weapon."

.I run out that way and I remember that all towns have a church. I run out and I jump over the church fence and I appear automatically with my mate [partner], together, entering the church. Automatically, exactly as I jump over the fence, I feel like a relief, a harmony, very distinct from what I had felt before.

Someone comes up to me and tells me: "Come, you have to fill out the papers before you go in." I say to him: "Go to hell! Leave me alone; there is no need for 'papers' here. I am coming here because ... I am being chased and now I am going to go in here."

So then I go into the church and there is a kind of half-darkness ... a lot of tranquility. And there is a kind of priest; I don't understand what he says, he is simply making sounds: *Eo ... Oh ... Eh ...* (a kind of religious chant). Suddenly, I go and sit on a chair with Nikaro, my mate, and suddenly there is a person beside us, and I look and say: "This one must be a nun, because in a place like this she must be a nun." And I look at her more, and no, she is a priestess. I begin to look her up and down and I say: "Fuck! She looks like Fenicia." I look at her right hand and I see a ring that has a circle with a serpent that is almost biting its own tail. And there the dream ends.

Claudio: Did you like the end? Was it good?

T: Yes, I liked it. Better than the fuckers chasing me.

C: Although there was a kind of pleasure in the other part also. The pleasure of an 8 before the imminence of death.

T: Yes.

C: The church seems to do you well.

T: Yes, the church was good for me.

C: Put yourself in the church. Let's go a little further into the dream from that point on — the salvation episode.

Imagine yourself sitting there in the church, beside this priestess, and go a little further into whatever it is that she suggests. How is it, to be sitting there next to her?

T: She is related to sexuality. I have two sensations. One is older, earlier. I have tasted promiscuity, that is, allowing my instinct to go wherever it may, and the time came when I stopped (twelve months ago) doing this, and I said: "Now I am going to try another way and I am going to observe what happens. And somehow, through sex, transcend it." That is what comes to me.

C: Monogamy provides better conditions for using sex as a way to ascend.

T: I feel more peaceful. I feel myself in that space of peace and as if there were something missing to make it complete.

C: What could that be?

T: What comes to me is to do more tantric sex with my partner/mate. We have spent twelve months without sexual relations, and it's like having to start another process.

C: That is not easy to carry into practice, but if you put yourself in the dream ... There you are sitting beside the priestess. Is something missing?

T: Something is missing; as if the priestess were in between, between my wife and I.

C: Between or as a bridge?

T: Yes, she is a kind of bridge, but one that is not consummated.

C: She is like a symbol of possibility.

T: Yes.

C: What do you think about doing that imaginatively? How would that tantric union with N. be? The ecstacy of sexualized spiritual communion.

T: The sensation that I begin to feel is as if my spinal column were to begin to stretch; and as if my chest were going to explode. I feel in the nape of my neck and before my forehead a kind of sun ... And on top of my head ... and toward the sides ... and my hands too [*his hands orbit making expressive gestures*]. As if all my body were now vibrating. As if it were rising.

C: Go on with that ... The halo of light ... The sensation before your fore-

435

head ... your nape ... the trembling ...

T: Heat, a lot of heat behind. I feel a halo of light from the bottom to the top [*he points to his spinal column, and he is moved*] and something that comes from above all ... A light. And it is like being before a mystery which frightens me a little. I am trembling, and now I am sort of trembling inside.

C: What is that, that comes from above?

T: Like a ray of light, it comes from in front of me.

C: Where does it go?

T: It goes here and here [*he points between his eyebrows and to his heart*].

C: Allow it to penetrate.

T: [*A position of open arms and hands. He begins to breathe heavily, to vibrate, to open his chest, his arms ... he makes movements. He passes his hands over his legs, his chest, his face, as if he were cleaning himself.*]

C: What is happening?

T: I feel as if all my wounds were being washed or healed. As if the venom (poison) I carry within me, here, in my guts, were being cleaned.

C: I won't ask you anymore. Go on with the process.

T: [*He covers his eyes and face and he breathes deeply.*]

C: Allow yourself to get in the experience.

T: [*He begins making movements, from down — up; and others — opening himself, closing himself. It is like a prayer in movement, a ritual ...*]: YOU ARE GOD. You are God.

C: What are you speaking about? What entered you!

T: [*tears in his eyes and in a very sweet voice*]: Now I feel a great compassion. It's like seeing with the eyes of a child. To feel that only this relieves my pain, the suffering, the separation.

C: Only by doing this. Will you know how to repeat it?

T: Yes.

C: Had it happened to you before?

T: Sometimes. Not so much like that … Sometimes.

C: You seem to have tapped into a process of which this is a beginning, but you could navigate further if you can only surrender to it.

T: I told myself, "Good, this far."

C: Magnificent!

T: This is my quest, my search. Also this morning when I got up [*tears in his eyes*] I picked a card from the Tarot — The Star. It was the search, the question. Today when I got up I said: "Today is the time to come out." And it was Tagore's story, to search for God. And as if each time I get close, He pulls away. When I have found the door, if I call and He opens to me, everything is over. Like a kind of suicide.

C: But now it was you who opened the door to Him and it didn't look like a suicide. It looked like a beginning of a journey to another level. A guided journey. What more for today!

T: [*laughs*] I, when I am in this state … But when I am seated there, in the ordinary state, I search for something terrible. I look for something painful.

C: You forget what you are looking for.

T: I don't allow it to happen.

C: The time before you said you were very angry; you were in the realm of the pursuer and the pursued. Yet the alternative is very much at hand, it seems.

The effect of this session, in which Tristan imaginatively enacts an act of tantric sex, might be compared to the manner in which the pondering of archetypal material in the Jungian analysis of dreams has a spiritualizing effect on a person's life. From Tristan's production of spontaneous *mudra** and the phenomena of activation of the *chakras* that he naively describes, as well as from the content itself, I have no doubt that the archetypal experience of the ritually sacralized *eros* has brought him to a real taste of a consciousness more elevated than that of the hunted hunter (of his dream) in the lust syndrome.

Just as I have known an E8 whose life improved dramatically through the channeling of his predatory aggression into a martial art, in this case Tristan has felt helped through further exploration of his intuition about the practice of ceremonial sex (in which sacralization counteracts the E8 perspective of sex as forbidden, and forbids invasively overstepping boundaries). I cannot help thinking that perhaps the denigration of sex, intrinsic in lusty sex, finds a particularly appropriate remedy in the visualization and evocation of sacredness in tantric ceremonies, in which impulse is subjected to a balance between expression and containment. I cannot help thinking of Rasputin (a notable E8) whose spiritual realization came about after his joining a Christian sect where promiscuous sexuality was turned into spiritually relevant work.

9

ENNEATYPE 9

In that remarkable pageant of characters that is Chaucer's *Canterbury Tales*, we find our E9 in the host:

> Our Host gave us welcome; everyone
> was given place and supper was begun.
> He served the finest victuals you could think,
> The wine was strong and we were glad to drink.
> A very striking man our Host withal,
> And fit to be a marshal in a hall.
> His eyes were bright, his girth a little wide;
> there is no finer burgess in Cheapside.
> Bold in his speech, yet wise and full of tact
> there was no manly attribute he lacked,
> What's more he was a merry-hearted man.[1]

The role of host seems congruent with the character, and Chaucer's observation that "everyone was given a place" seems intended to enhance the sense of the host's generosity. Also, the emphasis given to food (supper, victuals, wine) impresses us as a part of an indirect and impressionistic character description rather than as a mere feature of the story-line, as is confirmed by "his girth a little wide." And, through the narrator's opinion that "there is no finer burgess ..." Chaucer conveys that this host's combination of nurturance, a good appetite, gregariousness, tact, straightforwardness in speech and jollity is something appreciated by his social group.

The social value placed on generosity and the socially adaptive orientation of E9 make the pathological aspect of this character less visible than that of others. E9 people appear to be more healthy than others, for they have become relatively deaf to their suffering and do not make problems for those near them. They have learned to cope with life not through seduction or aggression but through resignation and conformity. The way they have found to cope with suffering is to ignore their own inwardness, and their real desires, as they turn with excessive readiness to the satisfaction of desires of others.

Just as E2 and E7 can be called oral-receptive, E4 and E8 oral-aggressive, E1 and E5 anal, and E3 and E6 phallic, I have proposed calling E9 "pseudo-genital": for, in the psychoanalytic vocabulary, genitality means true maturity, and an E9 is one who has matured artificially — from the outside in, through an excessive adaptation rather than from the inside out, as is the case in organic development.

Most people seem to love themselves more than they love their neighbor. By contrast, we can say that type 9 "love" their neighbor more than themselves. They defer too much to others. The loss of contact with their own depth, which complicates their over-adjustment, is dimly conscious to them as a loss of being that needs to be made up for somehow — and thus arises a polarity between spartan forbearance and a craving for company or amusement; stoicism and the love of comfort and food.

If these seem incompatible, one only has to think of somebody like George Washington, the wealthiest man of Virginia, who was able to endure the horrible privations of Valley Forge.

In their passion for psychological comfort E9 may seem to resemble E7. Yet E7 pursues the indulgence of desires and joy for the positive side of things, whereas E9 does not. Comfort, rather, is achieved through an inner deadening. Over-adjustment or conformity serves the passion for not "rocking the boat" and the price is boredom. No better name for the artificial peace of E9 than Gurdjieff's expression: a "self-calming devil."

Among the traditional capital sins, sloth corresponds to E9; but, it is worth pointing out that the meaning of "sloth" changed in the course of religious history from the original one of an inner or psychological inertia to that of physical laziness — which need not be an E9 symptom. More characteristic is the phlegmatic quality of the character and an over-stability manifesting in conservative tendencies and resistance to change. If sloth or *acedia*, to use the early Latin word of the Church Fathers, is the ruling passion (a passion no less "dispassionate" than avarice), and compulsive unselfishness the most striking behavioral trait, at the cognitive level the main characteristic is a loss of psychological mindedness. Along with it there is an experiential impoverishment, a compulsive extroversion and an excessive concreteness.

Because selfishness is a taboo for E9, and because psychotherapy is perceived as a selfish act, type 9s feel it is being too concerned with oneself. While type 8 also has little inwardness, because of its pursuit of external things: sex, food, power; and E1 is more inclined to do some kind of good in the world than deal with psychological issues; in E9 the issue becomes colored by a peculiar rejection of complexity. Other than feeling that therapy is a selfish act, it is a *complication*. There is in E9 an over-simplification of life, with loss of awareness of conflicts. To make peace inwardly is ever more basic than being a peacemaker in the human environment. E9 does not like conflict, does not tolerate it, and reacts to it through an over-simplification of life.

E9 people *idealize* simplicity. They say: "But if life is so simple, why do people complicate things? Why do people have so many problems when everything is so simple?" But this is a simplicity achieved with an impoverishment, with a loss of awareness of certain aspects of inner life. And when E9 people begin to mature, then things are not so simple anymore. I can think of somebody who, after taking a long step ahead in therapy, felt it a hellish thing that now everything had two faces. Everything was one thing ... and at the same time it appeared to be the opposite. The normal thing is to be able to see things from at least two different points of view, but this person was not used to this, which for her was intolerable. She was in that transition to a greater complexity.

There are more complex types and there are simpler ones; E4 and E7 are among the most complex — they hold in mind many things, simultaneously. Type 9 are very simple. Sancho Panza is an example. Like E9 in general, he is practical and is full of sayings, i.e., very inclined to quote popular proverbs. He is also a follower — not that he worships Don Quixote, but he seems too innocent, too trusting. A feature of simplicity is not questioning too much.

❦

When I undertook the task of collecting jokes on the different characters, I could not find humor that had E9 as a target as readily as I found caricatures of rigidity, slyness, grandiosity and so on. I conjectured that traits such as abnegation and trust were easier to idealize than to laugh at — until I realized a well known category of jokes particularly fitting to the E9 pattern: *dumb* jokes, jokes about "fools." Of course we are all foolish, and it is wise to acknowledge it; and there are also congenital idiots and people with senile dementia. I don't think it is these that have inspired jokes about fools, but rather the excessive simple-mindedness, literalness or unawareness of E9. As in the one of a man who falls from a second floor. A passer-by runs to assist him, and on ascertaining that he is alive, asks him: "Are you okay?" Comes the answer: "I don't know, I just got here."

If Ichazo has said that type 9 are non-conformists, I disagree — though some of them of course are, and some are not and yet consider themselves to be so. He also said that one of type 9's traps is searching too much, yet I think that in E9 the typical tendency is not to search enough. This is the character of those who content themselves all too easily. When E9 people begin to search it is because they are waking up. When they feel empty it is because they are not so lost in conformity, in self-forgetfulness. Type 9 tend to be cheerful, generous, and not at all needy, and those who are most submerged in their neurosis are the most satisfied, while those who begin to feel that they lack something, and develop a true spiritual aspiration, are already maturing.

In the clinical world, E9 was described by Kretschmer as "cyc-tothymia" — with its propensity to depression and "hypomania" — a jolli-ness that is a defense against the acknowledgement of sadness. Since Kurt Schneider, it has been recognized by European psychiatry as an "abulic psy-chopathy" — a character lacking in initiative and excessively prone to exter-nal influences; today I believe the more problematic E9 individuals tend to be classified (along with some E6 and E4) as "dependent." None of these terms addresses the dynamic core of the character, however, and some-times other traits are more striking. Among the characters described by Theophrastus, for instance, is "the rustic," in whom the salient trait is sim-plemindedness; and among those is one designated as a *bumpkin* (a word denoting insignificance), in whom stands out the characteristic of being opinionated — which many E9 people share. Also significant to the personality in question is the observation of Samuel Butler that his characteristic is "a native only of his own soil, and a foreigner of all other places" — a reference to provincialism.

Among the classical fictions, one of the most tragic is Balzac's *Old Goriot*, who lets himself be exploited to death by his beloved daughters. He renounces everything for them — with whom he lives vicariously, in virtue of a psychological symbiosis.

> I wait for them to pass; my heart beats fast when their carriages come; I admire them in their fine dresses; they throw me a little smile as they pass and then the sun seems to come out and gild all nature for me. I wait, for they will come back the same way, and I see them again! … Every man loves in his own fashion; mine does no harm to anyone, so why should people trouble themselves about me? I am happy in my own way. [2]

When somebody asks him, "When your daughters have such splendid houses, how can you live in a hole like this?" he explains that his life is lived through his two girls.

> If they are enjoying themselves, if they are happy and finely dressed, and have carpets to walk on, what does it matter what sort of cloth covers me, or what sort of place I sleep in? I don't feel cold if they are warm, and I am never dull if they are laughing. The only troubles I have are their troubles. (p. 153)

Yet Balzac seems to idealize E9, both here and in many descriptions of E9 women, of which the best known is Eugenie Grandet.[3]

More perception of the limitation and pathology of E9 may be found in Sinclair Lewis's Babbitt, where it is conformity, group dependency and an insignificance under the veneer of pomposity that are emphasized;[4] and in Pollyanna, where there is compulsive contentedness.[5] It is interesting to note that the names of these two literary creations have become part of our vocabulary. Not only can we say that someone is a Babbitt, but the

443

word has found its way into the English dictionary, along with "Pollyannaish." I insert a quote from Eleanor Porter's classic — a passage in which the orphaned child explains:

"You don't seem ter see any trouble bein' glad about every-thin'," retorted Nancy, choking a little over her remembrance of Pollyanna's brave attempts to like the bare little attic room.

Pollyanna laughed softly.

"Well, that's the game, you know, anyway."

"The — *game?*"

"Yes; the 'just being glad' game."

"Whatever in the world are you talkin' about?"

"Why, it's a game. Father told it to me, and it's lovely," rejoined Pollyanna. "We've played it always, ever since I was a little girl, little girl. I told the Ladies' Aid, and they played it — some of them."

"What is it? I ain't much on games, though."

Pollyanna laughed again, but she sighed, too; and in the gathering twilight her face looked thin and wistful.

"Why, we began it on some crutches that came in a mission-ary barrel."

"*Crutches!*"

"Yes. You see I'd wanted a doll, and father had written them so; but when the barrel came the lady wrote that there hadn't any dolls come in, but the little crutches had. So she sent 'em along as they might come in handy for some child, sometime. And that's when we began it."

"Well, I must say I can't see any game about that," declared Nancy, almost irritably.

"Oh, yes; the game was to just find something about every-thing to be glad about — no matter what 'twas," rejoined Pollyanna, earnestly. "And we began right then — on the crutches."

"Well, goodness me! I can't see anythin' ter be glad about — gettin' a pair of crutches when you wanted a doll!"

Pollyanna clapped her hands.

"There is — there is," she crowed. "But I couldn't see it, either,

Nancy, at first," she added, with quick honesty. "Father had to tell it to me."

"Well, then, suppose *you* tell *me*," almost snapped Nancy.

"Goosey! Why, just be glad because you *don't — need — 'em!*" exulted Pollyanna, triumphantly. (pp. 42-44)

Surveying the domain of famous lives I find E9 especially among statesmen, and sometimes among military. A willingness to serve and to sacrifice, as well as a willingness to receive orders, surely contributes to military suitability; additionally, the sensory-motor disposition of E9 enables such people (when not obese) as soldiers, but also as athletes. An orientation to the concrete side of life usually entails a good sense of economic realities, and this may contribute to the success of E9 as politicians, administrators and bankers. Honesty, consciousness, and a willingness to mind other people's affairs surely are factors that explain the prevalence of E9 among statesmen, for in many instances it is obvious that they attract people's confidence through selflessness and lack of guile.

I cannot doubt that E9 is an important component of every bureaucracy, and it is not difficult to see a resonance between the E9 personality style and the "bureaucratic phenomenon" with its characteristic inertia. Indeed, E9 is "passive aggressive" — i.e., tends to express anger indirectly through negligence, forgetfulness, procrastination or unconsciously motivated accident-proneness. Understandably, generalized passive aggression is striking in public services as an unconscious rebellion to excessive hierarchy and meaninglessness.

The Organization Man, written in the 1950s, explores the congruence of a character (recognizable as our E9) with the needs of corporations.[6] We also find a sociological reference to our E9 in David Riesman's "tradition directed" personality in *The Lonely Crowd*.[7]

Heeding tradition more than current opinion or principles involves conservatism, of course; and just as E9 is often conservative, the conservative movement is also sustained, to an important degree, by E9 individuals. More fundamental, however, is the connection between the E9 pathology of psychospiritual inertia and the social pathology of over-conformity: an alienated conformity that involves a loss of individuality.

With the critical danger posed today by institutional rigidity and generalized *status-quo* (in view of rapidly changing conditions), what at the individual level is an almost *invisible* pathology takes its toll at the societal level; so that widespread individual over-adaptation results in society's failure to adapt and evolve.

YALOM'S "IN SEARCH OF THE DREAMER"

Though E9 individuals are self-deadening and insensitive to their subtle psychological experiences to the point of blindness, they may have dreams with rich potential insight, just as in the following case, where a patient's insightlessness coexists with the alienated language of his half-conscious night life.

The title that Yalom has given to his report couldn't be more appropriate: it suggests that the therapeutic process is, in this case, one of coming to heed, reown and eventually re-identify with the split-off dreamer.

I quote below the first eighteen pages of Irvin Yalom's masterpiece — "In Search of the Dreamer" — which constitutes the tenth and last chapter of *Love's Executioner & Other Tales of Psychotherapy*.[8]

"Sex is at the root of everything. Isn't that what you fellows always say? Well, in my case you may be right. Take a look at this. It'll show you some interesting connections between my migraines and my sex life."

Drawing a thick scroll from his briefcase, Marvin asked me to hold one end, and carefully unrolled a three-foot chart upon which was meticulously recorded his every migraine headache and every sexual experience of the past four months. One glance revealed the complexity of the diagram. Every migraine, its intensity, duration, and treatment was coded in blue. Every sexual rush, colored red, was reduced to a five-point scale according to Marvin's performance: premature ejaculations were separately coded, as was impotence — with a distinction made between

inability to sustain an erection and inability to have one.

It was too much to absorb in a glance. "That's an elaborate piece of work," I said. "It must have taken you days."

"I liked doing it. I'm good at it. People forget that we accountants have graphic skills that are never used in tax work. Here, look at the month of July: four migraines and each one preceded by either impotence or a grade-one or -two sexual performance."

I watched Marvin's finger point to the blips of migraine and impotence. He was right: the correlation was impressive, but I was growing edgy. My timing had been thrown off. We had only just begun our first session, and there was much more I wanted to know before I would feel ready to examine Marvin's chart. But he pressed it before me so forcefully that I had no option other than to watch his stubby finger trace out the love leavings of last July.

Marvin at sixty-four had suddenly, six months ago, for the first time in his life, developed disabling migraine headaches. He had consulted a neurologist, who had been unsuccessful in controlling Marvin's headaches and then referred him to me.

I had seen Marvin for the first time only a few minutes earlier when I went out to my waiting room to fetch him. He was sitting there patiently — a short, chubby, bald man with a glistening pate and owl eyes which never blinked as they peered through over-sized, gleaming chrome spectacles.

I was soon to learn that Marvin was particularly interested in spectacles. After shaking hands with me, his first words, while accompanying me down the hall to my office, were to compliment me on my frames and to ask me their make. I believe I fell from grace when I confessed ignorance of the manufacturer's name; things grew even more awkward when I removed my glasses to read the brand name on the stem and found that, without my glasses, I could not read it. It did not take me long to realize that, since my other glasses were now resting at home, there was no way that I could give Marvin the trivial information he desired, so I held out my spectacles for him to read the label. Alas, he, too, was nearsighted, and more of our first minutes together was consumed by his switching to his reading glasses.

And now, a few minutes later, before I could proceed to interview him in my customary way, I found myself surrounded by Marvin's meticulous red-and-blue-penciled chart. No, we were not off to a good start. To compound the problem, I had just had a poignant but exhausting session with an elderly, distraught widow whose purse had recently been stolen. Part of my attention was still with her, and I had to spur myself to give Marvin the attention he deserved.

Having received only a brief consultation note from the neurologist, I knew practically nothing about Marvin and began the hour after we completed the opening eyeglass ritual, by asking "What ails?" That was when he volunteered that "you fellows" think "sex is at the root of everything."

I rolled up the chart, told Marvin I'd like to study it in detail later, and attempted to restore some rhythm to the session by asking him to tell me the whole story of his illness from the beginning.

He told me that about six months ago he, for the first time in his life, began suffering from headaches. The symptoms were those of classical migraine: a premonitory visual aura (flashing lights) and a unilateral distribution of excruciating pain which incapacitated him for hours and often necessitated bed rest in a darkened room.

"And you say you have good reason to believe that your sexual performance touches off the migraine?"

"You may think it strange — for a man of my age and position — but you can't dispute the facts. There's the proof!" He pointed to the scroll now resting quietly on my desk. "Every migraine of the last four months was preceded within twenty-four hours by a sexual failure."

Marvin spoke in a deliberate, pedantic manner. Obviously he had rehearsed this material beforehand.

"For the last year I have been having violent mood swings. I pass quickly from feeling good to feeling that it's the end of the world. Now don't jump to conclusions." Here he shook his finger at me for greater emphasis. "When I say I feel good, I do not mean I' tried to treat me for manic-depressive disease with lithium —

didn't do a thing except screw up my kidneys. I can see why docs get sued. Have you ever seen a case of manic-depression starting at sixty-four? Do you think I should have gotten lithium?"

His questions jarred me. They were distracting and I didn't know how want to get involved with that. Too many things to deal with. I made an appeal to efficiency.

"I'd be glad to come back to these questions later, but we can make best use of our time today if we first hear your whole clinical story straight through."

"Right you are! Let's stay on track. So, as I was saying, I flip back and forth from feeling good to feeling anxious and depressed — both together — and it is always in the depressed states that the headaches occur. I never had one till six months ago."

"And the link between sex and depression?"

"I was getting to that —"

Careful, I thought. My impatience is showing. It's clear he's going to tell it his way, not mine. For Chrissakes stop pushing him!

"Well — this is the part you'll find hard to believe — for the last twelve months my moods have been totally controlled by sex. If I have good sex with my wife, the world seems bright. If not, bingo! Depression and headaches!"

"Tell me about your depressions. What are they like?"

"Like an ordinary depression. I'm down."

"Say some more."

"What's to say? Everything looks black."

"What do you think about in the depressions?"

"Nothing. That's the problem. Isn't that what depression is all about?"

"Sometimes when people get depressed, certain thoughts circle around in their mind."

"I keep knocking myself."

"How?"

"I start to feel that I will always fail in sex, that my life as a man is over. Once the depression sets in, I am bound to have a migraine within the next twenty-four hours. Other doctors have told me that I am in a vicious circle. Let's see, how does it work?

When I'm depressed I get impotent, and then because I'm impotent I get more depressed. Yep, that's it. But knowing that doesn't stop it, doesn't break the vicious circle."

"What does break it?"

"You'd think, after six months, I'd know the answer. I'm pretty observant, always have been. That's what good accountants get paid for. But I'm not sure. One day I have good sex, and everything's all right again. Why that day and not another day? I haven't a clue."

And so the hour went. Marvin's commentary was precise but stingy, slightly abrasive, and larded with clichés, questions, and the comments of other doctors. He remained remarkably clinical. Although he brought up details of his sexual life, he expressed no embarrassment, self-consciousness, or, for that matter, any deeper feelings.

At one point I tried to get beneath the forced "hale fellow" heartiness.

"Marvin, it must not be easy for you to talk about intimate aspects of your life to a stranger. You mentioned you had never talked to a psychiatrist before."

"It's not a matter of things being intimate, it's more to do with psychiatry — I don't believe in psychiatrists."

"You don't believe we exist?" A stupid attempt at a feeble joke, but Marvin did not note my tongue in cheek.

"No, no, it's not that. It's that I don't have faith in them. My wife, Phyllis, doesn't either. We've known two couples with marital problems who saw psychiatrists, and both ended up in the divorce court. You can't blame me for being on guard, can you?"

By the end of the hour, I was not yet able to make a recommendation and scheduled a second consultation hour. We shook hands, and as he let my office I became aware that I was glad to see him go. I was sorry I had to see him again.

I was irritated with Marvin. But why? Was it his superficiality, his needling, his wagging his finger at me, his "you fellows" tone? Was it his innuendoes about suing his neurologist — and trying to draw me into it? Was it that he was so controlling? He took over the hour: first with that silly business of the glasses, and then with his determination to stick that chart in my hands whether I wanted it or not. I thought of tearing that chart to shreds and enjoying every moment of it.

But so much irritation? So Marvin disrupted the pace of the hour. So what? He was up front, he told me exactly what was troubling him as best he could. He had worked hard according to his conception of psychiatry. His chart was, after all, useful. I would have been pleased with it had it been my idea. Perhaps it was more my problem than his? Had I grown so stodgy, so old? Was I so rigid, in such a rut that if the first hour didn't proceed just the way I wished it to, I grew cranky and stomped my feet?

Driving home that evening I thought more about him, the two Marvins — Marvin the man, Marvin the idea. It was the flesh-and-blood Marvin who was irritating and uninteresting. But Marvin the project was intriguing. Think of that extraordinary story: for the first time in his life, a stable, if prosaic, previously healthy sixty-four-year-old man who has been having sex with the same woman for forty-one years suddenly becomes exquisitely sensitive to his sexual performance. His entire well-being soon becomes hostage to sexual functioning. The event is severe (his migraines are exceptionally disabling); it is unexpected (sex never presented any unusual problems previously); and it is sudden (it erupted in full force precisely six months ago).

Six months ago! Obviously there lay the key and I began the second session by exploring the events of six months ago. What changes in his life had occurred then?

"Nothing of significance," Marvin said.

"Impossible," I insisted, and posed the same question many different ways. I finally learned that six months ago Marvin had made the decision to retire and sell his accountancy firm. The information emerged slowly, not because he was unwilling to tell me about retirement, but because he attached little importance to the event.

I felt otherwise. The markers of one's life stages are always significant, and few markers more so than retirement. How is it possible for retirement not to evoke deep feelings about the passage and passing of life, about the meaning and significance of one's entire life project? For those who look inward, retirement is a time of life review, of summing up, a time of proliferating awareness of finitude and approaching death.

Not so for Marvin.

"Problems about retiring? You've got to be kidding. This is what I've been working for — so I can retire."

"Will you find yourself missing anything about your work?"

"Only the headaches. And I guess you can say I've found a way to take them with me? The migraines, I mean." Marvin grinned, obviously pleased with himself for having stumbled upon a joke. "Seriously, I've been tired and bored with my work for years. What do you think I'll miss — the new tax forms?"

"Sometimes retirement stirs up important feelings because it is such an important milestone in life. It reminds us of life passages. You've been working for how long? Forty-five years? And now you suddenly stop, you pass on to a new stage. When I retire, I think it will bring home to me more clearly than I've ever known that life has a beginning and an end, that I've been slowly passing from one point to another, and that I am now approaching the end."

"My work is about money. That's the name of the game. What retirement really means is that I've made so much money I don't need to make any more. What's the point of it? I can live on my interest very comfortably."

"But, Marvin, what will it mean not to work again? All your life you've worked. You've gotten your meaning out of working. I've a hunch there's something scary about giving it up."

"Who needs it? Now, some of my associates are killing themselves piling up enough money so they can live on their interest's interest. That's what I call crazy — *they* should see a psychiatrist."

Vorbeireden, vorbeireden: we talked past each other, past each other. Again and again I invited Marvin to look within, to adopt, even for a moment, a cosmic perspective, to identify the deeper concerns of his existence — his sense of finitude, of aging and decline, his fear of death, his source of life purpose. But we talked past each other. He ignored me, misunderstood me. He seemed pasted to the surface of things.

Weary of traveling alone on these little subterranean excursions, I decided to stay closer to Marvin's concerns. We talked about work. I learned that, when he was very young, his parents and some teachers had considered him a math prodigy; at the age of eight, he had auditioned, unsuccessfully, for the "Quiz Kids" radio show. But he never lived up to that early billing.

I thought he sighed when he said this, and asked, "That must have been a big wound for you. How well did it heal?"

He suggested that perhaps I was too young to appreciate how many eight-year-old boys auditioned unsuccessfully for the "Quiz Kids."

"Feelings don't always follow rational rules. In fact, usually they don't."

"If I would have given in to feelings every time I was hurt, I'd never have gotten anywhere."

"I notice that it is very hard for you to talk about wounds."

"I was one of hundreds. It was no big deal."

"I notice, too, that whenever I try to move closer to you, you let me know you don't need anything."

"I'm here for help. I'll answer all your questions."

It was clear that a direct appeal would be of no value. It was going to take Marvin a long time to share his vulnerability. I retreated to fact gathering. Marvin grew up in New York, the only child of impoverished first-generation Jewish parents. He majored in mathematics at a small city college and briefly considered graduate school. But he was impatient to get married — he had dated Phyllis since he was fifteen — and, since he had no financial resources, decided to become a high school teacher.

After six years of teaching trigonometry, Marvin felt stuck. He arrived at the conclusion that getting rich was what life was all about. The idea of thirty-five more years of slender high-school-teacher paychecks was unbearable. He was certain the decision to teach school had been a serious mistake and, at the age of thirty, set about rectifying it. After a crash accountancy course, he said goodbye to his students and colleagues and opened an accounting firm, which ultimately proved to be highly lucrative. With wise investments in California real estate, he had become a wealthy man.

"That brings us up to now, Marvin. Where do you go in life from here?"

"Well, as I said, there's no point in accumulating any more money. I have no children" — here his voice turned gray — "no poor relatives, no desires to give it to good causes."

"You sounded sad when you talked about not having children."

"That's past history. I was disappointed then, but that was a long time ago, thirty-five years ago. I have a lot of plans. I want to travel. I want to add to my collections — maybe they're my substitute for children — stamps, political campaign buttons, old baseball uniforms, and *Reader's Digests*."

Next, I explored Marvin's relationship with his wife which he insisted was extremely harmonious. "After forty-one years I still feel my wife is a great lady. I don't like being away from her, even for one night. In fact, I feel warm inside when I see her at the end of the day. All my tension disappears. Perhaps you could say that she's my Valium."

According to Marvin, their sex life had been wonderful until six months ago: despite forty-one years, it seemed to have retained luster and passion. When Marvin's periodic impotence began, Phyllis had at first shown great understanding and patience but, during the last couple of months, had become irritable. Only a couple of weeks ago, she had grumbled that she was tired of "being had" — that is, being sexually aroused and then left unsatisfied.

Marvin gave much weight to Phyllis's feelings and was deeply troubled when he thought he had displeased her. He brooded for days after an episode of impotence and was entirely dependent upon her to regain his equilibrium; sometimes she brought him around simply by reassuring him that she still found him virile, but generally he required some physical comforting. She lathered him in the shower, she shaved him, she massaged him, she took his soft penis into her mouth and held it there gently until it throbbed into life.

I was struck in the second interview, as in the first, by Marvin's lack of wonderment at his own story. Where was his curiosity that his life had changed so dramatically, that his sense of direction, his happiness, even his desire to live was now entirely dictated by whether he could sustain tumescence in his penis?

It was time now to make a recommendation to Marvin about treatment. I did not think that he would be a good candidate for a deep, uncovering type of psychotherapy. There were several reasons. I've always found it difficult to treat someone with so little curiosity. Although it is possible to assist in the unfolding of curiosity, the subtle and lengthy process would be incompatible with Marvin's wish for a brief and efficient treatment. As I thought back over the two hours, I was also aware that he had resisted every one of my invitations to dip deeper into his feelings. He didn't seem to understand, we talked past each other, he had no interest in the inner meaning of events. He also resisted my attempts to engage him more personally and directly: for example, when I had asked him about his wound or pointed out that he ignored any of my attempts to get closer to him.

I was about to offer my formal recommendation that he begin a course of behavioral therapy (an approach based on changing concrete aspects of behavior, especially marital communication and sexual attitudes and practice) when, almost as an afterthought, Marvin mentioned that he had had some dreams during the week.

I had inquired about dreams during the first interview; and, like many other patients, he replied that, though he dreamed every night, he could not recall the details of a single dream. I had suggested he keep a writing pad by his bed to record dreams, but he seemed so little inner-directed that I doubted he would follow through and I neglected to inquire about them in the second session.

Now he took out his notepad and began to read a series of dreams:

Phyllis was distraught that she hadn't been good to me. She left to go home. But when I followed her there, she was gone. I was afraid I would find her dead in this large castle on a high mountain. Next, I was trying to get into the window of a room where her body might be. I was on a high narrow ledge. I couldn't go any farther, but it was too narrow to turn around and go back. I was afraid that I'd fall, and then I grew afraid that I'd jump and commit suicide.

Phyllis and I were undressing to make love. Wentworth, a partner of mine, who weighs two hundred fifty pounds, was in the room. His mother was outside. We had to blindfold him so we could continue. When I went outside, I didn't know what to say to his mother about why we blindfolded him.

There was a gypsy camp forming right in the front lobby of my office. All of them were filthy dirty — their hands, their clothes, the bags they were carrying. I heard the men whispering and conspiring in a menacing way. I wondered why the authorities would permit them to camp out in the open.

The ground under my house was liquefying. I had a giant auger and knew that I would have to drill down sixty-five feet to save the house. I hit a layer of solid rock, and the vibrations woke me up.

Remarkable dreams! Where had they come from? Could Marvin have possibly dreamed them? I looked up, half expecting to see someone else sitting across from me. But he was still there, patiently awaiting my next question, his eyes blank behind his gleaming spectacles.

We had only a few minutes left. I asked Marvin whether he had any associations to any aspect of these dreams. He merely shrugged. They were a mystery to him. I had asked for dreams, and he had given them to me. That was the end of it.

The dreams notwithstanding, I proceeded to recommend a

course of marital therapy, perhaps eight to twelve sessions. I suggested several options: to see the two of them myself; to refer them to someone else; or to refer Phyllis to a female therapist for a couple of sessions and then for the four of us — Phyllis, Marvin, I, and her therapist — to meet in conjoint sessions.

Marvin listened attentively to what I said, but his facial expression was so frozen that I had no hint of what he felt. When I asked for his reaction, he became strangely formal and said, "I'll take your suggestions under consideration and let you know my decision."

Was he disappointed? Did he feel rejected? I couldn't be sure. It seemed to me at the time that I had made the right recommendation. Marvin's dysfunction was acute and would respond, I thought, to a brief cognitive-behavioral approach. Furthermore, I was convinced he would not profit from individual therapy. Everything weighed against it: he was too resistant; in the trade language, he had simply too little "psychological mindedness."

Nonetheless, it was with regret that I passed up the opportunity of working in depth with him: the dynamics of his situation fascinated me. I was certain that my first impression had been close to the mark: that his impending retirement had stoked up much fundamental anxiety about finitude, aging, and death, and that he was attempting to cope with this anxiety through sexual mastery. So much was riding on the sexual act that it was overtaxed and, ultimately, overwhelmed.

I believed that Marvin was entirely wrong when he said that sex was at the root of his problems; far from it, sex was just an ineffective means of trying to drain off surges of anxiety springing from more fundamental sources. Sometimes, as Freud first showed us, sexually inspired anxiety is expressed through other devious means. Perhaps just as often the opposite is true: *other anxiety masquerades as sexual anxiety*. The dream about the giant auger could not have been more clear: the ground under Marvin's feet was liquefying (an inspired visual image for groundlessness), and he was trying to combat that by drilling, with his penis, sixty-five feet (that is, sixty-five years) down!

The other dreams gave evidence of a savage world beneath Marvin's placid exterior — a world seething with death, murder, suicide, anger toward Phyllis, fears of dirty and menacing phantoms erupting from within. The blindfolded man in the room where he and Phyllis were to make love was particularly intriguing. When investigating sexual problems it is always important to ask, Are there more than two people present during lovemaking? The presence of others — phantoms of parents, rivals, other lovers — vastly complicates the sexual act.

No, behavioral therapy was the best choice. It was best to keep the lid of this underworld sealed. The more I thought about it, the more pleased I was that I had restrained my curiosity and had acted selflessly and systematically in the best interests of the patient.

But rationality and precision in psychotherapy are rarely rewarded. A few days later, Marvin called and asked for another appointment. I had expected that Phyllis would accompany him, but he arrived alone, looking anxious and haggard. No opening ceremonies that day. He came right to the point.

"This is a bad day. I feel miserable. But first, I want to say that I appreciate your recommendation last week. To be honest, I'd expected you to advise me to come to see you three or four times a week for the next three or fours years. I'd been warned that you psychiatrists did that regardless of the problem. Not that I blame you — after all, you guys are running a business and gotta earn a living.

"Your advice about couples therapy made sense to me. Phyllis and I do have some communication problems, more than I really told you about last week. Actually, I understated the case to you. I've had some difficulties with sex — not as bad as now — which caused me to flip back and forth in my moods for twenty years. So I decided to take your advice, but Phyllis will not cooperate. She flat out refuses to see a shrink, a marriage therapist, a sex therapist — anyone. I asked her to come in one time today to talk to you, but she has dug in her heels."

"How come?"

"I'll get to that but, first, there are two other things I want to cover today." Marvin stopped. At first I thought it was to catch his breath: he had been racing through his sentences. But he was composing himself. He turned away, blew his nose, and wiped his eyes surreptitiously.

Then he continued. "I'm way down. I had my worst migraine ever this week and had to go to the emergency room night before last for an injection."

"I thought you looked drawn today."

"The headaches are killing me. But to make things worse, I'm not sleeping. Last night I had a nightmare which woke me up about two in the morning, and I kept replaying it all night long. I still can't get it out of my mind."

"Let's go over it."

Marvin started to read the dream in such a mechanical manner that I stopped him and employed the old Fritz Perls device of asking him to begin again and to describe the dream in the present tense, as though he were experiencing it right now. Marvin put aside his notepad and from memory recited:

The two men are tall, pale, and very gaunt. In a dark meadow they glide along in silence. They are dressed entirely in black. With tall black stovepipe hats, long-tailed coats, black spats and shoes, they resemble Victorian undertakers or temperance workers. Suddenly they come upon a carriage, ebony black, cradling a baby girl swaddled in black gauze. Wordlessly, one of the men begins to push the carriage. After a short distance he stops, walks around to the front, and, with his black cane, which now has a glowing white tip, he leans over, parts the gauze, and methodically inserts the white tip into the baby's vagina.

I was transfixed by the dream. The stark images took form immediately in my own mind. I looked up in amazement at Marvin, who seemed unmoved and unappreciative of the power of his own creation, and the notion occurred to me that this was not, could not be, his dream. A dream like that could not have sprung from him: he was merely the medium through whose lips it was expressed. How could I, I wondered, meet the dreamer?

Indeed, Marvin reinforced that whimsical notion. He had no sense of familiarity with the dream and related to it as though it were some alien text. He still experienced fear as he recited it, and shook his head as though he were trying to get the dream's bad taste out of his mouth.

I focused on the anxiety. "Why was the dream a nightmare? Precisely what part of it was frightening?"

"As I think about it now, the last thing — putting the cane in the baby's vagina — is the horrible part. Yet not when I was having the dream. It was everything else, the silent footsteps, the blackness, the sense of deep foreboding. The whole dream was soaked in fear."

"What feeling was there in the dream about the insertion of the cane into the baby's vagina?"

"If anything, that part seemed almost soothing, as though it quieted the dream — or, rather, it tried to. It didn't really do it. None of this makes any sense to me. I've never believed in dreams."

I wanted to linger with the dream but had to return to the needs of the moment. The fact that Phyllis was unwilling to talk to me, even once, to help her husband, who was now in extremis, belied Marvin's account of his idyllic, harmonious marriage. I had to proceed with delicacy here because of his fear (which Phyllis obviously shared) that therapists snoop out and fan marital problems, but I had to be certain that she was inexorably opposed to couples therapy. Last week I had wondered if Marvin hadn't felt rejected by me. Perhaps this was a ploy to manipulate me into seeing him in individual therapy. How much of an effort had Marvin really made to persuade Phyllis to participate with him in treatment?

Marvin assured me that she was very set in her ways.

"I told you she doesn't believe in psychiatry, but it goes far beyond that. She won't see any doctor, she's not had a GYN exam in fifteen years. It's all I can do to get her into the dentist when she's got a toothache."

Suddenly, when I asked for other examples of Phyllis being set

461

in her ways, some unexpected things came pouring out.

"Well, I might as well tell you the truth. No sense of spending good money and sitting here and lying to you. Phyllis has her problems. The main thing is that she's afraid of going out of the house. That has a name. I've forgotten it."

"Agoraphobia?"

"Yeah, that's it. She's had it for years and years. She rarely leaves the house for any reason unless" — Marvin's voice grew hushed and conspiratorial — "it's to escape another fear."

"What other fear?"

"The fear of people visiting the house!"

He went on to explain that they had not entertained guests at home for years — indeed, for decades. If the situation demanded it — for example, if family members visited from out of town — Phyllis was willing to entertain them in a restaurant: "An inexpensive restaurant, since Phyllis hates to spend money." Money was another reason, Marvin added, that she opposed psychotherapy.

Moreover, Phyllis did not permit Marvin to entertain at home either. A couple of weeks ago, for example, some out-of-town guests called to ask if they could view his collection of political buttons. He said he didn't bother to ask Phyllis: he knew she'd raise hell. If he tried to force the issue, it would be, he said, "a month of Sundays" before he "got laid again." Consequently, as he had done many times before, he spent the better part of a day packing up his whole collection to exhibit it in his office.

This new information made it even more clear that Marvin and Phyllis very much needed marital therapy. But there was a new twist now. Marvin's first dreams had so teemed with primitive iconography that, the week before, I had feared individual therapy might break the seal of this seething unconscious and thought marital therapy would be safer. Now, however, with this evidence of severe pathology in their relationship, I wondered whether couples therapy might also unleash demons.

I reiterated to Marvin that, all things considered, I still believed the treatment of choice to be behaviorally oriented couples therapy. But couples therapy requires a couple, and if Phyllis was not yet willing to come in (as he immediately reaffirmed), I told him I would be willing to see him in a trial of individual therapy.

"But be forewarned, individual treatment will most likely require many months, even a year or longer, and it will not be a rose garden. Painful thoughts or memories may emerge which will temporarily make you more uncomfortable than you are right now."

Marvin stated that he had thought about it during the last few days, and wished to begin immediately. We arranged to meet twice weekly.

It was apparent that both he and I had reservations. Marvin continued to be skeptical about the psychotherapeutic enterprise and showed little interest in an inner journey. He agreed to therapy only because the migraine had brought him to his knees and he had nowhere else to turn. I, for my part, had reservations because I was so pessimistic about treatment: I agreed to work with him because I saw no other viable therapy option.

But I could have referred him to someone else. There was another reason — that voice, the voice of that being who had created those astonishing dreams. Buried somewhere within Marvin's walls was a dreamer tapping out an urgent existential message. I drifted back into the landscape of the dream, back into the silent, dark world of the gaunt men, the black meadow, and the black-gauzed baby girl. I thought of the incandescent tip of the cane and the sexual act that was not sex but merely a futile attempt to dispel the dread.

I wondered, if disguise were unnecessary, if the dreamer could speak to me without guile, what might he say?

"I am old. I am at the end of my life's work. I have no children, and I approach death full of dread. I am choking on darkness. I am choking on the silence of death, I think I know a way. I try to pierce the blackness with my sexual talisman. But it is not enough."

But these were my reflections, not Marvin's. I asked him to associate to the dream, to think about it, and to say anything that came to mind. Nothing came. He merely shook his head.

"You shake your head no almost instantaneously. Try again. Give yourself a chance. Take any part of the dream and let your mind wander with it."

Nothing whatsoever.

"What do you make of the white-tipped cane?"

Marvin smirked. "I was wondering when you'd get around to that! Didn't I say earlier that you fellows see sex at the root of everything?"

His accusation seemed particularly ironic because, if there were one conviction I had about him, it was that sex was not the source of his difficulty.

"But it's your dream, Marvin. And your cane. You created it, what do you make of it? And what do you make of the allusions to death — undertakers, silence, blackness, the whole atmosphere of dread and foreboding?"

Given the choice of discussing the dream from the perspective of death or of sex, Marvin, with dispatch, chose the latter.

"Well, you might be interested in something sexual that happened yesterday afternoon — that would be about ten hours before the dream. I was lying in bed still recovering from my migraine. Phyllis came over and gave me a head and neck massage. She then kept on going and massaged my back, then my legs, and then my penis. She undressed me and then took off all her clothes."

This must have been an unusual event: Marvin had told me he initiated sex almost all of the time. I suspected that Phyllis wanted to expiate her guilt for refusing to see a couples therapist.

"At first, I wouldn't respond."

"How come?"

"To tell you the truth, I was scared. I was just getting over my worst migraine, and I was afraid I'd fail and get another migraine. But Phyllis started sucking my cock and got me hard. I've never seen her so persistent. I finally said, 'Let's go, a good lay might be just the thing to get rid of some of this tension.'" Marvin paused.

"Why do you stop?"

"I'm trying to think of her exact words. Anyway, we started making love. I was doing pretty well, but just as I was getting ready to come, Phyllis said, 'There are other reasons for making love than to get rid of tension.' Well, that did it! I lost it in a second."

"Marvin, did you tell Phyllis exactly how you felt about her timing?"

"Her timing is not good — never has been. But I was too riled up to talk. Afraid of what I'd say. If I say the wrong thing, she can make my life hell — turn off the sexual spigot altogether."

"What sort of thing might you say?"

"I'm afraid of my impulses — my murderous and sexual impulses."

"What do you mean?"

"Do you remember, years ago, a news story of a man who killed his wife by pouring acid on her? Horrible thing! Yet I've often thought about that crime. I can understand how fury toward a woman could lead to a crime like that."

Christ! Marvin's unconscious was closer to the surface than I thought. Remembering I hadn't wanted to take the lid off such primitive feelings — at least not this early in treatment — I switched from murder to sex.

"Marvin, you said you're frightened also by your sexual impulses. What do you mean?"

"My sex drive has always been too strong. I've been told that's true of many bald men. A sign of too much male hormone. Is that true?"

I didn't want to encourage the distraction. I shrugged off the question. "Keep going."

"Well, I've had to keep it under rein all my life because Phyllis has got strong ideas about how much sex we will have. And it's always the same — two times a week, some exceptions for birthdays and holidays."

"You've got some feelings about that?"

"Sometimes. But sometimes I think restraints are good. Without them I might run wild."

That was a curious comment. "What does 'running wild'

mean? Do you mean extramarital affairs?"

My question shocked Marvin. "I've never been unfaithful to Phyllis. Never will be!"

"Well, what *do* you mean by 'running wild'?"

Marvin looked stumped. I had a sense he was talking about things he had never discussed before. I was excited for him. It had been one hell of an hour's work. I wanted him to continue, and I just waited.

"I don't *know* what I mean, but at times I've wondered what it would have been like to have married a woman with a sex drive like mine, a woman who wanted and enjoyed sex as much as me."

"What do you think? Your life would have been very different?"

"Let me back up a minute. I shouldn't have used the word *enjoy* a few minutes ago. Phyllis enjoys sex. It's just that she never seems to *want* it. Instead, she... what's the word?... dispenses it — if I'm good. These are the times when I feel cheated and angry."

Marvin paused. He loosened his collar, rubbed his neck, and rolled his head around. He was getting rid of tension, but I imagined him to be looking around the room, as though to assure himself no one else was listening.

"You look uncomfortable. What are you feeling?"

"Disloyal. Like I shouldn't have been saying these things about Phyllis. Almost like she'll find out about it."

"You give her a lot of power. Sooner or later we're going to need to find out all about that."

Marvin continued to be refreshingly open during the first several weeks of therapy. All in all, he did far better than I had expected. He was cooperative; he relinquished his pugnacious skepticism about psychiatry; he did his homework, came prepared for the sessions, and was determined, as he put it, to get a good return on his investment. His confidence in therapy was boosted by an unexpected early dividend: his migraines mysteriously and completely disappeared as soon as he started treatment (although his intense sex-spawned mood swings continued).

During this early phase of therapy, we concentrated on two

issues: his marriage and (to a lesser extent, because of his resistance) the implications of his retirement. But I was careful to tread a fine line. I felt like a surgeon preparing the operative field but avoiding any deep dissection. I wanted Marvin to explore these issues, but not too searchingly — not enough to destabilize the precarious marital equilibrium he and Phyllis had established (and thus drive him immediately out of therapy) and not enough to evoke any further death anxiety (and thus ignite further migraines).

At the same time as I was conducting this gentle, somewhat concrete therapy with Marvin, I was also engaged in a fascinating discourse with the dreamer, that vastly enlightened homunculus housed — or, one might say jailed — by Marvin, who was either ignorant of the dreamer's existence or allowed him to communicate with me in a spirit of benign indifference. While Marvin and I strolled and casually conversed on superficial levels, the dreamer drummed out a constant stream of messages from the depths. (pp. 230-248)

What kind of an E9 is Marvin? It is clear that there is nothing more important to him than sexual relationships, which he experiences as a sort of Being-transfusion through sex — even though to his conscious mind the peace it brings him may seem more a tranquilizer than an injection of meaning:

"I don't like being away from her, even for one night. In fact, I feel warm inside when I see her at the end of the day. All my tension disappears. Perhaps you could say that she's my Valium," he says.

Marvin's most salient passion is for union — and his therapeutic progress may be viewed as a transition from confluence to relationship proper.

A pathological trait that attracts our attention before any other, as we read Yalom's account of his first meeting with Marvin, is what I would call an invasive dispersion. Concern with detail is only an aspect of it; another is how this serves to perpetuate his blindness; and still another is the distraction of attention from the "center of things" to the periphery. Furthermore, Marvin *pushes* his trivial concern onto the therapist — as magnificently illustrated by the funny episode (through which precious time from the first therapeutic session is successfully diverted into an unsuccessful attempt to find out the brand of the therapist's eye glasses.) Or, consider the scene in which Marvin presses his chart so forcefully upon Yalom that the latter retains a vivid impression of his patient's "stubby finger ... [tracing] out the love leavings of last July." There is something akin to a reaction-formation in this covering over of blindness with attention to detail — and certainly a displacement of psychic energy. This trait is an aspect of a deliberate and pedantic character style — somewhat reminiscent of Dickens's portrait of Mr. Micawber in *David Copperfield*.

The expansiveness of both Marvin and Micawber seems built upon a denial of insignificance and depression — and in Marvin the denial is so successful that only his body and dreams signal a problem. He has a masked pre-retirement neurosis of the same nature as the transient Sunday neurosis so common in the Swiss bourgeoisie.

In one case as in the other (the pre-retirement neurosis and the Swiss Sunday neurosis), the meaninglessness of life becomes apparent, and thus critical, without acknowledging itself as that. When the distraction of work is not there, an inner deadness cannot fail to be confronted, and becomes intolerable. (I don't think the problem is that retirement signals that only a short life remains; this would not matter much if Marvin's remaining life were truly a *life*!)

Marvin had so little interest in the inner meaning of events, so little curiosity about his life, scarce interest in an inner journey and "lack of wonderment at his own story" that Yalom is perfectly accurate when he translates all this into the statement that, "he had simply too little psychological mindedness," and that "he seemed pasted to the surface of things."

Clearly, the patient's disconnection from his experience involves resignation: "If I would give into feelings every time I was hurt I would have never gotten any where," he says; and in response to, "I noticed it was very hard for you to talk about wounds," Marvin replies: "I was one of hundreds; it was no big deal."

Resignation is also echoed in Yalom's feedback: "Whenever I tried to move closer to you, you let me know you don't need anything."

The nature of Marvin's plans at the time of beginning therapy — travel, collections of political campaign buttons, old baseball uniforms and *Reader's Digests* — is strikingly symptomatic, particularly since they appear to constitute a displacement of his earlier wish to have children (and in this way a means to support denial of his disappointment), as the dialogue suggests.

During the therapy thus far reported, Dr. Yalom had concentrated on two issues: marriage and the implications of Marvin's retirement. Dreams continued to convey more insight than the conscious mind of the patient, sometimes reflecting or foreshadowing events in the therapy and reiterating the theme of ontological anxiety. But also, as therapy began to really drill its way to Marvin's subterranean psyche, dreams also reflected the new life that this awakening involved. In another dream he meets a woman who tells him she is a long-forgotten daughter whom he didn't know he had, and they agree to correspond. Yalom understands that this is a sign of communication with a more sensitive side of himself. In a third, two baby-kittens have just been born — a still more direct statement about birth and new life.

Then we come upon a dream in which Yalom detects a transferential content. It is about having a heart transplant, and noticing that the surgeon is being accused of being involved only in his job and uninterested "in the messy circumstances of how he got the heart from the donor." Yalom translates the heart transplant metaphor for psychotherapy, and takes this to be a message to himself — that he has not been interested enough in the circumstances of Marvin's character formation in the course of early life.

For me, one of the most interesting aspects of the report is the extent to which the therapist allows himself to be guided by his patient's dreams, taking these as advice and supervision. This leads Yalom to uncover the interpersonal circumstances of Marvin's early life and present intrapsychic dynamics. Yalom tells us that one of the most interesting things he learned is that when Marvin was seven or eight "a cataclysmic secret event shattered his family and resulted in his mother banishing his father permanently from her bedroom." (p. 252) So, we realize that Marvin's present situation is a replay of that to which he was an empathetic spectator.

After his father's exile, in the long run, it fell upon Marvin, the youngest son, to become his mother's constant companion: it was his job to escort her to all her social functions. For years he endured his friend's jibes about dating his mother.

Needless to say, Marvin's new family assignment did not increase his popularity with his father, who became a thin presence in the family, then a mere shadow, and soon evaporated forever.

Here is Yalom's brief summary of these understandings:

Obviously, the foundation was in place for major oedipal problems in Marvin's relations with women. His relationship with his mother had been exclusive, overly intimate, prolonged in its closeness and had disastrous consequences for his relationship with men; indeed, he imagined he had, in some substantial way, contributed to his father's disappearance. It was not surprising, then, to learn that Marvin had been wary of competition with men and inordinately shy with women. His first real date, with Phyllis, was his last first date: Phyllis and he kept steady company until their marriage. She was six years younger, equally shy and equally inexperienced with the opposite sex. (p. 252)

After this, Marvin became aware of how "he had re-created part of his parent's pattern in his own marriage — his wife, like his father's wife, wielded control by cutting off sexual favors." (p. 252-253)

But soon enough, "he lost interest in past origins of current life patterns." The awareness of his deadness and the consequent anxiety about it came to the foreground. There were dreams — with dead people and with a skull, for instance — and after considering them he declared that, "he had been temperate, too temperate. He'd known for a couple of years that he had deadened himself all his life." (p. 253)

Picking up an issue of "Psychology Today" at a dentist's office, Marvin was once stimulated by what he read there to hold imaginary conversations with the more important people who had died in his life.

> One day when he was alone, he tried it. He imagined telling his father how much he had missed him and how much he would have liked to have known him. His father didn't answer. He imagined saying his final goodbye to his mother, sitting across from him in her familiar bentwood rocker. He said the words, but no feelings came with them. He gritted his teeth and tried to force feelings out. But nothing came. He concentrated on the meaning of *never* — that he would *never, never* see her again. He remembered banging his fist on his desk, forcing himself to remember the chill of his mother's forehead when he kissed her as she lay in her casket. But nothing came. He shouted aloud, "I will *never* see you again!" Still, nothing. That was when he learned that he had deadened himself. (p. 256)

Yalom reported that Marvin cried that day, in the therapy office, for all that he had missed during his years of deadness. Clearly this was the mourning of one who had come to feel alive. Naturally, Marvin's sense of having awakened to this deeper experience, and to meaningfulness, didn't quite solve the situation of having little time before him in which to make something meaningful out of his life. Here is a transparent dream about it:

> I am climbing a mountain trail. I see some people trying to rebuild a house at night. I know that it can't be done, and I try to tell them but they can't hear me. Then I hear someone calling my name from behind. It is my mother trying to overtake me. She said she has a message for me. It is that someone is dying. I know that it is me who is dying. I wake up in a sweat. (p. 258)

Yalom tells us that Marvin came to learn "that deep inside there is a rich teeming world which, if confronted, brings terrible fear but also offers redemption through illumination." (p. 259) And it is noteworthy that as he became concerned with the inevitability of death he lost interest in his collection of stamps and the *Reader's Digest*. I quote his therapist again:

So Marvin and I reached a crucial point, a juncture to which full awareness inevitably leads. It is the time when one stands before the abyss and decides how to face the pitiless existential facts of life: death, isolation, groundlessness, and meaninglessness. Of course, there are no solutions. One has a choice only of certain stances: to be "resolute," or "engaged," or courageously defiant, or stoically accepting, or to relinquish rationality and, in awe and mystery, place one's trust in the providence of the Divine. (p. 260)

Yalom quotes his patient as saying that "he'd learned more about himself in the past five months than in his previous sixty-four years!" — and as a consequence of this learning, his relationship to Phyllis became one of greater honesty and deeper communication. (p. 261) I get the picture that she is an E5 to whom this communication from Marvin was a remedial stimulus, and that she began healing as well. As a consequence of her own greater awareness and interest in further self-understanding, there was a time when she came to therapy. I quote her now:

But watching Marvin change over the last several weeks has been impressive. You may not realize it, but the mere fact that I'm here today, in a psychiatrist's office, talking about myself is in itself a big, big, step. (p. 265)

Her joining Marvin in this therapeutic process was a further help to both in that a new situation became explicit: Marvin's retirement meant staying at home, which she dreaded as he would see how little she did and would lose respect for her. His anxiety about retirement was also connected to the dreaded alternative, but more essentially still, served to crystallize a commitment to working over the relationship itself, toward a more loving one.

After seeing both as a couple a few more times, all were satisfied with the work that had been done and felt that Marvin's change had initiated an adaptive spiral. His migraines had never returned and his anguish dreams had stopped. "Phyllis continued and solidified her improvement in individual therapy with another therapist over the next year." (p. 268)

Yalom comments: "Marvin and the dreamer had fused, and I spoke to them now as to a single person." (p. 269)

Next time patient and therapist met was a year later. Marvin listened to a ten minute recording of his initial interview, and smilingly remarked, "who is that jerk anyway?" (p. 269)

If insight is the remedy E9 needs most, this case was successful: the patient came to see his blindness, and to feel the feelings of the dream-self. Now he no longer needed physical symptoms to urge him to pay attention to his inner truth.

DISCOVERING THE NEED TO DECIDE:
An Annotated Dream Session

My first choice of a therapy transcript to document character-focused Gestalt on an E9 did not receive publication approval by my patient, as in the previous cases in this series. My alternative choice has conveniently fallen on a piece of dreamwork from the 1980s. I commented upon this piece in response to an invitation of *The Gestalt Journal* before I came across the Dick Price* transcript that I eventually submitted, in view of its pertinence, to the anniversary volume dedicated to him.[9] I then planned to include this piece of dreamwork as an appendix to my chapter on Gestalt and Protoanalysis in *Gestalt Therapy: The Attitude and Practice of an Atheoretical Experientialism* before realizing that the book had already become too thick.[10] Now that it felicitously serves the more specific purpose of illustrating E9 in this present volume, I only want to remark that the context of the recorded transcript was not a Gestalt therapy group, as in other instances, but a workshop of dreams. Because of this, and the didactic situation implied, I at times invited the patient to free-associate, and was once on the verge of interrupting and returning to the group agenda.

I turn to the transcript now, which begins with the dream narrative:

Placida: I am going along in my car, and I see it very vividly, in full color. I am driving, and near me there is another car, in which there are people. I don't know who they are, but we are all going along together. We go along a street, rushing, and it looks like I am following them. I come to a corner

473

where there is a stoplight and lots of traffic and people. When I come to the corner, for a moment I doubt. I don't know which way to go. Then I lose sight of the other car. I have two alternatives: like two streets. I look towards the side, and I see my husband, on a bicycle, and in a tennis outfit; he is in a happy mood, having a very good time, and all this makes me want to laugh. I sound the horn so he sees me. In the meantime, I have to decide where I am going. I'm there, and I don't know anything more, because that's as far as I go; that's the end of the dream.

So, she is going somewhere, and there is the sense of disconnection from another car, a loss of direction. She is going somewhere and "like ... following." Personality-wise there is also a going in a certain direction and a following, it would seem; going in the direction others are going; not going by herself, but with a group of people, a somewhat indistinct group of people. So I thought, as I looked at her and was under the impression that I was in the presence of an E9 individual: "Could there be a better symbol for that mode of being of an E9 that I have characterized as a 'going along with the stream?'" She doesn't know well where she is going, I would say, and is concerned that she loses the connection with others that gives her direction; and then suddenly she finds herself among lots of people, lots of traffic and chaos, feeling that she doesn't know which direction to go. We sense an organic development from losing sight of the other car to finding herself in this traffic situation, where there is a choice to be made. And, while this situation is there (of a choice to be made), she suddenly sees her husband who is, oh, so amused ... in such a good mood ... going to play tennis. She calls to him; she wants to connect with him; and of course, it would make sense for her to want to make contact with him in view of finding out which way to go. It is as if the normal reaction of asking him for help were obliterated by a more available response. One would imagine that her feeling state at that point is one of alarm, at any rate. Not knowing which way to go is an uncomfortable feeling, and one would imagine that making contact with another person at that moment would be a protection from that alarm; all the more so if that person happens to be her husband. Yet, I am intrigued that her reaction as a dreamer seems so phlegmatic: "I sound the horn so that he looks at me ..." She wants somebody; she as the dreamer has made her husband appear there, and as dream-self

474

wants to connect … and then there is something of an anti-climax. The dream leaves us in a situation of suspense, with her feeling of not knowing where to go.

She continues:

P: Okay. The emotion is "I don't know which way to go." On the one hand, I want my husband to see me, and on the other hand, I must make a decision as to which way to go.

There is a conflict between her making a decision and finding refuge in the contact with a loved person, while also incorporating his good feeling. Though I have translated the Spanish *"entretenido"* as *"in a happy mood,"* the word literally means amused or entertained.

"And what are you laughing at?" I ask.

P: This dream was from the night before last. I said to myself, "I have to produce a dream for this workshop" and I see that this dream is too evident. I laugh at how evident it would seem for me. I don't know whether it is so evident [to others], but for me it is too evident."

I was, at the time, not seeing a meaning that she found obvious, and it seemed that if a meaning was obvious to her I would be better off understanding that before "Gestalting" the dream through enactment. So I began by asking her self-interpretation.

Claudio: So, let us begin with your telling us what you see in the dream, and then we'll see whether your associations reveal something further. How do you understand that dream? And how do you come out of not knowing which way to go?

P: What is clear … what I understand is that I am not clear as to which way to go. And that I pay a lot of attention as to whom to follow, and that I am more oriented to following than to knowing where I want to go.

Then she began to weep, and I felt she well knew that she was describing something basic about herself. I remember her as a 9, and that I was particularly interested that she was aware of not knowing which way to go, of being more a follower than somebody with inner direction. Her use of the expressions: "I don't see," "It is not clear to me," is congruent with the blindness of E9 and deafness to their inner voices ... their confusion.

P: What also comes to me is that I see myself in the car as if I am in a hurry. Doing something ... I don't know what it is ... because I don't know where I am going; and there is my husband, who knows where he is going, and who is on his bicycle, and is okay. He is well ... all right. In other words, from the car I have the intuition that he knows where he is going, and that he is doing okay in that regard.

There is a very nice polarity between the healthy attitude conceived by the self-ideal and her pathological self.

P: What calls my attention about the dream is that it made me want to laugh. I don't feel anger or sorrow. I laughed at seeing him so immersed in what he is doing, and so happy with it.

Here is further allusion to her not knowing where she is going, the positive quality corresponding to her lack. "Seeing him so much in what he is doing." "So much in himself," I think we might say, in contrast to her dispersion or distraction.

It strikes her as remarkable that seeing him happy she feels like laughing, "Because, in real life that sometimes makes me sorry ... [To see him] sure of his way and myself so far from knowing mine." Once more she weeps. My guess is that she is now weeping not only because of her distance from that okay place, but also because of her laughing it away: at the part of her that is looking away from the situation, disowning her sorrow, laughing at herself — the E9 trait of making light of things.

Increasingly, she's been coming into her feelings and into an awareness of herself (throughout the time she has been answering my questions), and now she concludes:

P: That is what I understand of the dream.

C: And what do you feel as you do this, this very moment? [*I think she must have laughed right then, so I was asking: "How do you feel while you do this laughing at your dream or your understanding of it?"*]

P: In the dream, I feel like laughing; it's like funny. As when you meet some-body you know at an intersection and you wave to say hello; that's what catches my attention — that my reaction is one of humor in this contact.

So, she has been weeping; she has understood her lack of self-direction; and when I ask her, "How do you feel *now*?" she understands this to mean "in the dream" — a lack of understanding or a miss-hearing which allows her to revert to the superficial self.

Now, in the dream she doesn't quite feel like laughing; the dream scene here is just one where she smiles or she waves hello. "I wave to him as if to say hello," she says, and I comment (in the spirit of collaborating with her unconscious), just in case she picks up the thought: "This calls my attention. It would seem it also distracts your attention from thinking where you're going."

I am, of course, pointing to a mechanism of self-distraction, hypothesizing that precisely by being outer-directed she is creating a prob-lem for herself. I turn back to the transcript:

P: Of course, and I am now terribly in doubt as to where I go and where I am going. I not only don't know in which direction I am going, I don't even know *for what* I am going.

C: Well, this distracts you from where you are going, which is... [*I am telling her what she experienced in the dream. Of course, I can be mis-taken, for this is something that she has not told but I have inferred; and she confirms it, though not very explicitly. "Well," she says, "Of course, and now I have a terrible doubt," which confirms that now the situation is worse.*]

Since this was part of a workshop on dreams in which I wanted to demonstrate the use of various resources, I now invited her free-association.

C: Free associate further with this intersection at which you are, and about the direction to follow, and the stoplight.

P: Indecision … I don't know where to go. I see two streets. I don't know which is the one the other car followed …

She has only gone back to describing the dream … not endeavoring to produce an association; which, in a person so inclined to follow, may tell us that she is resisting. I choose to stimulate her:

C: How is this of having lost the other car? How is this feeling? With what is it linked in your experience; what is the connection?
Here you are: the other car has left you behind; you are now separate from the car you were following, from the people you were following. Is this now a way familiar to you, that you are following a car and that, suddenly, you are lost, in the dream as in real life? You are going well, perhaps on automatic; then you feel amused and you find yourself stopped while the other car disappears?
What is your *feeling* at this point?

Perhaps the extent to which I am being helpful reflects my perception that I am not with an altogether easy person; that in spite of her having produced valuable material, she needs to be stimulated and prodded.

P: It is like … sad … I don't know… frustration. I don't know which way to go. The others are faster than I; the others didn't hesitate, they knew which way to go, and I got distracted.

C: Yes, you became distracted. [*I just echo what reiterates the theme of distraction, significant to E9.*]

P: And the light changed, and I know that they recognize I will not know which way to go.

C: Do you have any sense of being interfered with by the stoplight? There is a block there. Have you any association to that, being stopped?

478

P: Yes, like being ... like tied up. The others did not hesitate, I got distracted. The bottom sensation is that the truth is I have never really known the way. I was not clear as to which was the way.

Now she is connecting with that in the dream — that she never knew; that she was always relying on and following where others were going. There followed a long silence, a pregnant silence, I felt, filled with experiential flow that I did not need to interfere with, and then:

P: What comes to me next is that I don't see the solution: I know the solution is in myself. It is up to myself to decide which is my way.

C: Continue with that. Repeat and amplify: "I must decide what my way is." Or simply: "I need to decide."

P: My first reaction is that it is easier to follow. This is what happens to me, that if I don't know which my way is... [*weeping*]...I am very lost.

Now she is coming to an understanding that it is not "good business," emotionally, not to know; that it is a terrible source of unhappiness; that she would be better off knowing, or choosing. Now she knows that, at this point, it is not good enough to enjoy the sight of somebody who has autonomy — for her husband only knows where he goes.

P: I never know which way to go. And what I am feeling now is that I need to know. And this calls for daring. [*Again she weeps.*]

The therapy which has taken place thus far is that she has owned her therapeutic impulse, voiced a motivation, the absence of which constituted a "hole" in her puzzle. Let me backtrack.

First, she presents a polarity — enjoying somebody else's well-being and laughing light-heartedly, versus being sad about being lost. Then, as she explores making light of it, she comes to appreciate the conflict between not knowing where to go and relying on somebody else. Thirdly, she has taken sides, and feels she needs to know which way she is going. In wanting to become somebody who knows where to go, she is taking the side of the healthy self.

Now I suggest: "Repeat and amplify, 'I must decide which my way is'" as a way of reversing her habitual passivity, and getting in touch with her disowned therapeutic course (i.e., "I need to decide")

Her first reaction is that it is "easier to follow (than to decide)" and then adds, "Oh, but I feel so lost!"

"Ah, very lost?"

"Of course, because at any moment I don't know where to go. And what I feel behind all this is that I need to know." And then she weeps.

"I need to know which my way is ... This I associate with having courage, daring," so she understands that to take the step is work, and that a price is involved; a price in courage. Already seeing that she *must* ... reflects a willingness to suffer, and a shift from automatic accommodation.

C: What is your weeping about? What makes you cry when you say, "I must find my way. I must decide?"

P: I feel sadness; I cannot know well.

I don't know whether she means she is being pessimistic about her being able to know where to go, or whether she means she does not know very well what this is about. But now, the last time she says it, there is a slight hesitation in her voice. I say: "Sadness at acknowledging that you don't know?" Today, I question my speaking of acknowledgement, which was present from the beginning of what she said. Perhaps it could have been useful to say: "Sadness, from fear of not being able to find your way? ... Hopelessness? Stuckness connected to some hopelessness?"

After a pause, I continue:

C: As you don't dare, you distract yourself, and find it easier to laugh, and in this sounding the horn for your husband there is an evasion, a superficialization.

I am suggesting, "Are you perhaps sad that you see how you escaped into the superficial?" I have the hunch: I think that my suggesting that her sadness has to do with her perception of herself as becoming superficial (…as making light) that, even if the sadness was now (which I thought that perception was), I was suggesting, "It would be *worth* getting sad," like "There *is something* to be sad about"; … some kind of confrontation smuggled in there. It is a strange sadness.

C: I think that this is the experience of separation. When I said to you: "What do you associate with?" I was surprised that this did not come up — the experience of separation from the car suggesting a primal separation. You are very attached to the other, but at a distance; like an attachment through a very long umbilical cord that can be severed any moment.

P: Yes, at a great distance..

C: Next time, don't let yourself be stopped by that light. It's better that you follow that car at any cost. Because I do believe you want to follow that car.

P: More than the stoplight, what stops me is this pointing to another direction. [*Meaning, her being distracted by her husband.*]

C: Okay. Go on with this alternative direction..

P: The first thing that occurs to me is: I go with this car, and I see Eugenio on his bicycle, and I find it's so funny that he be there in a tennis outfit, in the middle of all the traffic, and so absorbed in that. That's what I find so funny.

It may be interpreted that this was funny to her in the Freudian sense; that is, according to the Freudian interpretation of humor: using fun to make light of the expression of the repressed. Just as she is distracted, he is absorbed and just as she is over-influenced by the environment, he, in his lack of hurry and in his tennis outfit, is incongruous with the traffic around him.

P: That's what I find so funny. I am rushing. And so there is a conflict between the amusement and lightness of his going on a bicycle in a tennis outfit, almost to Avenida Providencia; and I am rushing.

We know that part of the psychology of E9 is to have a passion for comfort, for relaxation and lightness; and how an over-relaxation makes up for the tension — for there is an intolerance for tension. This pseudo-ease of E9, which is not deep spontaneity, is akin to the jolliness that covers up a sadness.

C: You don't seem very enthusiastic about this going along; and you are entertained by the scene where there seems to be plenty of time.

P: No time, right; there's no time. It's like timelessness, a lack of concern for time. Yes, I am in time, I am moving in time; Eugenio is in no-time. I am urged forward.

C: Now I would like to ask you to *be* your husband going on his bicycle.

P: [As Eugenio] Oh, that's wonderful, this is much fun to go on a bicycle in a tennis outfit. I'm having a wonderful time on this bicycle. I am not in a hurry; there is no time for me.

C: What do you call fun? [*"Entretenido" in Spanish is often used with the meaning of "fun" but literally means "entertaining."*]

P: It's like amusing.

[*It is interesting that in Spanish, "divertido" (amusing) comes from "diversión," i.e., deviating attention from, or distraction. So the defensive role of amusement is here implicitly.*]
Amusing is not having anything to do. It's having all the time in the world to ride a bicycle. (How is this for defensive laziness? One may say that she is seeking refuge in health in a way that is unhealthy — not only because it is vicarious, but because it is a distraction from her feeling pressured.)

P: It is having all the time in the world to ride your bicycle.
I suggest to her: "You are free. Imagine there is a sense of freedom from constraint, freedom from a topdog that says, 'Hurry.'"

P: Yes, it's wonderful!

C: It would seem to be what you are yearning for. It would seem to be an ideal, the opposite of this rushing along … you know not where. But the way you relate to this ideal is one of being distracted.

P: Yes, it's like I am neither with the bicycle nor the other situation.

C: Now let's try the experience of continuing the dream. The dream ended there, it didn't go beyond the stoplight. But what happens if you go on dreaming?

P: I'll begin to build it along as I imagine … What occurs to me is that the light changes, and, well, I have to go on. I am in the car and, okay, he did not see me. And it's like I say: "Well, next time." And I go left. I don't have images, only sensations. It is as if this road is the opposite of the one before; there is less traffic. It's like the outskirts of the city. And the sensation is of aridity, not of …

C: It seems to me that you are feeling cold as you fantasize this.

P: Cold?

C: Aren't you feeling cold? You are shivering.

P: Yes, but it is not cold.

C: I see, you are just shaking.

P: Yes.

C: And you are driving through this arid place.

P: It is a long way, and I feel it is wide, and I go just the same, and I don't know where I go.

C: And how do you feel as you don't know where you are going?

P: I feel that I'll *get to know*. I feel I *will* know. This is new.

> She is now conceiving that she can live without knowing — that she doesn't have to know beforehand in order to go; that the way to go is *to go*, and the way to make decisions is not on the basis of the kind of knowledge that she was missing. Since she cannot avoid not knowing, she has now allowed herself the space of not knowing. Allowed herself to *act* without knowing.

C: Let's see what else presents itself, what else comes up.

> Since there is only silence, I inquire: "Where do you want to go?"

P: I'd like to go to the beach.

C: To the beach?

P: Yes. [*And then there is silence.*]

C: What happens there?

P: I just have sensations rather than images. It's *going*, just *going*; I don't see anything else.

C: Perhaps it is good that you are not seeing anything and you are not concerned, for it looks that you have been always waiting for things to come from outside; that something presents itself and prompts you rather than taking the reins in your hands and saying, "I go where I want to go; I create my images." What's missing for you is that you take charge of your life; that you own your power.

P: Yes, it is a thing of power. It has to do with decision and power.
C: Perhaps this aridity results from your sense of powerlessness.

P: I feel that I am [facing] alternatives — between accepting to humbly receive from others, or embracing my solitude (to face it, and to seek by myself alone), or to getting into somebody else's car and daring to go without having to know where.

C: Or going to the beach. You never got there. Perhaps you didn't because you felt that if you didn't choose, something better may come to you from outside. That if you follow your wish, your decision would not be good enough.

P: Yes. [*She weeps.*]

C: These have been variations around what you already saw at the beginning: that you have to decide. I hope that the attention given to the issue now brings some inspiration to your life.

AFTERWORD

I set out to document the psychology of the enneatypes with observations from the intimate situation of psychotherapy, both through "macroscopic" or "longitudinal" accounts of the therapeutic process as reported in the literature, and through verbatim "microscopic" cross-sectional or "horizontal" accounts of my own work, in the domain of what might be called Protoanalytic Gestalt.

My intent, other than illustration, was to invite perceptions, rather than to ask a priori questions; it was certainly not my ambition to arrive at any conclusions about the nature of therapy or the laws of personality change through such a limited set of cases.

When I first completed the project and looked back on what I had written (as if to read what it might be saying *beyond* what had been my intention to say), I saw a gaping hole in the book: four of the case reports (E1, E2[1], E5 and E6) could be said to be therapeutic failures; and, no longer satisfied with a one-sided interest in character, I now wanted my case report selection to illustrate transformation as well. How this gap was filled I have told throughout the successive chapters, and also how happy I am about this, I have mentioned already in the Foreword.

My tendency, both in books and other ventures, is not to interrogate reality, but rather approach it with an eye of open curiosity; and what I have learned from what I have undertaken (as in life itself) is something I have had to discover *after* the fact.

What I observed along the way, concerning the clinical material I have quoted, is still another matter, already shared throughout the chapters, or stated implicitly in the design of the case-report mosaic. Yet, as I once more look panoramically at the series of case reports, a new "hole" catches my attention — one that was already there but has become more apparent recently in browsing the literature, i.e., the absence of a substantial E7 published case. Karl Abraham, who first drew attention to the oral-optimistic syndrome, left us no story; and what illustrates the therapy of "narcissistic personality disorders" in the books and journals is anything between E3 and E8, *except* E7 (which I had specially expected). It is true that the generalized description in DSM-III (which I had before me when I wrote *Character and Neurosis*) best fit the E7 pattern in the repertory, but a recent report[2] to the effect that diagnosed "narcissists" score low in the factor of agreeableness[3] (according to the Big Five factor model of personality), tells us it is E8 rather than E7 who receives that diagnosis in contemporary practice.[4] Though I am sure that some E7s are diagnosed as narcissistic, I find no significant report to quote. Probably because E7 (like E3) is just not very problematic — hypomania being less of a concern to people than depressive moods, and the sense of aloofness less questionable than the sense of all-wrongness — E7 is missing from the DSM-IV.

Just as an E7 case was originally missing in the book, and was later provided by Peñarrubia's sober pages, the E1 case is so much longer than any other that I was on the verge of cutting it down. In the end I didn't, however, thinking that the Anna O. case deserved the emphasis, and imagining that the reader would be more interested in the details of the case than in this book having regular proportions.

I hope that my equally unsystematic comments regarding the relevance of a therapist's personality in the task of helping another person to know and transcend his or her's have stimulated some interest in the subject. After many years of training therapists through a method that involves a peer-therapy laboratory of therapeutic exercises, I have formed the impression that the matching or mismatching of personalities in the therapeutic situation is a variable that (along with the therapist's soundness) may override training. I am glad that this subject (as well as that of inter-subjectivity) is beginning to receive the attention it deserves,[5s] and cannot doubt that much clarity will come from an enneatype-conscious approach to the subject.

My enneatype-conscious Gestalt transcripts were, of course, intended from the very beginning to present both character and character transformation, and I am pleased that this component of the book will serve to call attention to a valuable resource.

Gestalt therapy today is comparatively forgotten in the U.S., but those of us with a psychoanalytic background who were privileged to see the early work of Fritz Perls at Esalen Institute had no doubt that we were witnessing something quite beyond what we had seen or even heard before. So deeply felt was the insight gained and so clear were the shifts in people's attitudes through the guided adventure offered by this master therapist, that Gestalt soon came to be regarded as at least as important as psychoanalysis; while its adherents agreed with Perls's contention that it could go beyond the limitations of psychotherapy in its day. Though the therapeutic power of Gestalt opened the way to the humanistic approaches, and its spirit has inspired existential, eclectic and group therapists in general, the fact that the approach has lost attraction, if not vitality, seems to contradict its early promise. As I have discussed the matter in "Gestalt After Fritz," the last chapter of *Gestalt Therapy: Attitude and Practice of an Atheoretical Experientialism* (Nevada City, CA: Gateways, 1990), an ossification, the outcome of a contra-revolutionary movement in Gestalt history, has contributed to this, along with an over-emphasis of a poorly supported theoretical orientation and a reliance on dogmatic ideas.

Yet, I think that the theory of neurosis and character offered by enneatype psychology provides the theoretical support to Gestalt practice that outsiders to Gestalt have missed and insiders have erroneously believed they had. In view of this and of the sharpening of character perception that enneatype psychology makes possible, I am sure that an experiential acquaintance with protoanalysis makes for increased therapeutic effectiveness. Already at the time of writing the chapter on protoanalysis in my *Gestalt Therapy* book I remarked on how this body of knowledge had helped therapists; and ten years later, after extensive experience training therapists in Spain and Italy, I have reason to hope that this new formulation, inspired by an ancient wisdom, may save this precious approach from further decadence.

NOTES

Introduction

1. Should the reader be interested in further information on the Ennegram-based typology and the enneatypes, I suggest consulting *Character and Neurosis: An Integrative View*. Nevada City, CA: Gateways, 1994.

Chapter 1

1. Naranjo, Claudio. *Ennea-type Structures*. Nevada City, CA, 1990.
2. Theophrastus. *Caracteres*. Spanish Version, Ed. Gredos, 1988.
3. Chaucer, Geoffrey. *The Canterbury Tales*. Baltimore, MD: The Penguin Classics, 1961, pp. 20-21.
4. Butler, Samuel. *Characters*. Cleveland OH: The Press of Case Western Reserve University, 1970.
5. Naranjo, Claudio. "On Puritanical Character." *American Journal of Psychoanalysis*. New York: Agathon Press, vol.XLII, number 2, 1982.
6. Naranjo, Claudio. *Eneagrama de la Sociedad/Males del Mundo*. Males del Alma. Madrid: Temas de Hoy, 1995.
7. Dostoyevsky, Fyodor. *The Brothers Karamazov*. New York: The Modern Library, Random House, 1950, p. 131.
8. Weber, Max. *The Protestant Ethic and The Spirit of Capitalism*. New York: Simon and Schuster, 1980.
9. Which she has received not only through Lucy Freeman but, more recently, through *Bertha Pappenhiem/Freud's Anna O.* by Dora Edinger. Illinois: Congregation Solex, 1968.

10. Freeman, Lucy. *The Story of Anna O.* New York: Walker and Company, 1971.
11. Breuer, Josef and Sigmund Freud. *Studies on Hysteria.* Strachey edition. New York: Basic Books, Inc., 1957, pp. 21-28.
12. Freud quoted this sentence, not quite verbatim, in a footnote to the first edition of his *Three Essays on the Theory of Sexuality* (1905), Standard Ed., 7, 164 and in Chapter 11 of his autobiography (1925).
13. the French term
14. in English in the original
15. in English in the original.
16. In English in the original.
17. Freud, Sigmund. *Introductory Lectures on Psychoanalysis.* New York: Liveright, Publishing Corp., 1989.
18. Freeman, Lucy. *The Story of Anna O.* New York: Walker and Company, 1971, pp. 31-34.
19. Since I proposed it in 1971 it has been wisely recognized that in stress situations a person's character may shift so that it includes traits from the character that follows in the ennegram's "inner flow."
20. Berg, Charles. *The Case Book of a Medical Psychologist.* New York: W.W.Norton & Company, Inc., 1948.
21. A joke involving a Spanish saying that means finding the cause of something. In this case "the mother of the lamb" happens to be the patient's mother.

Chapter 2

1. Butler, Samuel. *Characters.* Cleveland, OH:The Press of Case Western Reserve University, 1970.
2. Austen, Jane. *Pride and Prejudice.* New York: Penguin Books, 1979.
3. Ibsen, Henrik. *Ibsen Plays.* New York: Penguin Books, 1980.
4. Ludwig, Emil. *Obras Completas de Emil Ludwig, Biografias.* Barcelona: Editorial Juventud, 1957, p. 39.
5. Dickens, Charles. *David Copperfield.* New York: Signet Classics, 1962, pp. 642-644.
6. Fromm, Erich. *The Sane Society.* New York: Owl Book edition, 1990, p. 164.

7. Campbell, Colin. *The Romantic Ethic and The Spirit of Modern Consumerism*. Oxford, U.K. and New York: Basil Blackwell, 1987.
8. Peck, M. Scott. M.D. *People of the Lie*. New York: Simon & Schuster, Inc., 1985.
9. Easser, Barbara R. and Lesser, Stanley R. "Hysterical Personality: A Reevaluation." In: Manfred F. R. Kets de Vries and Sidney Perzow (editors). *Handbook of Character Studies*. Madison, CT: International Universities Press, 1991.
10. Andrews, John D.W. "Psychotherapy with the Hysterical Personality." *Psychiatry*. vol. 47, August 1984, pages 228-230.
11. Kramer, Peter. *Moments of Engagement: Intimate Psychotherapy in a Technological Age*. New York: W.W. Norton and Co., 1989.
12. Akeret, Robert U. *Tales from a Travelling Couch*. New York: W.W. Norton & Company, 1995.

Chapter 3

1. de La Bruyere, Jean. *The "Characters."* London: John C. Nimmo, 1885.
2. Mansfield, Katherine. *Collected Stories*. London: Constable & Co.Ltd., 1945.
3. Thackeray, William M. *Vanity Fair*. London: J.M.Dent & Sons LTD., 1976.
4. Mailer, Norman. *Marilyn/A Biography*. New York: Warner Books, 1975, p. 17.
5. MacCann, Graham. *Marilyn Monroe / El Cuerpo del Delito*. Madrid: Espasa Calpe, 1992, p. 49.
6. Lowen, Alexander. *Narcissism/Denial of the True Self*. New York: MacMillan Publishing Company, 1983.
7. In bioenergetic analysis, a bed is used instead of a couch because the expressive exercises such as hitting or kicking the bed cannot be done on a couch.
8. Lowen: "I believe the Oedipal situation is more or less universal in our culture but that does not make it natural. As I pointed out in my previous book, *Fear of Life,* it derives from the power struggles in the family. It is natural for every child to have sexual feelings for the par-

ent of the opposite sex, but these feelings do not, in my opinion, lead to a competitive situation with the parent of the same sex. That situation results from the parent's jealousy at the attention showed the child by the other parent who is seductive with the child. Once seduction occurs, the child is placed in a competitive position with the parent of the same sex."

9. O'Neill, Cherry Boone. *Starving for Attention, A Young Woman's Struggle and Triumph Over Anorexia Nervosa*. Center City: MN: Hazelden, 1992.
10. She belonged to a Jewish family at a time of Nazi domination.
11. At the age of seven she was given a doll.
12. She abandoned the field of mathematics — a profession she had in common with her first partner — and went over to humanities, where she could accompany her second husband and take part in his work.

Chapter 4

1. Attar, Farid Ud-Din. *The Conference of the Birds*. New York: Samuel Weiser, Inc., 1969.
2. Flaubert, Gustave. *Madame Bovary*. New York: Random House, 1957, pp.156-7, 161-2.
3. Miller, Milton L. *Nostalgia: A Psychoanalytic Study of Marcel Proust*. Port Washington, N.Y. and London: Kennikat Press, 1969, p. 6.
4. Buenaventura, Ramón. *Rimbaud*. Madrid: Ed. Hiperión, 1985, p. 75.
5. Graves, Richard P. *Lawrence of Arabia and His World*. London: Thames and Hudson, 1976.
6. Lindner, Robert. *The Fifty Minute Hour*. New York: Bantam Books, 1979, p. 79.

Chapter 5

1. Attar, Farid Ud-Din. *The Conference of the Birds*. New York: Samuel Weiser, 1969, pp. 26-27.
2. Chaucer, Geoffrey. *The Canterbury Tales*. Baltimore, MD: The Penguin Classics, 1961, p. 25.

3. Leites, Nathan. "Trends in Affectlessness." In Kluckhohn, Clyde and Murray, Henry A. (editors). *Personality in Nature, Society and Culture.* New York: Alfred A. Knopf, Inc., 1964.

4. Melville, Herman. *Billy Budd, Sailor and Other Stories.* New York: Bantam Books, 1986.

5. Bergman, Ingmar. *Four Screenplays of Ingmar Bergman.* New York: Simon and Schuster, 1966.

6. Sheldon, William. *The Varieties of Human Temperament.* New York: Harper Brothers, 1942.

7. Canetti, Elias. *Earwitness: Fifty Characters.* New York: The Seabury Press, 1979.

8. Strachey, Lytton. *Biographical Essays.* New York: Harcourt, Brace and World, Inc., 1949, p. 43.

9. Moreno, Alfonso M. *Martin Lutero.* Bilboa: Ed. Mensojero, 1985, pp. 137-139.

10. Zweig, Stefan. *Obras Completas - III - Biografias.* Barcelona: Ed. Juventud, 1961, p. 424.

11. Kovel, Joel. *The Age of Desire: Case Histories of a Radical Psychoanalyst.* New York: Pantheon Books, 1981, pp. 86-97.

12. Naranjo, Claudio. *Character and Neurosis: An Integrative View.* Nevada City: CA:Gateways, 1994.

Chapter 6

1. Naranjo, Claudio. *Character and Neurosis: An Integrative View.* Nevada City, CA: Gateways, 1994.

2. Naranjo, Claudio. *Ennea-type Structures.* Nevada City, CA: Gateways, 1991.

3. Dostoyevsky, Fyodor. *Crime and Punishment.* New York: Bantam Books, 1971.

4. Carr, E.H. *Dostoevsky 1821-1881.* London: Unwin Books, 1962.

5. Kytle, Calvin. *Gandhi, Soldier of Nonviolence.* Washington, D.C.: Seven Locks Press, 1983.

6. Gandhi, Mohandas K. *The Story of My Experiments with Truth, an Autobiography.* Boston: Beacon Press, 1957.

7. Berg, Charles. *Deep Analysis:The Clinical Study of an Individual*

Case. New York: W.W. Norton and Co., Inc., 1947.

8. Wallerstein, Robert S. *Forty-Two Lives in Treatment: A Study of Psychoanalysis and Psychotherapy.* New York: Guilford Press, 1986.

9. de Vries, Manfred F. Kets and Perzow, Sidney. *Handbook of Character Studies.* Madison, CT: International Universities Press, 1991.

10. This chapter originally appeared in the *International Journal of Psycho-Analysis.* 41:59-69, 1960 and in Chatto and Windus, *Psychoanalysts and Beyond.* London: Chicago: University of Chicago Press. Reprinted (in de Vries and Perzow) by permission of the author and the publishers.

11. in de Vries and Perzow, pp.557-569.

Chapter 7

1. Chaucer, Geoffrey. *The Canterbury Tales.* Baltimore, MD: The Penguin Classics, 1961, p.24.

2. Abraham, Karl, *Selected Papers.* "Oral Eroticism and Character." London: Leonard and Virginia Woolf, The Hogarth Press, first ©1927; 1968, p. 401.

3. Flaubert, Gustave. *Madame Bovary.* New York: Random House, Inc., 1957, pp. 92-93.

4. Sanders, Lawrence. "McNally's Secret." In: *Book Digest.* New York: Time-Life, Time Warner Inc., 1992, p. 7. Used with permission.

5. Molière, Jean Baptiste. *Tartufo / Don Juan.* Madrid: Alianza Editorial, 1986.

6. Gurdjieff's expression of suffering that is deliberately accepted as part of working toward one's evolution.

Chapter 8

1. Canetti, Elias. *EarWitness/Fifty Characters.* New York: The Seabury Press, 1979, pp. 82-83.

2. Naranjo, Claudio. *Ennea-type Structures.* Nevada City, CA: Gateways, 1990.

3. Bey, Essad. *Stalin, la carrera de un fanatico.* Santiago de Chile:

Ediciones Extra, Empresa Letras, 1932, pp. 19-20.

4. quoted in: Blumenberg, Werner. *Marx.* Barcelona: biblioteca Salvat de grandes biografías, 1984, p. 92.

5. Rosal, Tania. *Los Amores de Carlos Marx.* Mexico: Los Caballos de Aquiles, 1982.

6. Chaucer, Geoffrey. *The Canterbury Tales.* Baltimore, MD:The Penguin Classics, 1961, p. 32.

7. Balzac, H. *Old Goriot.* London: Penguin Books, 1980, pp. 39-40.

8. Lindner, Robert. *The Fifty Minute Hour.* New York: Bantam Books, 1979.

Chapter 9

1. Chaucer, Geoffrey. *The Canterbury Tales.* Baltimore: MD: Penguin Classics, p.37.

2. Balzac, Honore. *Old Goriot.* New York: Penguin Books, 1986, p. 139.

3. Balzac, Honore. *Pere Goriot and Eugenie Grandet.* New York: Modern Library, 1946.

4. Lewis, Sinclair. *Babbitt.* New York: New American Library, 1961.

5. Porter, Eleanor H. *Pollyanna.* Boston: The Page Company, 1914.

6. White, William Hollingsworth. *The Organization Man.* New York: Simon and Shuster, 1956.

7. Riesman, David. *The Lonely Crowd.* New Haven and London: Yale University Press, 1961.

8. Yalom, Irvin D., M.D. *Love's Executioner and Other Tales of Psychotherapy.* New York: Basic Books, Inc., 1989.

9. *Dick Price: A Memorial Baptism.* Claudio Naranjo (editor). The Gestalt Journal, Vol X, No., 1, 1987.

10. Naranjo, Claudio. *Gestalt Therapy: The Attitude and Practice of an Atheoretical Experimentalism.* Nevada City, CA: Gateways, 1990.

Afterword

1. Originally, a report of Scott Peck's "Charlene, A Teaching Case." from his book, *The People of the Lie.* New York: Simon and Shuster, 1985.

2. Corbitt, Elizabeth M. "Narcissism from the Perspective of the Five

Factor Model." In: *Personality Disorders and the Five Factor Model of Personality.* (Costa, Paul T., Jr. and Widiger, Thomas A., editors.) Washington D.C.: American Psychological Association, 1994.

3. Widiger, Thomas A., Trull, Timothy J., Clarkin, John F., Sanderson, Cynthia and Costa, Paul T., Jr. "A Description of the DSM-IV Personality Disorders with the Five-Factor Model of Personality." In: *Personality Disorders and the Five-Factor Model of Personality.* (Costa, Paul T., Jr. and Widiger,Thomas A., editors). Washington, D.C.: American Psychological Association, 1994.

4. After writing the above I see in the revised edition of *Disorders of Personality: DSM-IV and Beyond.* (Millon, Theodore with Roger Davis, editors; New York: John Wiley & Sons, Inc., 1996) a formulation of "Narcissistic Personality Disorder." Perfectly coherent with the social E8 subtype (while the pathological extremes of the sexual and self-preservation subtypes are echoed in the formulations of the sadistic and anti-social syndromes).

5. A survey of the topic may be found in: Berzins, Juris I. "Therapist-Patient Matching." In: *Effective Psychotherapy: A Handbook of Research.* (Gurman, Alan S. and Razin, Andrew M., editors.) New York: Pergamon Press, 1977.

GLOSSARY

C: Capital sins – Deviations from spiritual consciousness that result in a loss of virtue and damage. Since Gregory the Great they are listed as pride, envy, wrath, sloth, avarice, gluttony and lust

Chakras – energy centers in the body described in the tantric teachings.

F: Fixation – in Ichazo's Protoanalysis, distorted views that are part of the lower intellectual center.

G: Gurdjieff, George – Master of wisdom who taught self-remembering, self-knowledge and attention development in Russia, France and the U.S.

H: Holy idea – aspects of reality, mapped by the enneagram of the higher intellectual centers, that are taken as meditation objects to counteract the wrong assumptions implicit in the fixations.

Hysterical personality – expression now mostly abandoned, and subsumed under "hystrionic personality disturbance." Chief among the traits of "hysterical (and hystrionic) personality" are "plasticity" (role playing ability), emotional expressiveness, seductiveness and an inclination to fantasy.

M: Mudra – ritual hand gestures.

Murshid – Sufi guide.

N: Nasruddin or Mulla Nasr Eddin – legendary Sufi to whom are attributed many jokes used as esoteric teaching devices.

P: Perls, Fritz – originator of Gestalt Therapy who had a deep influence in Humanistic Psychology and the spirit of the sixties.

Price, Richard – vice-president of Esalen Institute and disciple of Perls.

Protoanalysis – name under which Oscar Ichazo presented a body of psychological theory reputed to have originated in the Sarmouni brotherhood. The particle "proto" here has a double reference: 1) a fundamental structure of the personality that needs to be discerned through self-inquiry, and 2) that such analysis is a foundation or first step for ulterior work according to the system of self-development he proposed. Protoanalysis, as a theoretical system, involves the application of the Enneagram as a map of the passions, cognitive distortions or fixations and patterns of instinctual conditioning -- as I have partly elaborated upon in Character and Neurosis: An Integrative View.

Protoanalytic Gestalt – the practice of Gestalt therapy in light of protoanalytic understanding; or, in other words, Gestalt therapy conducted with a practical understanding of enneatype psychology.

R: Retroflexion – term introduced by Perls and now current in Gestalt Therapy to describe doing to oneself what one originally wanted to do to another. By undoing the retroflexion is meant, usually, redirecting anger to its original target in the outer world.

S: SAT – an integrative psycho-spiritual school active in the U.S. in the 1970s, and the source of SAT programs in various countries today.

Subtype – according to Ichazo's original formulation of personality structure in light of the enneagram, each basic type of ego (character- ized by a single passion and fixation) comprises three varieties according to the predominance of the sexual, self-preservation or social drive.

T: Tantra/tantric – spiritual schools in Buddhism and Hinduism that have in common a synthesis of yoga and devotionalism, an emphasis in a subtle body and the kundalini phenomenon.

Topdog – Perls's slang for super-ego, became a technical term in Gestalt Therapy.

Totemic – allusive to a totem-pole, here a metaphor for the more and yet less than human ideal of the social subtype of E5.

U: Underdog – Perls's word for the part of the mind that is the target of the topdog's accusations and demands.

BIBLIOGRAPHY

Abraham, Karl. *Selected Papers.* "Oral Eroticism and Character," London: Leonard and Virginia Woolf, The Hogarth Press, first ©1927; 1968.

Akeret, Robert U. *Tales from a Traveling Couch.* New York: W.W. Norton & Company, 1995.

Andrews, John D. W. "Psychotherapy with the Hysterical Personality," *Psychiatry,* vol. 47, August 1984, 228-230.

Attar Farid Ud-Din. *The Conference of the Birds.* New York: Samuel Weiser, 1969.

Austen, Jane. *Pride and Prejudice.* New York: Penguin Books, 1979.

Balzac, Honoré. *Old Goriot.* New York: Penguin Books, 1986.

Balzac, Honoré. *Père Goriot and Eugenie Grandet.* New York: Modern Library, 1946.

Berg, Charles. *Deep Analysis: The Clinical Study of an Individual Case.* New York: W.W. Norton and Co., Inc., 1947.

Berg, Charles. *The Case Book of the Medical Psychologist.* New York: W.W.Norton & Company, Inc., 1948.

Bergman, Ingmar. *Four Screenplays of Ingmar Bergman.* New York: Simon and Schuster, 1966.

Berzins, Juris I. "Therapist-Patient Matching." In: *Effective Psychotherapy: A Handbook of Research.* (Gurman, Alan S. and Razin, Andrew M., editors) New York: Pergamon Press, 1977.

Bey, Essad. *Stalin, la carrera de un fanatico.* Santiago de Chile: Ediciones Extra, Empresa Letras, 1932.

Breuer, Josef and Sigmund Freud. *Studies on Hysteria.* Strachey edition. New York: Basic Books, Inc., 1957.

Buenaventura, Ramón. *Rimbaud.* Madrid: Ed. Hiperión, 1985.

Butler, Samuel, *Characters.* Cleveland, OH: The Press of Case Western Reserve University, 1970.

Campbell, Colin. *The Romantic Ethic and the Spirit of Modern Consumerism.* Oxford, U.K. and New York: Basil Blackwell, 1987.

Canetti, Elias. *Earwitness: Fifty Characters.* New York: The Seabury Press, 1979.

Carr, E.H. *Dostoevsky 1821-1881.* London: Unwin Books, 1962.

Chaucer, Geoffrey. *The Canterbury Tales.* Baltimore, MD: The Penguin Classics, 1961.

Costa, Paul T., Jr. and Thomas A. Widiger, eds., "A Description of the DSM - IV Personality Disorders With the Five Factor Model of Personality," by Widiger, Trull, Clarkin, Sanderson and Costa. In: *Personality Disorders and the Five Factor Model of Personality.* Washington, D.C.: American Psychological Association, 1994.

Corbitt, Elizabeth M. "Narcissism from the Perspective of the Five Factor Model." In: *Personality Disorders and the Five Factor Model of Personality* (Costa, Paul T., Jr. and Widiger, Thomas A., editors) Washington D.C.: American Psychological Association, 1994.

de La Bruyere, Jean. *The Characters.* London: John C. Nimmo, 1885.

de Vries, Manfred F. Kets and Perzow, Sidney. *Handbook of Character Studies.* Madison, CT: International Universities Press, 1991.

Dickens, Charles. *David Copperfield.* New York: Signet Classics, 1962.

Dostoyevsky, Fyodor. *Crime and Punishment.* New York: Bantam Books, 1971.

The Brothers Karamazov. New York: The Modern Library, Random House, 1950,

Easser, Barbara R. and Lesser, Stanley R. "Hysterical Personality: A Reevaluation." In: Manfred F. R. Kets de Vries and Sidney Perzow (editors) *Handbook of Character Studies.* Madison, CT: International Universities Press, 1991.

Flaubert, Gustave. *Madame Bovary.* New York: Random House, 1957.

Freeman, Lucy. *The Story of Anna O.* New York: Walker and Company, 1971.

Freud, Sigmund. *Introductory Lectures on Psychoanalysis.* New York: Liveright, Publishing Corp., 1989.

Fromm, Erich. *The Sane Society.* New York: Owl Book edition, 1990.

Gandhi, Mohandas K. *The Story of My Experiments with Truth, an Autobiography.* Boston: Beacon Press, 1957.

Graves, Richard P. *Lawrence of Arabia and His World.* London: Thames and
Hudson, 1976.

Ibsen, Henrik. *Ibsen Plays.* New York: Penguin Books, 1980.

Kluckhohn, Clyde and Murray, Henry A. (editors) *Personality in Nature, Society and Culture.* New York: Alfred A. Knopt, Inc., 1964.

Kovel, Joel. *The Age of Desire: Case Histories of a Radical Psychoanalyst.* New York: Pantheon Books, 1981.

Kramer, Peter. *Moments of Engagement: Intimate Psychotherapy in a Technological Age.* New York: W.W. Norton and Co., 1989.

Kytle, Calvin. *Gandhi, Soldier of Nonviolence.* Washington, D.C.: Seven Locks Press, 1983.

Leites, Nathan. "Trends in Affectlessness." In Kluckhohn, Clyde and Murray, Henry A. (editors) *Personality in Nature, Society and Culture.* New York: Alfred A. Knopt, Inc., 1964.

Lewis, Sinclair. *Babbitt.* New York: New American Library, 1961.

Lindner, Robert. *The Fifty Minute Hour.* New York: Bantam Books, 1979.

Lowen, Alexander. *Narcissism / Denial of the True Self.* New York: MacMillan Publishing Company, 1983.

Ludwig, Emil. "Cleopatra." In: *Obras Completas de Emil Ludwig,* Biografias. Barcelona: Editorial Juventud, 1957.

MacCann, Graham M. *Marilyn Monroe/ El Cuerpo del Delito.* Madrid: Espasa Calpe, 1992.

Mailer, Norman. *Marilyn: A Biography.* New York: Warner Books, 1975.

Mansfield, Katherine. *Collected Stories.* London: Constable & Co. Ltd., 1945.

Melville, Herman. *Billy Budd, Sailor and Other Stories.* New York: Bantam Books, 1986.

Millen, Theodore and Roger Davis. *Disorders of Personality: DSM-IV and Beyond.,* New York: John Wiley & Sons, Inc., 1996.

Miller, Milton L. *Nostalgia: A Psychoanalytic Study of Marcel Proust.* Port Washington, N.Y. and London: Kennikat Press, 1969.

Molière, Jean Baptiste. *Tartufo / Don Juan.* Madrid: Alianza Editorial, 1986.

Moreno, Alfonso M. *Martin Lutero.* Bilboa: Ed. Mensojero, 1985.

Naranjo, Claudio "On Puritanical Character." *American Journal of Psychoanalysis*. New York: Agathon Press, vol.XLII, number 2, 1982.
(editor) "Dick Price: A Memorial Baptism," *The Gestalt Journal*, Vol. X, No. 1, 1987.
Eneagrama de la Sociedad/Males del Mundo, Males del Alma. Madrid: Temas de Hoy, 1995.
Character and Neuroses: An Integrative View. Nevada City, CA: Gateways, 1994.
Ennea-type Structures. Nevada City, CA, 1991.
Gestalt Therapy: The Attitude and Practice of an Atheoretical Experientialism. Nevada City, CA: Gateways, 1990.
O'Neill, Cherry Boone. *Starving for Attention: A Young Woman's Struggle and Triumph Over Anorexia Nervosa*. Center City: MN: Hazelden, 1992.
Peck, M. Scott. *People of the Lie*. New York: Simon & Schuster, Inc., 1985.
Porter, Eleanor H. *Pollyanna*. Boston: The Page Company, 1914.
Riesman, David. *The Lonely Crowd*. New Haven and London: Yale University Press, 1961.
Rosal, Tania. *Los Amores de Carlos Marx*. Mexico: Los Caballos de Aquiles, 1982.
Rycroft, Charles. "The Analysis of Paranoid Personality." In: de Vries, Manfred F. Kets and Perzow, Sidney. *Handbook of Character Studies*. Madison, CT: International Universities Press, 1991.
Sanders, Lawrence. "McNally's Secret." In: *Book Digest*. New York: Time -Life, Time Warner Inc., 1992.
Sheldon, William. *The Varieties of Human Temperament*. New York: Harper Brothers, 1942.
Strachey, Lytton. *Biographical Essays*. New York: Harcourt, Brace and World, Inc., 1949.
Thackeray, William M. *Vanity Fair*. London: J. M. Dent & Sons LTD., 1976.
Theophrastus. *Caracteres*. Spanish Version, Ed. Gredos, 1988.
Wallerstein, Robert S. *Forty-Two Lives in Treatment: A Study of Psychoanalysis and Psychotherapy*. New York: Guilford Press, 1986.
Weber, Max. *The Protestent Work Ethic and The Spirit of Capitalism*. New York: Simon and Schuster, 1980.
White, William Hollingsworth. *The Organization Man*. New York: Simon

and Schuster, 1956.

Yalom, Irvin D., M.D. *Love's Executioner and Other Tales of Psychotherapy.* New York: Basic Books, Inc., 1989.

Zweig, Stefan. *Obras Completas - III - Biografias.* Barcelona: Ed. Juventud, 1961.

INDEX OF PROPER NAMES
AND
LITERARY OR NON-TECHNICAL WORKS

COPYRIGHT PERMISSIONS

RETAIL ORDER FORM FOR HOHM PRESS HEALTH BOOKS

Name_____ Phone (   ) _____

Street Address or P.O. Box _____

City _____ State _____ Zip Code _____

	QTY	TITLE	ITEM PRICE	TOTAL PRICE
1		**THE ALCHEMY OF LOVE AND SEX**	$16.95	
2		**THE ALCHEMY OF TRANSFORMATION**	$14.95	
3		**ENNEATYPES IN PSYCHOTHERAPY**	$14.95	
4		**THE JUMP INTO LIFE**	$12.95	
5		**PLAYING WITH FIRE**	$16.95	
6		**TOWARD THE FULLNESS OF LIFE**	$12.95	
7		**TRANSFORMATION THROUGH INSIGHT**	$24.95	
8		**WHEN SONS AND DAUGHTERS...**	$14.95	
			SUBTOTAL:	
			SHIPPING: (see below)	
			TOTAL:	

SURFACE SHIPPING CHARGES

1st book $4.00

Each additional item $1.00

SHIP MY ORDER

☐ Surface U.S. Mail—Priority

☐ 2nd-Day Air (Mail + $5.00)

☐ UPS (Mail + $2.00)

☐ Next-Day Air (Mail + $15.00)

METHOD OF PAYMENT:

☐ Check or M.O.   Payable to Hohm Press, P.O. Box 2501, Prescott, AZ 86302

☐ Call 1-800-381-2700 to place your credit card order

☐ Or call 1-520-717-1779 to fax your credit card order

☐ Information for Visa/MasterCard order only:

Card #_____–_____–_____–_____

Expiration Date_____

ORDER NOW!
Call 1-800-381-2700 or fax your order to 1-520-717-1779.
(Remember to include your credit card information.)

ADDITIONAL TITLES OF INTEREST FROM HOHM PRESS

THE JUMP INTO LIFE: *Moving Beyond Fear*
by Arnaud Desjardins
Foreword by Richard Moss, M.D.

"Say Yes to life," the author continually invites in this welcome guidebook to the spiritual path. For anyone who has ever felt oppressed by the life-negative seriousness of religion, this book is a timely antidote. In language that translates the complex to the obvious, Desjardins applies his simple teaching of happiness and gratitude to a broad range of weighty topics, including sexuality and intimate relationships, structuring an "inner life," the relief of suffering, and overcoming fear.

Paper, 216 pages, $12.95, ISBN: 0-934252-42-4

• • •

TOWARD THE FULLNESS OF LIFE: *The Fullness of Love*
by Arnaud Desjardins

Renowned French spiritual teacher, Arnaud Desjardins, offers elegant and wise counsel, arguing that a successful love relationship requires the heart of a child joined with the maturity of an adult. This book points the way to that blessed union. Topics include: happiness, marriage, absolute love and male and female energy.

Paper, 182 pages, $12.95, ISBN: 0-934252-55-6

• • •

PLAYING WITH FIRE—*A Search for the Hidden Heart of Rock & Roll*
by Steve Ball

From Atlanta, Georgia 1967 ... to Bombay, India 1986 ... to Berlin, 1989 and '90 ... Steve Ball explores the "hidden heart of Rock & Roll" as he tells his own story—that of a Southern-born, starry-eyed young churchgoer turned rock musician and then D.J. who finds "liberation" through the music of his day; a liberation which takes him around the world and back in his quest for something "Real." Explores the question: "What's the connection between Rock & Roll and the spiritual search?"

Paper, 325 pages, photos; $16.95, ISBN: 0-934252-72-6.

TO ORDER, PLEASE SEE ACCOMPANYING ORDER FORM.

ADDITIONAL TITLES OF INTEREST FROM HOHM PRESS

ENNEATYPES IN PSYCHOTHERAPY
by Claudio Naranjo, M.D.

World-renowned Gestalt therapist, educator and Enneagram pioneer Dr. Claudio
Naranjo conducted the First International Symposium on the Personality
Enneagrams in Pueblo Acantilado, Spain, in December 1993. This book derives
from this conference and reflects the direct experience and lively testimony of
notable representatives of a variety of therapeutic disciplines including:
psychoanalysis, Gestalt, Transactional Analysis, bodywork, and others. Each
writer describes how the Enneagram holds invaluable keys to understanding
personality and its special relevance to those whose task is helping others.

Paper, 160 pages, $14.95, ISBN: 0-934252-47-5

• • •

WHEN SONS AND DAUGHTERS
CHOOSE ALTERNATIVE LIFESTYLES
by Mariana Caplan, M.A.

A guidebook for families in building workable relationships based on trust and
mutual respect, despite the fears and concerns brought on by differences in
lifestyle. Practical advice on what to do when sons and daughters (brother,
sisters, grandchildren...) join communes, go to gurus, follow rock bands around
the country, marry outside their race or within their own gender, or embrace a
religious belief that is alien to yours. "Recommended for all public libraries."—
Library Journal. "Entering an arena too often marked by bitter and wounding
conflict between worried parents and their adult children who are living in non-
traditional communities or relationships, Mariana Caplan has produced a wise
and thoughtful guide to possible reconciliation and healing...An excellent
book."—Alan F. Leveton, M.D.; Association of Family Therapists, past president

Paper, 230 pages, $14.95; ISBN: 0-934252-69-6.

TO ORDER, PLEASE SEE ACCOMPANYING ORDER FORM.

ADDITIONAL TITLES OF INTEREST FROM HOHM PRESS

THE ALCHEMY OF TRANSFORMATION
by Lee Lozowick
Foreword by: Claudio Naranjo, M.D.

"I really appreciate Lee's message. The world needs to hear his God-talk. It's insightful and healing."—(John White, author, and editor, *What is Enlightenment?: Exploring the Goal of the Spiritual Path.*
A concise and straightforward overview of the principles of spiritual life as developed and taught by Lee Lozowick for the past twenty years in the West. Subjects of use to seekers and serious students of any spiritual tradition include: • From self-centeredness to God-centeredness • The role of a Teacher and a practice in spiritual life • The job of the community in "self"-liberation • Longing and devotion. Lee Lozowick's spiritual tradition is that of the western Baul, related in teaching and spirit to the Bauls of Bengal, India. The Alchemy of Transformation presents his radical, elegant and irreverent approach to human alchemical transformation.

Paper, 185 pages, $14.95, ISBN: 0-934252-62-9

• • •

THE ALCHEMY OF LOVE AND SEX
by Lee Lozowick
Foreword by Georg Feuerstein, Ph.D., author of *Sacred Sexuality*

Discover 70 "secrets" about love, sex and relationships. Lozowick recognizes the immense conflict and confusion surrounding love and sex, and tantric spiritual practice. Preaching neither asceticism nor hedonism, he presents a middle path—(one grounded in the appreciation of simple human relatedness. Topics include: • what men want from women in sex, and what women want from men • the development of a passionate love affair with life • how to balance the essential masculine and essential feminine • the dangers and possibilities of sexual Tantra • the reality of a genuine, sacred marriage. . .and much more. The author is an American "Crazy Wisdom teacher" in the tradition of those whose enigmatic life and madcap teaching styles have affronted the polite society of their day. Lozowick is the author of 14 books in English and several in French and German translations only. " ... attacks Western sexuality with a vengeance." —*Library Journal.*

Paper, 300 pages, $16.95, ISBN: 0-934252-58-0

TO ORDER, PLEASE SEE ACCOMPANYING ORDER FORM.